C# & C++

5 books in 1 - The #1 Coding Course From Beginner to Advanced

MARK REED

C++

The Ultimate Beginners Guide to Learn C++ Programming Step-by-Step

TABLE OF CONTENTS

BOOK 1

C++

The Ultimate Beginners Guide to Learn C++ Programming Step-by-Step

BOOK 2

C++

The Ultimate Beginners Guide to Effectively Design, Develop & Implement a Robust Program Step-by-Step

BOOK 3

C#

The Ultimate Beginners Guide to Learn C# Programming Step-by-Step

BOOK 4

C#

The Ultimate Intermediate Guide To Learn C# Programming Step-By-Step

BOOK 5
C#

The Ultimate Advanced Guide To Master C# Programming

INTRODUCTION

This book is fit for beginners and for coders who are interested in getting into backend programming. Although C++ is sometimes portrayed as a specter of days past, the language is still with us and it continues to be behind some of the biggest technologies we use today–not mentioning its big imprint in the gaming world. Its power and versatility continue to make it one of the most important languages of our time. It is not going anywhere and learning it will expand your horizons.

C++ is often utilized as a backend language for big data because of its little processing overhead. Companies like Spotify, Adobe, YouTube, and Amazon power their backend with C++, and you will soon see why.

C++ is also behind powerful gaming engines. Gaming engines allow programmers to build a game without coding everything from scratch and to effectively render content. The Unity Game Engine and the Unreal Engine are examples of gaming engines that run on C++.

C++ is a beautiful, efficient language because of the favorable power/hardware ratio: it uses little hardware for the amount of power it gives us. This is why those who learn it love it.

In this book we will cover the following topics:

- Programming terminology and principles in programming
- Setting up a C++ environment
- Getting Started: Syntax, Data Types, and Variables
- Power of C++: Operations, Loops, Switches, and Decision Making
- Creating custom functions in C++

You will also find a useful glossary at the end so that you can use the book as a reference once you get cracking.

CHAPTER 1:

Setting up a C++ Development Environment

At its most basic, programming is writing a list of instructions in code that the machine can understand. The code resides in executables files. These files come with file extensions that tell a compiler what language is in the file. These extensions are the suffixes you often see at the end of the file, like ".js". ".cpp" or ".hpp".

To write code and save it in an executable file you need the following things:

1. A **text editor**: this will allow you to write and edit the code.
2. A **language compiler**: This program takes the code you have written and translates it into machine language that your computer can understand and follow.

All programming languages work like this except HTML, CSS, and JavaScript - these programs are interpreted and executed by the browser ("Introduction," n.d.). This means browser languages like JavaScript are software-based, while C++ is compiled and then run directly on your machine, not in a software environment.

This means C++ is an assembly language. **Assembly languages** are low-level programming languages that need a compiler so they can run on a machine (Lithmee, 2018). In this context, the word low-level does not carry a bad connotation; it is descriptive, meaning that the language is closer to the machine or just a step away from it.

As you can probably guess, C++ is a general-purpose language that can run almost anywhere. This means it can be assembled and compiled in several different ways. This will largely depend on your operating system and the creation utilities you are using.

Our C++ exercises will be compiled on an online IDE. IDE stands for **Integrated Development Environment** and it is used to edit and compile code. I bet that description sounds familiar. Yes, an IDE is an example of a text editor, but unlike a plain text editor, it has extra features that are important to the programming process. An IDE can do things like compile code, debug code, highlight code, warn you of syntax errors, and more.

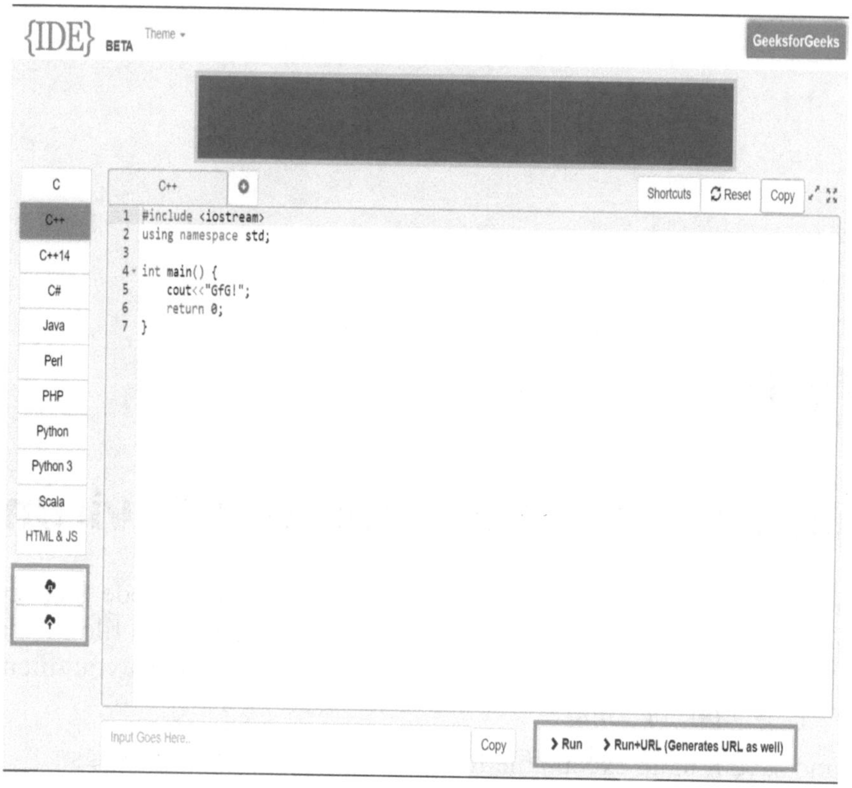

Geeks for Geeks IDE: A web-based Program Compiler

This IDE can be found at https://ide.geeksforgeeks.org/ and has several programming languages. We will be focusing on C++. This IDE has many coding utilities: a tabbed working space, an input box, and a code manager. *This code manager includes the two bottom buttons highlighted on the left.* These code manager buttons allow you to download and upload code as files with their corresponding file extension. This IDE also allows you to run and generate a URL that saves the result. We'll be using these generated URLs to manage our lessons.

In this book, we will use a Geeks for Geeks web-based IDE, but you should learn to set up a local IDE. For the majority of your programming career, that is where you will be working. Plus, you can customize the IDE to fit your needs and spruce up your code.

Setting up Your Text Editor

IDE environments that are focused on programming always have to have a text editor and a compiler within them. Non-IDE environments separate compilers and plain text editors. The text editor serves as a programming interface in non-IDE setups; this simply means the text editor will be the place you tinker with the code.

> **Note:** If you have a Linux, you will already have a text editor as Linux is a console-based environment. Console-based environments use a **command-line interface (CLI),** where you interact with programs by issuing lines of code. IDE for Linux may include a **graphical user interface (GUI)**. A GUI allows you to interact with programs through visual indicators such as clicking
> .

When looking for a text editor, you need one with syntax highlighting and indenting as all programming languages follow their syntax. This is because you want to be able to read your code easily and you want collaborators to be able to do so, too. These text editors help by improving readability. This is especially important because coding is no longer and has never been a solitary task. There is no one-man genius like in the movies.

Github and Pastebin are code aggregators that have syntax highlighting add-ons enabled. Github will allow you to host your entire project on their site, while Pastebin only allows code snippets. On these platforms, you can save code in a variety of languages.

They are very useful to programmers because they allow programmers to share code, collaborate, test, and so forth. Learning how to deploy a project to Github is one of the most important things in programming because it has become so standardized. So, maintaining a Github profile has also become important, as it holds all the projects you are working on, have worked on, and your activity (Peshev, 2017). To a potential employer or collaborator, this information is invaluable.

C++ 0.25 KB

```
#include "stdafx.h"
#include <iostream>

using namespace std;


int main()
{
        int num = 0;
        int result = 0;
        cin >> num;
        for (int i = 2;i<num+1; i+=2)  {
                result += i;

        }
        cout << endl << result << endl;
        system("pause");
        return 0;
}
```

C++ Code Syntax Example

This is a screenshot from Paste Bin with syntax highlighting enabled ("C++ Code," 2015). Syntax highlighting and tabbed spacing help with making the code more comprehensible. All text editors with syntax highlighting will use this scheme: libraries in green, and functions, data types, and data in blue. Strings will show up as red.

When you are working locally you will not have luxuries like these readily available. The first text editor you will find on your system if you are using windows is Notepad. Wordpad is another one that has more GUI features. What you will notice as you open these programs is how plain and boring they are. They are like Word but worse, because they shouldn't be simple word processors if writing efficient, elegant code is important to us. Their word processor-like aspects make them more suitable for writing words in them, not code, although you can code in them.

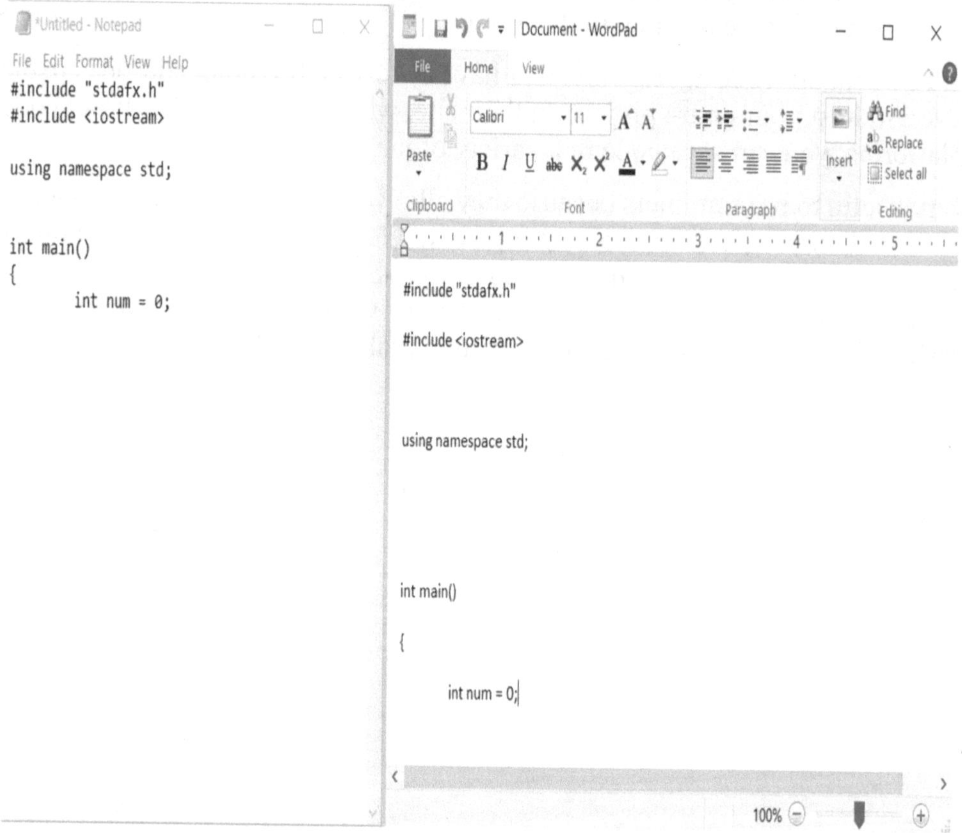

Side-by-side comparison of Windows' Notepad utility and Wordpad utility

This is a screenshot that features two of Windows' built-in utilities, Notepad on the left and Wordpad on the right. Wordpad has more Microsoft suite GUI features that may be more recognizable to you, including Microsoft's quick access bar located above the highlighted "File" tab. Notepad is very bare-bones in comparison. Both utilities, unlike word processors, allow you to save in different file extensions. However, Wordpad is more similar to a word processor than

Notepad, saving files in rich text format (.rtf). Wordpad will warn you that you will lose formatting if you save in an extension other than rich text format.

What makes Notepad and Wordpad unique is that they can save files in a variety of file extensions, while word processors cannot. File extensions are important because they tell the compiler how to interpret what is written in the file, and that leads to the machine having a set of instructions it can understand and execute.

Despite their abilities, these two programs lack crucial text editor features like syntax highlighting. You might think this is no big deal, but it is; the same words in code can mean different things because of how and when they appear, so highlighting helps us distinguish what they refer to. So if everything is plain, black and white, you have to work harder to figure out what a piece of code refers to. It sounds complex now, but once you code this will become obvious and necessary.

Notepad++, not to be confused with Windows 'Notepad, has highlighting features but you will have to activate them like so:

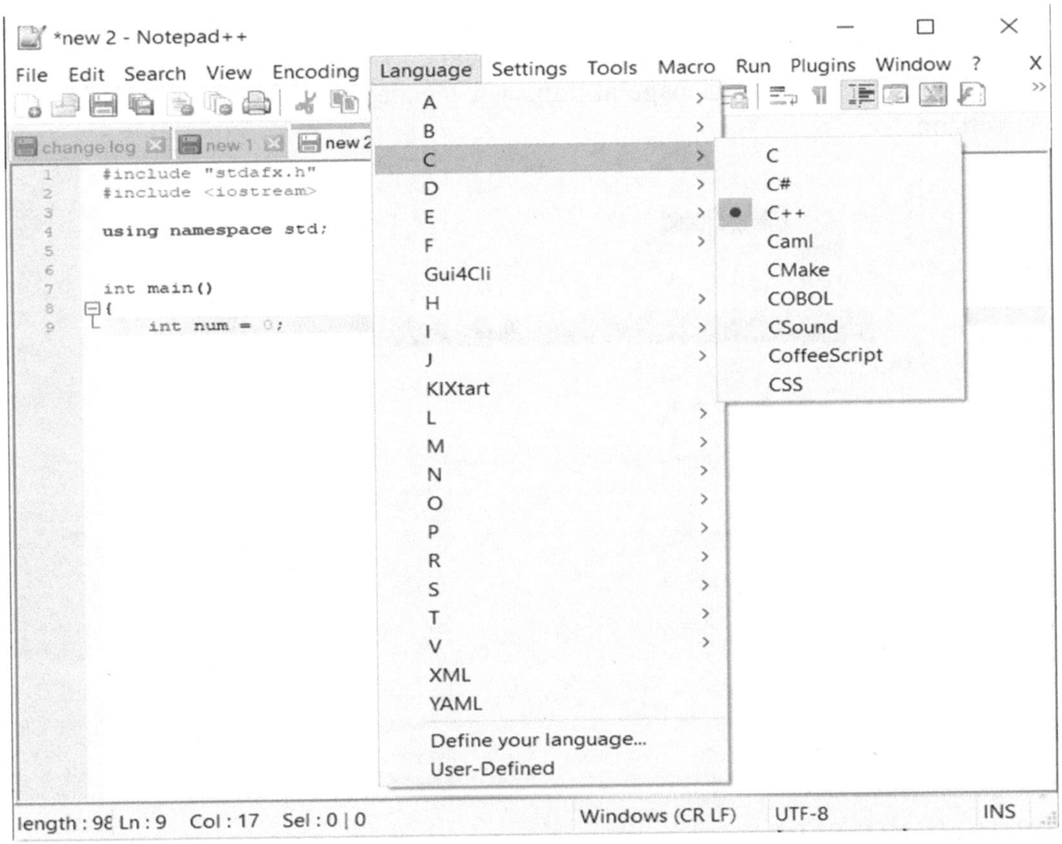

Screenshot of Notepad ++ with C++ Syntax

Notepad ++ is free and, as the name suggests, was programmed in C++. This screenshot illustrates how to enable language syntax. C++ syntax can specifically be enabled by going to language >"C" > and navigating to C++. Notepad++ is only available on the Windows platform (Orin, n.d.).

Bluefish is a more advanced text editor that comes with more features ("Bluefish Editor: Features," n.d.). Unlike Notepad++, Bluefish is available on multiple platforms other than Windows. But I would not recommend Bluefish for beginners because it has a lot of features that can be overwhelming to a complete beginner. If you are not new to programming you can go give it a shot; you will find it has many of the GUI features typical of an IDE text editor.

Once in the text editor, you must select a compiler. Now let me show you how you would set up your local environment on three platforms: Windows, Linux, and Mac.

Windows IDE Installation and Setup

All you need to do is to install an IDE. Just remember that it has to have a text editor and a compiler within it. **Code::Blocks** is a useful, open-source IDE made for C++ and it easily fits with a variety of compilers including Microsoft's Visual C++. Installing Code::Block is easy. You just have to go to their downloads page at http://www.codeblocks.org/downloads/26 and select the latest version.

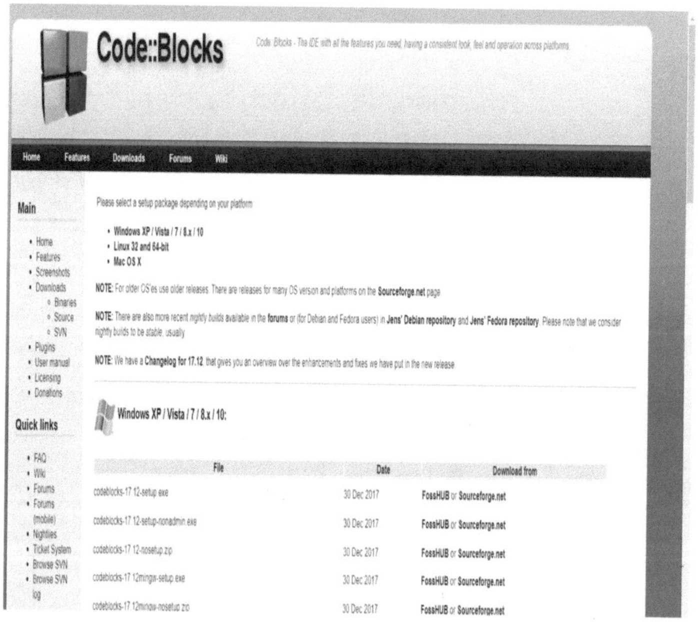

Code::Blocks Download Page

As of this writing, Code::Blocks has version 20.03 for Windows and Linux distributions. The page also includes helpful notes for installation.

Once the program is installed, you are set. You can use it to write C++ programs. To do so you have to follow three steps: creating a file, building the program, and running the program.

Creating a new file is a bit more nuanced. Here is what you have to do:

- Go to File > New
- Select "Create an empty file" and input your code
- Save the file with a ".cpp" extension

And, needless to say, you have to build a program before you can run it. You can do this by going to Build > "Build and Run" in the menu.

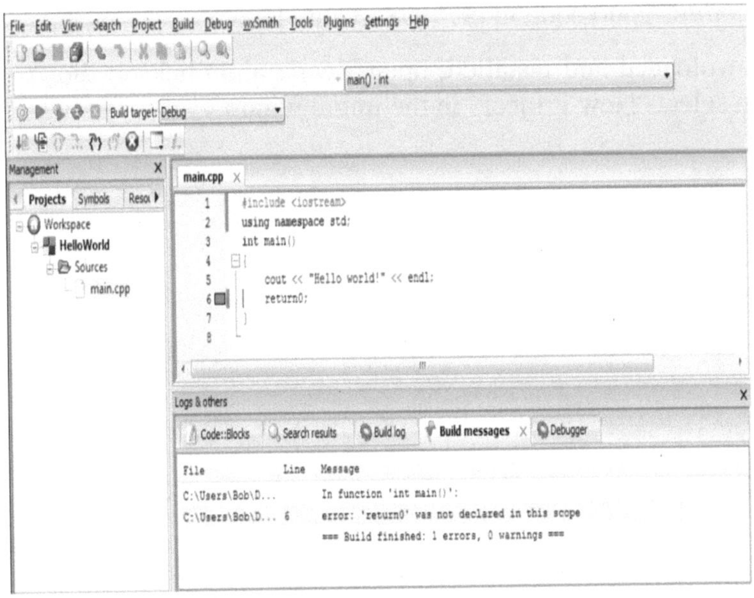

Screenshot of "Hello World" in Code::Blocks

This is a live screenshot of our "Hello World" program in code blocks. After this program is run, an error shows up in the Build Messages of the code. Code::Blocks highlights the error on line 6. Given your knowledge of C++ syntax from the earlier section, you should see how to repair the code. How can we repair the code?

Hint: Data and functions are supposed to show up in blue.

By the way, this program is very lightweight for the amount of work it allows you to do. Code::Block is available on Windows and Linux, but there is no Mac version.

Mac OS IDE Installation and Setup

For Mac, you will need to get **Xcode**. It is a free IDE software development suite for macOS. You can get it on the Mac App Store. Xcode supports a variety of other languages like Java, Python, and Ruby.

It is geared toward developing software for macOS operating systems; this can be for the tvOS for AppleTV, watchOS for Apple watches, and the iPadOS for iPad tablets ("What's New in Xcode 9," n.d.). Xcode offers a variety of **software development kits** (SDKs) for different MacOS platforms to help programmers through Apple's proprietary programming schemes. SDKs are a set of tools, provided by hardware and software vendors, used for developing applications for specific platforms ("What's New in Xcode 9," n.d.). SDKs allow developers to be fully integrated within a development community, like Apple's or Android's.

Mac uses proprietary compilers that will only work with Xcode, so if you are on Mac you have little choice but to develop with C++ using Xcode. You can download and install Xcode by following this link:

https://apps.apple.com/us/app/xcode/id497799835?mt=12

Once the file is downloaded and installed, open Xcode and click on the "Create a new Xcode Project" icon. Then select "New Project" in the initial window.

Initial Screen for Xcode: Select a new project

These screenshots feature an Xcode build from version 8.3.3 (Patel, 2017). Therefore, our examples might look different from a more up-to-date build. As of this writing, the most current version is 12.1, which mostly includes updates to the various macOS platform SDKs ("Xcode," n.d.). Despite these differences, these screenshots will still help you orient yourself in the more current build. Our instruction will still yield results.

After you do this, a prompt window will appear that will ask you to choose a template. This window will guide you through the rest of the setup. Select the macOS sections and go to the Application section; in there, choose the Command Line Tool.

It looks something like this:

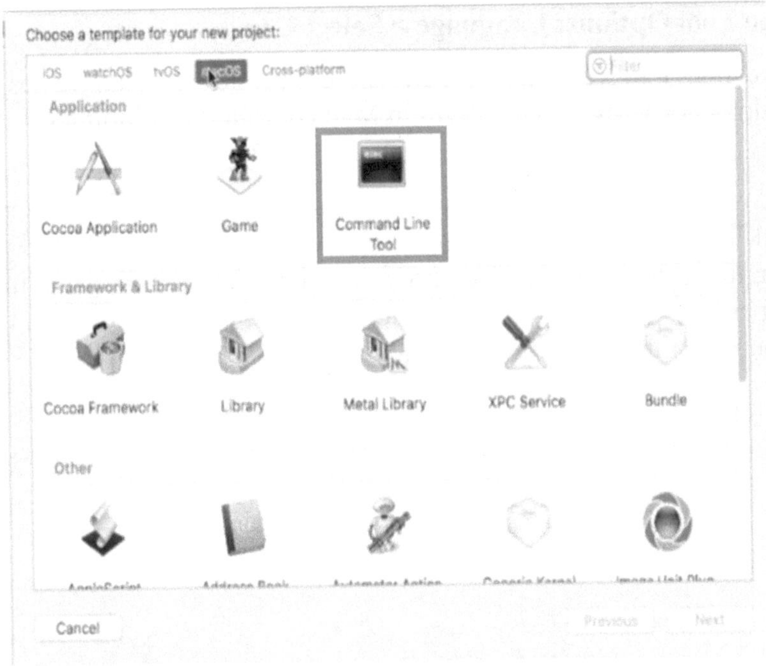

1. Project Selection Screen: macOS > Application > Command Line Tool

Xcode has many built-in code utilities for running programs on various Apple platforms. Therefore, to run a test program you would have to select macOS for it to run on your program. Further, to access assembly language software development needed for C++, you would have to use Xcode's command-line tool. This command-line tool can handle Objective-C and C languages as well.

After you select a template, the guide will present options for the command-line tool. Here, you can name the project, add your organization's name, use a bundle identifier, and select a programming language.

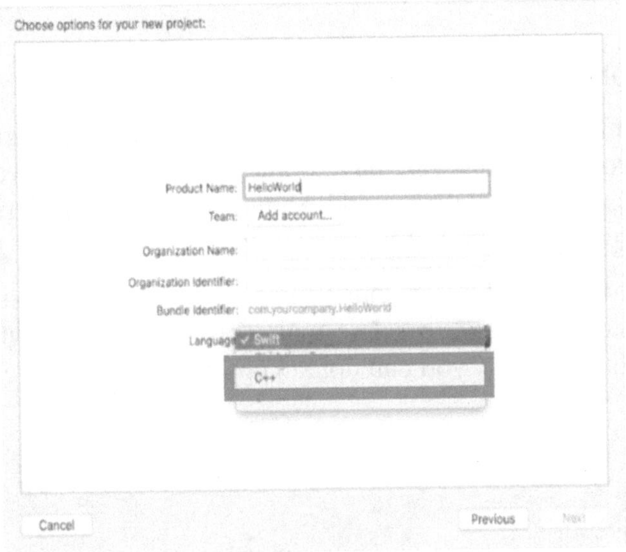

2. Command Line Tool Options: Language > Select C++

Xcode's command-line tool can handle Microsoft's proprietary languages like Swift. This program can run alongside C-based languages in Mac compilers, including C++. Swift is selected by default.

In the same window, you will be required to add an organization identifier. Remember that Xcode's command-line tool is a programming template for proprietary macOS operating systems, so the organization identifier is used to create a unique idea for your program in Apple databases: the Apple Developer Website and iCloud Container, iTunes connect portal in the Appstore. This will streamline your app into a proprietary macOS framework.

3. Command Line Tool Options: Organization Identifier > "cpp"

The organization's identifier is a naming convention that helps programmers integrate their projects into Apple's proprietary software development scheme. Here, we are using "cpp" as our identifier, which generates "cpp.HelloWorld" as our bundle identifier. Once we indicate an identifier, the guide allows us to proceed to the next step.

Now, save your project in a directory of your choice. On the left-hand side pane, Xcode will be able to open the file. You will have to select main.cpp to access the global C++ file for your program in Xcode. If you so desire, you can upload cpp files into the directory, and edit them.

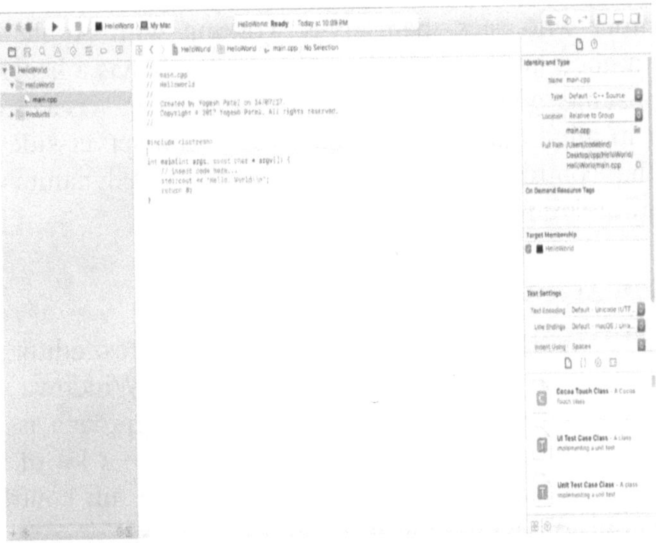

3. Xcode Command Line Tool: "main.cpp"

This screenshot features the IDE style Xcode Command Line Tool workspace. It has the *main.cpp* opened in the text editor (Patel, 2017).

Once you have written some code and you want to run it, you select Product and click on Run. Also, you can run and build the program by selecting the button.

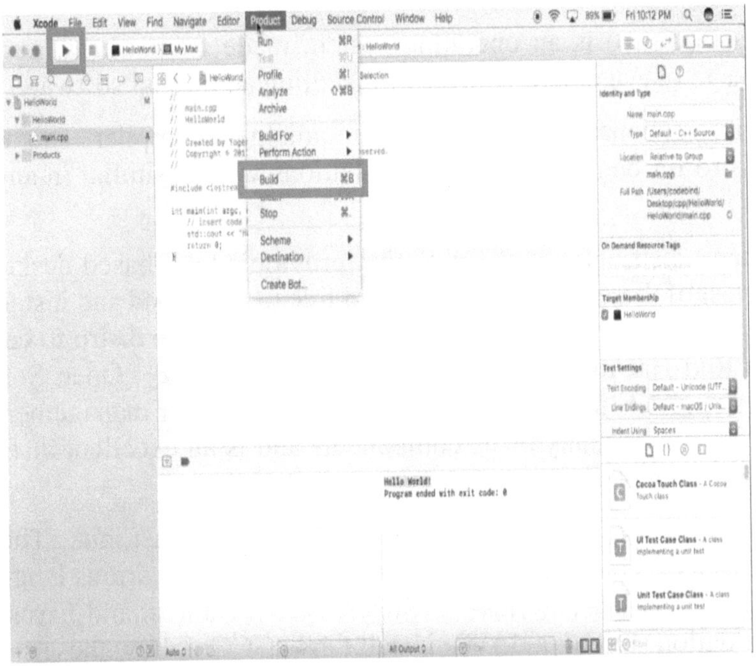

4. Xcode Command Line Tool: "Hello World" Build and Run

Similar to the Code::Blocks IDE, you will also have to build and then run your program. This screenshot also features the results of "Hello World" and the return value (Patel, 2017).

If you are a programmer who sees themselves working with Apple devices, working and practicing in Xcode is a good investment. For instance, Apple has a healthy share of the market in a wide variety of consumer goods and services like streaming services and devices. With that said, you should keep in mind that C++ is used mostly as a server-side language. Server-side programming is code that controls how content is delivered to a dynamic website like YouTube. Most server-side programming is done on Linux machines.

Linux Compiler Installation

Linux is a console-based operation system, so it does not need a text editor. Instead, we will focus on installing and setting up a programming compiler. Mac and Windows automatically initialize a compiler within the IDE, but in Linux, a more hands-on approach is required. You will be required to execute a backend initialization. It might seem like a lot of work, but in the great scheme of things, it allows those working with Linux to have full control of the development procedure and unlock more computing power.

Because Linux is an operating system that uses a console interface, it will be strange to beginners or anyone who is used to Windows or Mac. This is because users are often used to a GUI. The GUI-lessness of Linux allows more computing power to be freed for programming – a GUI takes some computing power to produce and maintain. This is why many servers and other programming environments have console interfaces. Also, many of them use **Linux distributions**.

A Linux distribution (distro) is an operating system made from Linux kernel-based software collection and package management system for installing additional software.

The following are instructions for installing and initializing a compiler. This will be for Ubuntu, a popular Linux distro for beginners. These installations will be similar in any Linux distro you will be using.

Note: There are many distributions of Linux that provide a GUI based desktop experience that many users love. Most of these are open-source and free to download and install. You can explore these distros and create console interfaces to practice on. One free distro to consider is **CentOS**, which is based on Red Hat for server management ("Centos-faq | Open Source Community," n.d.). **Red Hat Enterprise Linux (RHEL)** is used in many server management setups and is not free. However, CentOS uses many of its components and is an excellent distro for preparing to work in Red Hat environments.

In this example, we will use the **GNU Collection Compiler** on Linux. The GNU Collection Compiler is a Linux-based compiler that supports C++ and other various languages like Fortran, Ada, and Java ("GCC 7 Release Series—Changes, New Features, and Fixes—GNU Project—Free Software Foundation (FSF)," n.d.). To install GNU GCC, follow these steps:

- In the console, enter the following commands:

Check first if there is a version already installed on your machine by entering this command: gcc –v

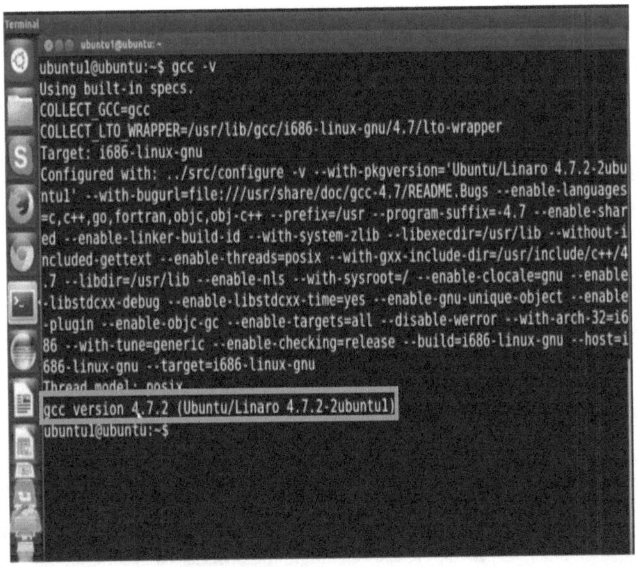

A. Check for GNU GCC in Ubuntu Console

You should check your system for a copy of the GCC. This screenshot features a system with GCC already installed (Patel, 2014). After using the command, if there is no copy of GCC in your system, it will be missing this line. If there is a copy, it will have a similar line. Most likely, your version will be more recent.

The following commands will install GCC on your system (Agarwal, 2017b):

sudo apt-get update

sudo apt-get install GCC

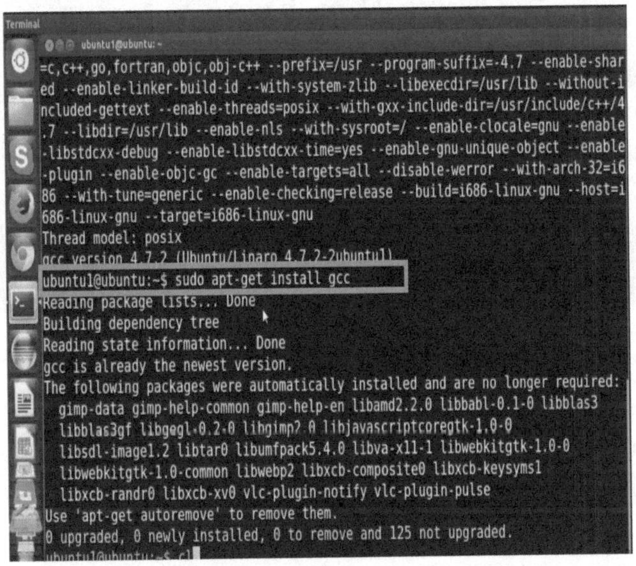

B. Install GNU GCC in Ubuntu Console

In the screenshot, a GNC GCC is already present. Running the highlighted command will install the GNU GCC on your system if it isn't there (Patel, 2014). The console will prompt you to type "Y" for it to begin the installation. You also are offered package management features like the ability of the terminal to inform you of outdated or unnecessary packages. It will also suggest commands that will make your system more efficient. This explains the popularity of Linux with programmers; although wordy, it allows them to troubleshoot with ease, gives them more control, and it is easy to navigate when compared to GUIs. This is because programmers are more likely to remember a line of code than where something resides in the GUI.

The following command will install all the libraries required to compile code and eventually run C++:

sudo apt-get install build-essential

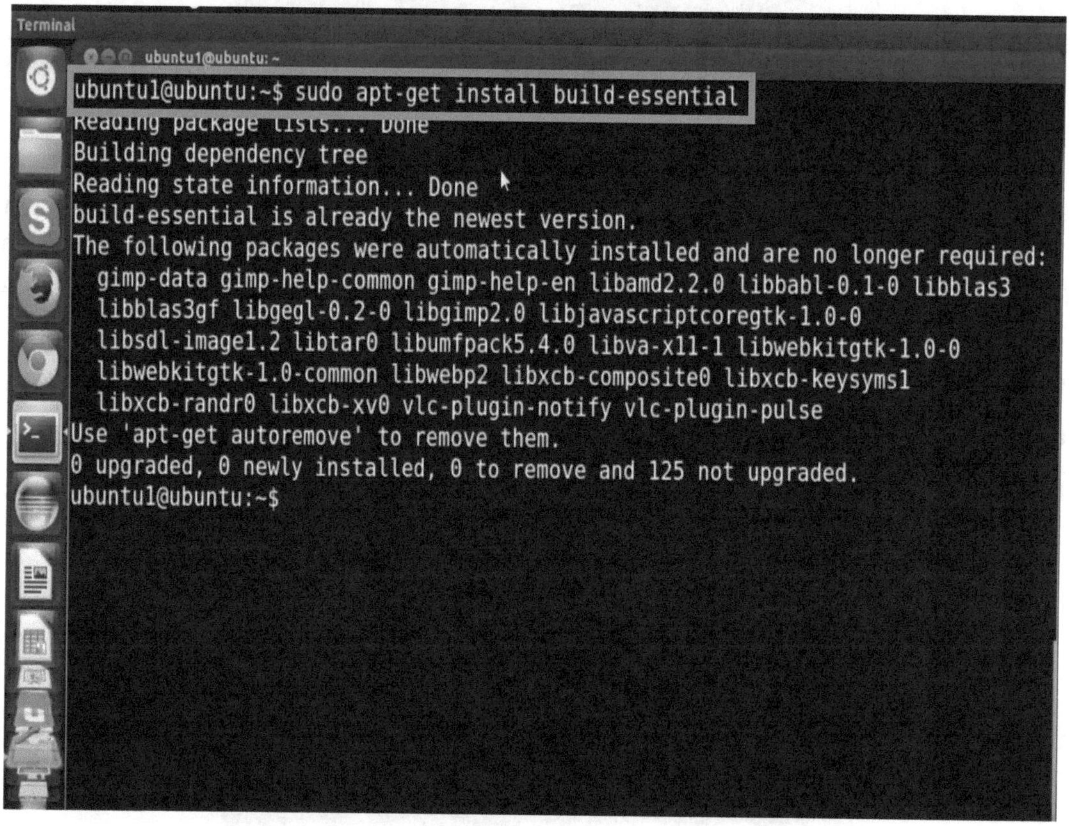

C. Install GNU GCC in Ubuntu Console

This screenshot shows a system with the build-essential libraries installed and inputting the highlighted installation command (Patel, 2014). Just as with installing the GCC, after using the command and finding there is no copy of the build-essential libraries in your system, it will prompt you to install. Type in "Y" and the terminal will install libraries.

- Check the installation with the following command:

g++ --version

If all went well it will tell you what version of GCC is installed.

Because Linux has a built-in text editor you will have to use the following command to access the GUI for the text editor:

gedit

You will be free to write your program as you see fit. Remember to save the programs with the ".cpp" extension so that they will be compiled correctly.

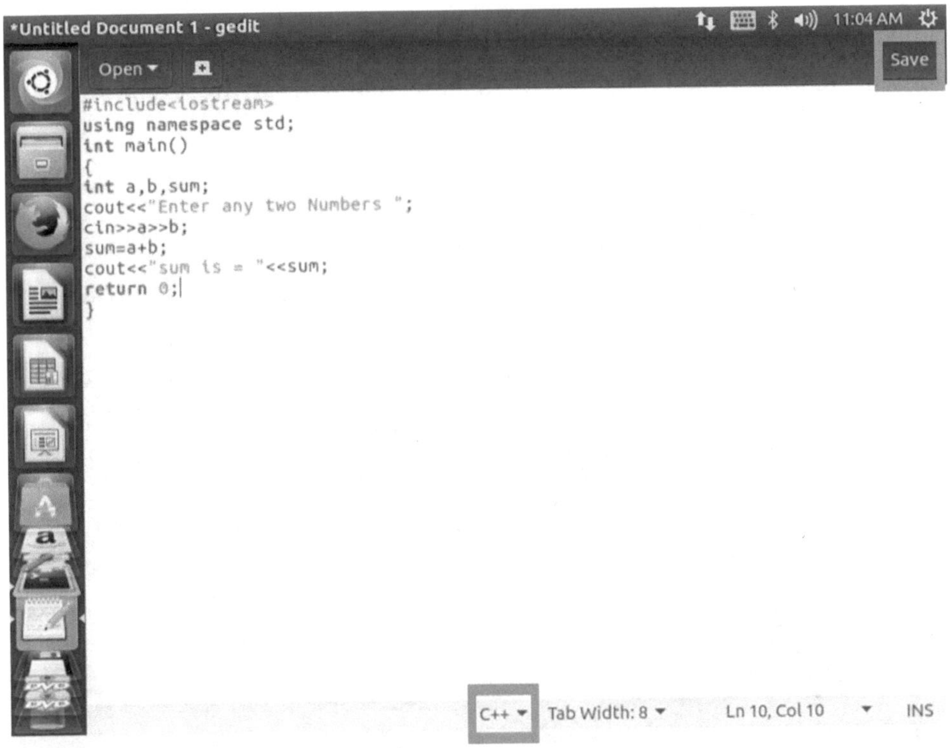

Gedit in Ubuntu

This screenshot features Linux's built-in text-editor, Gedit ([Running C, C++ Programs in Linux] Ubuntu 16.04 (Ubuntu Tutorial for Beginners), n.d.). Gedit is a Linux programming text editor utility that has syntax highlighting and tabbed spacing features for a diverse array of programming languages. Be sure to have "C++" selected from the highlighted dropdown menu. You can save your program file in the GUI by clicking the "save" button. Be sure to list which directory you have your file saved, as you will have to point the compiler to that directory to compile and run the code.

To test and run your code you must follow these instructions:

1. Lead the terminal to the files directory

To do this use this command. Enter it in the directory repeatedly until the .cpp file is revealed.

ls

2. Compile and test the program file

Use these commands to do so:

$$g + \pm otest[filename].cpp$$

If there are any errors this command will tell you which line contains the error just like you would expect from an IDE. Then you can open the program file through “gedit [filename.cpp]” and fix the line of code.

3. Run the program file

The compiler will create an executable file called “test” that will run the program. You can execute it by entering “. /test” in the terminal.

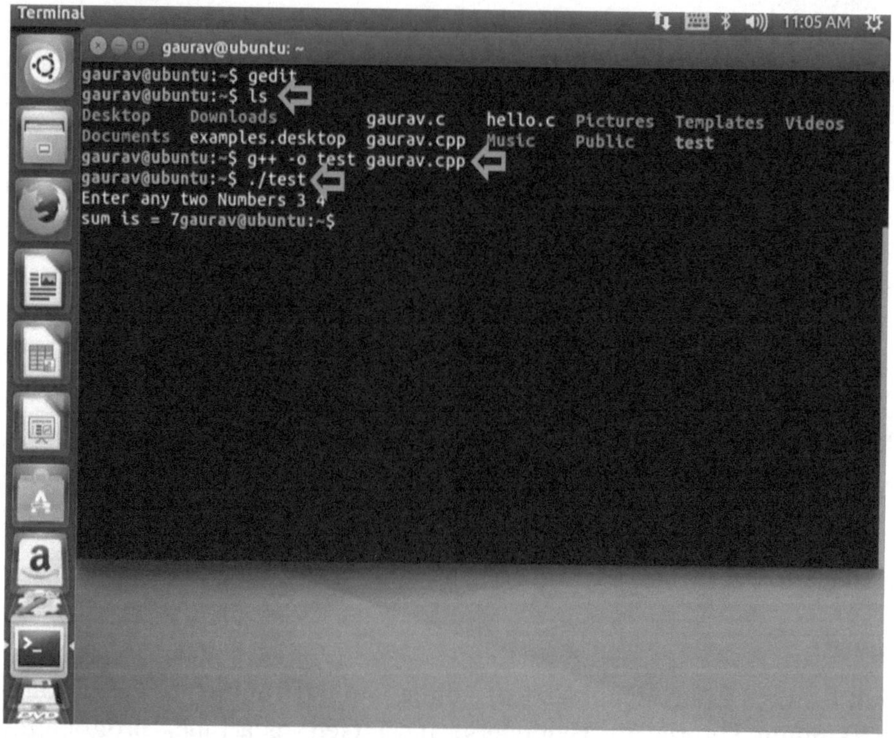

Testing, Compiling and Running a .cpp file in Ubuntu

This screenshot features the terminal testing, compiling, and running the example code written in gedit (*[Running C, C++ Programs in Linux] Ubuntu 16.04 (Ubuntu Tutorial for Beginners), n.d.*).

Linux distros are verbose console-based systems and most of them can handle programming in any language through the terminal. Learning to work in the Linux environment is beneficial as it exposes you to server-side programming.

Note: The process for installing GCC and compiling on CentOs is similar. To install, you instead use “*yumgroupinstall"DevelopmentTools*. This command automatically installs the needed libraries as well. The steps for composing, compiling, testing, and running the program are all the same.

Creating your own programming environment helps prepare you for real-world scenarios in a way that online coding spaces cannot. In this book, we will be using an online IDE. This is because everyone will have the same learning environment with standardized outputs and interfaces. It simplifies things.

CHAPTER 2:

Basics of C++, Principles of Programming

Programming languages are like any other human language: they have structure, syntax, and rules. It is not enough to know the words of another human language. Knowing how to use them and how they function in that language is an integral part of communicating effectively in that language. Programming languages function the same way, but the communication they care about trying to help is one between man and machine. While machines, at least today, can never be as clever and capable as we are, there is a lot they can understand at a rate and with an efficacy that is alien to us. All programming is a set of instructions. These instructions can be rules, they can be actions you want the machine to perform, or something else. But all this communication is possible because we follow the rules of a programming language.

Programming rules, or syntax, are a list of delineating symbols used to communicate aspects of a program like functions and variables. Syntax is important to the compiler because it tells the compiler what instructions it should give to the machine.

Before we start, it is worth keeping a few things in mind. Unlike Python or other high-level programming languages, C++ does not resemble the language of humans quite easily. High-level languages like JS, Python, and C# are made this way because it makes them easy to read and manage. C++, despite being this way, is easier for machines to understand precisely because it is not so abstracted. This is why when working with C++ you only need a compiler and text editor, whereas languages like Python need their environments installed.

Principles of Programming

C++ has many ways of completing the same task. Just like with human languages, there are many ways of saying the same thing, but some ways are best suited for certain occasions and some aren't. C++ is the same way; some methods are great because they reduce program overhead. Many developers will want that because it increases the performance of the entire application, and that is the first principle of programming: complete a task with the least amount of functions as possible. Do not make things more complicated than they need to be. In most cases, this means using a loop or a switch statement in a frugal way.

The best way to do this is by understanding the nature of the problem first and how best to implement the solution. In other words, you will need to write an algorithm – a list of instructions that you want the machine to follow to fix the problem.

Your designs should always begin with the thing you want the program to do. This will also include your algorithm, or at least the problem that your algorithm will fix. The algorithm will always look something like this:

4. Input: data coming, where applicable
5. Processing: operations performed on the data and declaration of variables
6. Output: the results, or the action you want performed.

Here is a verbose example of a C++ program for displaying "Hello World". This is to illustrate how C++ programs are composed:

```
// Simple C++ program to display "Hello World"
// Header file for input output functions
#include<iostream>
using namespace std;
// main function -
// where the execution of program begins
int main()
{
    // prints hello world
    cout<<"Hello World";

    return 0;
}
```

Here is the structure:

- Call header file for input and output functions
- Call the main function where the execution happens
- Print "Hello World"
- Terminating statement that indicates the state of the machine

We can see how verbose C++ is, because most of the steps regard the backend aspects of C++ that are needed to execute the code, such as calling the library files. Your algorithms don't need to be this detailed most of the time.

Despite being simple, this algorithm illustrates how developers take tasks and translate them into code. In the next chapter, we will use this algorithm to write our program.

As you have noticed in the example, there are comments in the code that explain what each part of the code does. These comments are preceded by "//". The compiler will not read any lines of code preceded by // because they don't do anything but help other people working on the code read what the code does. It is good practice to include comments in your code so people know what each line of code does.

Overview of the C++ Syntax

We have talked about the importance of syntax for the compiler, but it is also important to understand the syntax of a programming language because it will allow you to debug the code. Just like with human languages, if you know the rules of a language you can correct yourself easily when you make mistakes. **Debugging** is the process of finding and removing errors and abnormalities in the code, also known as "bugs" ("What is Debugging?" n.d.). It is a process of correction.

IDEs have debugging tools that highlight where errors occur in the code, but these features aren't always reliable. For instance, leaving out a semicolon to terminate a line of code is a common error, but the debugger will highlight the error in the (.h) file instead of the code where the mistake happens in the program file (.cpp). Most debuggers are not intelligent enough to detect an absence of something and will throw the verbose error that the compiler gives when the unterminated line violates a rule in the library. However, a programmer will pick up the error simply when they notice the red semicolon line delimiter is missing from one of the lines.

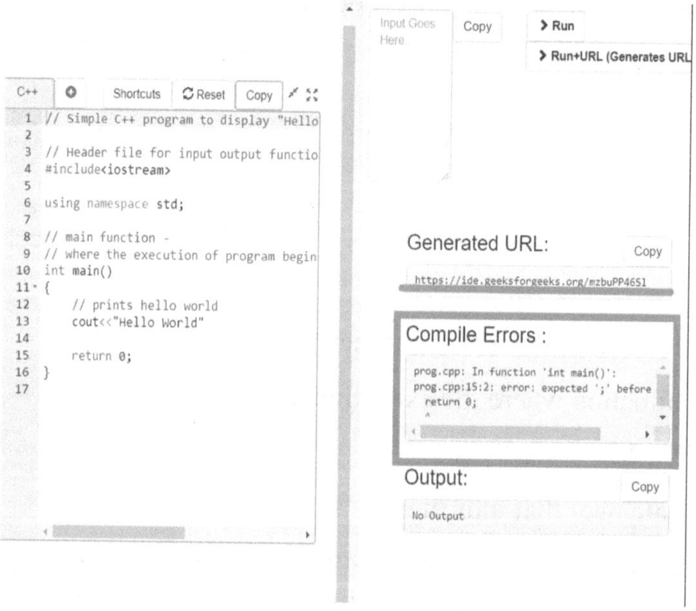

"Hello World" program in GeeksforGeeks IDE without a line delimiter

This screenshot features "Hello World" with a missing delimiter. Immediately you will notice that the IDE has different syntax highlighting for C++ than the programming environments we explored in the previous chapter. Syntax can vary from platform to platform. This is why we are standardizing the process with GeeksforGeeks IDE. In our chosen IDE, semicolons are not highlighted. However, the IDE can make up for this by recognizing and annotating missing semicolons, as highlighted in the screenshot. You can practice and explore this program by going to its generated URL: https://ide.geeksforgeeks.org/mzbuPP46Sl.

It is easy to see this when the code is small, but when working on a larger project the task can be difficult. I have heard of programmers who spend a week and or more trying to find or fix a line in their code only to discover it is something very minuscule like a missing letter or mismatch in case. To make debugging easier, it is advised that you separate code into smaller modules ("What is Debugging?" n.d.). Many errors can be found and easily dealt with in this way.

Let us look at the "Hello World" program and study its syntax in detail. While syntax highlighting may vary across different platforms, these aspects of code are consistently highlighted on all platforms.

Comments: As I said, these are the lines of code that the compiler will ignore. They are used to annotate code and leave helpful explanations for other programmers. This is great because normally when we code we collaborate with others. It advised that you leave comments in your algorithm to simplify it for others. In most platforms comments will be highlighted green. Comments are always preceded with (//).

Header File Library: Lines that start with (#) are used by the compiler to call library functions. These lines are very essential, so they appear in every program. In the "Hello World" example we call a library that is used to manage strings. These lines of code will be highlighted in different colors across different platforms. In GeeksforGeeks the color is purple.

Statements: Statements describe the beginning of a line of code with instructions that the compiler recognizes. This includes declaration handling instructions, like "*using...*" or "*return...*" in our Hello World program. They are also highlighted differently across multiple platforms. On GeeksForGeeks they are highlighted purple.

Functions: This is code that encapsulates instructions. It may take inputs and output a result. Every function is written like this: "[*function_name*] () "followed by curly braces {}. Anything in the curly braces is the set of instructions that will be executed. In our example, *main*() is the function that initiates the instructions that will output "Hello World" with cout<<. In a ".cpp" program, *int main* () must always appear for the program to **function.**

> **Note:** Recalling our discussion about algorithms from the previous section, your algorithm will mainly describe what instructions occur within the curly brackets of*intmain*(). More detailed algorithms may explain the sorts of data types needed for inputs, outputs, and other data. We'll discuss data types in detail in Chapter 3.

Data: These are variables and other kinds of data functions and statements. In the GeeksforGeeks IDE, they are highlighted blue.

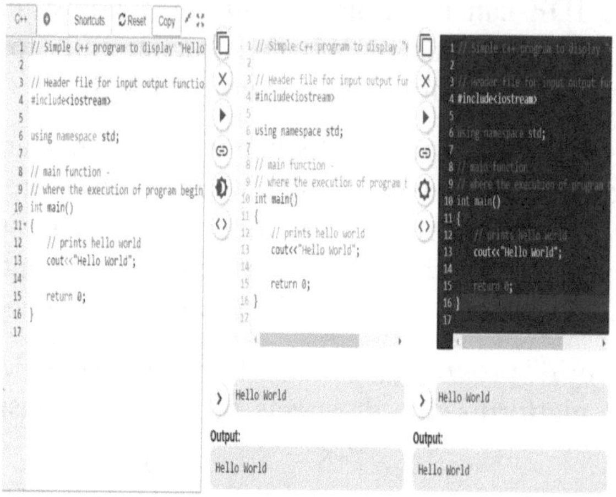

Comparison of "Hello World" program in GeeksforGeeks IDE and the GeeksforGeeks Embedded Program Articles

This screenshot features a successful run of "Hello World" with the memory used to run the program. This IDE has light syntax highlighting, focusing mainly on comments, statements, and operand data. Compared to GeeksforGeeks' embedded code in their articles, their embedded code is much more detailed ("Writing first C++ program," 2017). The two screenshots on the right feature the "light-mode" and "dark-mode" views of the same code embedded in their articles. These views are more detailed, highlighting comments, functions, and distinguishing different statements. For example, data types such as ***int are distinguished with a different color from other statements such as using namespace.*** Also the embedded views, unlike the IDE, distinguish strings from other data. This is a perfect example of how syntax highlighting can vary across different platforms.

Earlier we saw a Code::Block example with an error in it. Below is the very same code next to one that is corrected. Immediately you can begin to appreciate the syntax and what went wrong in the Code::Block example.

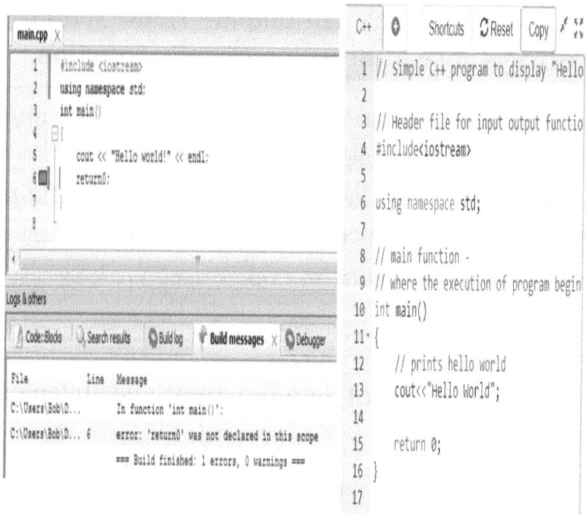

Comparison of "Hello World" in Code::Blocks with GeeksforGeeks IDE

This screenshot features a side-by-side comparison of the previous example, "Hello World" in Code::Blocks with errors, and the same corrected code in GeeksforGeeks IDE. Upon studying both, you should be able to see that the last instruction in the intmain()function was incorrectly entered in the Code::Blocks.As a result,the compiler could not recognize the return statement.

I will admit that it is not as impressive in a few code lines like this, but being able to notice errors and explain them is one of the most important skills for programmers. At this point you should not worry much about being able to do this. The more you code and learn, the better equipped you will be to notice and fix errors. Software and web development are industries with a high failure rate because of this. To succeed as a developer you need to solve problems quickly, find bugs more efficiently, and fix them. This also applies on the administrative side, because being able to find, fix, and explain bugs is a large part of desk service level agreements.

In tech, **Service Level Agreements** (SLAs) are agreements between a service provider and a client. They agree upon aspects of the service, like support, quality, availability, and responsibilities (Wieder, Butler, Theilmann, & Yahyapour, 2011). Comprehensive SLAs offer a debugging debriefing, where every error is logged and listed with its cause, workaround, and solution. This is the best way to do it in technology management firms and development stages. However, administrators have more resources to dedicate to debugging than developers themselves. They are compensated at a higher rate as well. For instance, web developers make approximately $60,000 a year in the US; web administrators, those in charge of SLAs, make about 1/3 more at $90,000 a year ("15-1199.03—Web Administrators," n.d.). This level of expertise is valuable because it understands how the compiler translates C++.

First Program: Output and Basic Strings

"Hello World" is every programming language's beginner project; its aim is to show the learner the basic syntax of the program and how it functions. As you learn more languages you will write many "Hello World" programs. In the previous section, we used it to explore topics like algorithms, syntax, and C++ programming environments. In this section we will go further: we will manipulate the code.

C++ uses the *cout* object from the *iostream* library. An object is a method that a computer uses to manage data. In our example, *cout* was used to tell the compiler to print "Hello World with the >> operator. Don't freak out; we will discuss operators and objects in later chapters. For now, it's enough to understand that the compiler reads *cout* as specific instructions because that instruction is defined in the *iostream* library that we declared.

Now, let's look at "Hello World" and the cout object by changing the print out. Find the original code here so you can use it as a reference:

https://ide.geeksforgeeks.org/eA8ZMEKiDO

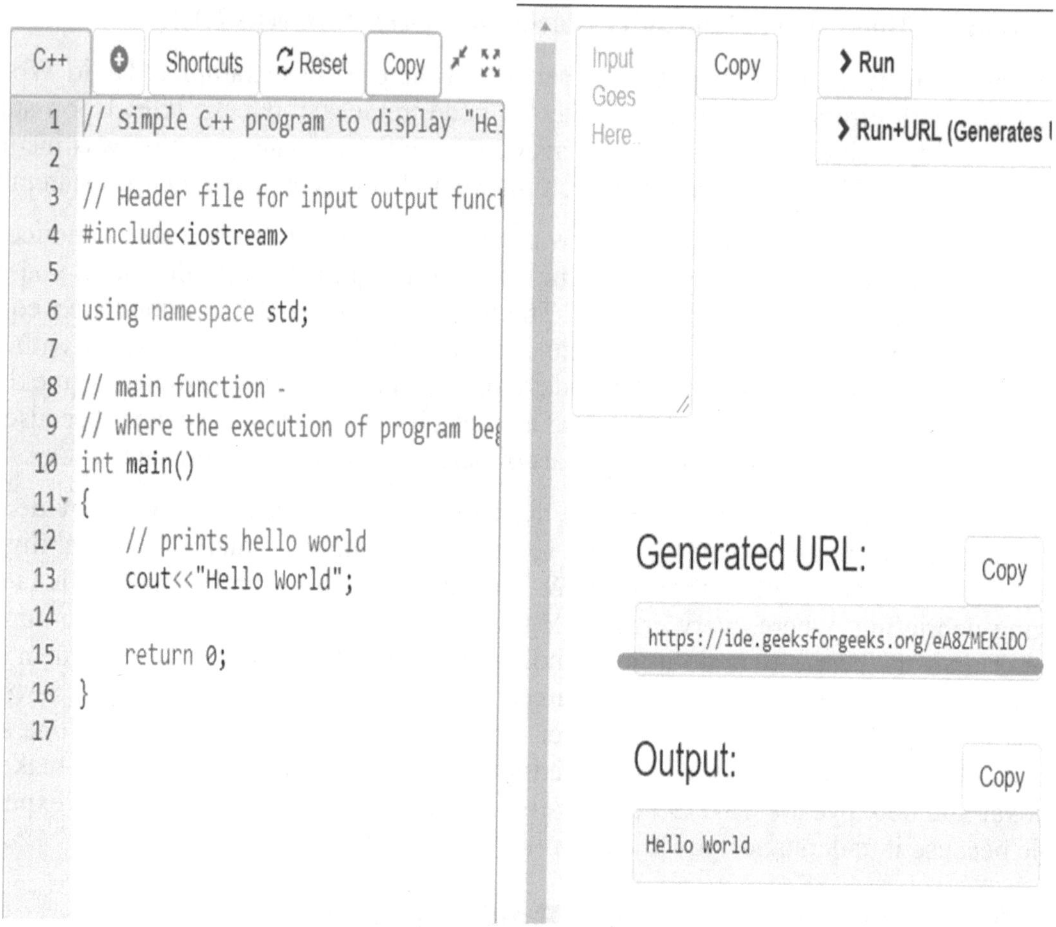

"Hello World" program in GeeksforGeeks IDE

This screenshot is the successful run of "Hello World" in split-screen mode. As we begin to use the IDE for coding exercises, note the input and output boxes. While there are no inputs for this program, you will input data into the top box labeled "Input Goes Here…" when prompted by the program in the output below.

You can access this program in the saved IDE here: https://ide.geeksforgeeks.org/eA8ZMEKiDO.

You can also view a copy of the code in the index.

Using Cout

The *cout* object uses the << operator to print values and text, and we can have as many of them as we like. Using the IDE in your browser, change the code to print out:

```
Hello World
I am learning C++
```

Like this:

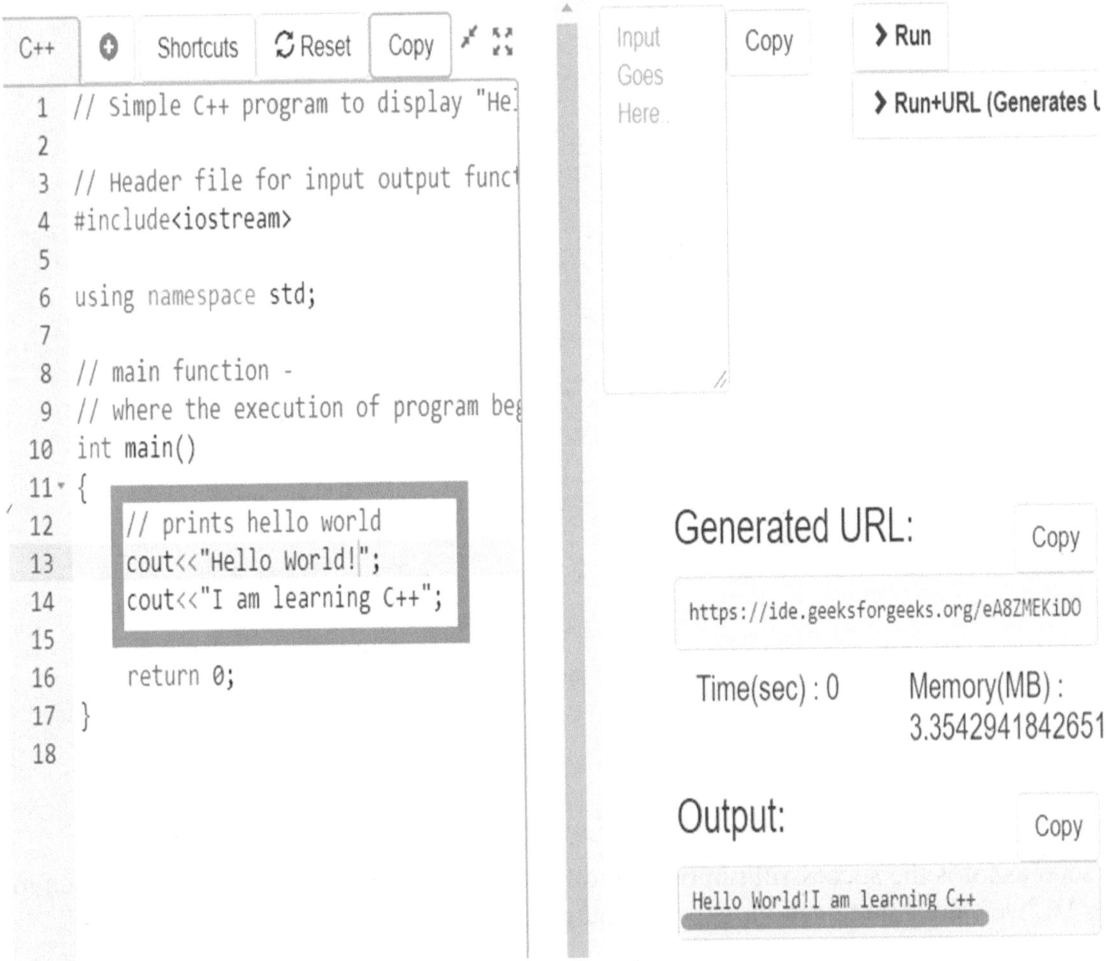

Adding cout objects

This screenshot is the successful run of our edited "Hello World" program in split-screen mode. While the program ran without any errors, it didn't produce the result we wanted. Observing the output, the printed text is missing a new line. We will have to instruct the compiler to add the new line to get the desired result.

Adding lines can be done in several ways: we can add delimiters within the strings or use another manipulator object from the *iostream* library.

Using Escape Sequences

Although it might be tempting to write a string within cout and enter a line, it will not work. It will break the code and it will not run. Don't believe me? Test it!

You can add a new line by using an escape sequence. **Escape sequences** are used in many instances where you need to introduce special characters within strings and character streams. It can also add lines, like so:

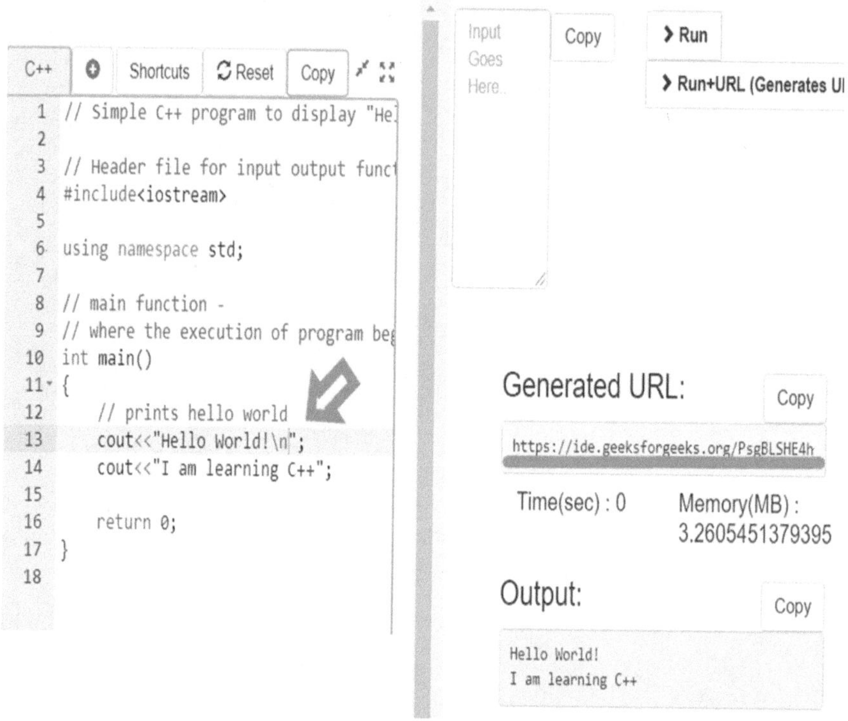

Using in-string escape sequences to delimit and manipulate the output

This screenshot is the successful run of our edited "Hello World" program in split-screen mode. Using \n, we were able to get our expected output.

As you look at the code, you can see that doubles quotes are used. So, if you want to add double quotes in a string, you will have to use an escape sequence so that the compiler knows that is not a part of the code. Not doing so may cause unforeseen errors or bugs. This is why escape sequences matter. Here is a list of the many instances where they can be used ("Escape sequences—Cppreference.com," n.d.):

"'": Used for single quotes

"\"": Used for double quotes

"?": Used for question marks

"\\": Used for backslashes

"\f": Stands for "form feed" and is used to go to the next "page"

"\n": Stands for "line feed" and is used to go to the next line

"\t": Stands for "horizonatal tab" and adds 5 spaces horizontally

"\v": Stands for "veritical tab" and is used for spacing in vertical languages

Note: If you decide to try different escape sequences as text delimiters, be sure to only use the *Run* button. This will save the workspace.

If you want to save some of your results for later, you can use the *Run + URL* ... button to save your work at another URL to return to later. To return to our exercise, you can use our saved IDE workspace URL (https://ide.geeksforgeeks.org/PsgBLSHE4h).

You can also access this code in the index.

Using Endl: Input/Output Manipulators

Like we have said, programming languages are as versatile as human language. You can express one instruction in many ways, and terminating a string is no exception. The difference between an escape sequence and *endl* is that *endl* flushes and refreshes the buffer used to store the string. Programmers use *endl* to clear memory after printing a lot of text. You can see why this is useful in memory management. *Endl* is an example of an input/output manipulator. **Input/Output manipulators** are functions that allow you to control input/output streams using the "<<" operator or the ">>" operator ("Input/output manipulators—Cppreference.com," n.d.).

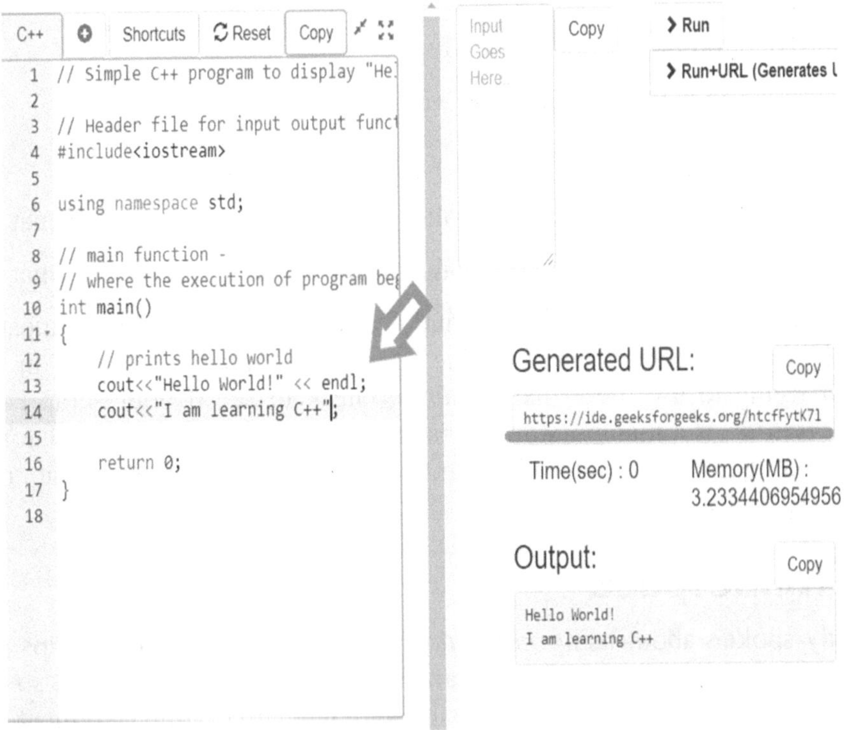

Using an input/output manipulator to delimit and manipulate the output.

This screenshot is the successful run of our edited "Hello World" program in split-screen mode. Using *endl* we were able to get our expected output. In a program this small, it is difficult to see the effects of using a memory manipulator. Manipulators only begin to make a difference when using them in called functions. You can access the code at this URL: https://ide.geeksforgeeks.org/htcfFytK71.

Like escape sequences, there are many more input/output manipulators that give programmers more control over data types or strings. Many of them will make sense once we talk about data types and structuring classes. Here are some of them ("Input/output manipulators—Cppreference.com," n.d.):

"$\frac{boolalpha}{noboolapha}$": Switches between using "0/1" to "false/true" for Boolean values

"$\frac{showbase}{noshowbase}$": For mathematical outputs, controls whether a prefix is used to indicate a numeric base

"$\frac{showpos}{noshowpos}$": Controls whether the " +" sign is used to indicate non-negative numbers

"$\frac{uppercase}{nouppercase}$": Controls the usage of uppercase characters with particular output formats

"$ends$": Outputs "\0"

"$flush$": Flushes the output stream

"$endl$": Outputs "$\backslash n$" and flushes the output stream

"get_{money}": Receives an input as a monetary value

"put_{money}": Formats and outputs a monetary value

"get_{time}": Receives an input as a date/time value according to a specified format

"put_{time}": Receives an input as a date/time value according to a specified format

Note: Recall our conversation about C++11 and C++14. As of this writing, most programming IDEs use C++11 as their default version. The "get/put…" functions are all in C++11. If you receive an error trying to use these manipulators, check to see if your setup is using C++11. Additionally, "$quoted$" is a manipulator that is in C++14 only. This manipulator allows you to insert and extract quoted strings with embedded spaces ("Input/output manipulators—Cppreference.com," n.d.).

Omitting Namespace

We have already spoken about using *namespace* statements. We said it helps declare strings globally, but when it comes to a small program like "Hello World" it is not so important. For larger programs that use several functions, it is good practice to use the statement to declare each string separately. This saves memory space in the compiler, or you will find yourself in a situation where the compiler is bogged down unnecessarily, having to pull the entire string namespace library to print code. Declaring each string separately might make your code wordier, but it will reduce compiler overhead, and it focuses your instructions. *Std namespace* has multiple objects and definitions that can make it difficult for the computer to find the appropriate way to manipulate and define a string. The namespace convention is important when you have functions that are going to be called by multiple programs. So putting it in there unnecessarily has the potential of making your functions poorly defined and causing recognition errors between them.

Let's make our code more efficient by removing the using *namespace* from our code.

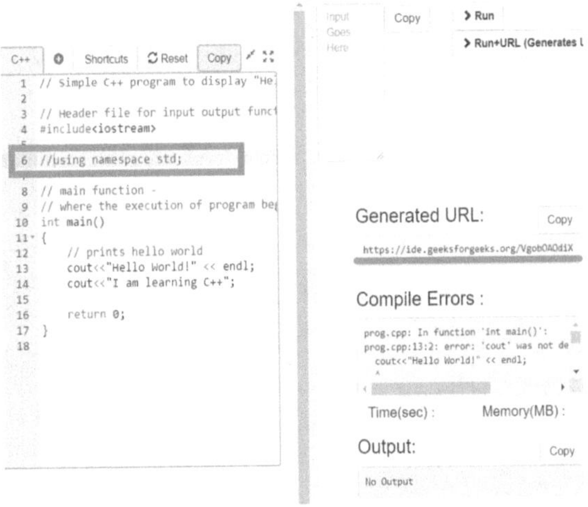

Testing Stability: Using a comment to remove "using namespace"

This screenshot is an unsuccessful test run of the "Hello World" program with *usingnamespacestd;*removed. You can access this saved IDE space through the following URL: https://ide.geeksforgeeks.org/VgobOAOdiX.

"Commenting out" lines of code is a highly efficient way of testing the stability of code. You can delete the double forward slashes to remove the comment and restore the line of code at any time. This allows you to test the code without destroying it. Once you have completed testing, it is good practice to delete any unwanted lines of code. During your testing, you can always return to this saved instance by using the URL above. You can also access the raw code in the index.

When you remove *using namespace* std the following error occurs:

```
prog.cpp: In function 'int main()':
prog.cpp:13:2: error: 'cout' was not declared in this scope
  cout<<"Hello World!" << endl;
  ^
prog.cpp:13:2: note: suggested alternative:
In file included from prog.cpp:4:0:
/usr/include/c++/5/iostream:61:18: note:   'std::cout'
   extern ostream cout;  /// Linked to standard output
                  ^
prog.cpp:13:26: error: 'endl' was not declared in this scope
  cout<<"Hello World!" << endl;
                          ^
prog.cpp:13:26: note: suggested alternative:
In file included from /usr/include/c++/5/iostream:39:0,
                 from prog.cpp:4:
/usr/include/c++/5/ostream:590:5: note:   'std::endl'
     endl(basic_ostream<_CharT, _Traits>& __os)
     ^
```

Looking closely, the compiler tells us that we need to declare *cout* and *endl.* It even makes suggestions, like declaring them as *std.* Let's do as the compiler asks and see what happens.

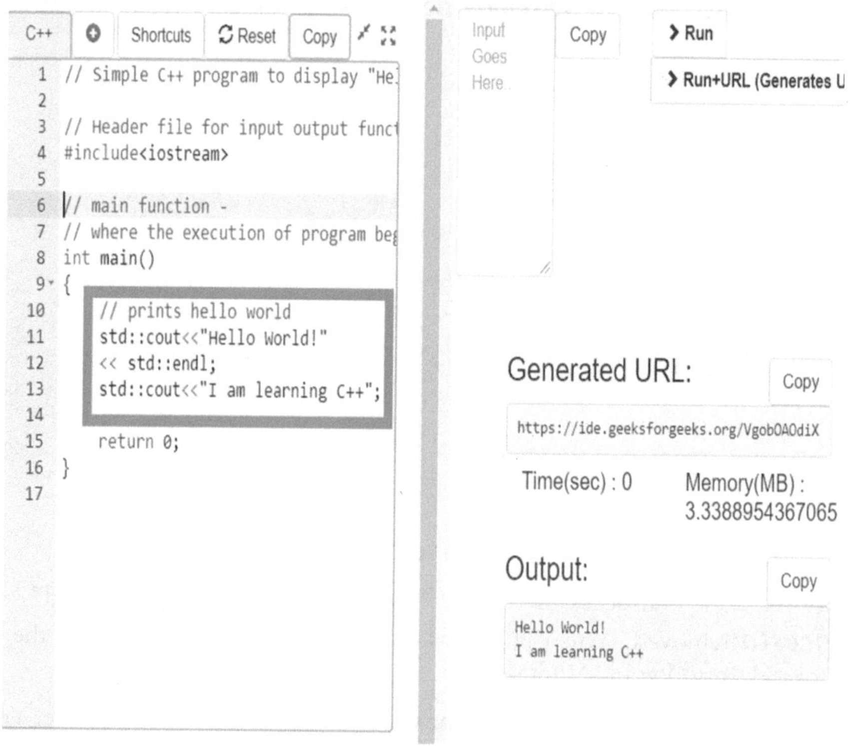

Declaring the iostream objects and manipulators

This screenshot is a successful test run of the "Hello World" program with *usingnamespacestd*;removed. Once the iostream objects and manipulators were successfully declared, the unneeded line was removed.

If you would like to practice, you can use this URL: https://ide.geeksforgeeks.org/VgobOAOdiX

Note: If you are having multiple errors during your practice, we will always provide a saved IDE workspace with a successful run of the program to help you troubleshoot. To begin the troubleshooting session, open up another window, and navigate to the successful run. Compare your current workspace with the successful run workspace. You can find a successful run of "Declaring the iostream objects and manipulators" at this link: https://ide.geeksforgeeks.org/a5zOdSWoQU.

CHAPTER 3:

Variables and Data Types

We have talked about how low-level programming closely resembles machine language, but they differ because they still use elements that are reminiscent of human languages like syntax, structures, and variables. **Variables** are a mathematical concept that humans use to convey meaning to machines. A huge chunk of computer science is recognizing that speech is a series of mathematical concepts. This includes AND and OR gates that enable machines to make decisions on a single data bit level. At a very small scale, bitwise functions can help with many computing processes, from controlling displays to switching traffic on a server. We will discuss these advanced topics later in Chapter 4. For now, let's deepen our understanding of C++ by looking at variables.

Variables are one of the most important aspects of any programming language - functions, and other operations of a programming language, generally operate on variables. We have said that not all programs need input or output, but all programs will have some variable that they are working on or there is nothing to work on. The outcome of a function is always a state change. A state change is when a machine changes from one decision or operational phase to another. This term was used to describe operations in old mainframe computers, but we still use it in computer science to describe how programs work. In our example, the IDE started with an initialized *main*() state before the program ran. Then it switched states to execute the output command.

State changes are discussed often in lower-level languages because of how close they are to machine language. Lower-level languages are also called **compiled languages** because they are compiled into machine language. This is in contrast to high-level languages like Python. If you remember, we spoke of how higher-level languages do not need variables to be declared with their data types because of their built-in libraries. For instance, Python uses a Python environment to recognize variables and their data types. In C++ variables and the data types have to be declared. A **data type** tells the compiler how to treat the data. Data types make more sense when you think of vectors in math; unlike integers, which communicate amounts, vectors tell us the size and direction of space. Therefore, vectors are a different data type than an integer. Properties like these are used in software like Photoshop to help with rendering.

Note: Vector-based images can be manipulated without losing the quality of the image. This is because files like .jpeg or .png store pixel location of an image as integers on a grid. Vector files such as svg or .pdf use vectors to describe their pixel locations. Therefore, when the image is made larger, the vectors indicate how the colors should expand while the regular image files do not. This is what causes the pixelation and distortion when manipulating non-vector image files.

Input and Output: Declaring Variables

In the previous chapter, we declared some things as we were learning how to use *cout*. In this section, we are going to look at examples of data types and how they are declared. Below are examples of variable declarations and what they stand for ("C++ Variables," n.d.). Keep in mind that variables essentially store types of data:

"*int*": Keyword is short for "integer" and stores whole numbers, without decimals. This keyword includes positive and negative integers.

"*double*": Stores numbers with decimals, both positive and negative numbers.

"*char*": Keyword is short for "character" and stores single characters regardless of their capitalization. Char values are single quoted.

"*string*": Stores text, such as in our "Hello World" example. String values are double quoted.

"*bool*": Keyword is short for "Boolean" and stores values with two states: true or false. As previously discussed, these values can be expressed as either "0/1" or "false/true."

In the next section, we will discuss them in detail. Now let us look at examples of these. To create a variable you have to assign it a value after the "=" operator. Their syntax looks like this:

```
[Datatype][Variable_name] = [value];
```

Note: Each $[Variable_{name}]$ must be unique within your function. Otherwise, it will cause an error.

Now let us create a variable called "*myNum*" with the *int* data type and a value of 10, then have our program print it out.

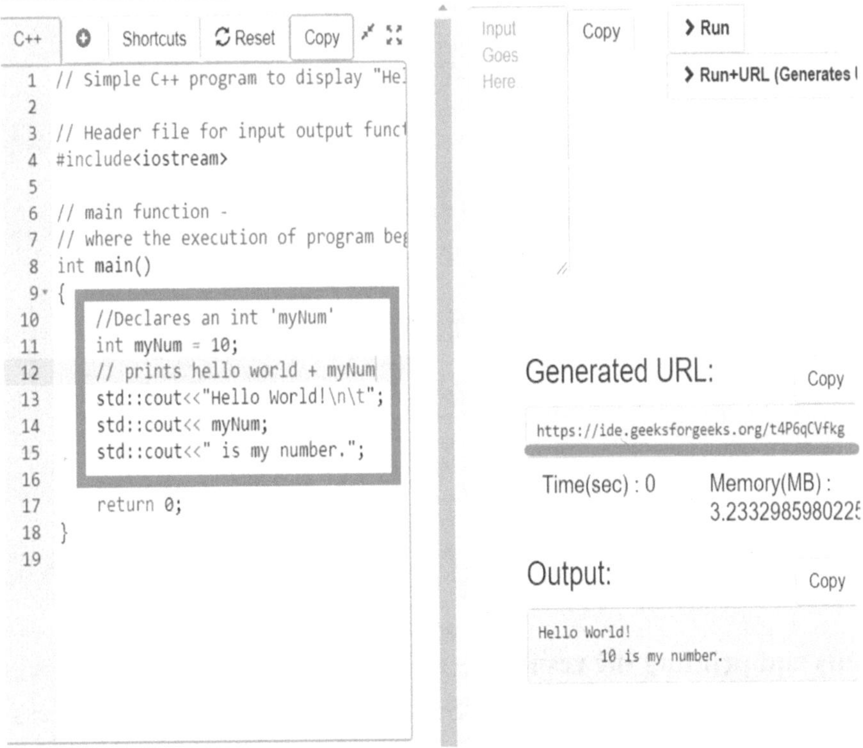

Declaring int numbers

This screenshot is a successful test run of the "myNum" program. You can access the saved IDE workspace with the following URL: https://ide.geeksforgeeks.org/t4P6qCVfkg.

This code was implemented without *usingnamespacestd*;as it's the best practice. You should practice implementing the same code successfully with the namespace. Remember that you can reset the workspace to a successful state by using the URL.

We had our share of *cout* examples in our code. Let's use the input box in the top right and the *cin* object so our program takes in inputs and operates on them.

We can do this by writing programs that take two numbers and adds them together. To do this, we have to declare two variables that will store our inputs for our program to operate on.

We will declare multiple variables:

- Two *int* variables named *x* and *y*,
- One *int* variable named sum.

We can also tell the program to prompt the user to give two inputs.

Note: In our IDE, you must enter the inputs *before* you run the program. Each input should be on its own line.

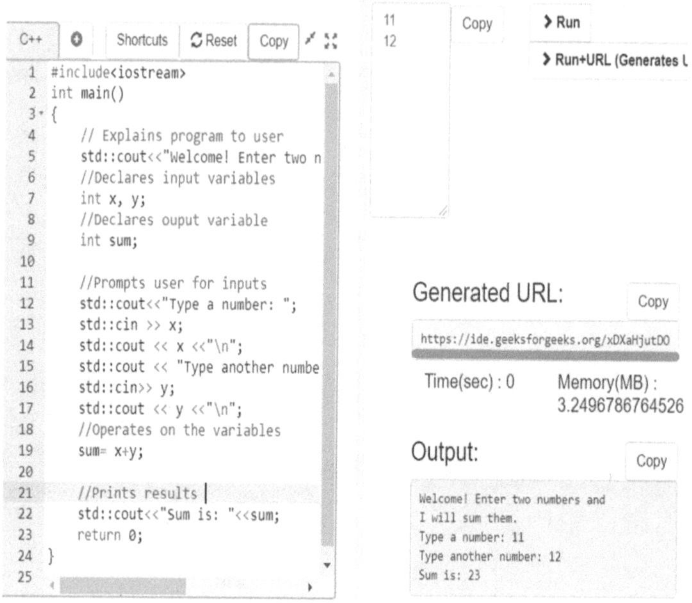

Summing inputs and printing the result

This screenshot is a successful test run of our "Summing" program. You can access the saved IDE workspace with the following URL: https://ide.geeksforgeeks.org/xDXaHjutDO. This exercise had to be modified for our IDE's input system. Therefore, we included additional *cout*lines that confirm our inputs.

This code was implemented without *usingnamespacestd*; as it's the best practice. You should practice implementing the same code successfully with the namespace. Remember that you can reset the workspace to the successful state by using the URL.

Basic Data Types

Data types specify the size and types of information stored in a variable. Each has its own keyword and an associated size ("C++ Data Types," n.d) :

"*int*": Keyword is short for "integer" and stores whole numbers. Has a size of 4 bytes.

"*float*": Stores decimal numbers with 7 decimal digits. Has a size of 4 bytes.

"*double*": Stores decimals numbers with 15 decimal digits. Has a size of 8 bytes.

"*char*": Keyword is short for "character" and stores single characters regardless of their capitalization. Has a size of 1 byte.

"*bool*": Keyword is short for "boolean" and stores values that have a state of either being true or false. Has a size of 1 byte.

Note: Recall the "*string*" data type. We have worked with this special datatype extensively. String values can vary in size. Due to this, they are handled in the iostream library to apply more flexibility for text handling. We'll return to strings and discuss some advanced topics in the next section.

These sizes matter for data handling. For instance, when you use *int* with *float/double* all those numbers will be converted to *int.* It is because the compiler uses 4 bytes to calculate integers which have the allocation for decimals. The program will still run but your calculations will not be accurate. Let's explore this more by modifying our program and looking at the results. We are going to be using a long-popular decimal number (pi):

$\frac{22}{7} = 3.142857142857142857142857142857$1. It will test the limits of *float* and *double.*

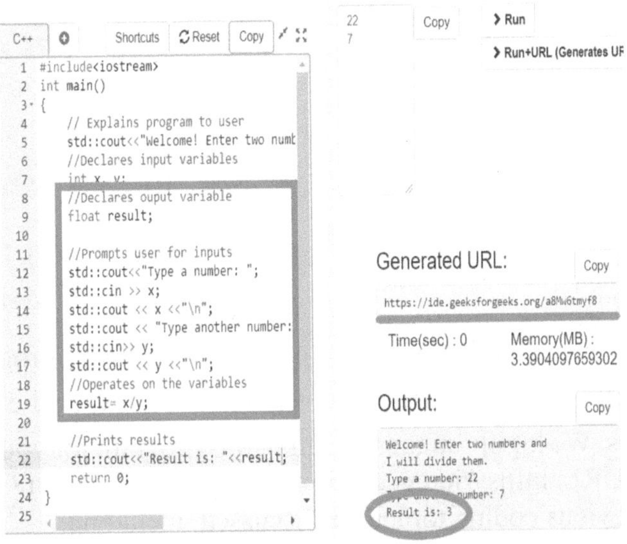

Using Int with Float or Double

This screenshot is a successful test run of our modified program calculating $\pi = \frac{22}{7}$. You can access the saved IDE workspace with the following URL:

$$\text{https:}\frac{\square}{\text{ide}}.\text{geeksforgeeks}.\frac{\text{org}}{\text{a8Mw6tmyf8}}.\text{This exercise also includes } \frac{22}{7} = 3.142857142857142857142857142857\ldots$$

but as you can see, the result is shown as 3. This is because the compiler calculated the inputs as *int*, which are not modified to store decimals. As a result, the result is missing the decimals.

To get the result we are looking for, it would be best to change the variable data types. Will using float data types differ from double data types? Can we expect a different result? Remember you can reset by going to a successful state of the workspace using the URL.

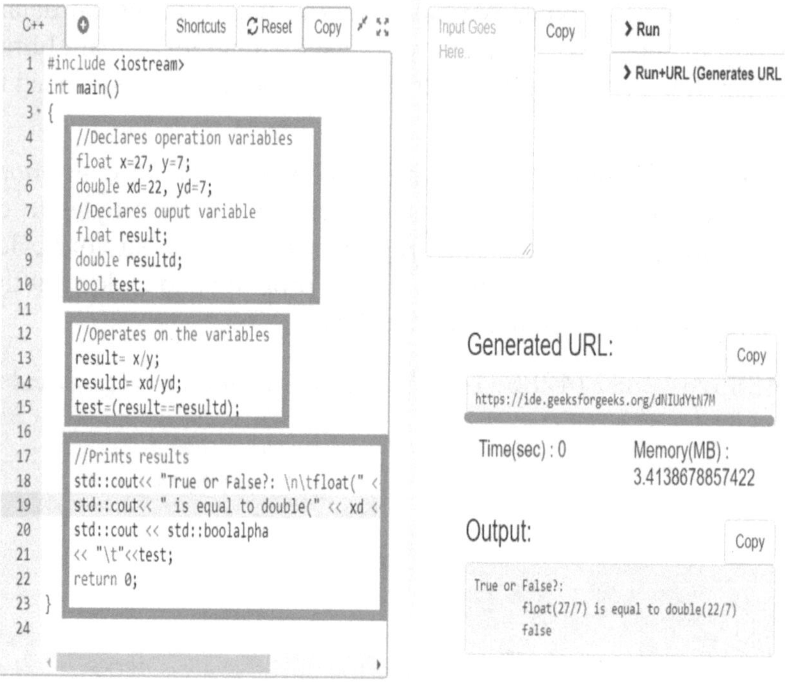

Comparing Float and Double

This screenshot is a successful test run of our modified program calculating $\pi = \frac{22}{7}$. To focus on comparing *float* and *double*, we have removed the input statements and rearranged our data types. We highly suggest creating this program for yourself using the previous program located at this URL: https://ide.geeksforgeeks.org/a8Mw6tmyf8. This exercise will give you practice in some previous coding topics we discussed, including:

1. "*bool*" data type keyword
2. "$\frac{boolalpha}{noboolapha}$" input-output manipulator

It will also give you some experience with a logical operator. We will discuss the logical operators in detail in the next chapter. Once you have manipulated the program, open a new window, and compare this to the successful run of the screenshot above. You can find the saved IDE workspace with the successful run at this URL: https://ide.geeksforgeeks.org/dNIUdYtN7M.

Power of C++: Advanced Strings

Another data type we are going to look at is strings. **Strings** are one of the most popular data types in computer science; they are sequences of characters. It might be helpful to think of them as sentences, but not every sentence represents a string. We have seen how they work with our "Hello World" app. Strings are a separate data type with their own library. To manipulate and work with them a program needs an appropriate header – the string library. These libraries have methods and features that allow the program to manipulate strings.

Operation: String Concatenation

String concatenation is when different strings are put together into one string. It is combining strings. This is one of the most common functions of a program. For instance, when you enter your name at a website or a game and then you switch to another page and the screen greets you "Hello, [your_name]!", the program has used concatenation to do that. It has combined "Hello," with your name and "!" in the end.

In C++, string concatenations are performed through the "+" operator. Let's see this in action by making a program that prints an imputed string with a greeting. For this to work, we must include the <string> library, which contains objects and statements needed for handling strings.

Open a fresh instance of the IDE we have been using and follow these steps:

- In addition to $\#include < iostream >$, also include the $< string >$ library
- Omit $usingnamespacestd;$
- Remove the current filler code within $intmain(\square)\{\ldots\}$
- Declare and set the variables $firstName = "John"$ and $lastName = Doe$
- Declare and calculate $fullName$ by adding $firstName$ and $lastName$ with the " +" operator
- Print out the result as "Hello John Doe."

It should look something like this:

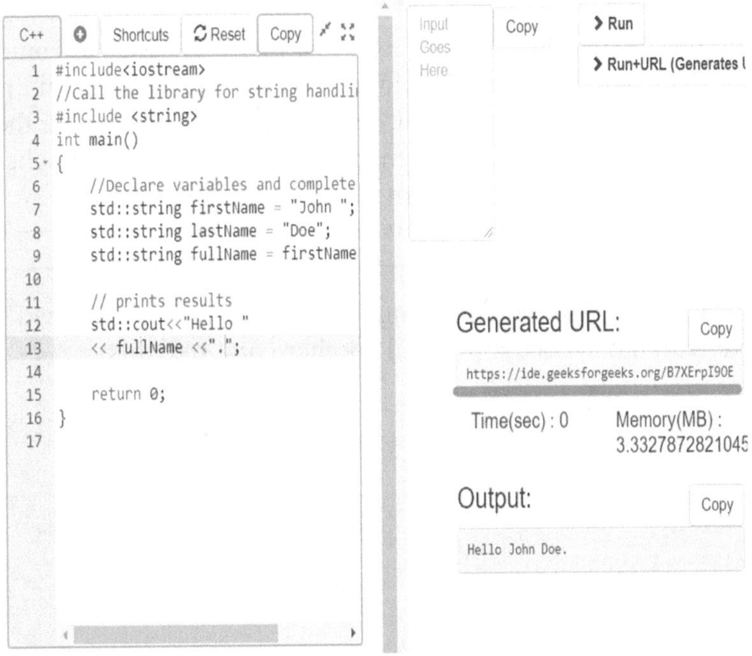

String Concatenation

This screenshot is a successful test run of our string concatenation program. We encourage you to open up this program in another window and compare it to your program. You can access the successful run at this URL: https://ide.geeksforgeeks.org/B7XErpI9OE.

Note: Be sure to annotate your code. You can shorthand the instructions and use them as an impromptu algorithm to annotate your code. This will help you keep the program in order.

Usually, in forums, the concatenated text input is kept small as possible and the formatting is done by the program. In the example, we manually have to add space after "Hello" and "John", but the program adds space. Now that you have seen how the "+" operator works, how might you add space? See if you can figure it out by playing with the code in your editor. If things fall apart you can always return to our successful IDE workspace by clicking on the URL.

Note:

The "+" operator is used for both adding numbers and concatenating strings.Trying to use the operator to add a string and a number will produce an error.You can test this on your own using a modified program from the previous chapter.You can also check out a successful run of the program here that shows how to concatenate numbers as strings at this URL:

https://ide.geeksforgeeks.org/glPmslDwF7.Uncomment the declarations to try to add numbers and strings to see the error for yourself.The error is very long and verbose,as it conflicts across the *<iostream>* and *<string>*libraries.

String Objects: Length() Attribute

We know from real-world experience that strings, like many things, can come in different sizes. This is unlike other data types we have explored so far. C++ makes this possible because it construes strings as objects with attributes. C++ defines a string length under the *Length*() attribute as you would expect in an object. To access length, the string must be attached to a variable and you must use the "." syntax. It should look something like this:

```
[string_name].length()
```

Let's return to our program and retrieve the length of *fullName*. We will need to modify our code by adding a new line with the syntax above and another *cout*, like this:

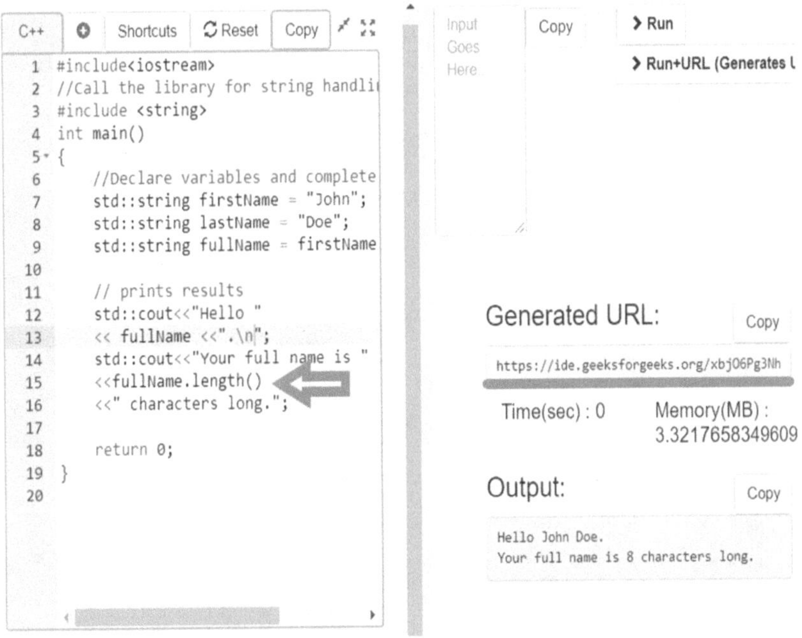

Print fullName.Length()

This screenshot is a successful test run of our modified string concatenation program. We encourage you to modify the program at this URL: https://ide.geeksforgeeks.org/B7XErpI9OE.

Once you have modified the program, you can compare it to this successful test run by opening it in another window. You can access this saved IDE window at the following URL: https://ide.geeksforgeeks.org/xbjO6Pg3Nh.

String Indexes and Arrays

Recall our conversation on objects. Vector arrays are also a special mathematical phenomenon with their own special attributes. An **array** is an orderly arrangement of objects – often rows, columns, or a matrix – where each has its own specific location. Strings are stored in arrays made up of characters. Therefore, a string array is orderly arrangements of characters where each character in a string is indexed in its own location. Arrays are accessed by using [ ] to find a character or any other items in an array. String indexes start with [0]. Let's see this in action by changing our program so that it prints out the 3rd character in *fullName*.

Note:

Remember that the index starts with [0].Therefore the 3rd character in the string array would be at [2], not 3.

We are going to use this syntax to do so:

```
fullName[x]
```

The *x* stands for the index of the character we would like to print out. Remember to also edit the cout to properly print the letter. You will also need to use escape sequences like this:

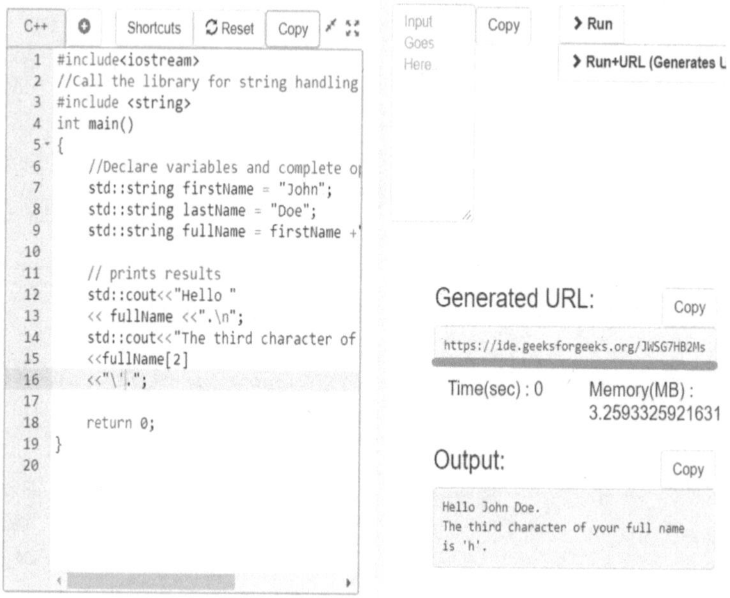

Access fullName String Array

This screenshot is a successful test run of our modified string attributes program. We encourage you to modify the program at this URL:

https://ide.geeksforgeeks.org/xbjO6Pg3Nh.

Once you have modified the program, you can compare it to this successful test run by opening it in another window. You can access this saved IDE window at the following URL: https://ide.geeksforgeeks.org/JWSG7HB2Ms.

In our examples we have relied a lot on cout capabilities, but, as I have alluded to, there are other strings handling capabilities used by programmers to field content from different sources. These are cin objects and the getline() function.

Cin and getline() function

In examples from the previous chapter, we have used cin. Like cout, cin is an object in the <iostream> library and it allows a program to receive input using the ">>" operator. Like cout, cin objects must be defined with the std data type. Let's modify our concatenation programs so that it receives the input of "John Doe". You can use your name if you like, as it can be fun to do so. You will need to follow these instructions:

- Navigate to the string concatenator program at the following URL:
- https://ide.geeksforgeeks.org/B7XErpI9OE
- Declare the variables
- Prompt the user for their name

- Calculate the operation by using the following code snippet:

  ....*fullName=firstName++lastName*...

- Print the results

If you find yourself stuck, here is how it should look:

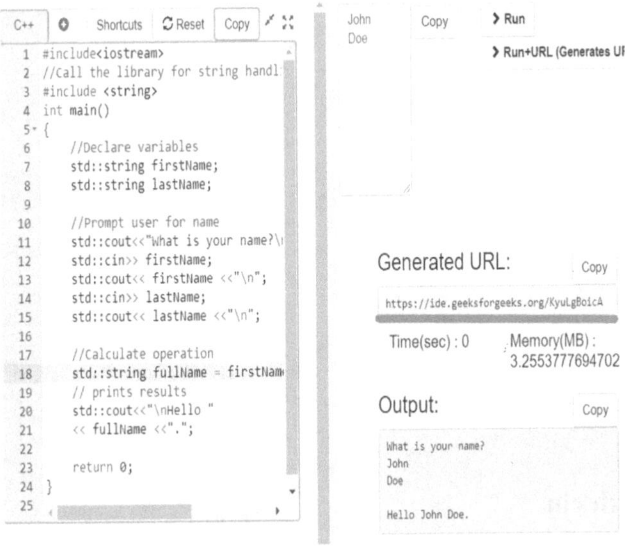

String Concatenation with cin

This screenshot is a successful test run of our modified string concatenation program using *cin*. We encourage you to open up this program in another window and compare it to your program. You can access the successful run at this URL: https://ide.geeksforgeeks.org/KyuLgBoicA.

Note: Be sure to annotate your code. You can shorthand the instructions and use them as an impromptu algorithm to annotate your code. This will help you keep the program in order.

The program will work only when the user enters their first and last name separately. But most peoples 'names are stored or put in as one single string. Let's change our program so that it greets the user when they enter their full name. You will need to follow these steps:

1. If not there already, or you need to reset the workspace, go to the previous workspace at the following URL:

   https://ide.geeksforgeeks.org/KyuLgBoicA

2. Declare only the *fullName* variable
3. Prompt the user for their full name using *cin*
4. Greet the user using *cout* and the input *fullName*

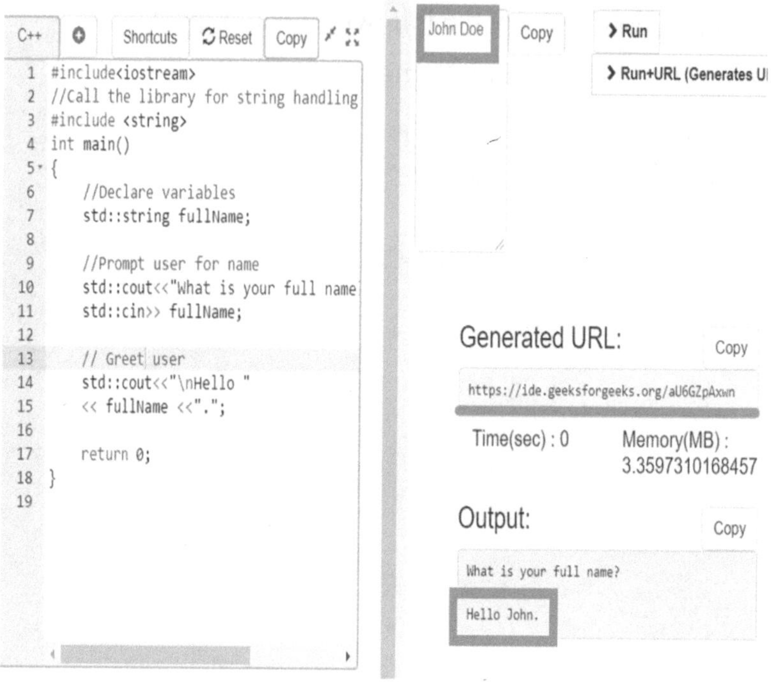

String Termination with cin

This screenshot is an unsuccessful test run of our modified string concatenation program using *cin*. While the program completed with no errors, we did not get an expected result. If your program had errors after your modifications or did not get a similar result, we encourage you to use our successful run to troubleshoot your workspace. Open up this successful run in another window and compare it to your program. You can access the successful run at this URL: https://ide.geeksforgeeks.org/aU6GZpAxwn.

You have witnessed typical *cin* behavior. When *cin* encounters a space it reads it as a string terminator and stops. This is why "Doe" is not added to the output. To get it to read the entire string with spaces, we must use the *getline*() function from the <string> library; it extracts all characters from the input and turns them into a string array.

Note:

getline()is usually preferred over *cin* to ensure that programs can read fielded text from secondary sources,particularly since *getline*() can read and aggregate different sorts of characters without errors.

Here is an example of *getline*() functions used well: https://www.geeksforgeeks.org/getline-string-c/

In this chapter, we have done quite a bit. We have looked at specialized functions, accessing objects, text manipulators, and operators. We will cover them in more detail in the coming chapters. I hope you have seen the role of operators in directing data and lending program functionality. In the following chapter, we are going to be looking at operators and how they give programs decision-making capabilities.

CHAPTER 4:

Operations in C++

We talked about how C++ is mainly a back-end, server-side language that is suited for controlling servers and other decision-making utilities for delivering content. In the last chapter, we looked at small ways that C++ handles data by looking at strings. In it, we saw the central role that operations play. Operations allow us to control loops and decision making in programs. A better understanding of operations allows us to add more functionality to our programs. **Functionality** is how programmers use methods and features of a language to achieve an end. We have seen how these string handling methods work, but what would be better is if we used those features in a context that allows us to achieve a particular end, like content management.

Note: "Operand" describes the value or variable being operated on. "Operator" describes the symbol indicating the sort of operation being carried out ("C++ Operators," n.d.).

The following is a list of operators in C++ ("Operators-In-C.png (800×533)," n.d.):

<table>
<tr><th>Operator</th><th>Type</th></tr>
<tr><td>+ +, −[] −</td><td>Unary operator > Arithmetic</td></tr>
<tr><td>+, −, *, /, %</td><td>Binary operator > Arithmetic</td></tr>
<tr><td><, <=, >, >=, ==, ! =</td><td>Binary operator > Relational</td></tr>
<tr><td>, ||. !</td><td>Binary operator > Logical</td></tr>
<tr><td>, |, <<, >>, ~, ∧</td><td>Binary operator > Bitwise</td></tr>
<tr><td>=, +=, −=, *=, /=, % =</td><td>Binary operator > Assignment</td></tr>
<tr><td>?:</td><td>Ternary or conditional operator</td></tr>
</table>

This table lists the operator symbols and categorizes them by (1) how many operands they accept at a time > (2) the type of operation they implement. For example, most arithmetic operators operate on two operands at a time.

All operators are characterized by how many operands they can operate on at a time and the types of operations they can execute. They are divided into three types:

Unary - operators that only accept 1 operand at a time

Binary - operators that only accept 2 operands at a time

Ternary - operators that accept more than 2 operands, or conditional operators with several arguments

They are further divided into 6 more types:

1. Arithmetic
2. Relational
3. Logical
4. Bitwise
5. Assignment operators
6. Other operators such as a conditional, address, and redirection

In this chapter, we will look at 5 types of operators and their functionalities.

Note: Operators have precedence, just as in mathematical equations. For example, parentheses, which are used to call a function, have higher precedence than addition or subtraction. However, you should try to keep your lines of code as simple as possible. This makes your programs easier to edit and debug. Having clean, uncomplicated code avoids bugs.

Binary Operators

Binary operators are the majority of operands you find in C++. They include 5 of the 6 types of operators. This makes them the perfect place to start. As the name suggests, binary operators compare two operands. They are perfect for decision-making and controlling switches.

Arithmetic Operators

They are the most common and well understood of all operators because of how much we use them even outside programming, since they are primarily mathematical. We use them to perform mathematical operations.

Note: In the string concatenation example, the "+" used to concatenate *was not an arithmetic function*. Instead, it was a function of the $< string >$ library that handled the concatenation.

Most operators in this category require two operands. The only exceptions are the unary "++" and " - -" operators which we use to increase or decrease within a loop. The binary operators are (Jaggi, 2015a):

"+": the addition operator that adds two operands

"−": the subtraction operator that subtracts one operand from another

"*": the multiplication operator that multiplies two operands

"$\frac{\square}{\square}$": the division "forward slash" operator that divides the first operand into the second

"%": the modulus operator that returns the remainder from dividing the first operand into the second

Let's make a *cout* program that demonstrates all of these 5 arithmetic operands. Create a new C++ workspace in the IDE and follow these instructions:

1. Declare two variables $a = 25$ and $b = 3$ as integers

2. Declare a variable, *result*

3. Print the variables a and b

4. Add a and b and print the result

5. Subtract a and b and print the result

6. Multiply a and b and print the result

7. Divide a and b and print the result

8. Calculate the remainder from dividing a and b and print the result

Here is how that looks.

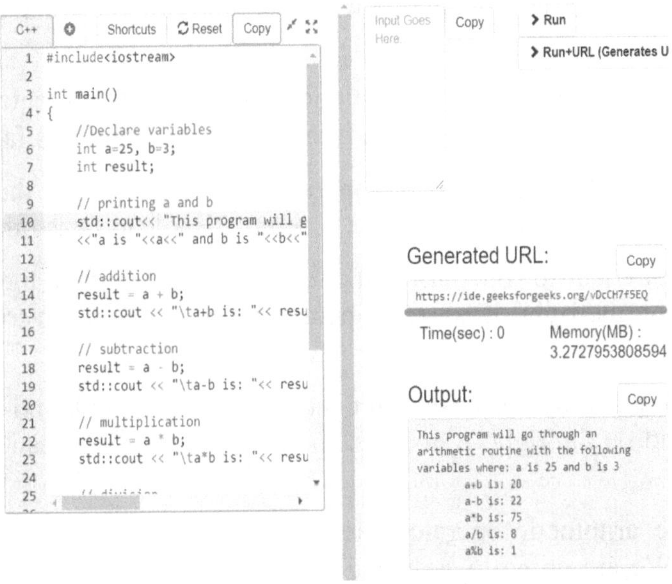

Arithmetic Routine Program

This screenshot is a successful run of the arithmetic routine program displaying all the arithmetic functions. You can access a copy of the raw code in the index.

If you get errors, I encourage you to use our successful run to troubleshoot your workspace. Open it up to compare the code. Here is where to find it:

https://ide.geeksforgeeks.org/vDcCH7f5EQ

Relational Operators

Most programs, not just in C++, use conditionals and loops to control flow. Operators in this section are used to perform conditional switching. For instance, in games, the game engine adapts to how the player interacts with the game. It gives the gamer more of an engaging and dynamic experience.

If the gamer completes challenges quickly, it might mean they find the game too easy. As a result, the game adjusts by increasing difficulty, but not too much. If the game is too hard, the engine might respond to that by making it a little easier to play. This is called dynamic gameplay, and it happens because coding languages have conditional switching. Conditional switching, the adaptation, happens through relational operators that compare two values. All relational operators are binary (Jaggi, 2015b). Here they are:

“==”: “Equal” operator that checks whether two given operands are equal. If the operands are equal, it returns a Boolean “true”; if not, it returns false.

“! =”: “Not-Equal” operator that also checks whether two given operands are equal or not. However, this operator returns a Boolean true if the operands are not equal and returns false if the operands are equal.

“>”: “Greater-than” operator that checks if the operand on the left is greater than the operand on the right. If so, this operator returns a Boolean true. Otherwise, it returns false.

“<”: “Less-than” operator that checks if the operand on the left is less than the operand on the right. If so, this operator returns a Boolean true. It returns Boolean false otherwise.

“>=”: “Greater-than or equal-to” operator that checks if the operand on the left is greater than or equal to the operand on the right. If so, this operand returns a Boolean true. If not, it returns a Boolean false.

“<=”: “Lesser-than or equal-to” operator that checks whether the operand on the left is less than or equal to the operand on the right. If so, this operand returns a Boolean true. If not, it returns false.

Like we did with the arithmetic operators, let’s create a *cout* program which demonstrates relational operators, We are going to be using conditional *if()* statements in our code. An *if()* statement executes the code within its curly braces when a specified condition is met. If the condition is not met it will execute the code in the *else*{} statement. The else does not have a condition to check; it executes when the specified condition in *if*() is not met. Conditional statements always use a relational operator to test a condition.

Note:

The *if*(*m*) and else statement is case sensitive.Both "if" and "else" must be lowercase.Additionally,while if() can be executed without an else,the missing else statement can cause an error if the condition is false.else statements also cannot be implemented without an if()statement.We will describe if()...else statements in more detail in later chapters

To create our program we have to follow the following steps.

1. Open and edit the arithmetic routine program using this URL:

a. https://ide.geeksforgeeks.org/vDcCH7f5EQ

2. Use the same variables from the arithmetic routine. Be sure to clean the code of any unneeded variables.

3. Print an explanation of the program

4. Test $if(a > b)$ and print the result

a. Create an if statement printing out the result if greater than

b. Create a nested else statement printing out the result if false

Note: For each $if(\square)$ ... *else* you will have to create a $cout$ for all possibilities. For our simple program, it is only two possibilities for each statement.

5. Test $if(a >= b)$ and print the result

6. Test $if(a < b)$ and print the result

7. Test $if(a <= b)$ and print the result

8. Test $if(a == b)$and print the result

9. Test $if(a! = b)$ and print the result

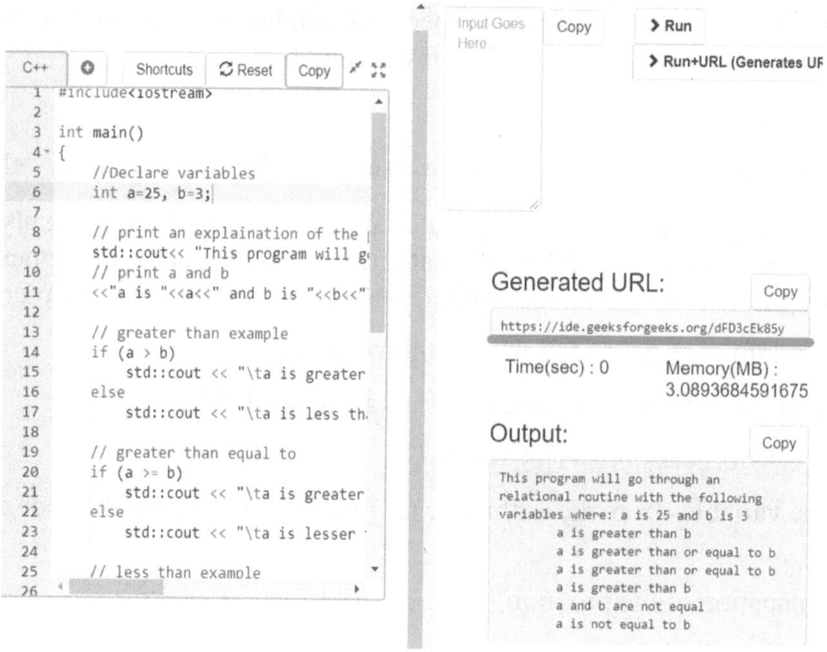

Relational Routine Program

This screenshot is a successful run of the relational routine program displaying all the relational functions.

If you did not get similar results, go look at our code here: https://ide.geeksforgeeks.org/dFD3cEk85y. Compare and figure out where you went wrong. An exercise like this one will equip you with debugging skills.

Also, take your time to appreciate the code and understand it.

Logical Operators

Logical operators add more complexity to relational operators. These are comparable to human ideas of "and" or "or". They also have qualities that switch the meaning of the relational operator. **Logical operators** are used in conjunction with relational operators to combine two or more conditions to describe a constraint. They make us catch a lot more and do a lot more with our conditionals. There are three logical operators (Jaggi, 2015b):

"": the logical "AND" operator returns a Boolean true when both the conditions are met and false if they aren't.

"|□|": the logical "OR" operator returns a Boolean true when one (or both) of the conditions are met, and false if none of the conditions are met.

"!": the logical "NOT" operator returns a Boolean true if the conditions in consideration are not satisfied. If one of the conditions is true, then it returns a Boolean false.

Logical operators are used a lot in machines. Imagine a "NOT" operator in the security system of a bank. Let's say locked doors are "0"[false], and unlocked doors are "1". Because the bank should stay secure, our default value is "0." This is called a failed closed system, because if things go wrong the doors will be closed (the default). All signals that go to the door are controlled by a "NOT" signal: If nothing is going on, the doors should remain locked, and if there is robbery they should also remain locked. Doors that open during a robbery will get a "NOT" signal to fail-close. But in a fire, these doors should open, so the fail-closed "NOT" signal will return true to open doors.

Let's explore logical operators by building a logical routine program. Follow these instructions:

1. Open and edit the relational routine program using this URL:

https://ide.geeksforgeeks.org/dFD3cEk85y

2. Edit these additional variables to test the logical operators:

$$a = 5, b = 0, c = 12, d = 24$$

3. Print an explanation of the program
4. Test if(a>b && c==d) and print the result

a. Create an if statement printing out the result if greater than

b. Create a nested else statement printing out the result if false

5. Test (a>b || c==d) and print the result
6. Test (!b) and print the result
7. Clean the code of any unnecessary lines

Here is how it looks:

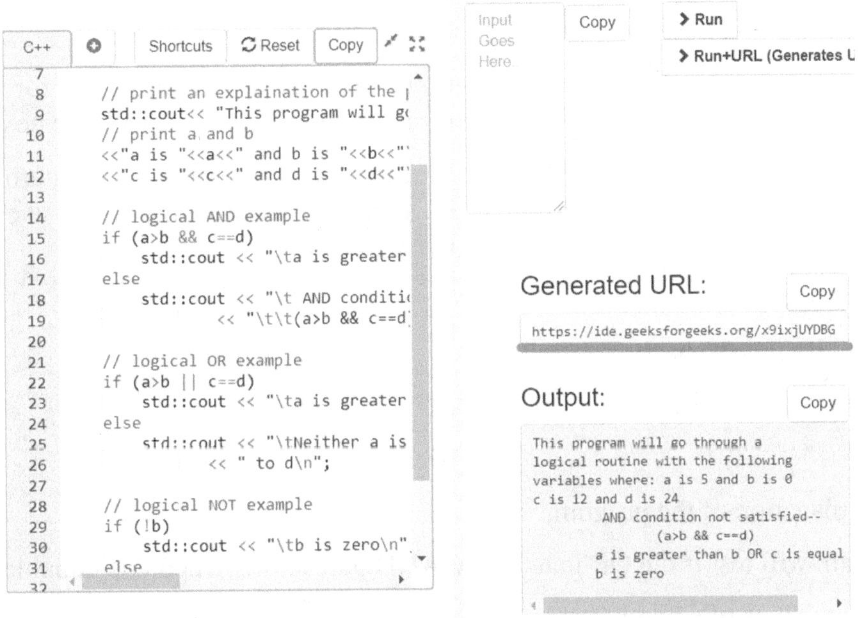

Logical Routine Program

This screenshot is a successful run of the logical routine program displaying examples of all the logical functions. You can access this workspace with this URL: https://ide.geeksforgeeks.org/x9ixjUYDBG

As you can see, the "AND" function may be difficult to print with just one $if(\square)\ ...\ else$ statement when producing a false – state. Either relational expression can be false to produce a false AND. However, the program can be fixed to produce an exact answer by nesting another 2 $if(\square)\ ...\ else$ statements. Modify this exercise to create a program that can explain itself better!
Hint: You only need one additional $if(\square)\ ...\ else$ *statement. You can check your work against ours with this URL -- https://ide.geeksforgeeks.org/nh8yYV9Kjy.*

Let's take a break from routines and explore other ways we can use logical operators. Logical operators are based on machine logic, especially logical gates. Logical gates are electronic circuits that have one or more inputs while having one output. Logical gates have the same function as logical operators. "AND" gates only pass "1" when all inputs are "1"; "OR" gates pass "1" when they receive a "1" from any of their inputs; "NOT" passes "1" when they receive a "0" as their input.

Logical gates can control the flow of data in a circuit, the same as our logical operations when combined with a conditional statement. It is called a **conditional short-circuit** in logical operators.

Logical AND operators and OR operators short-circuit. Recall how logical AND returns a true Boolean value when both relational operators are conditionally true. What's more, relational operators are assessed in the order that they appear in a conditional statement – if the first one is false the second one will not be evaluated, so it short circuits.

OR operators do this differently. Only one relational operator has to return true for it passes a true Boolean value. So if the first relational operator returns true, it won't check the next one.

This is very useful because we can give more complex instructions to a program about how to behave in what circumstances. OR and AND are short-circuit opposites. Let's use this to write a program that tells when a condition short-circuits AND and OR gates.

Follow these instructions:

1. Open a new IDE workspace
2. Declare two *int* variables:

$$a = 10, b = 4$$

3. Print an explanation of the program

a. This program will test if the OR gate or the AND gate shorts when a is equal to b.

b. Print current values of a and b

4. Declare and calculate two *bool* variables:
5. resAND = ((a == b) && std::cout << "OR circuit shorted")
6. resOR = ((a == b) || std::cout << "AND circuit shorted")

This is how it looks:

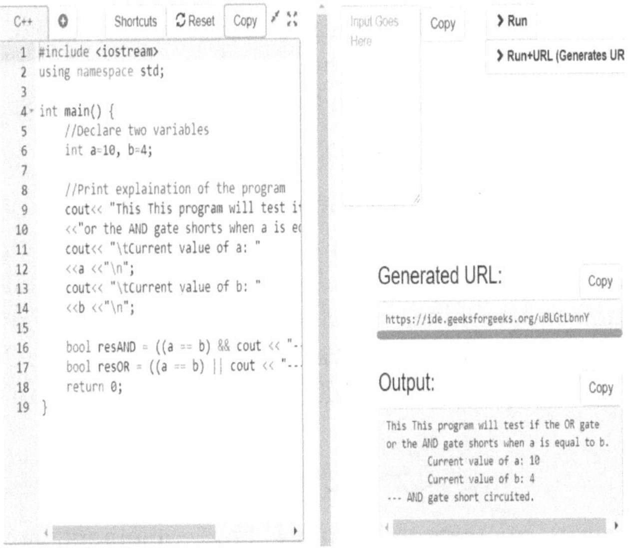

Short Circuit Detection Program

This screenshot is a successful run of our short circuit detection program. Using our knowledge of logical AND, logical OR, and their relationship to each other, we were able to develop a way to detect short circuits. You can access this workspace with this URL: https://ide.geeksforgeeks.org/uBLGtLbnnY

Try different values of *a* and *b* to see if you can trip the different "circuits."

Consider a short circuit detection program. How would we use it in the real world? I have alluded to systems like these playing a role in bank security. The question is how it would achieve those things? You can tell your program that if a condition is not ("NOT") met to refuse access, like if the password does not match.

An understanding of logical operators gives a good idea of how machines and systems make their decisions. Relational and logical operators give us more control over what happens in the program and how it relates to everything around it. We do this through various libraries, statements, and objects. So far we have written small programs, but in bigger programs using objective control like these can cause overhead for the compiler. That has a noticeable effect in programming environments and industries like gaming engines, content delivery, and others. Think about the servers at YouTube that have to deliver gigabytes of data per second and gaming engines that need to render in real-time: they have to reduce the amount of overhead while being able to utilize these control features. Thankfully, that can be achieved by using bitwise operators.

Bitwise Operators

On the circuit level, machines communicate by using AND and OR gates. It gives them decision-making capabilities at a single bit data level. **Bitwise operators** use those microscopic level calculations to access computing processes at the machine level, bypassing objective programming. In other words, they are logical operators operating on numbers at a binary level.

To use them, you will need to know about binary. Humans conceptualize numbers using **base-10** numbers, also known as the decimal system. For instance, a number like 543 is understood as five-hundreds, three tens, and 4 single units. In base 10 it looks like this:

$$5 * 10^2 + 3 * 10^1 + 4 * 10^0 = 534$$

In binary the same number would look like this 0b1000010110 – the “0b” is just for us humans to understand it is a binary number. Binary numbers are **base-2**, they just look different. All binary numbers are presented as a stream of bits, which can either be in two states: 1 or 0. Like in base-10, the position of the number determines its value. The 534 example shows a binary number that is 10 bits long. Looking closely at the 534 streams we can see that the 2nd, 3rd, 4th, and 10th bits are on (moving right to left), and all the other bits are off (1 is on, 0 is off). In base 2 we calculate this as:

$$2^9 + 2^4 + 2^2 + 2^1 = 534$$

It is not easy for us humans to calculate it, but this is how computers communicate, in streams of data bits. They are more adept at recognizing and counting these numbers just as easily as if they were base-10 numbers to humans. Therefore, using bitwise operators that function at the computer’s natural level improves speed and performance (Killian, 2012) because it skips the translation of objective programming into machine language. This is why you will find bitwise operations are often used in competitive programming. Below is a list of C++ bitwise operators (“Bitwise Operators in C/C++,” 2014):

“”: Bitwise AND takes two numbers (operands) and runs AND on every bit within the stream of those numbers. The results of the AND stream will be 1 if both are 1.

“|”: Bitwise OR takes two numbers(operands) and runs OR on every bit within the stream of those numbers. The results of the OR stream is 1 if any of the two is 1.

“∧” Bitwise XOR that takes two numbers as operands and does XOR on every bit within the stream of the two numbers. The result stream of XOR is 1 if the two bits are different.

“<<” Left shift operator takes two numbers and left shifts the bits of the first operand. The second operand is used to determine the number of places to shift.

“>>” Right shift operator takes two numbers and right shifts the bits of the first operand. The second operand is used to determine the number of places to shift.

“~” Bitwise NOT operator that takes one number and switches the state of all the bits (1s to 0s, 0s to 1s).

Note: Machines use registers and buffers to store the bits for calculation. A **register** is just an array of storage, where each bit gets its own place in the array. If you think of these data streams as an array, it will help you rationalize many of the bitwise operators, particularly the shift operators.

Let's write a bitwise routine program. First, we will need to create a bit register and study bit streams. This requires the bitset<x>() function for the *<bitset>* library. It allows you to print a binary stream with a length of <x>. Follow the instructions:

1. Open a new IDE C++ workspace
2. In addition to $< iostream >$, be sure to call the $< bitset >$ library as well
3. Declare the operand variables and their values

$$unsignedinta = 60; \frac{\frac{\square}{\square}}{60} = 00111100$$

$$unsignedintb = 13; \frac{\frac{\square}{\square}}{13} = 00001101$$

4. Declare register c for the calculations

$$intc = 0;$$

5. Print operand values and their registers:

$$cout \ll \text{Operandregistersa:} \ll a$$

$$\ll \text{andb:} \ll b$$

$$\ll \backslash n \backslash t\text{registera:-0b} \ll bitset < 8 > (a)$$

$$\ll \backslash n \backslash t\text{registerb:-0b} \ll bitset < 8 > (b) \ll endl;$$

Note: Since all numbers are less than 255, we will then use a bit stream of $< 8 >$ for the entire exercise.

6. Calculate Bitwise AND for a and b in register c

$$c = ab; \frac{\frac{\square}{\square}}{12} = 00001100$$

7. Print the result and the register in c

Note: Since we are using bitwise functions, it is better to use *endl;* to terminate our lines. This is because this function clears the buffer and prevents overflow. This makes the program a little slower, but it ensures that our registers are clear. The speed difference is made up by using bitwise functions.

8. Calculate Bitwise OR for a and b in register c

$$c = a|b;//61 = 00111101$$

9. Print the resulting value and the register in c
10. Calculate Bitwise XOR for a and b in register c

$$c = a^b;\frac{\square}{49} = 00110001$$

11. Print the resulting value and the register in c
12. Calculate Bitwise NOT for a in register c

$$c = \square a;\frac{\square}{-61} = 11000011$$

13. Print the resulting value and the register in c
14. Print a comparison register for a in register c

    This will make it easier to compare with the shifting bitwise operations

15. Calculate Bitwise Left Shift for $a << 2$ in register c

$$c = a \ll 2;\frac{\square}{240} = 11110000$$

16. Print the result and the register in c
17. Calculate Bitwise Left Shift for $a >> 2$ in register c

$$c = a \gg 2;\frac{\square}{15} = 00001111$$

18. Print the result and the register in c

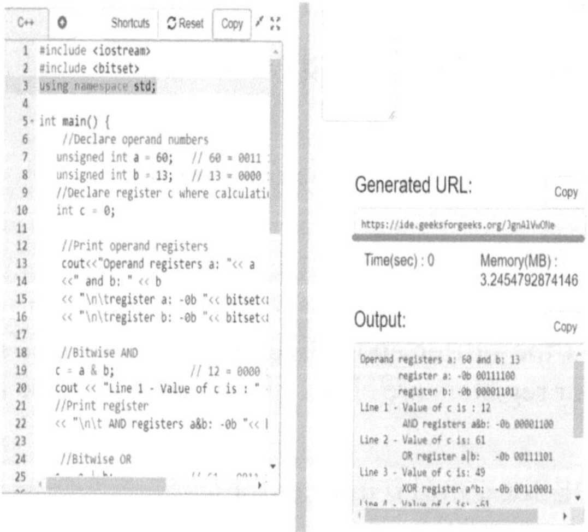

Bitwise Routine with Register Printing

This screenshot is a successful run of our bitwise routine program. The output features visuals of the *c*register array. This will allow you to see how each bitwise is calculated and how it changes the register. This is a long program with a very long output. To study it fully, you can access it on our saved workspace using this URL: https://ide.geeksforgeeks.org/JgnAlVwONe

Note:

This program uses *usingnamespacestd*; to simplify the program.It would be good practice to omit the namespace and declare each *cout* and *bitwise* object separately.

The last binary operators we will discuss are assignment operators. **Assignment operators** are used for assigning value and dynamically changing values. In principles of programming, we talked about programs needing to be as efficient as possible while using a few instructions as possible. Advanced assignments operators combine with equal assignments and other various operations to reduce lines of code. They are all **atomic operations**, meaning they allow programmers to manipulate stored values within variables, and reassign them. Below is a list of common assignment operators (Prabhu, 2018):

"=": Equal assignment operator assigns the value on the right to the variable on the left.

"$+=$ ": Operator for atomic addition, used to combine the ' $+$ ' and ' $=$ 'operators. This operator *adds* the value of the variable on the left to the value on the right. Then it saves the result to the variable on the left. For example, $x+= y$ would be a shorter way of writing $x = x + y$ without having to use a separate arithmetic operator.

"$-=$ ": The atomic subtraction used to combine the ' $-$ ' and ' $=$ 'operators. This operator *subtracts* the value of the variable on the left from the value on the right. Then it saves the result to the variable on the left.

"$*=$ ": Operator for the atomic multiplication, used to combine the ' $*$ ' and ' $=$ 'operators. This operator multiplies the value of the variable on the left with the value on the right and saves the result to the variable on the left.

"$\neq$ ": The atomic division operator is a combination of ' $\frac{⬚}{,}$and ' ' operators. This operator divides the value of the variable on the left by the value on the right and saves the result to the variable on the left. For example, $x \neq y$ would be a shorter way of writing $x = \frac{x}{y}$ without having to use a separate arithmetic operator.

Note: There are also bitwise atomic assignment operations: "= ","| = ", and " ∧=". We will focus on the arithmetic-atomic functions for now.

Let's create an assignment operator routine program to see how these assignment operations work. Follow these steps:

1. Open a new IDE workspace
2. Declare and initialize our variable

   int a = 10;

3. Print an explanation of the program and the starting value

Note: When making programs that print, always make them easy to read! Make sure your program can explain itself.

4. Atomically add 10 and print the result
5. Atomically subtract 10 from our variable and print the result
6. Atomically multiply 10 and print the result
7. Atomically divide our variable by 10 and print the result

Here is how it looks:

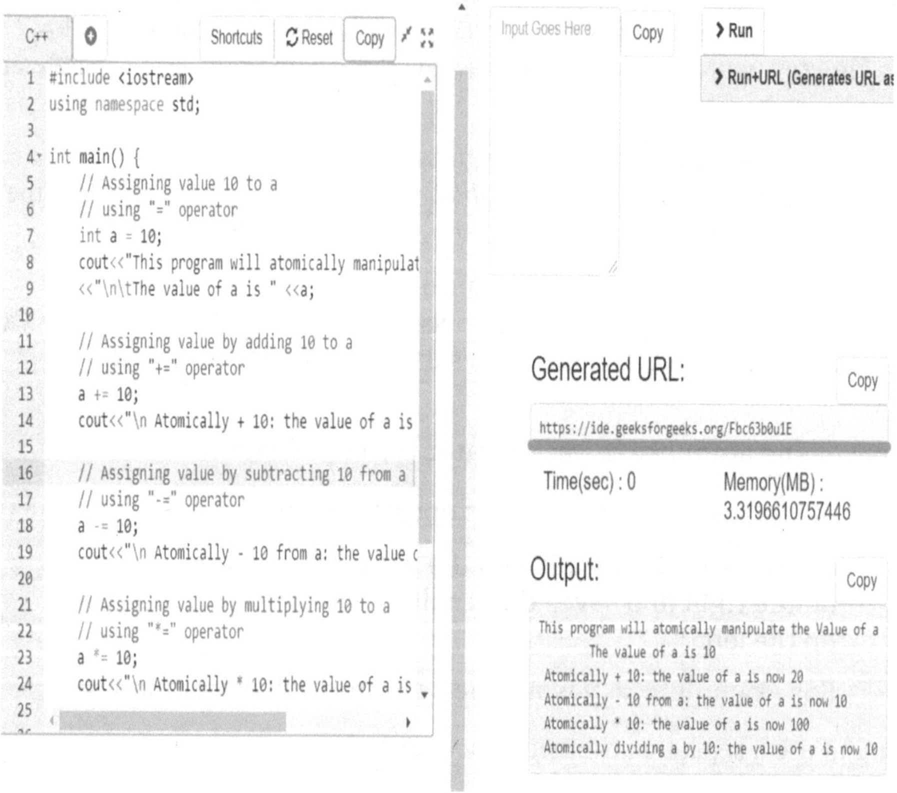

Assignment Routine

This screenshot is a successful run of our assignment routine program. This program has a sequential output, which means that each instruction impacts the result of the next instruction. This means if we were to change the order of the atomic operations applied to a that the output would be different. To study it fully, you can access it on our saved workspace using this URL: https://ide.geeksforgeeks.org/Fbc63b0u1E

These binary assignment operators combine assignments and arithmetic functions. They work well when controlling loops and conditional statements, too. Atomic assignment operators are closely related to unary arithmetic operators. Both are frequently used to control loops. Let's take a look at unary operations.

Unary Operations

Before we discuss unary operations, let's look at code that uses them.

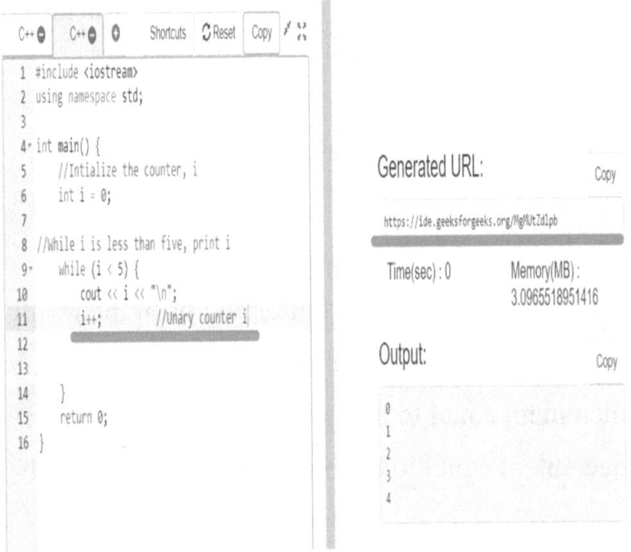

While Loop featuring a Unary Operator

This screenshot is of a simple while loop that prints the value of the counter, i. The unary operation performs $i = 1 + i$ for each iteration until $i = 5$ and the while loop ends. Omitting $i++$ will cause an error as the while loop would not be able to advance. We will talk about loops extensively in the decision making chapter. To study it fully, you can access it on our saved workspace using this URL: https://idc.gccksforgccks.org/MgMUtZdlpb

The *i* = 1 + i is the same as *i*++. Using the unary form makes the code neater because it precludes the + arithmetic operator and the = assignment operator. We can also use an atomic addition operator to complete the code: *i*+=1 is the same as *i*++. But a format like that would require the compiler to store and operate on an additional operand. **Unary operators** are there to simplify code by only having one operand. Remember, unary operators are those operators that use one operand. Here are some of the other examples of unary operators (Kumar, 2017) :

"+ +": Increment operator used to increase the value of an integer by 1. It can be placed in front of a variable to increment the value immediately or after to temporarily save the value before increment.

"– –": Decrement operator used to decrease the value of an integer by 1. Similar to the increment, programmers can also implement pre-decrement and post-decrement instructions.

"–": Unary minus operator that is used to change the sign of a variable or argument. Performing a unary minus operation on a negative integer will make it positive and vice versa.

"!": NOT operator is used to reverse the Boolean logical state of an operand. For example, if a variable $x$has a Boolean value of $false, !\, x$ will be $true$.

"": Address of operator that is used to point to the address of a variable.

Let's make a unary operator routine to see how the pre- and post-instructions work. Follow these instructions:

1. Open a new IDE workspace
2. Declare and initialize our variable and a buffer

   int a = 10, buf

3. Print an explanation of the program and the starting value
4. Calculate a post-increment equal to the buffer and print the result
5. Calculate a post-decrement equal to the buffer and print the result

8. Calculate a pre-increment equal to the buffer and print the result
9. Calculate a pre-decrement equal to the buffer and print the result

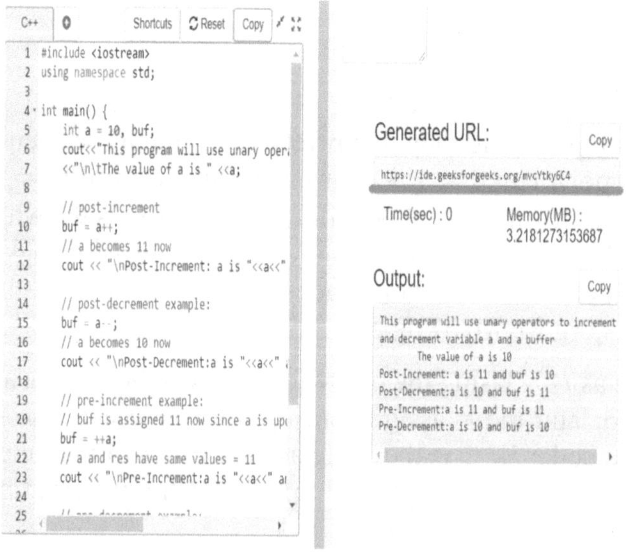

Unary Operator Routine with Post- and Pre-Operations

This screenshot is of our unary operator routine program. To study it fully, you can access it on our saved workspace using this URL: https://ide.geeksforgeeks.org/mvcYtky6C4

The program operates on *a* and while it calculates, it stores the value in a buffer we can observe. Comparing *a* with the buffer, the post-operation delays changing the value of a; in contrast, pre-operations change the value immediately.

On top of all this, we have the *sizeof*() operator. It looks like a function but it is categorized as an operator. It checks the size of an object and returns the size in bytes.

Recall our conversation about bit streams. What I didn't say is that they are often divided into a group of 8. One byte is a single 8-bit stream that can present 255 numbers. In our bitwise routine, our registers were 1 byte long, that was because we were working with numbers that were less than 255.

Let's write a program that can get the size of an array using *sizeof*(). Here we go:

- Open a new C++ IDE workspace

1. Declare and initialize our array

$$intarr[\ ] = \{1,2,3,4,7,98,0,12,35,99,14\}$$

2. Print an explanation of the program and the array

Note: To print the array you will have to create a for loop. We will discuss for loops in the next chapter. For now, just use these lines of code:

$$for(constautoe: arr)\{$$
$$cout << "[" << e << "]";$$
$$\}$$

3. Calculate the size of the array

$$intarsize = \frac{sizeof(arr)}{sizeof(arr[0])};$$

4. Print the size of the array

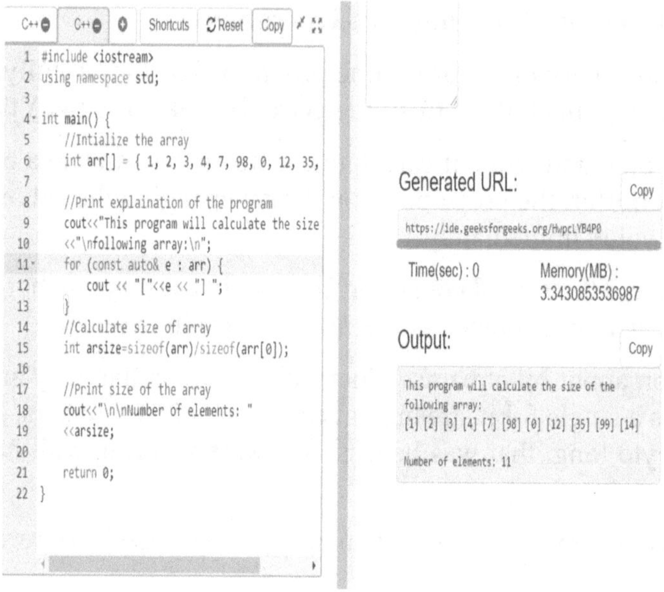

Array Size Reporting Program

This screenshot is of our array size reporting program. We encourage you to compare your result to ours. To study it fully, you can access it on our saved workspace using this URL: https://ide.geeksforgeeks.org/HwpcLYB4P0.

That was a good example of two unary operations: *sizeof*() and the address pointer &. The *for*(){} loop we used to print the array is called a copy constructor call. **Constructor copy calls** consist of a *for*() loop with an index variable, an *Addressof* operator, and a container object with an index. The copy constructor sets up [0]: [the size of arr] by using the *Addressof* pointer to automatically deduce the [size of arr] and print its contents. In simple words, a copy constructor uses *Addressof* to reduce the size of the program.

The *sizeof*() operator is an objective operation and it uses a single operand, the arr array object. They both have disadvantages and advantages. The *sizeof*() operator uses one operand and is easier to spot without esoteric memory registers. The call combination had to use an additional object (*e*), to print the array but it would have done with less incrementing operators. We are going to discuss loops and decision making features of C++ in more detail in the next chapter. For now, let's turn our attention to ternary operators.

Ternary Operators

C++ only has one ternary operator. **Ternary operators**, also called conditional operators, take 3 or more operands – they are Boolean logic-based operators. The result is always determined by whether or not the first expression is true, then the second will be evaluated; if the first expression is false, the third expression will be evaluated. If you recall our *if*()...*else* statement in the relational program routine, it had three parts: an initial expression that the function evaluates, an expression it evaluates if the initial expression is true, and an else statement which is evaluated when the initial expression is not true. Conditional operators have the same components as an *if()...else* statement. They are just more compact.

Let's make a program that illustrates these similarities:

- Open a new IDE C++ workspace
- To use the conditional operator you will have to call the $< \frac{bits}{stdc} + +.h >$ library
- Print an explanation for the conditional operator

This program will pick the greatest one using two methods: a conditional operator and an $if(\square) \ldots else$ statement

We expect a result of 5.

- Declare the variable and execute the conditional operator

```
int arsize=sizeof(arr)/sizeof(arr[0]);
```

Print an explanation for the $if(\square) \ldots else$

```
if(2 > 5) then print 2
else then print 5
```

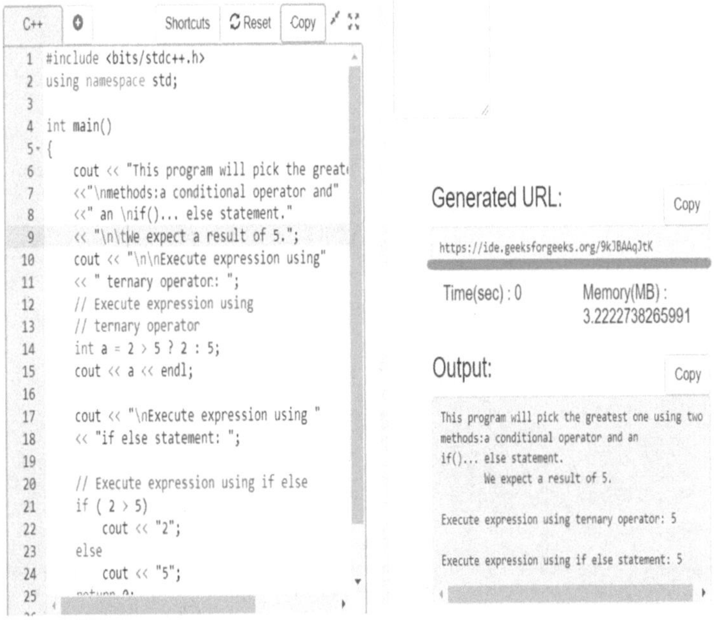

Conditional Operations Demo

This screenshot is of our conditional operations demo. This program has no real practical functionality. However, for our purposes, it does demonstrate the similar structures between conditional operators and $if(\square) \ldots else$ statements. To study it fully, we suggest that you access the copy of our saved workspace using this URL: https://ide.geeksforgeeks.org/9kJBAAqJtK.

In this chapter, we looked at 3 types of operators: unary, binary, and ternary. As you have seen, these operators allow programmers to apply powerful aspects of C++. For instance, binary operators allow machines to make logical decisions, compute values, and control processes by changing functions. Unary functions help us shrink and simplify complicated code. Ternary operators allow us to be more succinct in our code. They are all central to making decisions and switching in C++.

CHAPTER 5:

Decision Making in C++

We're going to talk about decision-making functions; these are functions like *if-else* loops. Programming rests a lot on decision making, and decision making is informed by logical expressions involving operators we have seen in chapter 4. Decision-making functions combined with logical expressions give machines the ability to make decisions based on criteria selected by programmers.

In our *sizeof*() exercise in Chapter 4 we used a *for*() loop in a copy constructor which fielded the array, printing all indices. The unary operator *Addressof* with an auto data type allowed us to implement the *for*() loop, without an additional counter for the loop. The simplicity of the copy constructor is not so obvious if you have never had the experience of initializing and implementing loops yourself.

Loops

Programmers spend a lot of time automating mundane, repetitive tasks through scripts and routines. What allows scripts and routines to achieve this are loops. As the name suggests, loops repeat the same instructions as long as a certain condition is met ("C++ While Loop," n.d.). Loops are often used to navigate aggregated objects with indices like arrays and vectors. For instance, you might write a loop that keeps searching an array until a specific item is found. There are two types of loops: entry-controlled loops and exit loops.

In our unary arithmetic example, we had a *while*() loop with a counter. The counter is an arbitrary variable that is used with a unary operator to increment an indicated expression. It is an example of an entry controlled loop – it tests a condition before it executes code. Let's modify that example into a *while*() loop to explore its components. We will use it to print out "Hello World" 10 times. Follow these instructions:

- Open the following IDE C++ workspace:

https://ide.geeksforgeeks.org/MgMUtZdlpb

- Print explanation of the program

This program will number and print 10 lines--

- Change the conditional test to $i < 11$
- Print "Hello World" 10 times with numbered lines

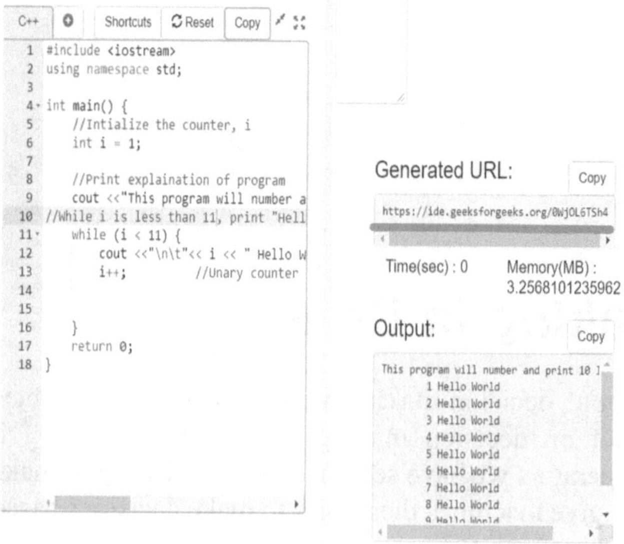

While Loop Demo

This screenshot is of our while loop demo. You can access a copy of our saved workspace using this URL: https://ide.geeksforgeeks.org/0WjOL6TSh4.

This program shows us how incremental counters work. For it to work, the number must start with 1, not 0. Most people are used to numbers working that way. To do this, we initialized the counter at 1. Yet if we set the condition to 10 it will give us 9 print outs. To get 10 we have to increase the number to 11.

Another example of a controlled loop is the for() loop function; it requires three expressions as inputs (Agarwal, 2017a):

1. An initialization expression that declares a data type and a variable. This variable can be either a counter or an indexing variable.
2. A test expression that produces a Boolean *true* or *false*. If the condition is true then the for loop will continue to loop its specified block of code.
3. An update expression that increments the counter or the indexing variable

Let's see how they work by writing a program similar to our *while*() loop example. Follow these instructions:

- Open the following IDE C++ workspace:

https://ide.geeksforgeeks.org/0WjOL6TSh4

- Print explanation of the program

This program will number and print 10 lines of Hello World

- Implement the for() loop

$$for(inti = 1; i < 11; i++)$$

- Print "Hello World" 10 times with numbered lines
- Clean the data of any unneeded code and comments

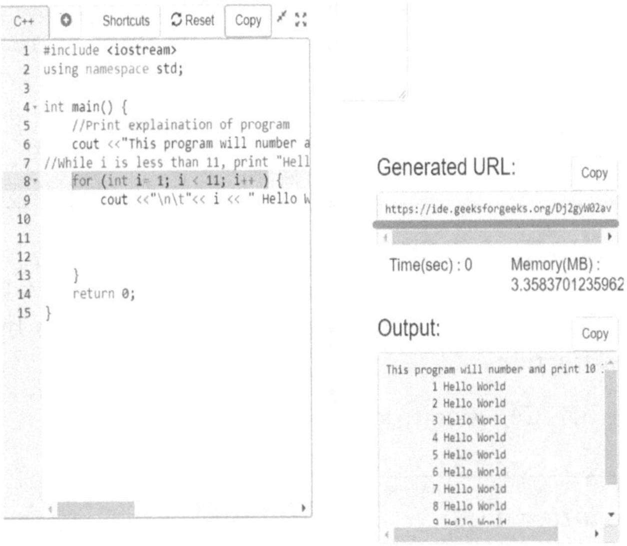

For Loop Demo

This screenshot is of our for loop demo. You can access a copy of our saved workspace using this URL: https://ide.geeksforgeeks.org/Dj2gyW02av.

Note: Make sure you clean your code of unnecessary lines and update your comments. While this does not impact the performance of your code, it can make things confusing for other programmers on your team that have to implement your code. Do you see a mistake here?

Now that we see how *for*() loops work and how they are constructed, let's look at the copy constructor we used earlier. The expression used for the copy constructor call was:

$$for(constautoe: arr)$$

"*E*" being the indexing variable and "*arr*" the variable array. We saw that the *for() loop* needs three expressions to work: the initialization, the test expression, and the update expression.

The copy constructor has an initializing function (*const auto& e*). When you look closely, you can see this expression also works as a test expression, because the & is an Addressof operator that points to *e* which stands for indices in the *arr* array. The : is an operator to break into class.

It allows the attributes of the container *arr* array to pass to the *e* variable. The *for()* loop will print the *e* until the end of the array is reached.

The copy constructor call is good for a situation where the size of the container is unknown and you want all items printed out. *For()* loops define the number of iterations that have to take place from the get-go, while copy constructors calls are defined by the size of the container. *While()* loops are best for the situation where the condition can change at any time, during which you want the iterations to stop.

The *do{}...while()* loop is for situations where the *while()* code may impact the test. *Do{}..while()* loops are exit controlled, meaning code is executed until a condition is met. The code is executed at least once before checking the test condition. Think back to that bank security example. The door will always fail-close, receiving a NOT signal, except when there is a fire. Here is how a *do{}..while* loop will look for that:

$$do\{Keepthedoorslocked\}$$
$$while(fire = false);$$

The door will remain closed as long as fire is not detected. *Do{}..while()* loops are useful for many fail-close systems. Other applications include data correction in servers where a correction routine is run when an error is detected. Let's code our first do while loop by changing our *while()* program. Follow these instructions:

- Open the following IDE C++ workspace:

  https://ide.geeksforgeeks.org/0WjOL6TSh4
- Initialize counter to $inti = 11;$
- Implement the do{} code block
- Set $while(i < 11);$
- Clean the data of any unneeded code and comments
- Check the results

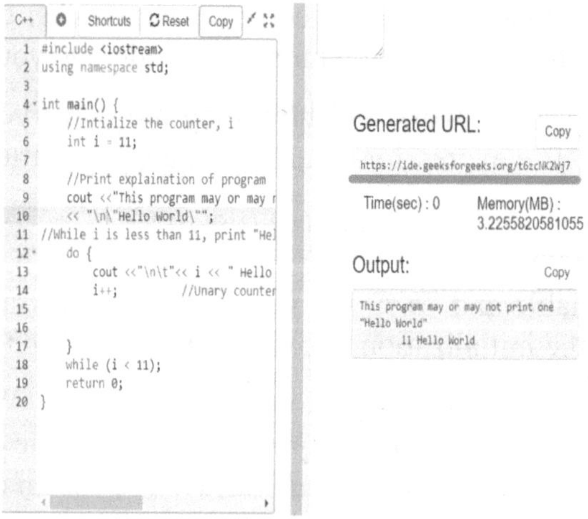

Do While Loop Demo exhibiting an exit controlled loop

This screenshot is of our do while loop demo. You should notice that, despite $i < 11$being $false$ for the entire duration of the program, the $do\{\dots\}$code block was executed. This is because the loop is an exit control loop: the condition is tested after the code block is executed. The code has the potential to execute. You can access a copy of our saved workspace using this URL: https://ide.geeksforgeeks.org/t6zcNK2Wj7.

See how the message was printed despite the conditions being false. You can apply it to data corrections in streams. Many error detection services pause the stream of data and a request for retransmission is sent. A *do{}...while* loop will allow the data stream to continue until an error is detected. These are the types of routines used by YouTube in server buffers. This shows how useful they are in controlling data. For single switching, we would use an *if()...else.*

If()...Else

So far we have used *if()...else* functions in our examples. They are easy to understand and their structure is pretty self-explanatory. An *if()...else* statement tests a condition and based on the result it executes one block of code or another. They are a combination of two separate distinct statements.

You can execute the *if()* function alone but the compiler expects an *else* statement. An *else* statement contains the code that accompanies the *if()* expression. An else statement can never be executed without the *if()* statement.

An *else if()* statement specifies another condition to test. It creates a chain of statements called nested *if-else* statements. If you are testing a lot of conditions, it is best to use a switch which we will discuss in the next section. Let's make our first nested *if-else* statement. Follow these instructions ("C++ | Nested Ternary Operator," 2018):

1. Open a new IDE C++ workspace
2. Print an explanation for the conditional operator

This program will go through a sequential list of numbers 2 through 4 and pick the greatest one using a nested $if(\dots)$ ... $else$ statement

We expect a result of 4.

3. Implement a nested if-else

```
if(2 > 3) then print 2
elseif(3 > 4) then print 3
else print 4
```

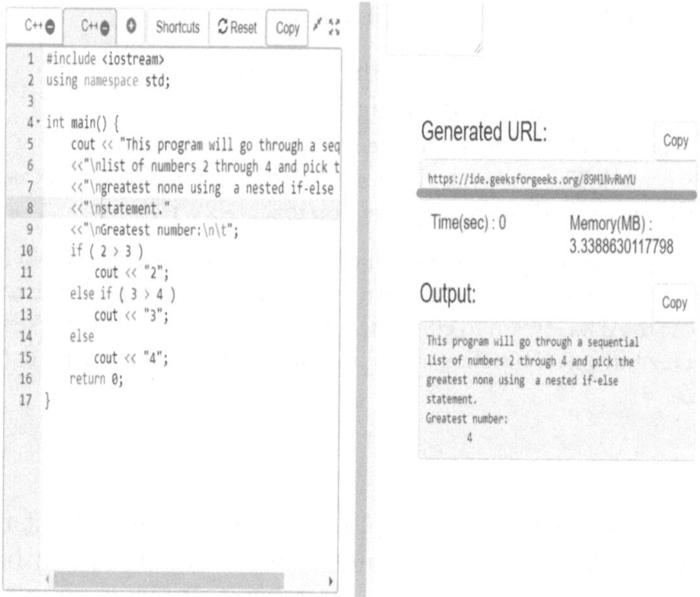

Nested If-Else Demo

This screenshot is of our nested if-else demo. Just like our other demos, this program has no functionality. However, for our purposes, this is an excellent exercise for implementing and understanding *if*(⬚) ... *else* statements. Despite us already knowing the answer, the *if*(⬚) ... *else* still requires code blocks for each statement. The code blocks should also correspond to the condition in order to create a functional program that fulfills its stated purpose. You can access a copy of our saved workspace using this URL: https://ide.geeksforgeeks.org/89MlNvRWYU.

Let's examine the exercise further. The nested *if-else* can be divided into two parts: the *if*() and *else* – *if*() statement that contains conditions and execution code. You notice that the blocks of code logically follow the state goal of the program, which is to find the largest number. It makes sense to print numbers in ascending order in case we change the conditional statement. Conditions within the *if*() statements and the blocks of code they contain are arranged in a way that allows the program to flow to the answer. For instance, if (2 > 3) is hardcoded to the next nested statement. The structure followed the nested conditional operator deliberately.

Nested Ternary If Else Operator

In the previous chapter, we talked about conditional operators, ternary operators that test conditions and execute an expression based on the results. We said the structure it uses is similar to an *if*()...*else* statement but more succinct. For instance, an *if*() statement tests a condition and executes one of the two blocks of code depending on the result of the test. If ()...*else* statements can be nested, and conditional operators can also be nested. Let's compare the structures of both. Follow these steps to participate ("C++ | Nested Ternary Operator," 2018):

1. If you had closed the nested if-else demo, open up the saved IDE C++ workspace with our program at this URL: https://ide.geeksforgeeks.org/89MlNvRWYU

2. Print an explanation for the program
1. This program will go through a sequential list of numbers 2 through 4 and pick the greatest one using two methods: a conditional operator and a nested *if*( ) ... *else* statement
2. We expect a result of 4.
3. Add a printed notification of the nested if-else
4. Print a notification for the conditional statement
5. Add the conditional operator code: declare the variable and execute the conditional operator

   int a = 2 > 3 ? 2 : 3 > 4 ? 3 : 4;

6. Clean the code of any unnecessary lines and correct any annotations

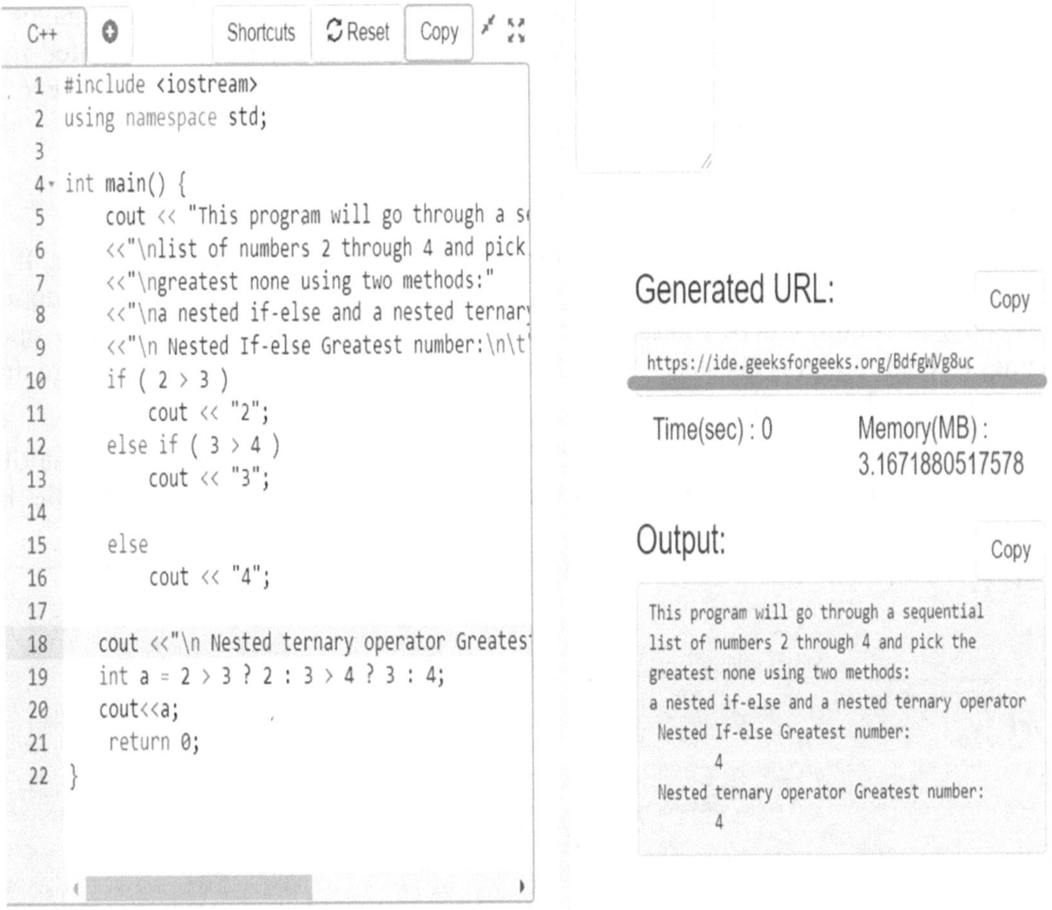

Nested If-Else and Nested Ternary Operation Comparison

This screenshot is of our modified nested if-else demo. We modified our demo by implementing a nested ternary operator for side-by-side comparison. As you may have experienced, the ternary operator was much easier to implement, using fewer statements. You can access a copy of our saved workspace using this URL: https://ide.geeksforgeeks.org/BdfgWVg8uc.

Let's talk about what we have just done there. In our previous discussion, we broke down the nested *if-else* statement into its components and a list of possible results. Even in the case where "2" and "3" were arbitrary values, if-else statements have to list all possible results to ensure great functionality regardless of the conditional statements results.

To see how conditional statement results of a nested *if-else match* with components of ternary operator, we have to take a close look at the ternary operator. Here is the syntax: $var = (expression)_1 ? [resultiftrue]_1 ⓔexpression)_2 ? [resultiftrue]_2 : [resultiffalse]_2$

Var is the variable used to print the result. The result of the nested if-else match expression before the ? indicators of the operator. The second expression executes when the first expression is false and corresponds to the *else if* () in the nested if-else. You can already see advantages to the compactness of ternary operators, but by their nature ternary operators are not suited for code blocks. With three or more expressions both get cluttered, so we need something else to handle multiple expressions: the switch statement.

Switch

As I have said, programmers need to strive for efficient, easily understandable code. It makes work easier for you and everyone else. Using switch over *if()..else* is one way you can achieve this, especially in circumstances where we are handling a lot of expressions. Ternary operators reduce lines of code, and it is because of this that they are not suited for situations where the code needs to span more than one line.

Switch statements offer a solution for both problems. Switch statements are multibranch statements that provide a clean way to execute a different block of code on one variable. Here is the syntax (Awasthi, n.d.):

$$switch(n)$$
$$\{$$
$$case1: \frac{-}{codetobeexecutedifn} = 1;$$
$$break;$$
$$case2: \frac{-}{codetobeexecutedifn} = 2;$$
$$break;$$
$$default: \frac{-}{codetobeexecutedifndoesn'tmatchanycases}$$
$$\}$$

Note: A switch can only evaluate an integer against case numbers. To add the conditional component, you must change the variable with an operation. The operator must produce an integer.

Let's create a switch demo practice the components of a switch:

1. Open a new IDE C++ workspace
2. Initialize a variable

$$intx = 2;$$

3. Print an explanation of the program
4. Initialize the switch

$$switch(x)$$

5. Print out "Choice is 1" for case 1
6. Print out "Choice is 2" for case 2
7. Print out "Choice is 3" for case 3
8. Print out "Program Exit" for the default;

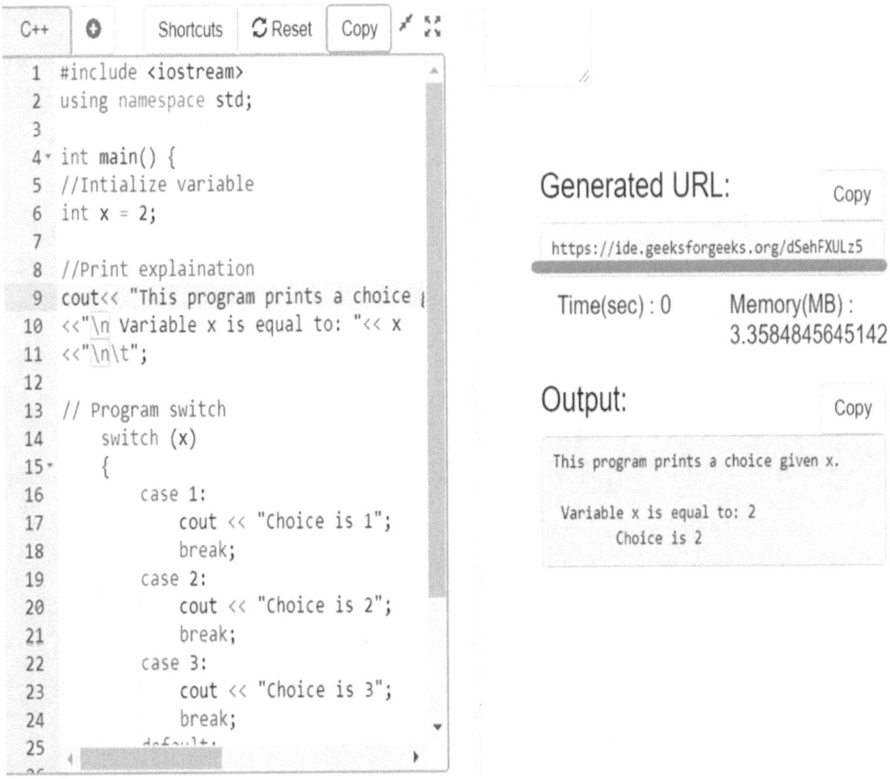

Switch Demo

This is a screenshot of our switch demo. You can access a copy of our saved workspace using this URL: https://ide.geeksforgeeks.org/dSehFXULz5. We highly suggest using this demo to convert one of our previous exercises into a switch. One excellent candidate is our relational routine program. It had **6** if()... else statements! This comes out to 12 different scenarios. How could you convert this program into a switch? Hint: Consider creating a menu for each relational routine using the input function. You can study the relational routine for yourself at this URL: https://ide.geeksforgeeks.org/dFD3cEk85y.

Now that we have seen what decision making functions are and how they work, let's turn our attention to functions and their role in programming.

CHAPTER 6:

CREATING FUNCTIONS

We talked about algorithms as a method of understanding problems and planning how your code will work to fix it. Algorithms receive inputs, perform actions, and then give a result which then causes a state change. A **function** is a block of code you can call multiple times without having to write the code again. The code is usually something that performs a desired task and has high re-usability. A function is composed of the header and a body. Here is how the syntax of a function looks:

```
[datatype]functi on_name(arguments)
{//statements
return0;
}
```

Like you have seen, and like many other programming languages, C++ is mostly just a series of functions, statements, and operators with objects and other data-holding elements for in-between. Everything we have written so far has used the *main*() function which uses syntax similar to the one above. So functions aren't new to you.

Every function must return a data type, just like the *main*() function returns the *int* 0. If a function does not do this, (void) is used as the parameter return type. As you might have guessed, the *return* is the statement that terminates the function.

The inputs that the functions receive are called parameters or arguments. Not all functions will take inputs as we have seen with *main*(); regardless of this, you can still pass parameters into the function for it to run. This is how libraries pass objects into *main*().

Create and Call a Function

To begin calling a function, you must declare it and define it before *main*(). This is because C++ executes sequentially. C++ practices take precedence and functions get priority. This is why you must declare them before *main*() so you can call them. They are also called this way because they make code more organized. Once a function is declared, we can define it anywhere outside of *main*()

Let's write a simple printing function so we can appreciate them more. Follow these instructions:

1. Open a new IDE C++ workspace
2. Declare your function

   void myFunction();
3. Call your function in main ()

   myFunction()
4. Define your function outside of main

$$\{cout \ll Ijustgotexecuted!;\}$$

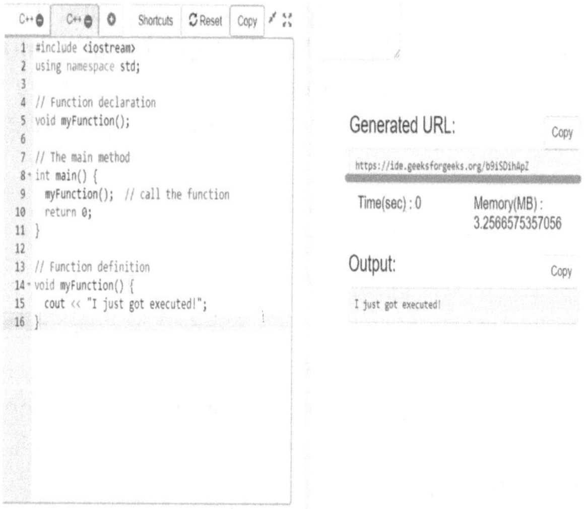

Function Demo

This screenshot is of our function demo. You can access a copy of our saved workspace using this URL: https://ide.geeksforgeeks.org/b9iSDihApZ. If you want more practice, we suggest using this exercise as a template to turn one of our past exercises into a function! Consider our exercise using *cin*and passing parameters to it. Any function with*cout* will do.

Separating the declaration and the definition falls under good programming practices. It makes it so you know all defined functions in the code that are available for calling. Having definitions at the bottom makes it easy to parse for errors within functions. Now let's turn our attention to parameter passing.

Parameter Passing

Functions are scripts that are given to the compiler. To complete the task and be useful, these functions need inputs to compute. To remind you, these inputs are called arguments or parameters. Programmers describe parameters differently based on where they originate or appear. Parameters that go into a defined function are called actual parameters. For instance, if you have a summing function called *mySum(x,y)*, when *main*() passes 2 and 3 into the functions those parameters are actual parameters. Conversely, x and y are formal parameters because they are variables that the data is going to be bound to. This applies to all other parameters before actual parameters are passed. There are two ways to pass parameters to functions ("Functions in C/C++," 2015):

Pass by Value: Values of actual parameters are copied into and stored in the function's formal parameters. Any changes made inside *main*() do not impact the actual parameters that were passed.

Pass by Reference: Both actual and formal parameters refer to the same locations. Therefore, any changes made inside the *main*() function will impact the actual parameters that were passed.

Let's practice parameter passing by writing our own code. Follow these instructions:

1. Open a new IDE C++ workspace
2. Declare your function

   int max(int x, int y)
3. Call your function in main ()
4. Initialize two actual variables

$$inta = 10, b = 20;$$

5. Initialize a variable and call the function

   int m = max(a, b);
6. Print the result
7. End main()
8. Define your function outside of main

i. This function should use an if() statement to check if x is greater than y.

ii. If x is greater than y, then return x

iii. Otherwise, return y.

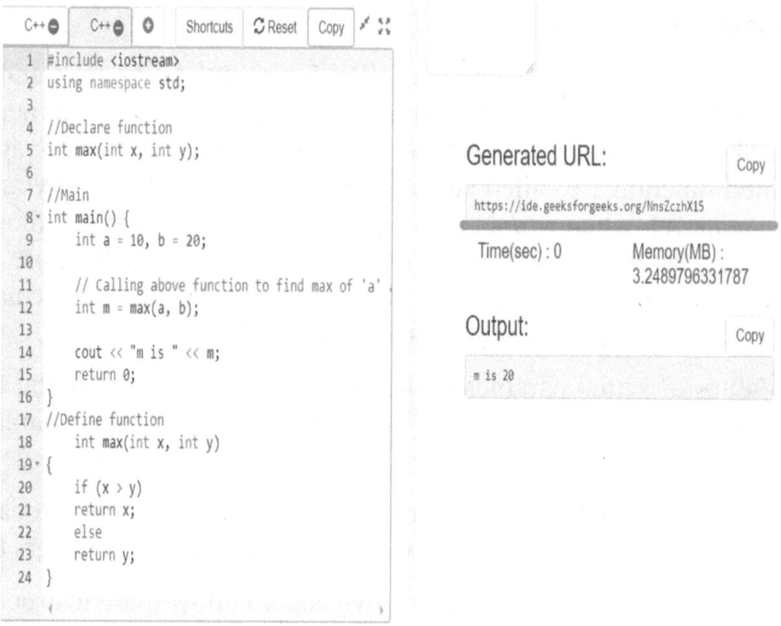

Functions with Parameter Passing

This screenshot is of our function demo. You can access a copy of our saved workspace using this URL: https://ide.geeksforgeeks.org/NnsZczhX15. If you want more practice, we suggest using this exercise as a template to turn one of our past exercises into a function! Consider our exercise using *cin*and passing parameters to it. We'll discuss how to pass parameters in the next section, but trying it first on your own will help you grasp the concept.

In our example, we have used value passing well. The variables used for *main* (*a,b*) are in a different location than those used in *max*(), (*x, y*). You can see how this can be very useful in larger programs where several complicated computations might take place in *main*(). It is preferred to pass values because it ensures that actual variables remain present until the function is called again.

Using a reference to pass arguments has its own advantages, especially in larger programs. References to pass inessential values may speed up the program and make it responsive. Scripting for automating functions is more likely to use references to pass parameters since automated processes are likely to happen repeatedly and quickly. These qualities are a selling point for reference-based structures. Let's now turn our attention to condensing and optimizing code.

Function Overloading

All defined objects and classes must have unique names. You cannot run a program that has two variables that have the same name or an error will be thrown. You might have seen this earlier while we're working on our routines and demos, especially when we had to modify a program. So keep this in mind: variables that are declared twice cause errors. But weirdly, multiple functions can have the same name as other functions as long as they have different parameters. This is only allowed in circumstances where the functions return different data types. It is better, given that, to overload a function to return multiple data types. This is what is called **function overloading**; a process where programmers combine functions to receive multiple data types. Why? Because it simplifies and consolidates the code. Take a look at the following code ("C++ Function Overloading," n.d.):

Program without function overloading

You can access a copy of our saved workspace using this URL: https://ide.geeksforgeeks.org/qkpHhZsqq5. The functions are declared and defined at the top of the file so that we can observe them better. You will be using this file to perform function overloading on your own. Remember that you can return to this workspace at any time if your code is damaged during editing.

The program above declares two separate functions that do similar computations. In a big program that is a waste of real estate and it is inefficient. It makes it harder to edit the code since either one of the functions are unlikely to be in the same place in a larger program. To make things more efficient, we should consolidate these functions under one name, and "stack" the data types. Here's how you can do this:

1. Open the saved IDE workspace at the following URL:

https://ide.geeksforgeeks.org/qkpHhZsqq5

2. Change double plusFuncdouble...to double plusFunc...
3. Call double plusFuncdouble... in place of double plusFunc...

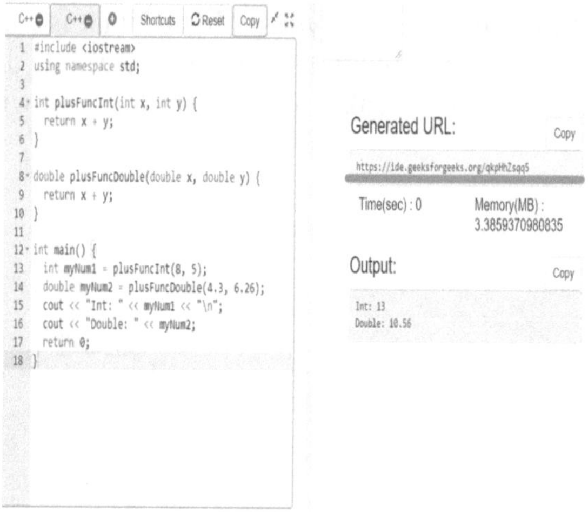

Program function overloading

You can access a copy of our saved workspace using this URL: https://ide.geeksforgeeks.org/e1qLzi3aGo. We kept the functions at the top of the file for easier editing. This overloading exercise requires a few small minute detail changes in order for this file to work. Use our workspace to compare your file in the event you get any long-standing errors. Remember that you can return to the original workspace at any time if your code is damaged during editing. You can access the original workspace at this URL: https://ide.geeksforgeeks.org/qkpHhZsqq5.

When you consolidate similar functions, you clean up your code. It is important, especially when you have to debug the code, since the compiler will likely point to functions when errors occur. The compiler does this because it is pointing to multiple libraries in the C++ code. Consolidating and overloading functions ensures that your compiler will have fewer functions to reference, making it easier for you to debug. Keep in mind that C++ is constantly updating so it becomes even easier to work with. New features are constantly added, and libraries are condensed and further organized. So an error is C+++7 would look different than an error in C++14. Updates bring new, easy ways to perform mundane tasks. For instance, the copy constructor call combinations are considered more modern for indexing containers such as arrays. To stay updated and reap the benefits of new C++ developments, you have to keep practicing, testing yourself, and asking questions.

CONCLUSION AND FINAL NOTES

Learning programming is a cognitive journey, one that is stimulating, exciting, and sometimes frustrating. As we come to the end of this book, it is important to go over some of the important lessons we learned. They are also going to be accompanied by final thoughts and suggestions that are meant to equip you with all you need to continue growing in this field.

Expanding Your Practice: Preparing Your Coding Environment

We have used an online IDE to make it so that everyone has the same experience. If you want to save your work you can use the Run+URL button to save it in another URL. You can also bookmark all these for later reference using your saved IDE workspace and URLs listed in this book. Use them as a reference or to fix broken code. I have done my best to show you the best coding practices in all the exercises we did. You have seen that in C++ there are many ways of doing something, so use that. Don't be afraid to experiment and try new things, and read up on how to do other things you are interested in. The exercises in his book are not definitive answers and nothing like that exists in programming. So come to this book for reference and explore other ways of doing something. We have our codes in the index of this ebook for quick reference.

There are many programming environments and text editors that can support C++. Some will have multiple versions of C++. As of writing this, the most up to date version of C++ is 17 but the most supported is C++14. C++ 14 is the evolved version of C++ and it features more comprehensible language features. C++14 is more intelligible to humans than its predecessor and you can expect this trend to continue. The oldest, widely available C++ version in most programming environments is C++11.

I encourage you to set up a local IDE and work on it. It will allow you to grow faster and get accustomed to real-world scenarios. We have spoken of Code::Blocks for Microsoft and Xcode of Mac. If you have Linux there are standardized options you can use across all distros. Linux is a console-based environment that is highly preferred by software developers because console-based environments are entrenched with many built-in features that directly interact with programs.

There are many distros that provide a GUI-based desktop that is preferable for many users. Most of them are open source, free to download and install. We highly recommend CentOS, a free Linux distro server management. CentOS uses many of Red Hat Enterprise Linux (RHEL) components. It is the best distro for preparing to work in Red Hat server management environments.

Coding Best Practices: Ownership of Learning and Collaboration

In our time together we have seen many techniques and best practices for software development. In the first chapter, we talked about how programs should fulfill their tasks with as little code as possible. Thankfully, with each new version of C++, more ways of doing this are added. The majority of beginner programming courses teach older, less efficient methods of implementing common programming tasks like parsing arrays, conditional statements, and calling functions. You will find most of these techniques are never used in actual programming situations. Most beginner courses are focused on equipping beginners with a strong grasp of the basics – the foundation of your knowledge is often as important as how you are going to progress. As you grow you will find more efficient ways of solving problems with your code, but this can only happen if you practice and study.

If you want to improve as a programmer you have to take ownership of your learning. Learn pre-development tools like algorithms. It is all about learning to fix problems. There are other pre-development tools you can try, like diagraming. Diagraming is good for individuals who are visual learners. All of these are great for growing as a programmer; it does not matter which you choose, as long as pre-developments tools are something you take advantage of.

Turning back to algorithms, more detailed algorithms will explain all sorts of data types required for inputs, outputs, and other data. The advantage of algorithms is that you can use them as a shorthand. You can also annotate and manage your code. These habits will help keep your code ordered and coherent to your team members. All these practices will help enhance how you see and think about programs.

Software developers work in teams, with several people working on the same piece of code at the same time. The importance of annotating your code becomes very apparent in such situations.

It also happens that working with others will accelerate your growth. When coding with others you learn from their experience and knowledge. As we have said, C++ has a variety of library objects, statements, and other tools. It is as rich as vocabulary in human languages because there are many ways of doing the same things. Your way of fixing a problem will depend on your ability to see efficient ways of doing so. But ultimately all programming and software developments are creative endeavors. Working with others will increase your programming "vocabulary" – you will learn from how creatively they fix problems and you will find insights of your own in the process. You should always keep in mind that everyone can contribute something and what they contribute is heavily influenced by the amount of experience they have. So even if you are new to C++, you still have a unique experience and approach to solving problems that other people don't have because you think differently. That in itself is valuable to any team, particularly if you learn to communicate your ideas well. I highly recommend you use the glossary as one of the ways to help you communicate clearly.

In addition to annotations, it is good practice to make your code as clean as possible. I have demonstrated how to comment lines of code to prevent breaking the code during editing. In your exercises, when you break the code beyond repair, you can always start over from our saved IDEs, or you can simply refresh the browser to start over (this will depend on the state you ran and generated the code). Only generate URLs when you need to save your code, not while you are developing.

We also stressed the importance of code structure. For instance, we talked about the importance of declaring and defining functions: the best practice is to declare your functions on the top and define them after the main() function. It is similar to declaring integers. The techniques ensure you have an inventory of functions, variables, and objects right at the beginning. It works like an index and can help you avoid definition errors.

Formatting and editing your code of unnecessary lines reduces the possibility of errors during development. You should always update your comments when you make a change. Unformatted code will not impact performance, the logic of the code will. It is a collaboration courtesy to format your code, not to mention how much easier it makes things for you. Other programmers on your team will be able to implement your code, or even improve it, and they will leave comments.

But these types of practices are not just good for you. As the world moves forward it is becoming more and more complicated, so it is good for programs to explain themselves to the user. If your program prints, make sure it is easy to read. We have seen how this can be done in this book. Use escape sequences like \n to create new lines and \t to create horizontal table so there is enough whitespace to your code. But as a back-end programmer working with servers and other equipment, you may not have to print out as often as a front-end programmer who serves content to the client. The only users who may need to see your print outs are other technicians and administrators managing those machines through the terminal. Formatting practices are often underused in backend programming, but it is still a good practice to have. It is valuable to administrators and technicians, who do not have the resources to navigate esoteric compiler-generated errors that programmers are used to when debugging. So a program that is formatted and gives this information clearly in the terminal or consoles is important.

Take Away: Computer Science Concepts in C++

In addition to programming, we also explored some basic computer science concepts. We looked at the behavior of machines and their language. We talked about how learning programming is like learning a new language: both have syntax and rules that ensure communication is possible. C++ is a back-end server language that is used for managing servers that control oceans of data. Unlike high-level languages like Python, which are more human, C++ wants programmers to be more detailed in their code. Each variable must be unique in a function or we will have an error. All functions and statements are case sensitive and have specific rules that govern them. We have implemented many *if()...else* statements and made nested *if-else* statements. We saw that conditional statements like *if()* can be executed without the *else*, but a missing *else* statement can cause an error if the condition is false. And just as a missing verb indicates a sentence is incomplete, *else* statements cannot be implemented without an *if()*.

We saw how computers communicate in binary numbers using logical math. We saw bitwise function work at the bit level, completing logical math computations like AND, OR, and NOT. All the other C++ functions that are object-based must be translated by the compiler into machine language. But *bitwise* functions are faster because they skip that step and communicate directly to the machine. They are often deployed in competitive programming to make highly agile programs and routines. Outside of competitive programming, bitwise functions have some functionality in managing big data.

The challenge with *bitwise* functions is that they are very difficult for humans to understand because they are binary. To see what computers see we had a brief computer science lesson on binary and binary math. We made a "byte-sized" stream of register with our bitwise routine program and we made dynamic buffers to store bits for bitwise computations. Those virtual buffers and registers are how servers manage terabytes of data. Think about this; our buffers and registers were all one byte long, but a terabyte is 10^{12} times larger than our buffer: 1,000,000,000,000 bytes. These numbers are small for websites like YouTube which bases its back – end computing on C + +. The data that YouTube deals with is astronomical. In 2018 it was 5.25 zettabytes (10^{21}bytes). It was serving over 3.25 billion hours of content ("How much data does YouTube store? - Quora," n.d.). Bitwise functions give these servers the ability to work with this load without interruption or massive delays. This is one of the best examples of the power of C++ and its ability to handle big complex systems. It is a useful language for programmers to learn. If you visualize these data streams as arrays of 8 slots, it will be easier for you to rationalize many bitwise operators, especially shift operators.

In addition to binary programming, we worked with different kinds of data and explored different aspects of object programming. We did plenty of exercises where we dealt with strings, for example. In fact, we used and deployed strings in every one of our exercises. We saw that strings are also arrays of data, and can be manipulated like objects except in a few ways. Strings have a length, size and can be parsed with various objects in the <string> library. Think of the copy constructor call combination we learned. To parse a container of any type, vector or array, you need a *for()*loop with an *Addressof* operator element. That task has a dedicated function in the <string> library where all you need is the index of the item you are parsing. If there is one thing you should take away from this book it is proficiency in handling strings: breakout escape sequences, handling strings through array indexing, and passing strings to different functions.

We also learned and discussed functionality and design considerations. We talked, for instance, about how and when to use loops. Our bank security example was best illustrated by our exit controlled loop example in a fail-close system. Banks, as we said, should always have their doors locked and closed; they fail-close. Most events in the bank require doors and exits to fail-close and the only time they should open it in a fire. The system should keep everything in check, where a condition is tested AFTER the routine. The exit control loops are also useful in other areas, like in data control. YouTube does data corrections as a secondary routine of normal operations. This makes sure the system is always running, not hunkered by resend-data requests.

As C++ is a backend-language it has to handle and work with multiple types of data. We have had a brief discussion about this when we spoke of vector-based images as an object class and their other object properties. Photo manipulation software like Photoshop is programmed in C++ where aspects like image manipulation take full use of the program's power. Vectors allow image manipulation without loss of quality, unlike .jped or .png that are arrays of pixels. Vectors like .svg or .pdf use vector containers to describe their pixel locations, which has more class features in C++ that allows preservation of the image.

This book is also meant to be reference, so I encourage you to use the glossary and the index to review topics. The glossary has all the terms bolded and some of the code snippets we looked at. It also includes the section where the terms are discussed in more detail.

Glossary

Term	Definition	Section
"+",	Binary, arithmetic operation that sums two variables. Also used to concatenate strings in the <string> library	Operation:String Concatenation
"++"	Increment operator used to increase the value of an integer by 1. This unary operator is often used to increase a variable within a loop.	Unary Operators
"--"	Unary operator that decreases a variable within a loop. This unary operator is often used to increase a variable within a loop.	Unary Operators
"-", Arithmetic Operator	Binary operator that subtracts one operand from another	Arithmetic Operators

"-", Unary Operator	Unary minus operator that is used to change the sign of a variable or argument. Performing a unary minus operation on a negative integer will make it positive and vice versa.	Unary Operators
"-="	The atomic subtraction used to combine the '-' and '=' operators. This operator first subtracts the current value of the variable on the left from the value on the right. It then assigns the result to the variable on the left. For example, x-=y would be a shorter way of writing x=x-y without having to use a separate arithmetic operator.	Assignment Operators
"!", Binary Operator	Binary logical "NOT" operator that returns a Boolean true if the conditions in consideration are not satisfied. If one of the conditions is true, then it returns a Boolean false.	Logical Operators
"!",	NOT operator is used to reverse the Boolean logical state of an operand. For example, if a variable x has a Boolean value of false, !x will be true.	Unary Operators
"!="	"Not-Equal" operator	Relational Operators

	that also checks whether two given operands are equal or not. However, this operator returns a Boolean true if the operands are not equal and returns false if the operands are equal.	
"*"	Binary operator that multiplies two operands. The order of the operands does not matter.	Arithmetic Operators
"*="	Operator for the atomic multiplication, used to combine the '*' and '=' operators. This operator first multiplies the current value of the variable on the left to the value on the right and then assigns the result to the variable on the left. For example, x*=y would be a shorter way of writing x=x*y without having to use a separate arithmetic operator.	Assignment Operators
"/"	Binary division "forward slash" operator that divides the first operand into the second.	Arithmetic Operators
"/="	Atomic division operator is a combination of '/' and '=' operators. This operator first divides the current value of the	Assignment Operators

	variable on the left by the value on right and then assigns the result to the variable on the left. For example, x/=y would be a shorter way of writing x=x/y without having to use a separate arithmetic operator.	
“\?” Escape Sequence	Used for question marks.	Using Escape Sequences
“\’” Escape Sequence	Used for single quotes.	Using Escape Sequences
“\”” Escape Sequence	Used for double quotes.	Using Escape Sequences
“\\” Escape Sequence	Used for backslashes.	Using Escape Sequences
“\f” Escape Sequence	Stands for “form feed” and is used to go to the next “page”.	Using Escape Sequences
“\n” Escape Sequence	Stands for “line feed” and is used to go to the next line.	Using Escape Sequences
“\t” Escape Sequence	Stands for “horizontal tab” and adds 5 spaces horizontally.	Using Escape Sequences
“\v” Escape Sequence	Stands for “vertical tab” and is used for spacing in vertical languages.	Using Escape Sequences
“&” Unary Operator	Addressof operator that is used to point to the address of a variable.	Unary Operators
“&”, Binary Operator	Bitwise AND that takes two numbers as operands and does AND on every bit within the stream of the two numbers. The result stream of AND is 1 only	Bitwise Operators

	if both bits are 1.	
“&&”	Binary logical “AND” operator that returns a Boolean true when both the conditions in consideration are satisfied. Otherwise, it returns false.	Logical Operators
“%”	Binary modulus operator that returns the remainder from dividing the first operand into the second.	Arithmetic Operators
“^”	Bitwise XOR that takes two numbers as operands and does XOR on every bit within the stream of the two numbers. The result stream of XOR is 1 if the two bits are different.	Bitwise Operators
“+=”	Operator for atomic addition, used to combine the ‘+’ and ‘=’ operators. This operator first adds the current value of the variable on the left to the value on the right. It then stores the result to the variable on the left. For example, x+=y would be a shorter way of writing x=x+y without having to use a separate arithmetic operator.	Assignment Operators
“<”	“Less-than” operator	Relational Operators

	that checks whether the first operand is less than the second operand. If so, this operator returns a boolean true. Otherwise, it returns false.	
“<<”	Left shift operator that takes two numbers and left shifts the bits of the first operand. The second operand is used to determine the number of places to shift.	Bitwise Operators
“<=”	“Lesser-than or equal-to” operator that checks whether the first operand is less than or equal to the second operand. If so, this operand returns a Boolean true. Otherwise it returns false.	Relational Operators
“=”	Equal assignment operator, used to assign the value on the right to the variable on the left.	Assignment Operators
“==”	“Equal” operator that checks whether two given operands are equal. If the operands are equal, it returns a Boolean “true”, if not it returns false.	Relational Operators
“>”	“Greater-than” operator that checks whether the first operand is greater than the second operand. If so, this	Relational Operators

	operator returns a Boolean true. Otherwise, it returns false.	
“>=”	“Greater-than or equal-to” operator that checks whether the first operand is greater than or equal to the second operand. If so, this operand returns a Boolean true. Otherwise, it returns a Boolean false.	Relational Operators
“>>”	Right shift operator that takes two numbers and right shifts the bits of the first operand. The second operand is used to determine the number of places to shift.	Bitwise Operators
“|”	Bitwise OR that takes two numbers as operands and does OR on every bit within the stream of two numbers. The result stream of OR is 1 if any of the two bits is 1.	Bitwise Operators
“||”	Binary logical “OR” operator that returns a Boolean true when one (or both) of the conditions in consideration are satisfied. If none of the conditions are satisfied, it returns false.	Logical Operators
“~”	Bitwise NOT operator	Bitwise Operators

	that takes one number and switches the state of all the bits (1s to 0s, 0s to 1s).	
“bool” Keyword	Datatype keyword that is short for “Boolean” and stores values with two states: true or false. Has a size of 1 byte. these values can be expressed as either “0/1” or “false/true" with a manipulator.	Basic Data Types
“boolalpha/noboolapha” Manipulator	Input-Output manipulator that switches between using “0/1” to “false/true” for Boolean values.	Using Endl: Input/Output Manipulators
“char” Keyword	Data type keyword that is short for “character” and stores single characters regardless of their capitalization. Has a size of 1 byte. Char values are surrounded by single quotes.	Basic Data Types
“cout” object	C++ programming object part of the <iostream> library that allows a program to print out values and text using the "<<" operator. This object must be defined with a datatype, usually "std".	Using Cout
“double” Keyword	Data type keyword that is used to store numbers with decimals with 15 decimal digits. Has a	Basic Data Types

	size of 8 bytes. This data type can hold more decimal numbers and is preferred for mathematical calculations.	
"else"	Statement is used to specify a code in the event that its accompanying if() expression is false. Else cannot be used without if ().	Loops
"endl" Manipulator	Input-Output manipulator that outputs "\n" and flushes the output stream.	Using Endl: Input/Output Manipulators
"ends" Manipulator	Input-Output manipulator that outputs "\0" [zero].	Using Endl: Input/Output Manipulators
"float" Keyword	Keyword data type that stores numbers with decimals with 7 decimal digits. Has a size of 4 bytes. This data type is preferred for holding monetary numbers.	Basic Data Types
"flush" Manipulator	Input-Output manipulator that flushes the output stream.	Using Endl: Input/Output Manipulators
"get_money" Manipulator	Input-Output manipulator that receives an input as a monetary value. This manipulator works in C++11 only and may cause errors in outdated C++ programming environments.	Using Endl: Input/Output Manipulators

"get_time" Manipulator	Input-Output manipulator that receives an input as a date/time value according to a specified format. This manipulator works in C++11 only and may cause errors in outdated C++ programming environments.	Using Endl: Input/Output Manipulators
"int" Keyword	Data type keyword that is short for "integer" and stores whole numbers. Has a size of 4 bytes. This keyword includes positive and negative integers.	Basic Data Types
"put_money" Manipulator	Input-Output manipulator that formats and outputs a monetary value. This manipulator works in C++11 only and may cause errors in outdated C++ programming environments.	Using Endl: Input/Output Manipulators
"put_time" Manipulator	Input-Output manipulator that receives an input as a date/time value according to a specified format. This manipulator works in C++11 only and may cause errors in outdated C++ programming environments.	Using Endl: Input/Ouput Manipulators
"quoted" Manipulator	Input-Output manipulator allows you to insert and extract	Using Endl: Input/Output Manipulators

	quoted strings with embedded spaces. This manipulator works in C++14 only.	
"showbase/noshowbase" Manipulator	Input-Output manipulator specifically for mathematical outputs that controls whether a prefix is used to indicate a numeric base.	Using Endl: Input/Output Manipulators
"showpos/noshowpos" Manipulator	Input-Output manipulator that controls whether the "+" sign is used to indicate non-negative numbers.	Using Endl: Input/Output Manipulators
"uppercase/nouppercase" Manipulator	Input-Output manipulator that controls whether uppercase characters are used with some output formats.	Using Endl: Input/Output Manipulators
"using namespace std;" Statement	Line of code frequently used to unilaterally declare the "std" datatype for iostream library objects and manipulators. This unilateral declaration makes the code easier to see. However, this is discouraged outside of practice because it can make string handling ill-defined in programs, thus, causing errors that are difficult to mitigate. Exercises in this book will avoid using this statement.	Omitting Namespace

[string_name].length() Attribute	Coding syntax for calling the "length" string object attribute .	String Objects: Length( ) Attribute
Actual Parameters	Parameters coming into a defined function.	Parameter Passing
Algorithm	An organizational tool used to plot out the aspects of a program including (1) data in, if applicable, (2) operations performed on declared variables, and (3) the result of running the program.	Principles of Programming
Arithmetic operators	Binary and unary operations that are used to perform common mathematical operations.	Arithmetic Operators
Assembly language	Describes a low-level programming language that requires a compiler to convert it into machine code.	Chapter 1: Setting up a C++ Development Environment
Assignment Operators	Used to assign a value to a variable and change values on the fly, reducing the number of instructions in a program.	Assignment Operators
Atomic Operations	Operations that combine assignments with other operations. Atomic operations allow programmers to manipulate a value stored within a variable and reassign it immediately.	Assignment Operators

Base-10	Number system used by human beings assign place value to numerals. Base-10 is also known as the decimal system because a digit's value in a number is determined by where it lies in relation to the decimal point. The value is multiplied by a base power of 10, where each point away from the left of the decimal is 10^(n+1) and each point to the right of the decimal is 10^(n-1).	Bitwise Operators
Binary Number System	See Base-2	Bitwise Operators
Binary Operator	Classification of operators that execute with two operands.	Chapter 4: Operations in C++
Bitwise Operators	Logic operators that operate on numbers at the binary level.	Bitwise Operators
Bluefish	A free software advanced text editor with a variety of tools for programming in general and the development of dynamic websites.	Setting up the Text Editor
Byte	Measurement of data composed of 8 bits. A byte can represent up to 225 numbers (0b 1111111).	Unary Operators
C++14	Advanced version of C++ that makes this version slightly more	Chapter 1: Setting up a C++ Development Environment.

	intelligible for humans to program in. "Standard C++" usually refers to C++11, also known as C++0x.	
CentOS	A free, community-supported. Linux distribution operating system that is functionally compatible with Red Hat Enterprise Linux (RHEL).	Linux Compiler Installation
Code	See Executable file	Chapter 1: Setting up a C++ Development Environment
Code::Blocks	A free open source IDE designed for C++. This IDE supports many C++ compilers including GCC, Clang, and Visual C++ in Microsoft. This IDE can program in C++, C, and Fortran.	Windows IDE Installation
Command-Line Interface (CLI)	Method of interacting with a computer program where the user controls the program with entering lines of code.	Setting up a Text Editor
Comments	Lines of code that are ignored by the compiler and indicated by a double slash at the beginning of the line in C++. Comments are used to annotate code and leave notes to guide	Overview of C++ Syntax

	other programmers studying your code.	
Compiled Language	See Low-Level Language	Chapter 3
Concatenation, String	A common programming feature that allows programmers to dynamically control text by fielding content from a source and serving it within their program. In C++ String Concatenation is done through "+", an arithmetic operator.	Operation:String Concatenation
Conditional Operator	Boolean logic based operator with three operand expressions. The outcome of the conditional operator depends on the first expression.	Ternary Operators
Conditional Short-Circuit	When program developers use logical operators and conditional statements to control how a program behaves.	Logical Operators
Copy Constructor Call	Method of searching and printing indexes. Consists of for() loop with an index variable with an Addressof operator, and a container object with an index such as an array.	Unary Operators
Counter	An arbitrary variable	Loops

	that is used in conjunction with an arithmetic unary operator to incrementally loop an indicated expression.	
Data	Operands, or the various kinds of data that the functions and statements are acting on	Overview of Syntax
Data Type	Attribute of a variable which tells the compiler or interpreter how the programmer intends to use the data. Common data types include real numbers, integers, and "true-false" Boolean variables.	Chapter 3
Debugging	Process of location and removing computer program errors and abnormalities, also known as "bugs." As a general rule, smaller, modularized code that calls on functions is easier to debug than larger files.	Overview of Syntax
Decimal Number System	See Base-10	Bitwise Operators
do {}...while() Loop	Exit controlled loop that tests a single condition and loops a block of code until the condition is met.	Loops
else if()	Conditional statement combination used to nest conditional if()... else statements.	Loops

	Programmers are advised to use a switch if there are numerous conditions to test.	
Escape Sequence	Special in-string character combinations that are used to represent certain special characters within strings and character streams. Escape sequences allow programmers to include symbols in strings without confusing the compiler.	Using Escape Sequences
Executable File	List of instructions that are used to perform the operations of a program.	Chapter 1
File Extension	File suffix that informs the code compiler what language the executable file is in. The C++ language is indicated by ".cpp" or ".hpp" extensions.	Chapter 1
First Principal of Programming	A program must be designed to complete a task in the smallest number of functions possible. This principle reduces overhead and increases performance of a program.	Principles of Programming
for() Loop	Entry controlled loop that has three inputs: an initialization expression, a test expression and an update expression. The for loop will execute its	Loops

	block of code until the test expression reports false.	
Formal Parameters	Variables used to define the initial arguments, and any arguments in the function before the actual parameters are passed.	Parameter Passing
Function	A block of code that takes inputs to perform an action and runs when called.	Chapter 6: Creating...
Function Overloading	Programming technique of consolidating code through stacking several data types onto one function.	Function Overloading
Functionality	How program features and utilities can be implemented in a code to achieve a specific result.	Chapter 4: Operations in C++
Functions	Code that encapsulates instructions that may take inputs and output some result. Every function "[function-name]()", where [function_name] is some arbitrary function, is always followed by curly brackets {} and every explicitly stated instruction within the curly brackets will be executed by the compiler.	Overview of Syntax
Gedit	Free, open-source,	Linux Compiler

	general-purpose text editor that includes tools for editing source code and structured text such as markup languages.	Installation
getline() function	C++ function from the <string> library that extracts all characters from an input string into a string array.	Cin and getline() function
GNU Collection Compiler (GCC)	An open source compiler system produced by the GNU Project supporting various programming languages. GCC is a key component of the GNU toolchain and is the standard compiler for most Linux projects.	Linux Compiler Installation
Graphical user Interface (GUI)	Method of interacting with a computer program that allows users to interact with graphical icons and visual indicators such as secondary notation instead of inputting commands.	Setting up Text
Header File Library	Lines that start with the pound sign (#) that are used by the compiler to call library functions.	Overview of Syntax
if() .... else Statement	Conditional statement function combination that tests a single condition and executes explicitly stated blocks of code based on the	Loops

	results of the test.	
if()... else statement	A nested function that executes all instructions within its curly brackets "{}" given a specified condition is met. Otherwise, it executes the items with the enclosed else {} statement. These statements always deploy a relational operand to test the condition.	Relational Operators
Integrated Development Environment (IDE)	Programming environment used to write code, test for errors and translate a program.	Chapter 1
Linux distribution (distro)	An operating system made from a Linux kernel based software collection and package management system for installing additional software.	Linux Compiler Installation
Logic Gates	Physical electronic circuits that have one or more inputs while only having one output. AND gates only pass a "1" when all inputs are "1"; OR gates pass a "1" as their output when they receive a "1" at any of their inputs; NOT gates pass a "1" when they receive a "0" at their input.	Logical Operators

Logical Operators	Binary operators used in combination with the relational operators combine two or more conditions to describe a specific constraint.	Logical Operators
Loops	Function that execute a block of code as long as a specified condition is reached	Loops
Low-Level Language	A programming language that closely follows a computer's instruction set architecture—commands or functions in the language map closely to processor instructions. This reduces the overhead for running the program as the compiler takes less resources to translate low-level languages into machine code.	Chapter 2
Machine Language	Coding language that is directly compiled and executed by a CPU. See "Assembler Language"	Chapter 1
Manipulator, Input/Output	Helper functions within the C++ iostream library that make it possible to control input/output streams using the "<<" operator or the ">>" operator.	Using Endl: Input/Output Manipulators
Notepad ++	Text editor and source code editor for use with Microsoft Windows.	Setting up Text

Object	A general computing term that describes a method that the computer uses to manage data.	First Program: Output and Basic Strings
Operand	Operation component that describes the value, object, or variable being operated on.	Note: Operand...
Operations	Features such as control loops that implement decision-making in programs.	Chapter 4: Operations in C++
Operator	Operation component that describes the symbol indicating the sort of operation being carried out. Operators are described by how many operands they can operate on at a time: unary, binary, and ternary.	Note: Operand...
Organization Identifier	Proprietary Apple naming convention that is used to create a unique ID for programs across various Apple databases: the Apple Developer Website, and iCloud Container, iTunes connect portal in the Appstore. The organization identifier is used as the first argument of a "reversed domain" that ensures that all developed projects can be streamlined into the	Mac IDE Installation

	proprietary macOS framework.	
Parameter Pass by Reference	Both actual and formal parameters refer to the same locations. Therefore, any changes made inside the main() function will impact the actual parameters that were passed.	Parameter Passing
Parameter Pass by Value	Values of actual parameters are copied into and stored in the function's formal parameters. Any changes made inside main() does not impact the actual parameters that were passed.	Parameter Passing
Red Hat Enterprise Linux (RHEL)	A commercial Linux distribution developed by Red Hat for the commercial market.	Linux Compiler Installation> Note: there are many distributions…
Register	An array of binary storage where each bit gets its own place in the array. Registers are used to calculate bitwise operators.	Bitwise Operators
Relational Operators	Binary operators that are used to compare two values and return a boolean response.	Relational Operators
Script	Supplementary list of commands executed by certain programs or scripting engines.	Chapter 6: Creating...
See Base-2	Number system used by	Bitwise Operators

	machines to calculate computations. Also known as the binary number system. binary numbers are represented as a stream of bits, where each singular bit can be one of the two states: 1 or 0. The position of the 1 bit in the stream determines the value of the number.	
Server-side programming	Writing code that negotiates and delivers content to a dynamic, or changing website. C++ is, majorly, a server side language.	Mac IDE Installation
Service Level Agreement (SLA)	Term in IT management that describes a commitment between the technology administrator, the one providing the service, and a client.	Overview of Syntax
sizeof()	Unary operation that queries the size of an object and delivers its size in bytes.	Unary Operators
Software Development Kit (SDK)	A set of tools used for developing applications provided by hardware and software providers.	Mac IDE Installation
Statements	General term to describe the beginning line of code with specific instructions that the compiler recognizes outside of functions.	Overview of Syntax

	How these are highlighted in language syntax environments depend on the type of the statement and the conventions of the programming environment.	
String Array	An orderly arrangement of characters where each character of the string is indexed in its own numerical location.	String Indexes and Arrays
Strings	A computer programming data type that represents a sequence of characters, either as a literal constant or as some kind of variable.	Advanced Strings
switch () Statement	Multibranch statement used to execute different code blocks based on the value of an evaluated expression	Loops
Ternary Operator	Classification of operators that accept more than 2 operands, or conditional operators with several arguments.	Ternary Operator
Text Editor	Program that enables editing of the code.	Chapter 1
Unary Operator	Classification of operators that execute with a single operand.	Unary Operator
Variables	A concept borrowed from mathematics to describe a symbolic	Chapter 3

	value who's associated value can be changed and operated upon. Variables are used to control a program through operational functions.	
while() Loop	Entry controlled loop that tests a single condition and loops a block of code until the condition is met.	Loops
Xcode	A free IDE software development suite for the macOS. This IDE has utilities for developing C++ based programs for MacOS oriented operating systems like tvOS for Apple TV, watchOS for Apple watches, and iPadOS for iPad tablets.	Mac IDE Installation

INDEX

For your convenience, all coding program exercises have been posted here.

"Hello World" program in GeeksforGeeks IDE

```
// Simple C++ program to display "Hello World"
// Header file for input output functions
#include<iostream>
using namespace std;
// main function -
// where the execution of program begins
int main()
{
    // prints hello world
    cout<<"Hello World";

    return 0;
}
```

Using in-string escape sequences to delimit and manipulate the output

```
// Simple C++ program to display "Hello World"
// Header file for input output functions
#include<iostream>
using namespace std;
// main function -
// where the execution of program begins
int main()
{
    // prints hello world
    cout<<"Hello World!\n";
    cout<<"I am learning C++";

    return 0;
}
```

Using a input/output manipulator to delimit and manipulate the output

```
// Simple C++ program to display "Hello World"
// Header file for input output functions
#include<iostream>
using namespace std;
// main function -
// where the execution of program begins
int main()
{
    // prints hello world
    cout<<"Hello World!\n";
    cout<<"I am learning C++";

    return 0;
}
```

Testing Stability: Using a comment to remove "using namespace"

```
// Simple C++ program to display "Hello World"
// Header file for input output functions
#include<iostream>
//using namespace std;
// main function -
// where the execution of program begins
int main()
{
    // prints hello world
    cout<<"Hello World!" << endl;
    cout<<"I am learning C++";

    return 0;
}
```

Declaring the iostream objects and manipulators

With namespace

```
// Simple C++ program to display "Hello World"
// Header file for input output functions
#include<iostream>
// main function -
// where the execution of program begins
int main()
{
    // prints hello world
    std::cout<<"Hello World!"
    << std::endl;
    std::cout<<"I am learning C++";

    return 0;
}
```

Without namespace

```
// Simple C++ program to display "Hello World"
// Header file for input output functions
#include<iostream>
//using namespace std;
// main function -
// where the execution of program begins
int main()
{
    // prints hello world
    cout<<"Hello World!" << endl;
    cout<<"I am learning C++";

    return 0;
}
```

Declaring int numbers

```
// Simple C++ program to display "Hello World"
// Header file for input output functions
#include<iostream>
// main function -
// where the execution of program begins
int main()
{
    //Declares an int 'myNum'
    int myNum = 10;
    // prints hello world + myNum
    std::cout<<"Hello World!\n\t";
    std::cout<< myNum;
    std::cout<<" is my number.";

    return 0;
}
```

Summing inputs and printing the result

Inputs

```
11
12
Code
#include<iostream>
int main()
{
    // Explains program to user
    std::cout<<"Welcome! Enter two numbers and \nI will sum them.\n";
    //Declares input variables
    int x, y;
    //Declares output variable
    int sum;

    //Prompts user for inputs
    std::cout<<"Type a number: ";
    std::cin >> x;
    std::cout << x <<"\n";
    std::cout << "Type another number: ";
    std::cin>> y;
    std::cout << y <<"\n";
    //Operates on the variables
    sum= x+y;

    //Prints results
    std::cout<<"Sum is: "<<sum;
    return 0;
}
```

Using Int with Float or Double

Inputs

```
22
7
Code
#include<iostream>
int main()
{
    // Explains program to user
    std::cout<<"Welcome! Enter two numbers and \nI will divide them.\n";
    //Declares input variables
    int x, y;
    //Declares output variable
    float result;

    //Prompts user for inputs
    std::cout<<"Type a number: ";
    std::cin >> x;
    std::cout << x <<"\n";
    std::cout << "Type another number: ";
    std::cin>> y;
    std::cout << y <<"\n";
    //Operates on the variables
    result= x/y;

    //Prints results
    std::cout<<"Result is: "<<result;
    return 0;
}
```

Comparing Float and Double

```
#include <iostream>
int main()
{
    //Declares operation variables
    float x=27, y=7;
    double xd=22, yd=7;
    //Declares output variable
    float result;
    double resultd;
    bool test;

    //Operates on the variables
    result= x/y;
    resultd= xd/yd;
    test=(result==resultd);

    //Prints results
    std::cout<< "True or False?: \n\tfloat(" << x << "/" << y <<")";
    std::cout<< " is equal to double(" << xd << "/" << yd <<")\n";
    //std::cout<<"Is Float is Equal to Double?: ";
    std::cout << std::boolalpha
    << "\t"<<test;
    return 0;
}
```

String Concatenation

```
#include<iostream>
//Call the library for string handling
#include <string>
int main()
{
   //Declare variables and complete operation
   std::string firstName = "John ";
   std::string lastName = "Doe";
   std::string fullName = firstName + lastName;

   // prints results
   std::cout<<"Hello "
   << fullName <<".";

   return 0;
}
```

Print fullName.Length()

```
#include<iostream>
//Call the library for string handling
#include <string>
int main()
{
    //Declare variables and complete operation
    std::string firstName = "John";
     std::string lastName = "Doe";
     std::string fullName = firstName +" "+lastName;

    // prints results
    std::cout<<"Hello "
    << fullName <<".\n";
    std::cout<<"Your full name is "
    <<fullName.length()
    <<" characters long.";

    return 0;
}
```

Access fullName String Array

```
#include<iostream>
//Call the library for string handling
#include <string>
int main()
{
    //Declare variables and complete operation
    std::string firstName = "John";
     std::string lastName = "Doe";
     std::string fullName = firstName +" "+lastName;

    // prints results
    std::cout<<"Hello "
    << fullName <<".\n";
    std::cout<<"The third character of your full name \nis \'"
    <<fullName[2]
    <<"\'.";

    return 0;
}
```

String Concatenation with cin

Input

```
John
Doe
Code
#include<iostream>
//Call the library for string handling
#include <string>
int main()
{
    //Declare variables
    std::string firstName;
     std::string lastName;

     //Prompt user for name
     std::cout<<"What is your name?\n";
    std::cin>> firstName;
    std::cout<< firstName <<"\n";
    std::cin>> lastName;
    std::cout<< lastName <<"\n";

    //Calculate operation
     std::string fullName = firstName + " "+ lastName;
    // prints results
    std::cout<<"\nHello "
    << fullName <<".";

    return 0;
}
```

String Termination with cin

Input

```
John Doe
Code
#include<iostream>
//Call the library for string handling
#include <string>
int main()
{
    //Declare variables
    std::string fullName;

    //Prompt user for name
    std::cout<<"What is your full name?\n";
    std::cin>> fullName;

    // Greet user
    std::cout<<"\nHello "
    << fullName <<".";

    return 0;
}
```

Arithmetic Routine Program

```
#include<iostream>
int main()
{
    //Declare variables
    int a=25, b=3;
    int result;

    // printing a and b
    std::cout<< "This program will go through an\narithmetic routine 
with the following\nvariables where: "
    <<"a is "<<a<<" and b is "<<b<<"\n";

    // addition
    result = a + b;
    std::cout << "\ta+b is: "<< result << "\n";

    // subtraction
    result = a - b;
    std::cout << "\ta-b is: "<< result << "\n";

    // multiplication
    result = a * b;
    std::cout << "\ta*b is: "<< result << "\n";

    // division
    result = a / b;
    std::cout << "\ta/b is: "<< result << "\n";

    // modulus
    result = a % b;
    std::cout << "\ta%b is: "<< result << "\n";

    return 0;
}
```

Relational Routine Program

```
#include<iostream>
int main()
{
   //Declare variables
   int a=25, b=3;

    // print an explanation of the program
    std::cout<< "This program will go through an\nrelational routine
with the following\nvariables where: "
    // print a and b
    <<"a is "<<a<<" and b is "<<b<<"\n";

    // greater than example
    if (a > b)
        std::cout << "\ta is greater than b\n";
    else
        std::cout << "\ta is less than or equal to b\n";

    // greater than equal to
    if (a >= b)
        std::cout << "\ta is greater than or equal to b\n";
    else
        std::cout << "\ta is lesser than b\n";

    // less than example
    if (a < b)
        std::cout << "\ta is less than b\n";
    else
        std::cout << "\ta is greater than or equal to b\n";

    // lesser than equal to
    if (a <= b)
        std::cout << "\ta is lesser than or equal to b\n";
    else
        std::cout << "\ta is greater than b\n";

    // equal to
    if (a == b)
        std::cout << "\ta is equal to b\n";
    else
        std::cout << "\ta and b are not equal\n";

    // not equal to
    if (a != b)
        std::cout << "\ta is not equal to b\n";
    else
        std::cout << "\ta is equal b\n";
    return 0;
}
```

Logical Routine Program

```
#include<iostream>
int main()
{
    //Declare variables
    int a=5, b=0, c=12, d=24;

    // print an explanation of the program
    std::cout<< "This program will go through a\nlogical routine with
the following\nvariables where: "
    // print a and b
    <<"a is "<<a<<" and b is "<<b<<"\n"
    <<"c is "<<c<<" and d is "<<d<<"\n";

    // logical AND example
    if (a>b && c==d)
        std::cout << "\ta is greater than b AND c is equal to d\n";
    else
        std::cout << "\t AND condition not satisfied--\n"
                  << "\t\t(a>b && c==d)\n";

    // logical OR example
    if (a>b || c==d)
        std::cout << "\ta is greater than b OR c is equal to d\n";
    else
        std::cout << "\tNeither a is greater than b nor c is equal "
                 << " to d\n";

    // logical NOT example
    if (!b)
        std::cout << "\tb is zero\n";
    else
        std::cout << "\tb is not zero\n";

    return 0;
}
```

Short Circuit Detection Program

```
#include <iostream>
using namespace std;
int main() {
    //Declare two variables
    int a=10, b=4;

    //Print explaination of the program
    cout<< "This This program will test if the OR gate \n"
    <<"or the AND gate shorts when a is equal to b.  \n";
    cout<< "\tCurrent value of a: "
    <<a <<"\n";
    cout<< "\tCurrent value of b: "
    <<b <<"\n";

    bool resAND = ((a == b) && cout << "--- OR gate short
circuited.\n");
    bool resOR = ((a == b) || cout << "--- AND gate short
circuited.\n");
    return 0;
}
```

Bitwise Routine with Register Printing

```
#include <iostream>
#include <bitset>
using namespace std;
int main() {
    //Declare operand numbers
   unsigned int a = 60;        // 60 = 0011 1100
   unsigned int b = 13;        // 13 = 0000 1101
   //Declare register c where calculations will take place
   int c = 0;

    //Print operand registers
    cout<<"Operand registers a: "<< a
    <<" and b: " << b
    << "\n\tregister a: -0b "<< bitset<8>(a)
    << "\n\tregister b: -0b "<< bitset<8>(b)<< endl ;

    //Bitwise AND
   c = a & b;              // 12 = 0000 1100
   cout << "Line 1 - Value of c is : " << c
   //Print register
   << "\n\t AND registers a&b: -0b "<< bitset<8>(c)<< endl ;

    //Bitwise OR
   c = a | b;              // 61 = 0011 1101
   cout << "Line 2 - Value of c is: " << c
   //Print register
   << "\n\t OR register a|b:   -0b "<< bitset<8>(c)<< endl ;
    //Bitwise XOR
   c = a ^ b;              // 49 = 0011 0001
   cout << "Line 3 - Value of c is: " << c
   //Print register
   << "\n\t XOR register a^b:  -0b "<< bitset<8>(c)<< endl ;
    //Bitwise NOT
   c = ~a;                 // -61 = 1100 0011
   cout << "Line 4 - Value of c is: " << c
   //Print register
   << "\n\t NOT register ~a:       -0b "<< bitset<8>(c)
   << "\n\t Compare to register a: -0b "<< bitset<8>(a)<< endl ;

    //Left Shift
   c = a << 2;             // 240 = 1111 0000
   cout << "Line 5 - Value of c is: " << c
   //Print register
   << "\n\t Left Shift register a<<2:  -0b "<< bitset<8>(c)<< endl ;
    //Right Shift
   c = a >> 2;             // 15 = 0000 1111
   cout << "Line 6 - Value of c is: " << c
   //Print register
   << "\n\t Right Shift register a>>2: -0b "<< bitset<8>(c)<< endl ;
   return 0;
}
```

Assignment Routine

```
#include <iostream>
using namespace std;
int main() {
   // Assigning value 10 to a
    // using "=" operator
    int a = 10;
    cout<<"This program will atomically manipulate the Value of a"
    <<"\n\tThe value of a is " <<a;

    // Assigning value by adding 10 to a
    // using "+=" operator
    a += 10;
    cout<<"\n Atomically + 10: the value of a is now " <<a;

    // Assigning value by subtracting 10 from a
    // using "-=" operator
    a -= 10;
    cout<<"\n Atomically - 10 from a: the value of a is now " <<a;

    // Assigning value by multiplying 10 to a
    // using "*=" operator
    a *= 10;
    cout<<"\n Atomically * 10: the value of a is now " <<a;

    // Assigning value by dividing 10 from a
    // using "/=" operator
    a /= 10;
    cout<<"\n Atomically dividing by 10: the value of a is now " <<a ;

    return 0;
}
```

While Loop featuring a Unary Operator

```
#include <iostream>
using namespace std;
int main() {
    //Initialize the counter, i
    int i = 0;

//While i is less than five, print i
    while (i < 5) {
        cout << i << "\n";
        i++;          //Unary counter i


    }
    return 0;
}
```

Unary Operator Routine with Post- and Pre Operations

```
#include <iostream>
using namespace std;
int main() {
    int a = 10, buf;
    cout<<"This program will use unary operators to increment \nand
decrement variable a and a buffer"
    <<"\n\tThe value of a is " <<a;

    // post-increment
    buf = a++;
    // a becomes 11 now
    cout << "\nPost-Increment: a is "<<a<<" and buf is "<<buf;

    // post-decrement example:
    buf = a--;
    // a becomes 10 now
    cout << "\nPost-Decrement:a is "<<a<<" and buf is "<<buf;

    // pre-increment example:
    // buf is assigned 11 now since a is updated here itself
    buf = ++a;
    // a and res have same values = 11
    cout << "\nPre-Increment:a is "<<a<<" and buf is "<<buf;

    // pre-decrement example:
    // res is assigned 10 only since a is updated here itself
    buf = --a;
    // a and res have same values = 10
    cout << "\nPre-Decrementt:a is "<<a<<" and buf is "<<buf;
    return 0;
}
```

Conditional Operations Demo

```
#include <bits/stdc++.h>
using namespace std;
int main()
{
   cout << "This program will pick the greatest one using two "
   <<"\nmethods:a conditional operator and"
   <<" an \nif()... else statement."
    << "\n\tWe expect a result of 5.";
    cout << "\n\nExecute expression using"
    << " ternary operator: ";
    // Execute expression using
    // ternary operator
    int a = 2 > 5 ? 2 : 5;
    cout << a << endl;

    cout << "\nExecute expression using "
    << "if else statement: ";

    // Execute expression using if else
    if ( 2 > 5)
        cout << "2";
    else
        cout << "5";
    return 0;
}
```

While Loop Demo

```
#include <iostream>
using namespace std;
int main() {
   //Initialize the counter, i
   int i = 1;

   //Print explanation of program
   cout <<"This program will number and print 10 lines--";
//While i is less than 11, print "Hello World"
    while (i < 11) {
        cout <<"\n\t"<< i << " Hello World";
        i++;          //Unary counter i


    }
   return 0;
}
```

For Loop Demo

```
#include <iostream>
using namespace std;
int main() {
    //Print explanation of program
    cout <<"This program will number and print 10 lines--";
//While i is less than 11, print "Hello World"
     for (int i= 1; i < 11; i++ ) {
          cout <<"\n\t"<< i << " Hello World";



     }
    return 0;
}
```

Do While Loop Demo exhibiting an exit controlled loop

```
#include <iostream>
using namespace std;
int main() {
   //Initialize the counter, i
   int i = 11;

   //Print explanation of program
   cout <<"This program may or may not print one \"Hello World\"";
//While i is less than 11, print "Hello World"
    do {
        cout <<"\n\t"<< i << " Hello World";
        i++;          //Unary counter i


    }
    while (i < 11);
    return 0;
}
```

Nested If-Else Demo

```
#include <iostream>
using namespace std;
int main() {
    cout << "This program will go through a sequential"
    <<"\nlist of numbers 2 through 4 and pick the "
    <<"\ngreatest none using  a nested if-else "
    <<"\nstatement."
     <<"\nGreatest number:\n\t";
     if ( 2 > 3 )
         cout << "2";
     else if ( 3 > 4 )
         cout << "3";
     else
         cout << "4";
     return 0;
}
```

Nested If-Else and Nested Ternary Operation Comparison

```
#include <iostream>
using namespace std;
int main() {
    cout << "This program will go through a sequential"
    <<"\nlist of numbers 2 through 4 and pick the "
    <<"\ngreatest none using two methods:"
    <<"\na nested if-else and a nested ternary operator"
     <<"\n Nested If-else Greatest number:\n\t";
     if ( 2 > 3 )
         cout << "2";
     else if ( 3 > 4 )
         cout << "3";

     else
         cout << "4";

    cout <<"\n Nested ternary operator Greatest number:\n\t";
    int a = 2 > 3 ? 2 : 3 > 4 ? 3 : 4;
    cout<<a;
     return 0;
}
```

Switch Demo

```
#include <iostream>
using namespace std;
int main() {
//Initialize variable
int x = 2;
//Print explanation
cout<< "This program prints a choice given x.\n"
<<"\n Variable x is equal to: "<< x
<<"\n\t";
// Program switch
    switch (x)
    {
        case 1:
            cout << "Choice is 1";
            break;
        case 2:
            cout << "Choice is 2";
            break;
        case 3:
            cout << "Choice is 3";
            break;
        default:
            cout << "Program Exit";
            break;
    }
return 0;
}
```

Function Demo

```
#include <iostream>
using namespace std;
// Function declaration
void myFunction();
// The main method
int main() {
  myFunction();  // call the function
  return 0;
}
// Function definition
void myFunction() {
  cout << "I just got executed!";
}
```

Functions with Parameter Passing

```
#include <iostream>
using namespace std;

//Declare function
int max(int x, int y);
//Main
int main() {
    int a = 10, b = 20;

    // Calling above function to find max of 'a' and 'b'
    int m = max(a, b);

    cout << "m is " << m;
    return 0;
}
//Define function
    int max(int x, int y)
{
    if (x > y)
    return x;
    else
    return y;
}
```

Program without function overloading

```
#include <iostream>
using namespace std;
int plusFuncInt(int x, int y) {
  return x + y;
}
double plusFuncDouble(double x, double y) {
  return x + y;
}
int main() {
  int myNum1 = plusFuncInt(8, 5);
  double myNum2 = plusFuncDouble(4.3, 6.26);
  cout << "Int: " << myNum1 << "\n";
  cout << "Double: " << myNum2;
  return 0;
}
```

Program function overloading

```
#include <iostream>
using namespace std;
int plusFuncInt(int x, int y) {
  return x + y;
}
//Change function
double plusFuncInt(double x, double y) {
  return x + y;
}
int main() {
  int myNum1 = plusFuncInt(8, 5);

  //Call function in place of the old one
  double myNum2 = plusFuncInt(4.3, 6.26);
  cout << "Int: " << myNum1 << "\n";
  cout << "Double: " << myNum2;
  return 0;
}
```

REFERENCES

[Running C,C++ Programs in Linux] Ubuntu 16.04 (Ubuntu Tutorial for Beginners). (n.d.). Retrieved from https://www.youtube.com/watch?v=A7Ny-ro1hT0

15-1134.00—Web Developers. (n.d.). Retrieved September 20, 2019, from https://www.onetonline.org/link/summary/15-1134.00

15-1199.03—Web Administrators. (n.d.). Retrieved October 1, 2019, from https://www.onetonline.org/link/summary/15-1199.03

Agarwal, H. (2017a, January 13). Loops in C and C++. Retrieved August 28, 2019, from GeeksforGeeks website: https://www.geeksforgeeks.org/loops-in-c-and-cpp/

Agarwal, H. (2017b, May 16). Setting up C++ Development Environment. Retrieved August 13, 2019, from GeeksforGeeks website: https://www.geeksforgeeks.org/setting-c-development-environment/

Awasthi, S. (n.d.). Switch Statement in C/C++—GeeksforGeeks. Retrieved October 3, 2019, from https://www.geeksforgeeks.org/switch-statement-cc/

Bluefish Editor: Features. (n.d.). Retrieved August 28, 2019, from Bluefish Editor: Features website: http://bluefish.openoffice.nl/features.html

C++ | Nested Ternary Operator. (2018, October 15). Retrieved October 3, 2019, from GeeksforGeeks website: https://www.geeksforgeeks.org/c-nested-ternary-operator/

C++ Code [Paste Site]. (2015, December 5). Retrieved August 28, 2019, from Pastebin.com website: https://pastebin.com/f7KKzVyf

C++ Function Overloading. (n.d.). Retrieved October 4, 2019, from https://www.w3schools.com/cpp/cpp_function_overloading.asp

C++ Functions. (n.d.). Retrieved October 3, 2019, from https://www.w3schools.com/cpp/cpp_functions.asp

C++ Operators. (n.d.). Retrieved August 28, 2019, from https://www.w3schools.com/cpp/cpp_operators.asp

C++ Variables. (n.d.). Retrieved August 28, 2019, from https://www.w3schools.com/cpp/cpp_variables.asp

C++ While Loop. (n.d.). Retrieved October 3, 2019, from https://www.w3schools.com/cpp/cpp_while_loop.asp

Centos-faq | Open Source Community. (n.d.). Retrieved September 30, 2019, from https://community.redhat.com/centos-faq/

Deb, R. (n.d.). What is the Base-10 Number System? Retrieved October 2, 2019, from ThoughtCo website: https://www.thoughtco.com/definition-of-base-10-2312365

Escape sequences—Cppreference.com. (n.d.). Retrieved October 1, 2019, from https://en.cppreference.com/w/cpp/language/escape

GCC 7 Release Series—Changes, New Features, and Fixes—GNU Project—Free Software Foundation (FSF). (n.d.). Retrieved September 30, 2019, from https://gcc.gnu.org/gcc-7/changes.html

How much data does YouTube store? - Quora. (n.d.). Retrieved October 4, 2019, from https://www.quora.com/How-much-data-does-YouTube-store

Input/output manipulators—Cppreference.com. (n.d.). Retrieved October 1, 2019, from https://en.cppreference.com/w/cpp/io/manip

Introduction. (n.d.). Retrieved August 28, 2019, from https://web.stanford.edu/class/cs98si/slides/overview.html

Jaggi, A. (2015a, July 28). Operators in C | Set 1 (Arithmetic Operators). Retrieved August 28, 2019, from GeeksforGeeks website: https://www.geeksforgeeks.org/operators-in-c-set-1-arithmetic-operators/

Jaggi, A. (2015b, July 29). Operators in C | Set 2 (Relational and Logical Operators). Retrieved August 28, 2019, from GeeksforGeeks website: https://www.geeksforgeeks.org/operators-in-c-set-2-relational-and-logical-operators/

Killian, J. (2012). Understanding Bitwise Operators. Retrieved August 28, 2019, from https://code.tutsplus.com/articles/understanding-bitwise-operators--active-11301

Kitowska, K. (2019, April 23). What is C++ used for? 10 extremely powerful apps written in C++ - Blog. Retrieved August 28, 2019, from BoostHigh Software Development Company website: https://boosthigh.com/10-extremely-powerful-apps-written-in-cpp/

Kumar, H. (2017, June 2). Unary operators in C/C++. Retrieved August 28, 2019, from GeeksforGeeks website: https://www.geeksforgeeks.org/unary-operators-cc/

List of game engines. (2019). In *Wikipedia*. Retrieved from https://en.wikipedia.org/w/index.php?title=List_of_game_engines&oldid=911528135

Lithmee. (2018, October 18). What is the Difference Between Machine Code and Assembly Language. Retrieved September 11, 2019, from Pediaa.Com website: https://pediaa.com/what-is-the-difference-between-machine-code-and-assembly-language/

Manideep, P. (2017, October 26). Server side and Client side Programming. Retrieved September 30, 2019, from GeeksforGeeks website: https://www.geeksforgeeks.org/server-side-client-side-programming/

Operators-In-C.png (800×533). (n.d.). Retrieved August 28, 2019, from https://www.geeksforgeeks.org/wp-content/uploads/Operators-In-C.png

Orin, A. (n.d.). Behind The App: The Story Of Notepad++ | Lifehacker Australia. Retrieved August 28, 2019, from https://www.lifehacker.com.au/2015/06/behind-the-app-the-story-of-notepad/

Patel, Y. (2014). *How do I install gcc on Ubuntu Linux*. Retrieved from https://www.youtube.com/watch?v=cotkJrewAz0

Patel, Y. (2017). *How to Create First C++ Hello World Project using Xcode Mac OS X*. Retrieved from https://www.youtube.com/watch?time_continue=21&v=-H_EyIqBNDA

Peshev, M. (2017, November 3). As a programmer, is it important to have a GitHub profile? - Quora. Retrieved September 11, 2019, from https://www.quora.com/As-a-programmer-is-it-important-to-have-a-GitHub-profile

Prabhu, R. (2018, December 11). Assignment Operators in C/C++. Retrieved August 28, 2019, from GeeksforGeeks website: https://www.geeksforgeeks.org/assignment-operators-in-c-c/

Programming software and the IDE - Revision 1—GCSE Computer Science. (n.d.). Retrieved September 11, 2019, from BBC Bitesize website: https://www.bbc.co.uk/bitesize/guides/zgmpr82/revision/1

Python vs C++—Find Out The 9 Important Differences. (2018, July 1). Retrieved September 30, 2019, from EDUCBA website: https://www.educba.com/python-vs-c-plus-plus/

What are Scripts? - Definition from Techopedia. (n.d.). Retrieved October 3, 2019, from Techopedia.com website: https://www.techopedia.com/definition/10324/scripts

What is a Software Development Kit (SDK)? - Definition from Techopedia. (n.d.). Retrieved September 29, 2019, from Techopedia.com website: https://www.techopedia.com/definition/3878/software-development-kit-sdk

What is Debugging? - Definition from Techopedia. (n.d.). Retrieved September 28, 2019, from Techopedia.com website: https://www.techopedia.com/definition/16373/debugging

What's New in Xcode 9. (n.d.). Retrieved September 28, 2019, from https://developer.apple.com/library/archive/documentation/DeveloperTools/Conceptual/WhatsNewXcode/xcode_9/xcode_9.html

Wieder, P., Butler, J. M., Theilmann, W., & Yahyapour, R. (2011). *Service Level Agreements for Cloud Computing*. Springer Science & Business Media.

Writing first C++ program: Hello World example. (2017, May 17). Retrieved October 1, 2019, from GeeksforGeeks website: https://www.geeksforgeeks.org/writing-first-c-program-hello-world-example/

Xcode. (n.d.). Retrieved September 29, 2019, from Mac App Store website: https://apps.apple.com/us/app/xcode/id497799835?mt=12

C++

The Ultimate Beginners Guide to Effectively Design, Develop & Implement a Robust Program Step-by-Step

INTRODUCTION

This object oriented programming course in C++ language presents learners with the concepts and techniques necessary to effectively design, develop and implement a robust program model. As a learner, you will be able to grasp practical knowledge on how to apply the fundamental concepts of object oriented analysis and design and solve various problems in your day to day activities.

You will learn how to apply the concept of data abstraction, encapsulation, inheritance and polymorphism when creating objects. You will be in a position to create classes that define an object and its behaviour, create objects from a class definition and also be able to establish communication between the objects. You will also learn how to apply the object oriented concepts in performing various tasks and the benefits of doing do.

This book will help you to understand function definition and declaration, how to pass arguments to the function and how to call both inline functions and member functions. Class and objects are an important feature in C++ programming and knowing how to create class definitions and declaring objects as instance of a class will make your program development process easier.

We will teach you to understand the concept of inheritance and polymorphism. You will be able to understand the importance of code reusability and how it makes your work more efficient. In the related chapter, you will learn various ways that inheritance is achieved and how to declare private, public and protected members in a class. Through the inheritance feature, you will be able to implement the concept of polymorphism.

Constructors and destructors is also another important concept in the C++ development framework. This tutorial will enable you to understand how to declare constructors and destructors. you will also be able to work with function uploads and managing dynamic data using the concept of constructors and destructors.

All programs created are stored in the disk drive and knowing how to manage file operations and handling the input/output system will make your work more effective. In this course, you will learn how to use various C++ streams, class streams, and how to use manipulators in managing input and output data. You will also be in a position to open an existing file, write into the file, and read from the file.

You will also be able to detect file errors using various error handling functions. At the end of the course, you will learn about exception handling mechanisms and how to use throw and catch errors techniques.

CHAPTER ONE:

Getting Started With C++ Programming

C++ is one of the most competitive general-purpose programming languages on the market. It has features of imperative programming paradigm and can operate in any platform.

Object Oriented Fundamentals

Object oriented programming (OOP) in C++ language revolves around data created using objects. Objects are real-time entities that represent data and methods or functions used in the manipulation of the data.

C++ language uses objects to execute programs. As the program is executed, objects communicate with each other through passing messages. Each object doesn't have to know the implementation details of another object.

C++ utilizes features of OOP to execute a program. The main key features include:

- Objects.
- Classes.
- Data abstraction and encapsulation.
- Inheritance.
- Polymorphism.

A true OOP language uses objects to represent data in any program. Although C++ supports all the OOP features, it is said to be a partial OOP language for the following three reasons:

1. Uses global variables

   C++ supports the concept of global variables. You can declare global variables outside of a class so that other entities of the program can access the variables. Though declaring global variables violates encapsulation concept, C++ can support encapsulation through the use of classes and objects.

2. Optional creation of classes or objects

   The main function is a mandatory feature in any C++ program and it should be created outside of the class. Therefore, it's not necessary to create classes or objects as long as you have the main ().

   Omitting classes or objects violates OOP language concept in that data is represented in the form of objects.

3. Supports friend function

   C++ allows you to create a friend class or function that enables you to access the protected members or private members of a certain class. This violates the features of OOP language.

   Even though C++ supports the above features, it is referred as a partial object oriented programming language because it sometimes works against the features.

Programming Paradigms

A programming paradigm is a programming model that uses distinct concepts to shape how programmers design, organize and write a program. Programming paradigms are aimed at solving certain problems using various programming languages.

There are different types of paradigms and each fulfils a specific function based on the programming language. These paradigms are divided into two: declarative programming paradigm; and imperative programming paradigm.

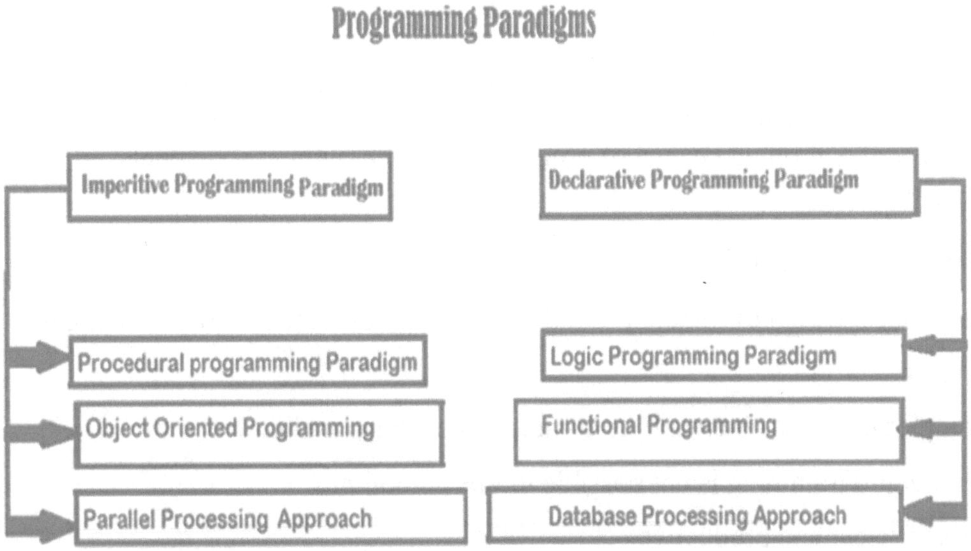

Declarative Programming Paradigm

A declarative programming paradigm is divided into three components: logic; functional; and database or data driven. Declarative programming expresses program logic without focusing on the control flow of the program. The programs developed focus on what to do rather than how to do it. These paradigms emphasize what action needs to be done and declares the results to be achieved. For example, expressing computations include:

Logic programming paradigm

This programming paradigm focuses on solving logical computation problems like a program to solve a puzzle or series of data. Logic programming paradigm relies on the knowledge base which is already known and passes it to a machine learning tool to produce results. The logic paradigm relies on artificial intelligence and machine learning to solve problems.

Functional programming paradigm

This is a language independent program and has its roots in mathematical functions. The main principle in this paradigm is execution of mathematical functions. Data is coupled into functions which hides the implementation details. The functions can be replaced with values and this doesn't change the meaning of the program.

Database or data driven programming paradigm

This programming paradigm focuses on the use of data and movement. All the program statements are defined using data. It is event driven and provides data operation mechanisms like file creation, writing into files, updating files and databases, producing queries and reporting. There are a variety of programs developed for database applications, like the Structured Query Language (SQL), among others.

Imperative Programming Paradigm

Imperative programming paradigm uses a step by step process to achieve a specific goal. It emphasizes how to do a particular task like how to execute several statements and store the results. The paradigm works through change of program state by assigning statements.

Advantages:

- Simple to implement
- Uses loops, variables, functions, and structures to execute program statements

Disadvantages:

- Complex programs increase the complexity of this paradigm
- Parallel programming is not possible in this paradigm
- Less efficient and productive

The imperative paradigm has three broad categories: procedural; parallel processing; and OOP.

Procedural paradigm

Just as the name suggests, this paradigm focuses on step by step processes for performing specific functions. It allows code reusability and it is very easy to implement. It is used to solve simple problems.

Parallel processing paradigm

In this type of paradigm, program instructions are processed using multiple processors. A parallel processing paradigm has several processors aimed at running a program in the shortest time possible. Some C++ library functions support this technique.

Object oriented programming (OOP)

This uses a collection of classes and objects to write a program. An object is the smallest entity where all computations takes place. The paradigm focuses on the use of data rather than procedures to solve real world problems. OOP slips the problem into a number of entities represented by objects and then builds data and functions based on these objects. It can solve complex problems about real life scenarios. C++ is a good example of OOP that attempts to eliminate some of the disadvantages of conventional programming languages.

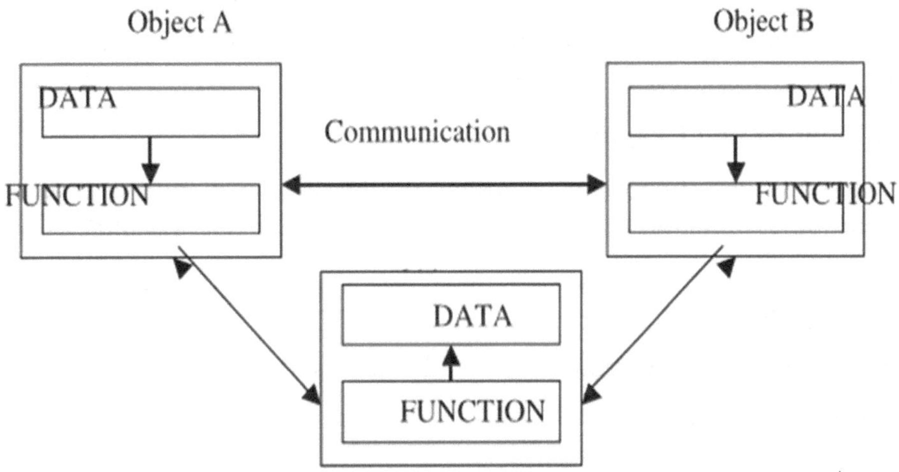

Each of the objects work independently and they're encapsulated within modules. Objects communicate with each other through 'message passing technique'. These objects are organized into several classes in which they can inherit methods and variables needed to perform certain functions such as:

- Advantages.
- Improved data security.
- Code reusability.
- Ability to use inheritance.

- Data abstraction.

Object Oriented Development Framework

Object Oriented Paradigm

An object oriented paradigm relies heavily on system theory as part of its conceptual background. A system represents a collection of entities that interact together to achieve a common objective. These entities may include an individual, an object or an equipment, and abstract entities such as data files and functions.

Object oriented paradigm focuses on objects that encapsulate data and procedures. These objects play a major role in the software development process.

Object Oriented Analysis

Object oriented analysis (OAA) involves techniques used in determining the software requirements of an object, its behavior and interactions. Object oriented design converts the software OOA requirements into specifications for the objects and generates a class hierarchy for object creation. Object oriented programming (OOP) implements the program using objects using OOP language like C++.

Developing program specifications ensures there is a clear and well organized statement of the project problem.

Object-oriented Notation and Graphs

The graphical notation is very important in project design and development processes. These notations represent objects, classes, subclasses and their inter-relationships. The common graphical notations include:

- Instances of objects.
- Message communication between objects within a class.
- Inheritance relationships.
- Hierarchical chart.
- Client-server relationship.
- Classification relationship.

Object oriented analysis provides us with powerful mechanisms to identify objects which are used as the building blocks in the development of the software. Analysis involves decomposition of the software problem into various component parts. It then establishes a logical model which evaluates the system functions.

Steps in object oriented analysis:

1. Identifying the project problem.
2. Creation of a requirement specification document for the users and the software itself.

3. Identifying the project objects and their attributes.
4. Identify what services each object is to perform.
5. Establishing communication between the objects. Objects should be able to interconnect with each other and exchange messages.

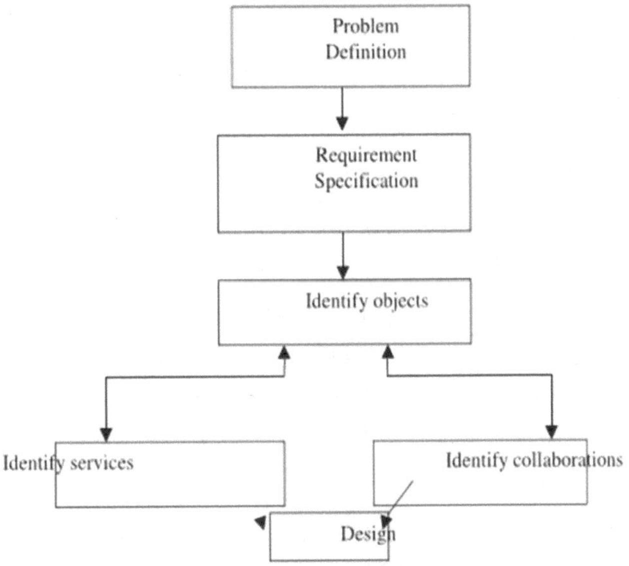

Problem definition

This is the first step in the system development life cycle. It involves understanding the problem the user is facing and writing a problem statement. The problem statement should be refined and redefined using computer system engineering. A well-defined problem statement enables the programmer to come up with a requirement specification document for both the user and the software.

Requirement specification

After clear definition of the problem, you need to understand the objectives of the proposed system and what it's supposed to do. This will help you to generate the system requirements and user requirements in the proposed system.

The requirement specification document should state:

- The outputs which are required.
- The processes to be used to in order to produce these outputs.
- The inputs required.
- The resources required to achieve desired results.

Object identification

This step involves the identification of real world objects and abstract objects. These objects can be found in the application and are analyzed by the use of data flow diagrams (DFD) and textual analysis (TA).

Data flow diagrams

A data flow diagram uses various symbols that represent data, and they are used to indicate the flow of data from one point to another. The DFD has input/output symbols, decision symbol and the process symbol which acts as the data store for all objects.

Textual analysis

This includes a detailed textual description of the problem with one or two paragraphs or several sentences based on the complexity of the problem.

1. Identify object services: Once objects are identified, the next step is to determine the set of services each object is supposed to perform.
2. Establish a connection between objects: After determining what services each object will offer, a communication is established between objects based on the services each object offers and receives. You can use an entity relationship diagram or information flow diagram to list information being communicated by each object.

Object Oriented Design

The design process involves mapping out objects and creating a conceptual model of the system. This uses a bottom-up approach to build the system structure, or uses a top-down approach by designing the class member function that provides the services to the system.

When designing objects, it's important to come up with class hierarchies, identify any abstract class and the simply messaging passing process between the objects.

When mapping out content, put into consideration the reusability of classes if you had previous designs, and the classification of the objects into subsystems.

Steps in object oriented design:

1. Evaluate objects created during the analysis phase.

   Evaluating the objects identified in the problem space enables you to refine the objects based on their attributes and their operations. It also enables you to identify other objects that can help you obtain more solutions to the problem.

2. Specify class dependencies.

   Analysis of the relationship between the classes is very important, as it enables you to determine the appropriate class to represent the objects and establish relationships between the objects. The major relationships necessary in the design stage include:

   - **Inheritance relationship:** This allows a class to inherit the properties and behaviors of another class. In this case, an object can inherit some members from another class.
   - **Containment relationship:** In this type of relationship, an object of Class A is used as a member of Class B.

- **Use relationship:** This type of relationship provides information on the various classes a particular class uses and how it uses the classes. For example, Class A can use Class B and C in the following ways:
    - Class A reads the members of Class B.
    - Class A calls the members in Class C.
    - Class A uses new operator to create Class B.

If you're planning to override some attributes or functions, it is highly recommended to use an inheritance relationship.

3. Organize classes into hierarchies.

   After creating an inheritance relationship between the objects, you have to re-examine the relationships and create class hierarchies. This allows you to reuse data and functions that have been established. Identifying similar attributes and function within a group of related classes helps in organizing the classes into hierarchies. A new class can be formed from the related classes, and it's called the super class. The other classes are subordinate classes. If an object is created by combining all the class attributes, then it's called an abstract class.

4. Design classes.

   This step defines the methods to be used on the created class to make it more useful. Some of the functions used in a class include:

   - **Management functions:** How to create an object and how to destroy an object.
   - **Implementation function:** The operations performed on the class data types.
   - **Access functions:** This is a function of accessing the internal variables of a class.
   - **Utility function:** This involves how to handle errors and access control.

5. Design class member functions.

   Member functions define some of the tasks to be performed on an object. These functions work like other normal functions. You can use a top-down function decomposition approach to design member functions.

6. Determine the driver program.

   The main() function is the standard C++ driver program. All function calls are made in the main() function. The driver program is responsible for:

   - Receiving users' input.
   - Creating objects from a class definition.
   - Displaying program output based on the users' requirements.
   - Making calls to the member functions.

Program Implementation

This process involves coding and testing the developed program. The program code is written using class member functions and the driver program. Once you finish coding the program, you have to test it for errors and to determine whether it functions as expected.

Program testing is an essential feature in the software development process. You should come up with a detailed testing plan of what to test and how the testing will be carried out. Test all the class dependencies and interfaces for any errors. The ultimate goal of program testing is to ensure the program performs its functions as intended.

C++ Programming Building Blocks

Built-in Data Types in C++

When declaring variables, you have to define the data type for each variable. The data type indicates what kind of data is stored in the variable. In C++ programming, the compiler allocates memory space for each variable created based on the data type. Different data types require different memory sizes.

Data Types

There are three C++ data types:

1. Primitive data types
2. Derived data types
3. Abstract or user defined data types

Primitive data types/ built-in data types

A primitive data type is a predefined or built-in data type that is used directly to declare a variable. The most common built-in data types include:

Data Type	Keyword	Range
Character	Char	-127 to 127 and from 0 to 255
Integer	Int	-2147483648 to 2147483647
Floating point	Float	+-3.4e +/-38(7 digits)
Boolean expression	Bool	Stores value as either true or false
Double floating point	Double	+/-1.7e +-308(15 digits)
Valueless	Void	Indicates no type
Wide character	Wchar_t	1 wide character

Character and integer data types can be modified further using the following C++ modifiers:

- Signed
- Unsigned
- Short
- Long

These modifiers indicate how much memory space is needed to store these variables.

Specifying the data type for all variables created tells the compiler how much space to allocate for each variable. Any variable definition specifies the data type and the variable list.

Syntax

```
Datatype Variable_list;
```

Example:

```
int a, b, c;
char y, n;
float salary;
```

Derived data type

As the name suggests, this data type is derived from the built-in data types. They include:

- Arrays.
- Pointers.
- Functions.
- Reference.

Abstract data types

This is a data type defined by the user, thus the name user-defined types. These data types include:

- Enumeration.
- Structure.
- Union.
- Class.

Enumerated types

Enumerated data types use 'enum' variable to declare an optional data type and a list of identifiers that show the values of the data type.

```
Enum enum_name {list of names}
```

Where,

the enum_name is the enumeration data type name. You can have one or more lists of names separated by commas.

For example, we can define an enumeration for class rectangle and call it rectangle and pass variable l to be assigned to length.

```
Enum rectangle {length, width} l=length;
```

Variable Scope

A variable is declared either inside a function (local variables) or outside a function (global variables).

Local variables: Defined variables within a block or inside a function are known as local variables. Once declared, only statements within the functions can execute or access the variables.

Example:

```
#include <iostream>
using namespace std;

int main ()
{
   // Declaring local variables:
   int x, y;
   int Z;

   // Initialization of variables
   x = 20;
   y = 15;
   Z = x - y;

   cout << Z;

   return 0;
}
```

Global variables: Global variables are declared outside the function and can be called or accessed by any function. The variables are usually declared at the top of the program after the namespace library thus making it accessible throughout the entire program.

Example:

```
#include <iostream>
using namespace std;
 // Declaring global variables
int m;
int main ()
{
   // Declaring local variables:
   int x, y;

   // Initialization of variables
   x = 5;
   y = 10;
   m= x + y;

   cout << m;

   return 0;
}
```

C++ Arrays

If you have multiple variables to store values, you can create an array that allows you to declare a single variable instead of declaring individual variables for each value. An array is a data structure that stores a collection of variables of the same data type.

Arrays are accessed through the use of an index. Each array element is made of contiguous memory allocation with the lowest memory address allocated to the first element of the array, and the highest memory address allocated to the last element.

When declaring an array, you have to specify the data type, array variable name, and the number of elements to be stored in that array variable.

Syntax

```
Type ArrayName [ArraySize]
```

This type of an array is a single-dimension array. Type is the data type of the array element and ArraySize must be an integer number that is greater than 0. For example, to declare an array with 3 elements, you can write it as follows:

```
String cars [3];
```

Initializing Arrays

You can initialize the arrays created by allocating values to the array elements. These values are added inside braces { } and they shouldn't be larger than the number of elements declared between the square brackets [ ].

Syntax

```
Type ArrayName [size] = {Values}
```

Example:

```
String cars [3] = {"BMW", "RAV4", "Volvo"};
```

If you want to create an array for integer numbers, you can write:

```
 int num[5] = {5, 10, 25, 20, 35};
```

Declaring the array size tells the compiler to create a memory allocation to hold 5 elements. If you don't specify the array size, a huge chunk of memory is created to hold the initialized variables.

Arrays use index to represent variables with 0 index representing the first element. You can represent the above array as follows:

Index	0	1	2	3	4
num	5	10	25	20	35

Accessing Arrays

You can access array element by indexing the array name. This can be done by placing the index number of the element you want to access within the square brackets after the array name.

Example:

```
int num[5] = {5, 10, 25, 20, 35};
cout<< num[1];

// output 10
```

Using Loops in Arrays

You can use for loop to execute array elements.

Example:

```
#include <iostream>
#include <string>
using namespace std;

int main()
{
  string cars[3] = {"BMW", "RAV4", "Volvo"};
  for(int a = 0; a < 4; a++)
  {
    cout << cars[a] << "\n";
  }
  return 0;
}
```

// output

```
BMW
RAV4
Volvo
```

Multi-dimensional Arrays

Multidimensional is an array of arrays which stores data in the form of tables with both rows and columns (rows*columns), also known as the matrix. It can be either a two-dimensional or three-dimensional array.

Syntax

```
Type ArrayName [Size1] [Size2] … [SizeN];
```

Example:

```
Int M [5] [12];
Int N [2] [2] [3];
```

To get the number of elements stored in a multidimensional array, multiply the size of all array dimension. In the array of **int M [5] [12]**, you can store (5*12) = 60 elements.

Two-dimensional array

A two-dimensional array is the simplest array format. This array format uses 'r' number of rows and 's' number of columns to form a table. The table ranges from 0 to r-1 for the rows and the from 0 to s-1 for the column number range.

```
DataType ArrayName [r] [s];
```

Two-dimension elements in an array are represented by r[x] [y], where 'x' is the row number while 'y' is the column number.

The table below shows a two-dimensional array with three rows and five columns.

	Column 0	Column 1	Column 2	Column 3	Column 4
Row 0	r[0][0]	r[0][1]	r[0][2]	r[0][3]	r[0][4]
Row 1	r[1][0]	r[1][1]	r[1][2]	r[1][3]	r[1][4]
Row 2	r[2][0]	r[2][1]	r[2][2]	r[2][3]	r[2][4]

Example of two-dimensional array:

```
int x [2] [3];
```

You can initialize the array by passing values to the array element as follows:

```
int x [2] [3] = {0, 2, 3, 5, 8, 12}
```

This array can also be initialized as follows:

```
Int x [2] [3] =
{
        {0, 2, 3},
        {5, 8, 12}
        };
```

Example:

```
 #include <iostream>
using namespace std;
int main()
{
  int testingarray[3][3] =
    {
        {2, 3, 4},
        {4, 6, 8},
        {6, 4, 6}

    };
    for(int a = 0; a < 3; ++a)
    {
        for(int b = 0; b < 3; ++b)
        {
        cout<< testingarray[a][b]<<" ";
        }
        cout<<"\n";
    }
    return 0;
}
```

// output

```
2 3 4
4 6 8
6 4 6
```

Pointers

Pointers are very essential in the implementation of C++ programs. They help in the dynamic allocation of memory space, thus making it easy for the programs to execute efficiently.

When you declare a variable, a memory location is created to store the values. Each of the allocated memory has a defined address which makes it easy to access the variable. Using pointers simplifies program execution by holding the memory address of the stored variable.

A pointer variable points to the data type of the variable and it is created using the asterisk (*) operator. Therefore, before using pointers, you have to declare them.

Syntax

```
Type *variable-name;
```

Where,

type is valid C++ data type and variable-name is the pointer variable name.

Example 1: Let's create a pointer named 'ptr' that points to an integer variable.

```
int *ptr;
```

When assigning memory address to the pointer variable, an ampersand (&) operator is used.

```
int *ptr = &variable-name.
```

Example 2: Create a program that defines a pointer variable and assign memory address to the pointer variable. Add a code to allow the compiler access to the value of the pointer variable in the allocated address.

```
#include <iostream>

using namespace std;

int main ()
 {
   int  num = 12;
   int  *ptr;

    // assign memory address to pointer variable
   ptr = &num;

   cout << " The value of the num variable is: ";
   cout << num << endl;

   cout << "The memory address stored in ptr variable is: ";
   cout << ptr << endl;

   cout << " The value of *ptr variable is: ";
   cout << *ptr << endl;

   return 0;
 }
```

//output

```
The value of num variable is: 12
The memory address stored in ptr variable is: 0x28fef8
The value of *ptr variable is: 12
```

Dynamic Free Store Operators

Free store is unallocated memory dynamically assigned to a program during its execution time. Each program has a large pool of free memory it can utilize during its running time.

All objects allocated to the free store memory require pointers to indirectly manipulate them since the free store memory is unnamed. You also have to manually initialize the free store memory in order to use it.

Dynamic free store memory is manually allocated on the heap while non-static memory with local variables is allocated at the stack.

The allocation of free store memory is via the new operator, and it is deactivated using delete operator. The new and delete operators are system variables available for manipulation by the programmers.

When using data structures like lists and trees, dynamic allocation of free store memory is essential. The new operator is used to request dynamic allocation of free store memory.

Syntax

```
Pointer= new data-type;
 or
Pointer= new data-type [number-of-elements]
```

Where,

Pointer-variable specifies the pointer of type data type and datatype is any built-in C++ data type.

Number-of-elements is an integer value used when a sequence of several elements or an array of elements is needed. Otherwise, if you only need to allocate free memory for a single element, use **pointer= new type** expression.

Free store objects created using the **new** operator are independent within the scope and are available until destroyed by the **delete** operator.

OOP classes are dynamically allocated free store memory, and they're accessed through the use of pointers and references.

Example:

```
// a pointer initialized with null values
float *ptr = new  float;

// initialize memory using the new operator
int *ptr = new int(15);

// allocation of block memory with an array of 5 integers
int *ptr = new int[5]

// using delete operator for single expression
delete ptr;
// delete operator for an array of elements
delete[ ] ptr;
```

C++ Functions

A function or method is a group of statements that execute a particular task. C++ functions are divided into two:

1. Library functions
2. User-defined functions

Library Functions

These are pre-defined or built-in C++ functions that perform a number of tasks. For example, main (). You can use the library functions by directly invoking it order to execute an instruction.

Example:

```
#include<iostream>

#include<cmath>

using namespace std;

int main() {

        float num, squareRoot;

        cout<<"Enter a number to get the squareroot:";

        cin>>num;

        squareRoot=sqrt(num);

        cout<<"Squareroot of"<<num<<"="<<squareRoot;

        return 0;

}
```

// output

```
Enter a number to get the square root: 60
Square root of 60 = 7.74597
```

The **sqrt()** is a library function used to calculate the square root of a number. While **#include <cmath>** is the header file.

Every C++ program has the **main()** function. For any program to begin its execution, it has to make a system call to the **main()**. That is, the execution starts from the main function.

User-defined Functions

C++ program allow users to define their own functions. A user can specify a function and write a block of statements to be executed once the function is called.

Function Definition and Passing Arguments

Function declaration is very important when defining functions. It tells the compiler about the function name and how to call the function.

Syntax

```
Type function_name (arguments)
{
Function body/Statements;
}
```

Where,

Type is the data type returned by the function. If the function executes without any value to be returned after an execution, use void as the return type for the function.

Function_name is the actual name of the function executed.

Arguments or parameter is the value passed to the function. The parameters are optional since a function can have a list of parameters passed to it or not.

Statements or body of the function is a block of statements that explain what the function does.

Example:

```
//function call
float sum (float a, float b)
{
         float sum;
         sum= a+b;
         return sum;
}
```

In the above example, two parameters (**float a,** and **float b**) are passed to function when calling it.

Calling Function

When declaring a function, you have to state what the function will do on the block of statements. To use the declared function, you have to make a call to the function. When the program makes a call to the function, the full control of the program is transferred to that function. As a result, the function executes the defined task under its function body until the end of the function then returns the control back to the main program.

When calling the function, you can pass the parameters needed by the function to execute.

Example:

```
#include <iostream>
  using namespace std;
  // Declaring Function prototype
  float add(float, float);
  int main()  {
     float num1, num2, sum;
     cout<<"Enter two numbers:";
     cin >> num1 >> num2;
     // call to the Function
     sum = add(num1, num2);
     cout << "Sum = " << sum;
     return 0;  }
  // Function definition
  float add(float a, float b)  {
     float add;
     add = a + b;
     return add;
  }
```

// output

```
Enter two numbers: 10 6
Sum = 16
```

Function Prototype

If you want to define your own function (user-defined function), you have to do this outside the **main ()** otherwise the compiler will generate an error. The compiler doesn't recognize user-defined functions and their arguments passed through the main function.

To solve this, you can declare a function prototype outside the **main()**. Function prototype is declared without the function body to enable the compiler to know about the user-defined function in the program. In the above example, function prototype is declared as:

```
float add (float, float);
```

Therefore, it is important to define a function prototype if user-defined functions exist in the program and they should be defined before the **main ()** function.

Call by Value and Call by Reference

You can pass data to function using either a call by value or a call by reference. In a call by value, the original value of the function argument is not modified, while in call by reference, its original value is modified.

Call by value

In call by value, the passed value is locally stored in the stack memory. If you change the parameters, the changes only apply to the current function only. The value of the variable inside the **main ()** function will not change when you call the function.

Call by value is the most used method of calling functions, and any changes made to the function parameters will not have any effect on the call to that function.

In call by value, only a copy of the value is passed to the function.

Call by reference

When you pass parameters by reference, the original value of the variable changes. Passing arguments by references modifies the original address of the variable. The original address of the variable is modified with the new variables passed to the function.

When you change the value of arguments in a function, it changes the value of the variable both inside and outside of the **main ()** function.

Inline Functions

When you make a call to a function, the function takes some time to execute a block of statements and store the function return values in the predefined memory allocation before transferring the control back to the program. The program control is switched between the function call and function execution.

Sometimes a function call can take more time than the time it takes to execute a task. The switching time between the function call and the function execution time can create an overhead. To solve this problem, C++ programming implements the use of inline function to reduce the overhead time.

Inline functions reduce calling time for small functions. Whenever a call is made to the function, the compiler expands the function and replaces the function with a corresponding code that reduces overhead time on the function call.

Syntax

```
Inline return-type function-name (parameters)
{
Function body
}
```

When you insert an inline keyword before the function, it sends a request to the compiler and its not a command. The compiler can decide to decline the request based on the following conditions:

- The function has static variables.
- You're using recursive function.
- The function uses loop control structures like for, while, and do-while.
- You use switch or go-to statements in the function.
- There is no return statements and the function return type is not void.

Example:

```
#include <iostream>
using namespace std;

//declaring inline function
inline int area(int l, int w)
{
    return l*w;
}
int main()
{
    cout << "The area of rectangle is: " << area(3, 5) << "\n";
    return 0;
}
```

Inline functions can be used inside classes. Once you define a function inside a class it automatically becomes an inline function and all the restriction of inline function also apply to functions inside the class.

When defining inline function in a class, you have to declare the function inside the class then define it outside the class using the keyword **inline**.

```
Class Rectangle
{
Public:
int area (int l, int w)
};
Inline int Rectangle:: area(int l, int w)
{
 Return l*w;
}
```

Data Structures

Data structure is the collection of elements and variables within a single unit. All data elements of different data types need to be processed and stored together under one name. For example, a student's information file should have details about name, school id, contacts, course, class, marks, and grading information.

Structures work the same as arrays, and the only difference is that structures represent a collection of variables of different data types under a single name, while arrays represent a collection of variables of the same data type.

To declare structures, use the keyword **struct** followed by the structure name which is also called a "**tag**". Then define data members or variables inside the open and closing braces ({}). After the closing braces, enter the object name (structure-variables) although this is optional.

Syntax

```
Struct StructureName
 {
    Type MemberName1;
     Type MemberName2;
     Type MemberName3;
     .
     .
 } ObjectName;
```

The struct keyword tells the compiler that a structure is being defined. The object_name allows a user to directly declare an object of structure type, that is, be able to instantiate different objects in a single object.

Example 1:

```
Struct Person
 {
    Char FName[15], LName[15];
    Int age, code;
    Float salary;
 } Samuel, Anthony, Paul;
```

The above example defines a structure tag called person, and stores variables of different data types together with objects passed to the structure.

Example 2: Creating a structure with an array of 10 objects

```
Struct Products
 {
    Char ProdName [20];
    Int weight;
    Float price;
 } items [10];
```

How to Access Structure Memories

Once you define and declare structure variables, you can work directly with their members. To access structure members, use the **dot (.)** operator which is also known as the access operator.

The access operator is inserted between the **object_name** and the **member_name**.

```
Mango. Price;
```

Initializing Structure Elements

You can initialize the elements of a structure by assigning values to them. You can initialize the elements by using separate assignment statements or using array notation.

For example, if you want to assign value 50 to the price of mango fruit, this can be done as follows:

```
Mango.price = 50;
```

When using an array notation, you can initialize the elements as follows:

```
Type Student = {10, 15.6, 50.0, ‘B’};
```

The array type initialization only works if the structure variable is already defined. The type in the above statement is the data type specifier of the structure student which is declared and initialized simultaneously. All the values assigned to the structure members should be enclosed with open and closing braces.

Example:

```
#include<iostream.h>
#include<conio.h>
#include<stdio.h>

struct student
{
        int StudNo;
        char StudName[30], Course [20], class [2];
        float marks[4];
        char grade;
}student_var;

void main()
{
        float sum = 0;
        float average;

        cout<<"Enter student's number: ";
        cin>>student_var.StudNo;
        cout<<"Enter student's name: ";
        cin>>student_var.StudName;
        cout<<"Enter student’s course: ";
        cin>>student_var.Course;
        cout<<"Enter student's class: ";
        cin>>student_var.Class;
        cout<<"Enter student’s marks on 4 subjects:\n";
        for(int m=0; m<4; m++)
        {
                cout<<"Subject "<<m+1<<": ";
                cin>>student_var.marks[m];
                sum = sum + student_var.marks[m];
        }
        average = sum / 4;
```

```
        if(average<50)
        {
                student_var.grade = 'Fail';
        }
        else if(average<65)
        {
                student_var.grade = 'pass';
        }
        else if(average<80)
        {
                student_var.grade = 'Credit';
        }
        else
        {
                student_var.grade = 'Distinction';
        }
        cout<<"\nStudent Result:\n";
        cout<<"\nStudNo: "<<student_var.StudNo<<"\t\t\t Student Name:
"<<student_var.StudName;
        cout<<"\nCourse: "<<student_var.Course<<"\t\t\t Class:
"<<student_var.Class;
        cout<<"\nTotal Marks: "<<sum<<"\tGrade: "<<student_var.grade;

        Return 0;

}
```

// output

```
Enter student's number: 05
Enter student's name: Sebastian Monroe
Enter student's course: Economics
Enter Student's Class: B2
Enter student's marks on 4 subjects:
Subject 1: 68
Subject 2: 74
Subject 3: 86
Subject 4: 94

Students Result:
StudNo: 05                                       Student Name: Sebastian Monroe
Course: Economics                        Class: B2
Total Marks: 322                         Grade: Distinction
```

References in C++

C++ reference is an alternative name assigned to an existing variable. Once you initialize a variable name with a reference, you may use the variable name or the reference to call a variable.

There are three types of references supported in C++ programming language. They include:

- **Non-constant references:** These are simply called references and are declared to non-constant values.
- **Constant references:** These consist of constant values
- **R-value references:** These help to avoid repetitive copying and assist forwarding functions.

In non-constant references, variables are declared as references using the ampersand (&) operator which is declared between the variable name and the reference type.

```
Int &ref = {value};
```

The ampersand operator in this case will mean 'reference to' and not 'address of'. These references work the same as the values their referencing. That is, it acts as an alias of the referenced object.

Example 1:

```
int prd= {5};
int &x = {prd};
int &y = {x};
```

In the above example, 'x' is a reference to **prd** variable while 'y' is also a reference to 'x'.

Example 2:

```
#include<iostream>
using namespace std;

int main()
{
  double price = 100;

  double &ref = price;

  // change the price to 120
  ref = 120;
  cout << "price = " << price << endl ;

  // now change the price to 150
  price = 150;
  cout << "ref = " << ref << endl ;

  return 0;
}
```

// output

```
Price = 120
Ref = 150
```

Application of References

1. **To modify the parameters of a function:** If you want to change the parameters passed to a function during function call, you can reference the variables. In the above example, referencing the variable, modified the price value from the original 100 to 120.

2. **To avoid copying large structures:** If you have a function that executes a large number of objects, then passing parameters to it without referencing them creates a copy of object-variables. This results in wastage of CPU time and memory. To avoid this duplication of objects, you can use references.

Example:

```
Struct Employee
{
   string EmpNames, address;
   int EmpNo;
}
Void print (const Employee &em)
{
   Cout << em.EmpNames << " " << em.address << " " << em. EmpNo;
}
```

If we remove the reference to operator, it will create a new copy of the employee object. The **const** keyword prevents any accidental update to the program.

3. **To modify objects in for each loop:** You can use references to modify all elements in for loop or to avoid copying of objects when working with large objects.

Chapter Summary

C++ is a general purpose programming language and one of the most competitive object oriented programs in the market. The language utilizes features of object oriented programming to design a program and manipulate data. The commonly used features include: objects, classes, data abstraction, encapsulation, inheritance and polymorphism.

With the help of programming paradigms, programmers can easily design, organize and build a program that solves various problems. There are two types of programming paradigm; a declarative programming paradigm and an imperative programming paradigm. C++ language is an imperative programming language since it relies on OOP concepts to execute functions.

The major key elements in this chapter included:

- Learning various built-in data types and how to use them in writing a program.
- How to use user-defined types to execute complex programs.
- How to declare variables in C++ and allocate memory location for the user variables.
- How to declare arrays to hold data elements, initializing arrays, accessing array elements as well as know how to work with both two dimensional arrays and multidimensional arrays.

- Using pointers to point to a specific storage location and allow you to determine the reference address of the variable.
- Learning how to use dynamic free store operators to allocate memory space for your programs.
- How to use C++ functions to build programs and implement code reusability features to make complex programs more effective.
- Learn function definitions, how to declare functions, make function calls, and how to use function prototypes and inline functions.
- Learning how to use references when dealing with large objects to enable you reduce the overhead time in function calls. References will help you minimize CPU execution time and save on memory space since it prevents duplication of objects whenever a function call is made.
- How to use structures and references to access objects. Data structures allow you to work with variables of different data types under a single unit.
- Creating variables with different return types and data elements under a single name to avoid code repetition.
- Making calls to structure functions and pass arguments of different data types.

In the next chapter you will learn basic concepts of object oriented programming including the use of classes, objects, data abstraction and encapsulation, polymorphism and inheritance feature.

CHAPTER TWO:

Basic Concepts in Object Oriented Programming

It is necessary to understand the basic concepts used in object-oriented programming. See figure below.

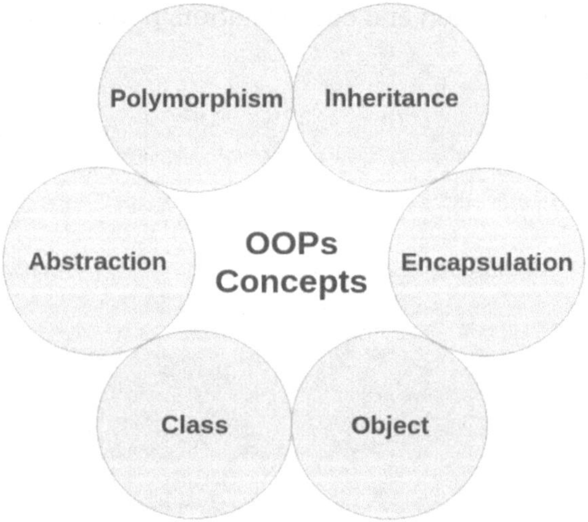

Class

A class is an expanded concept of data structure and a building block for C++ programming language. It consists of logical methods for organizing data and functions in the structure. The 'class' keyword denotes the data structure with functions represented as members.

A class consists of two parts: class header and body. A class header defines the class name and the base class, whereas the class body defines the class members supported by each class. The class uses user-defined data type to hold its own data members and member functions. Class members and functions are accessed by creating an instance of the class.

Class members: They represent the data variables in that class and specify how class objects are represented.

Member functions: Describes the function prototype used in manipulating these data variables. It specifies class operations which is also referred to as the instance of the class.

Both member functions and data members define the properties and behavior of an object in a class.

Class members fall under three access permissions: public, private and protected.

Public members: Data members in this class are accessible by every class member and from anywhere as long as the class is visible.

Private members: In this class, data members are only accessible by the class members or other members of the same class.

Protected members: These are only accessible within the class members and other members from a derived class.

Syntax

```
Class ClassName
{
Access Specifier:
Member(s);
Access Specifier 2:
Members(s);
Access Specifier n:
Member(s);
};
```

Where,

- **Class** is the keyword that denotes class declaration.
- **ClassName** is a valid name identifier of class.
- **Access Specifier** is the access permission granted to that class: either private, public or protected.
- **Members** defines the class members and member functions of the class.

Example:

```
Class Cars
{
Char CarName[30], brand[30];
Float SpeedLimit, Mileage;
Public:
Void getdata(void);
Void display(void);
};
```

In this example, the data members will be CarName, brand, SpeedLimit and Mileage. The member function is getdata, display, a function to apply breaks or even a function to increase the speed of the car.

From the above data, we can deduce that a Class is the blue-print that defines a group of objects with similar properties and behaviors.

Objects

In C++, an object is an entity or variable which possess some characteristics and behaviors. It represents an instance of the class. That is, when you define a class, there is no memory allocation but if the class is instantiated (declaring variables), a memory allocated is created and allocated to the specific objects created.

An object can represent a person, a car, or bank account. Objects include both data members and their associated member functions, known as methods.

When creating a class, you have to determine the attributes of the object you're creating, commonly known as the data members of the class. For example, Class Cars (object) has attributes like car model, year of manufacturer, engine power, and color. Its associated member functions or methods include; start(), stop() and move().

You may have more than one instance of the object created. The car objects include: Toyota, Rav4, Fielder, Land Rover, etc.

An instance is an actual object which is created during run time. For example, Toyota is an instance of Class Cars.

To determine the behavior components of the objects, you have to determine what message the objects can receive and what kind of operations need to be performed. The behavior component of the class type object describes a collection of member functions which send a message to the object and prompt a certain action to be taken.

Note: all messages are sent from one object to another by calling or invoking member functions.

Syntax

```
Identifier. Message ([arg1, arg2])
```

Where,

- **Identifier** is the object name.
- **Dot** represents the member access operator.
- **Message** is the type of message sent.
- **Arg** is an optional list of arguments to be returned or the message content.

The dot between the identifier and the message type is the member access operator that identifies the data members and member functions of the object.

For example:

```
Class Person
{
    Char FName [25], LName[25];
    Int age;
Public:
    Void getdetails()
    Void display()
};
Void Person :: getdetails()
    {
    Cout<<"Enter your first name and last name";
    Cin>>FName, Lname;
    Cout<<"enter your age";
    Cin>>age;
    }
Void Person :: display()
    {
    Cout<<"Your name is:"<<FName<<LName<<aged"<<age;
    }
Int main()
    {
    Person P; //P is an object
    p.getdetails(); //call to enter names and age function
    p.display(); // call to display your names and age
  Return 0;
    }
```

Objects created generate a memory space for storing data. When you run the above program, the objects interact by sending messages to each other through a **message passing** technique.

Each of the objects has data and the code needed to manipulate the data. Objects can send messages to one another without knowing the content of each other's data or the execution code.

The Class Person has two private member attributes (names and age), and public member functions (getdetails() and display()). These functions are declared within the class as the prototype.

The function name is followed by a double colon which identifies getdetails() and display() as function member to Class Person.

If a class is created, the class name defines a new data type called an **object p**.

From the example above, **Person P** is an object created of the Class Person where P sends a call to the function getdetails (P.getdetails();).

When you call this function, the compiler prompts you to enter the first name, last name and the age of the person and store them in the class private members.

P.display() is a call to retrieve the stored data on the names and age of the person.

Data Abstraction

Data abstraction is another important feature in C++ programming. Data abstraction provides needed information without presenting the entire details. It only displays the information needed while hiding the background data details.

Classes helps in implementing abstraction in C++. Using access specifiers, you can group a class based on member functions and data members. This makes it easy to know which data member will be visible to the users and what data remains hidden.

Abstraction can also be applied on header files. For example, when using **pow()** in calculating the power of a certain number you only call the function **pow()** from **math.h header file** and pass the parameters to it. You don't have to know how the functions work on the background, you're only interested in what the function does and the results of the calculation.

Data Encapsulation

Data encapsulation is the process of wrapping data and functions under a single unit called a **class.** That is, wrapping data together with its manipulation methods or functions.

In encapsulation, you can't access data directly. You can only access it via a function inside the class.

When working with data, encapsulation ensures data is not directly accessible and can only be accessed through a function prototype inside a class. This makes the concept of data hiding possible.

For example, if you're an accountant and want to obtain sales data for a particular week, you don't have access to all data in the sales section. You can contact the sales manager in charge of sales section and request him to retrieve sales for a specific week. The sales data and sales manager are wrapped under a single class called 'sales section'.

Encapsulation makes it easy to create the concept of data hiding or data abstraction. For example, hiding data that is not required in the sales class.

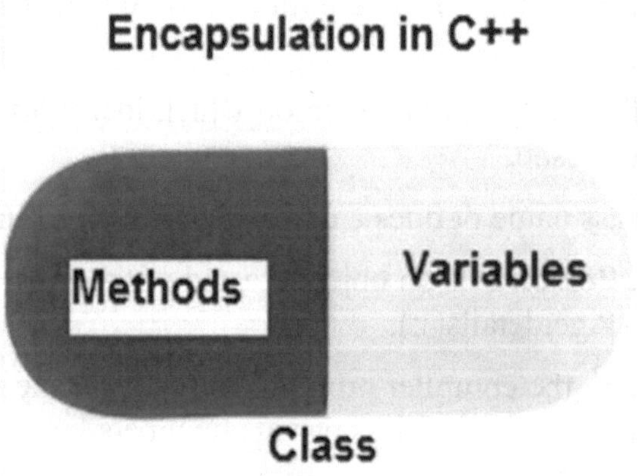

Polymorphism

Polymorphism is representation of data in more than one form. It allows functions and variables of different types to be used at different times. That is, a variable or function can exhibit a different behavior at different instances.

When performing an operation, a simple function call can give different results depending on the data type of the variables passed. Polymorphism allows operators to exhibit different behaviors.

There are two types of polymorphism:

- Operator overloading
- Function overloading

Operator overloading: This is where an operator show different results in different instances.

Function overloading: This is where a single function name performs different types of tasks.

Example: You can write a function to calculate a sum of numbers with different parameters. Create function 1 & 2 and pass two parameters of integer type to the first function, and supply the second sum function with three parameters of integer type. When you make a call to the sum function, it will give different instances. Therefore, polymorphism allows you to use the same method and pass different parameters to it.

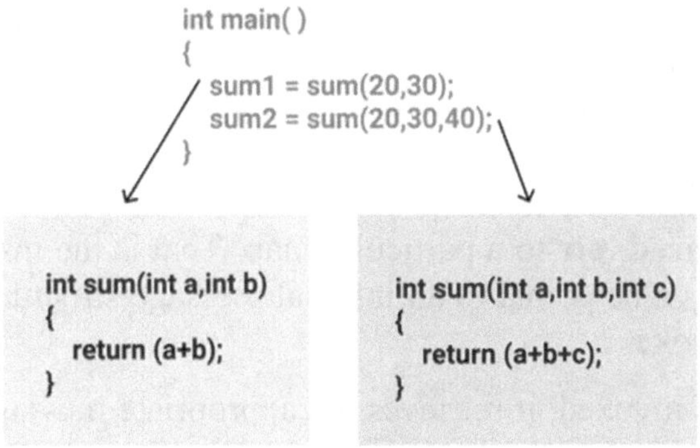

Inheritance

This is a concept where you develop a new class from an existing class or from a base class. The new class derived will have the characteristics of the base class. The base class will act as the parent or super class while the derived class will act as the child class or a sub-class.

The sub-class inherits all the properties and characteristics of the super class (parent class).

Inheritance supports the concept of code reusability. This is very important as it helps in reducing the overall code written to perform a certain task, thus making it a great feature in object oriented programming. If you want to create a new class that uses some of the code in another class, you can derive a new class from the existing class. This allows you to re-use the variables and methods in the existing class.

Other Features

Dynamic Binding

When you make a call to a function, the code to the function is executed at runtime. This process is known as dynamic binding. C++ uses virtual functions to support dynamic binding.

Message Passing

Message passing is a technique in which objects communicate with one another. An object sends a message to another object requesting execution of a certain procedure. This triggers a function in the receiving object to send back the desired results.

When an object is communicating with another object, it has to specify its name, the function name, and the message to be sent.

C++ language supports static message passing, that is, when you invoke an object's method, the target object should also have the invoked method. Otherwise, the compiler will generate an error message. Message passing is made through the help of **vtables**.

To use dynamic message passing on objects, you should:

- Declare a global function that will act as a signature to the message being passed between objects.
- Inherit object properties from dmp::object.
- Create a class constructor and add a single message or more to the object by using add_message method.
- Use invoke(signature, …parameters) to send a message to an object.

How Message Passing Works

Each C++ object has a **shared_ptr** to a particular map. That is the map's key act as a pointer to the message signature. Its value points to an internal message structure that holds the pointer of the message method to invoke.

Once the object method is invoked, it retrieves the appropriate message structure from the map. As a result, it invokes the object method using **this** as the object target.

The objects share the message map among themselves to increase efficiency among themselves. If the map is not unique, it will be duplicated after modification of a message map.

Chapter Summary

In this chapter, you have learned basic concepts of object oriented programming including:

- Learning how to work with C++ objects and initialize them.
- How to create classes and class definition.
- Applying the concept of data data abstraction and encapsulation to extend the power of programming language.

- Learning how programmers can create user-defined data types and how encapsulation and abstraction work in order to provide the needed information to the user without the need to present program details.
- Learning how the concept of data hiding is made possible through encapsulation.
- How to use OOP polymorphism feature to create objects with more than one data type or form.
- How to use function overloading and overloaded operator in polymorphism.
- Learning how C++ supports inheritance feature by allowing the properties and characteristics of a class (base class) be used in building another class (derived class).
- Dynamic binding feature and how message passing works.

In the next chapter you will learn how to build base classes and derived classes as well as how to work with data members and member functions.

CHAPTER THREE:

Working with Classes and Objects

In the previous chapter, you learned about classes as user-defined data type that acts as a blueprint for creating objects. Classes extended the concept of data structures and just like data structures, they have data members and additional member functions.

Using Classes

When working with complex class functions, defining member functions inside the class makes it difficult to manage the class.

Class Headers and Class Body

C++ programming language allows code reuse by putting class definition in the header file. This prompts code reuse in multiple files or projects. Just like declaring functions in the header file so as to use the function in multiple projects, a class definition is put in the header file with the same name as the class.

The member functions of this type of class are defined outside of the class and stored in a **.cpp** file with the same name as the class.

A class header file consists of class definition with its data members and member function prototypes.

Note: Putting all member functions inside the header file may cause clutter in your class definition. All functions defined inside a class are implicitly inline, and if you're dealing with a complex function that is invoked more often, it will slow down the execution time of the function code.

If you change some function code in the header file, then you have to make the same changes in every file that includes the header. Otherwise, it will affect the recompilation process of the project.

But if you change some function code in a .cpp file, you only need to recompile the .cpp file.

Definition and Declaration of Class

In C++, a class consists of related functions and data. Data and functions in a class are combined together to form a data type that is used in creating objects of the type. The classes created represent real world entities made of various data type properties and behavior (that is, their associated operations).

Syntax

```
Class class-name {
Access-specifier 1:
Member1;
Access-specifier 2:
Member 2;
...
} object-names;
```

Where,

- The class keyword specifier indicates the new data-type and it is followed by the class-name which is the specific name that identifies that class.
- The body of the class is made of both private and public access specifiers.

Private

The private access specifier helps in implementation of data hiding concept. This is achieved by using the keyword **'private'** when declaring member values. The data members and functions declared under the **Private** keyword can only be accessed from within that class itself.

The data hiding concept is a security technique that prevents unauthorized users from performing any data operation like read/write operation or modification of data. Therefore, **Private** data declaration, hides data from unauthorized users and any accidental manipulation.

Public

In public access specifier, both data and functions can be accessed outside the class. Member functions declared in the class are generally public and as a result, you can access them from outside the class.

Class definition for both private and public members is shown below.

```
Class class-name
{
Private: Variable declaration (data members);
           Function declaration (member function);

Public: Variable declaration;
          Function declaration;
```

```
Protected: Variable declaration;
               Function declaration;
};
```

Syntax

```
Class mytest
{
         Private:
                    int x;
                    double y;
                    string *name;
                    void getX () {x=25;}
                    ...;
         Public:
                    int count;
                    void getY () {y=15;}
                    ...;
 };
```

Where,

- In this example, x, y, and the names are defined inside the class thus, they are private members which can be accessed within that class.
- Count is a public data member which can be accessed from anywhere outside the class.

Data Members and Member Function Definitions

Data members are any variables declared in a class using the standard data types like **char, int, float, double**, etc. or using derived data types like **class, pointers**, and **structures**.

A class member function consists of function definition or prototype within the class. The function prototype works on any object of the class it is in and also has access to all other data members in the class. There are two types of member function definition: class; and class method

Class definition

This describes the data members and member functions of the class.

Class methods definition

This describes how a program is to perform certain tasks. It shows how member functions are coded. The member function code can be written in two ways:

- Using **inside class** definition
- Using **outside class** definition by the use of scope resolution operator (::)

In this case, the function code is the same but the function header is different in both cases.

Inside class definition

If you define a member function inside the class, there is no need to place the membership label within the function name. To easily implement this, you can use **inline functions**.

When you use inline functions, the compiler inserts the function body code at the specific point where the function is invoked or called. This ensures fast execution of the program.

Example: Creating class rectangle to access the class members using the member function instead of accessing the members directly.

Syntax

```
Class Rectangle
   {
         Public:
               Float length;
               Float width;
               Float getArea (void)
                     {
                        Return length*width;
                     }
   };
```

Outside class definition using Scope Resolution operator (::)

In this class defines, the function is declared outside the class as demonstrated below.

Syntax

```
Type class-name:: function-name(parameters)
{
Function body
}
```

The :: operator allows you to define member functions outside the class. The operator was earlier used to identify a global variable in situations where the global variable had the same name as the local variable.

Example:

```
Class Rectangle
   {
         Public:
               Float length;
               Float width;
               Float getArea (void)
   };
Float Rectangle ::getArea (void)
         {
            Return length*width;
         }
```

To call the member function, you have to use a dot operator (.) as shown in our previous chapter. The dot operator allow you to manipulate data in an object and make a function call to the object.

Syntax

```
Rectangle rect;              // create a rectangle object
Rect.getArea ();      // make a call to the member function of the
object
```

Example:

```
#include<iostream.h>
#include<string>
using namespace std;
class product
{
string prd_name;
float weight, price;

public:
void mgetdata()
void mfdisplay ()
} item;
 void product::mfgetdata()
         {
          cout<<"Enter the product name";
          cin>>prd_name;
          cout<<"Enter the product weight and price";
          cin>>weight>>price;
         }
 void product::mfdisplay()
         {
         Cout<<"product name is"<<prd_name<<"Weight is"<<weight<<"and
the price"<<price<<endl;
         }
//calling class member functions
int main()
{ product item;
item.mfgetdata();
item.mfdisplay();
return 0;
}
```

To access the private data members, you have to create **getter** and **setter function (mfgetdata()** and **mfdisplay())** in order to get and set the value of the private data members. The setter function sets the value of the parameter passed to the private data member while the getter function returns the value of the private data member that needs to be used. Both getter and setter functions must be defined public.

Using Protected Data Members

In a protected data member function, data members and member functions are used by that current class or by the derived class where they are declared.

You can access protected data members using the dot (.) operator within a subclass of the current class. Just like the public class, you can access protected members from a class, friend function, or from a derived class.

If class members are declared as protected then:

- Only the member functions of the original class that declared it can have access to the variables.
- Only the friends of the class that originally declared the members as protected access class members.
- They are accessed directly by a privately derived class that has private access to the protected members.
- Only classes derived with either public or protected access from a class where the data members were originally declared can use them.

When using base classes, then the protected keyword indicates that both the public and protected members of the base class are protected data members of the derived class.

The protected data members are not as private as the private data members or more public than the public data members which can be accessed from any function.

You can declare protected data members as static, meaning they will be accessible to friend function or member function of a derived class. If the members are not static, then they can be accessed in the friend function and derived member functions using pointers or references.

Types of Class Member Functions

There are several member functions which can be utilized to manipulate data members and functions in C++. These special member functions include:

1. Simple functions.
2. Static functions.
3. Const functions.
4. Inline functions.
5. Friend functions.

Simple Member Functions

These are the basic member functions declared in C++. They don't use any special keywords like static as they're prefix. The general format of the basic or simple member functions is shown below.

Syntax

```
Type function_name (arguments)
{
  Function body;
}
```

Static Member Functions

These member functions uses keyword **static** and it's associated with both data members and member functions. Static means something that holds the same position.

To make a function static, use the keyword static followed by the function name. Static functions works for the entire class rather than for a specific object of the class.

Static functions are called using object and direct member access operator (.). You can also call static member function using the class name, a scope resolution operator, or by itself.

Syntax:

```
Class S
 {
        Public:
        Static void fxn ()
        {…}
 };
 int main() {
        // call the member function directly with its class name.
        S::fxn ()
    }
```

The above function can only access static data members and static member functions. The ordinary data members or functions can't be accessed.

Const Member Functions

Const keyword is used to declare constant variables. Once a variable is defined as constant, its values can't be changed. When **const** is used with member functions, those functions can't modify the data objects or the related data members.

Syntax

```
Void x () const
  {
     // function body
  }
```

1. **Inline Functions**

   When you define member functions inside a particular class, the function automatically becomes an inline function.

2. **Friend Functions**

   Friend functions provides private access to non-class functions. These functions are not a class member function. Friend function allows you to declare a global function as a friend or a member function of another class as a friend.

Syntax:

```
Class friendclass
  {
        int x;
        Public:
        Friend void fn() //set global function as a friend
  ];
 Void fn()
    {
       Friendclass fc;
       // accessing private data member
       fc.x=10;
       cout<<fc.x;
     }
  Int main() {
     fn ()
    }
```

A friend function will be able to access the private member function through creation of class objects. You can also make your entire class as a friend class. If you make a class to be a friend class, then all the member functions automatically become a friend function.

Example:

```
class anotherfriendclass
{
    void fn();
};

class Friendclass
{
    private:
    int x;
    public:
    void getdata();  //

    // make the class function anotherfriendclass
    friend void anotherfriendclass::fn();

    // e complete class as friend
    friend class anotherfriendclass;
};
```

Building Classes

When creating classes, there are two types of classes you can create: base class and derived class.

Base Class and Derived Class

A base class is a class which allows building of other classes from it. That is, it allows other classes to be derived from it. A base class facilitates creation of a new class that reuses the code inherited from the original base class. The derived class inherits both properties and methods of the base class. You can extend the functionality of base class by overriding members in the derived class.

A base class is also called a parent class or super class while the derived class is called child or subclass.

Any class built from the base class inherits both the data and behavior of the base class.

Properties of a base class:

- Base classes are instantiated automatically before building derived class.
- During instantiation, a derived class communicates with base class through calling the base class constructor with similar parameter list.
- Members of the base class are accessed from the derived class by the use of an explicit cast.
- Defining abstract methods in the base class so that the class automatically becomes an abstract class. A non-abstract class from derived class can override data members in the abstract class.

The base class members have private, public, and protected access modifiers where the private members are accessible within the class. Public members are accessed outside the class while the protected members are accessed within the class or by a subclass.

A derived class can only access the public and protected members of the base class. Private members are inaccessible.

Chapter Summary

In this chapter you learned how to use classes to solve various problems, including:

- How to use class headers and class body when defining objects, and how to define and declare classes.
- How to differentiate between data members and member functions.
- How to declare both data members and member function, and determine whether they should be declared as private, public or protected members.
- How to access the private, public and protected members in a class, as well as make calls to the member functions.
- How to work with different class member functions when invoking specific functions.
- How to build classes using the base class and derived classes. From the base class or the parent class, you can derive a child class which inherits the behavior and properties of the base class.
- You will be able to know more detailed information about how the derived class inherits these properties in our next chapter.

In the next chapter you will learn about class inheritance, including how the derived class inherits properties. At the end of the chapter you will be able to derive new classes from an existing class, learn how to apply different types of inheritance to solving problems, identify relationships between classes, learn how to apply inheritance in constructors and destructors, and lastly be able to manage dynamic data.

CHAPTER FOUR:

Extending Classes via Inheritance

Deriving New Classes from Existing Classes

Inheritance is an object oriented programming feature that allows a class to borrow the members of other classes without repetition of its members. It allows one class (derived class or subclass) to acquire the properties and methods of another class (base class or superclass). A class whose properties are inherited is called the base, parent or superclass while the class that inherits these properties is called a derived, subclass or child class.

When a class inherits properties of another class, the variables and functions of the base class are available to the new class, hence promoting code reusability. The derived class inherits all members except the private members.

Importance of inheritance:

1. Supports code reusability
2. Support overriding method
3. Uses virtual keyword

Base Class and Derived Class

When inhering members of another class, the public members of the superclass will remain public while the protected members will remain protected. In a private inheritance, both public and protected members of a superclass will remain private in a subclass.

Syntax

```
Class subclass: access_mode superclass
```

The superclass should be declared first, that is, before you define the subclass. The access mode (private, public or protected) specifies what superclass properties are to be inherited by subclass.

For example, assume you have a class employee and class manager, where the manager is also an employee who has additional responsibilities. You can apply inheritance concept to avoid repeating data members and member functions in employee class to the manager class.

The manager class can be declared as shown below.

```
Class Manager: Public Employee
{
Public:
// additional manager member components
...
};
```

Inheritance helps you declare manager class without repeating those member components inside the employee class. Employee is the base class while manager is the derived class.

```
class student
  {
   char* studname, course;
   int age;
   char* department;
  Protected:
    student(char* studname);
   void display();
  };


  class HOD : Protected student
  {
   studentlist students;

  Protected:
   HOD(char* studname, student* people);
   void display();
  };
```

Types of Inheritance

Single Inheritance

Single inheritance is one of the simplest types of inheritance where a class is derived from a single class. The derived class will inherit member components from only a single class. For example, class B inherits properties and behaviors of class A. Class B inherits both the public and protected members of class A.

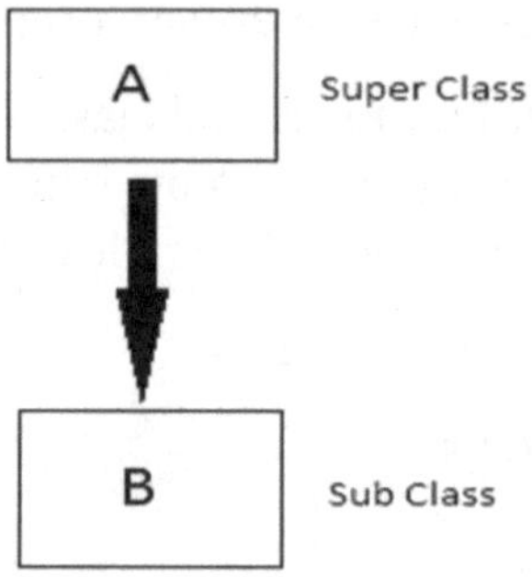

Syntax

```
Class B: public A {/*…*/};
Or
Class B: Protected A {/*…*/};
```

Multiple Inheritance

In multiple inheritance, a class can inherit members from two or more direct base classes. For example, you can create derived class C from class A & B base classes.

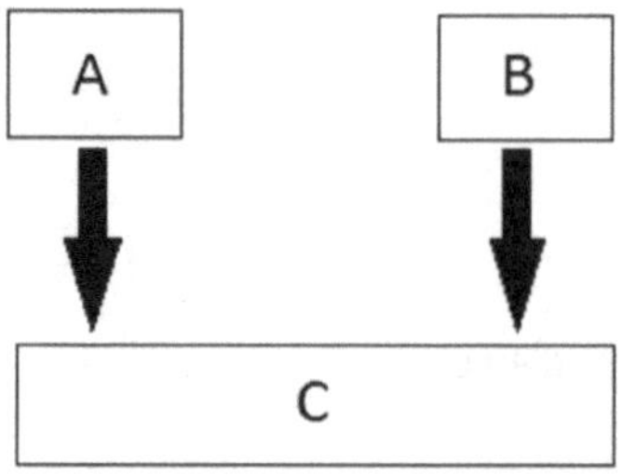

Syntax

```
Class C: public A, public B {/*…*/};
Example:
#include<iostream.h>
Class Polygon
{
protected:
   int width, height;
   Public:
        void setvalues (int w, int h)
        {
        width=w, height=h;
        }
};
Class output
{
public:
   void output (int);
};
```

```
void output::output (int i)
{
   cout<<'i'<<endl;
}
class rectangle:public polygon, public output
{
public:
   int area()
   {
         return width*height;
   }
};
class triangle: public polygon, public output
{
   int area()
   {return (width*height/2);}
};
int main()
{
   rectangle rect;
   triangle tri;
   rect.setvalues (6,4);
   tri.setvalues (6,4);
   cout<< "Area of rectangle is:"<<rect.output(rect.area);
   cout<< "Area of triangle is:"<<tri.output (tri.area);
   return 0;
}
```

Multi-level Inheritance

This is a where a derived class inherits from a class which also inherited properties of another base class. For example, if A is the base class of B while class B is the base class of C, then C will be the derived class of B and B will be a derived class of A.

Hybrid inheritance/virtual inheritance

Hybrid is a combination of several inheritance types. For example, class B and C are the derived classes of base class A. From the derived class B and C, you can create a new derived class D. This forms a hybrid inheritance since it combines multiple inheritance types to form a new class.

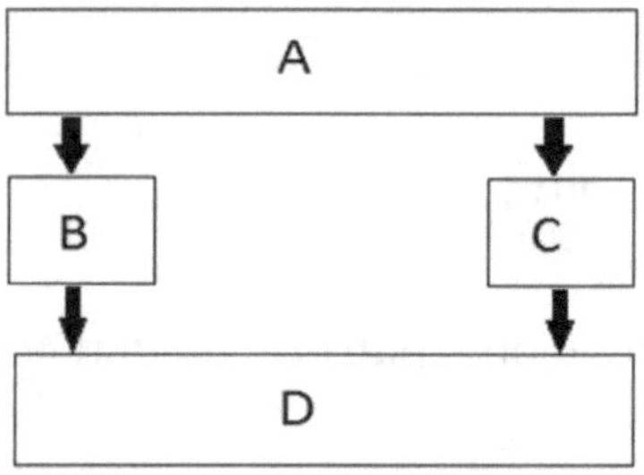

Hierarchical inheritance

Hierarchical inheritance has multiple subclasses which inherit properties of a single base class. Class B, C, and D inherit the properties of single class A.

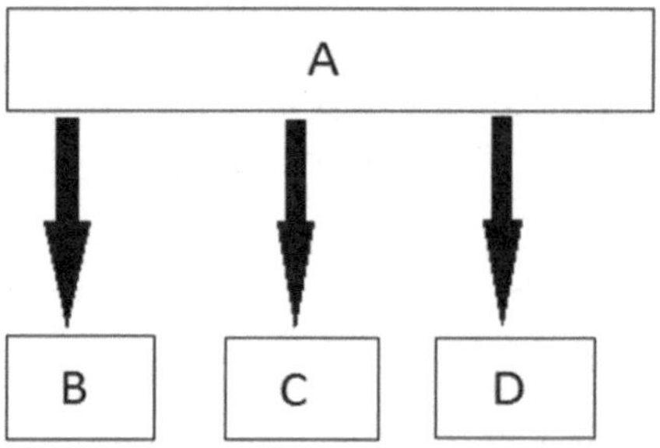

Relationships

C++ supports encapsulation in which data is bundled together with the specific functions that operate on it, thus forming a single unit. This process ensures data is only accessed by functions operating on it and not outside the class. This protects the class member functions from being accessible outside.

To access the private and protected members outside the class, you have to use the special feature called the friend function or class to access the private members. The friend function allows you to access non-public members of a class. That is, a class can allow other non-member functions and other classes to access its private members by making them friends.

To make the private and protected classes accessible, you have to declare a prototype of the external class allowing it to gain access to the private members of another class. The friend keyword is placed on the function declaration of the friend function and not in the function definition. The friend function is invoked without any object since the function has its own arguments as objects.

Syntax

```
Class class-name
{
…
…
Friend Type Function_name (arguments)
}
 Example:
#include<iostream.h>
class square;
class rectangle
{
   int length, width;
public:
   int area()
   {
        return (length*width);
   }
   void convert (square s);
};

class square
{
private:
   int side;
public:
   void setsize (int a)
   {
        size= a;
   }
   friend class rectangle
};
void rectangle::convert (square s)
{
   length= s. length
   width=s.side;
}

int main()
{
    rectangle.rect
   square. sqr

    sqr.setvalues (a);
   rect. convert (sqr);
    cout<<rect.area();
   return 0;
}
```

Example 2:

```
#include <iostream.h>
class XYZ
{
private:
    int x, y;
public:
    void text()
    {
        x=50, y=75;
    }
    friend int compute (XYZ E1,E2)
};
int compute (XYZ E1)
{
    return int (E1.x+E2.y)-5;

}
int main()
{
   XYZ E
   E.test
   cout<< "The result is:"<<compute(E)
   return 0;
}
```

Construction and Destruction of Derived Objects

Constructors and destructors are C++ tools used for creating objects. Constructors initialize member variables in an object while a destructor is used in destroying that object. Whenever an instance of a class is created, it invokes the constructor method.

Constructors use the same name like class and no return type, while a destructor uses the same form of naming as class but it has '~' at the beginning of the class declaration.

During program execution, the compiler automatically calls the constructor and destructor variables. If the base class has no parameters passed to it, then the derived class doesn't need any constructor. If the base class has a parameter list, then the derived class should have a constructor.

The derived constructor class will pass its arguments to the base class constructor. When using inheritance concept, you can declare objects using the derived class. Once you declare objects in a derived class, the constructor of the base class and derived class are automatically executed.

Constructors and Destructors in Base and Derived Classes

Inheritance of destructor objects execute in reverse order during execution of a constructor. When the object gets out of scope, the destructor is executed. See below for an example of constructor and destructor program using multiple inheritance.

Syntax

```
#include<iostream.h>
#include<constream.h>

class Base1
{
        Public:
        base()//constructor with zero arguments
         {
           cout<<"Zero arguments constructor /n";
         }
        ~base()
         {
           cout<<"Destructor of base1 class/n";
         }
};

class Base2
{
        public:
        base2()
         {
           cout<< "Zero argument constructor for base2 class/n";
         }
        ~base3()
         {
           cout<< "Destructor of base2 class/n";
         }
};

class Base3: Public Base1, Public Base2
{
        public:
        base3()
         {
           cout<<"Zero argument constructor for a derived class /n";
         }
        ~base3()
         {
           cout<<"Destructor of the derived class /n";
         }
};

int main ()
 {
   clrscr ();
   Base3 obj; //declaring object
   return 0;
 }
```

//output

```
Zero arguments constructor
Destructor of base1 class
Zero argument constructor for base2 class
Destructor of base2 class
Zero argument constructor for a derived class
Destructor of the derived class
```

In the above program, base1 and base2 are the superclass while base3 is the derived class. The constructors of the superclass are executed first before executing the derived class. The destructor of the derived class is executed before executing the superclass.

You can call the superclass constructor in a derived class constructor. When you create a derived class object from an existing base class, the base class becomes a constructor by default, and it is executed first then followed by the derived class.

When making a call to a base class constructor with parameters inside the derived class constructor which also has parameters, then you have to explicitly mention it when declaring the parameters of the derived class constructor.

Base class is the default constructor which is present in all types of classes. See example below.

Syntax

```
class construct
{
    int x;
    public:

     construct()
    {
        cout << "Building default constructor\n";
    }
};

class Child : public construct
{
    int y;
    public:

    Child()
    {
        cout << "Default derived  constructor\n";
    }
    // constructor with parameters
     Child(int z)
    {
        cout << "Parameterized derived constructor\n";
    }
};
```

```
int main()
{
    construct c;
    Child c1;
    Child c2(10);
}
```

//output

```
Building default constructor
Default derived  constructor
Building default constructor
Parameterized derived constructor
```

In the above example, the base class is the default constructor class which is called together with objects from derived/child class. The example below shows base class constructor with parameters.

Syntax

```
class construct
{
    float x;
    public:

    construct(float i)
    {
                    x=i;
        cout << "Parameterized constructor\n";
    }
};

class Child : public construct
{
    float y;
    public:

    Child(float j): construct(j)
    {
        y=j;
                    cout << "Parameterized derived constructor\n";

    }

};

int main()
{
  Child (10);
}
```

// output

```
Parameterized constructor
Parameterized derived constructor
```

An explicit call to the parameterized base constructor class permits a call to the parameterized derived class constructor. A constructor base class is called inside the derived class. This allows the constructor to initialize the object in the class.

A derived class constructor can only access its own class members while a derived class object inherits the characteristics and properties of the base class. A base class constructor initializes the members of the base class.

Upcasting in C++

The use of superclass reference or a pointer to point to a subclass object is known as upcasting. That is, converting the subclass reference address or pointer to its superclass reference address.

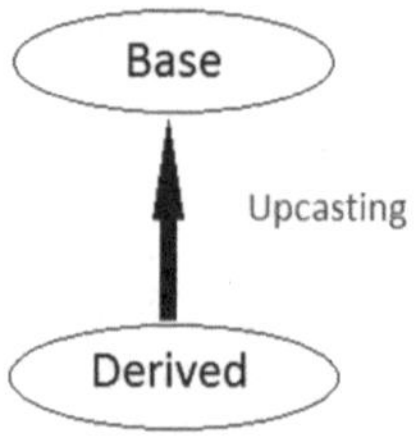

Syntax

```
class baseclass
{
    int i;
    public:
    void Base()
    {
            cout << "This is a Superclass";
    }
};

class derived:public baseclass
{
    int j;
};

int main()
{
    baseclass* ptr;   // pointer to base class
    derived obj;
    ptr = &obj;

    baseclass &ref;   // baseclass's reference address
    ref=obj;
}
```

In a downcasting, the base class's reference or pointer is converted into a derived class reference or its pointer.

Note: Constructors and destructors are not inherited. The assignment operator (=) can be overloaded but it cannot be inherited by a subclass.

Inheritance and Static Functions

1. The static functions can be inherited into the derived class.
2. If static member functions are redefined in a derived class, then other overloaded functions in the super class are hidden.
3. All static member functions cannot be virtual.

Hybrid Inheritance and Virtual Class

When a derived class inherits properties of more than one base class, it results in multiple inheritance. See example below.

Syntax

```
class BaseA
{
   void print();
};

class BaseB:public BaseA
{
   // derived class definition
};

class BaseC:public BaseA
{
   // derived class definition
};

class BaseD:public BaseB, public BaseC
{
   // class definition
};

int main()
{
   D obj;
   obj.print();
}
```

Class BaseB and BaseC inherit the **print()** function in class BaseA. Class BaseD inherits two copies of the **print()** function. When you call the **print()** in the **main()** function, it results in ambiguity since the compiler doesn't know which **print()** function to call. To avoid this, a virtual function is used. This is done by inserting the virtual keyword when the class is being inherited.

```
class BaseB: virtual public BaseA
{
    // derived class definition
};

class BaseC: virtual public BaseA
{
    // derived class definition
};

class BaseD:public BaseB, public BaseC
{
    // class definition
};
```

The virtual keyword tells the compiler to call any of the two functions.

Managing Dynamic Data

C++ allows you to dynamically allocate memory space for your program. Initially, a programmer can determine the memory space of the program by defining the variables before the program executes. There are cases where the memory can only be determined during run time or it is based on user input needs. In this case, the memory is dynamically allocated to programs. Dynamic memory determines how the data is processed and stored.

Pointers are also used for memory allocation and hold the memory address of a variable. When you declare a variable it has two components:

- The address of the variable
- The value which is stored in the variable. For example: int y= 200.

The above example tells the compiler to:

1. Create a space in memory to store the value of the variable.
2. Associate the variable ***y*** with the reserved memory location.
3. Store value 200 at the reserved memory location.

Pointers is one of the useful features in C++ language, and once utilized in a program, it enables:

1. Direct access and manipulation of the memory location.
2. Allocation of dynamic memory into a variable.
3. Improvement of efficiency in some routine programs.

Allocating and Deallocating Memory with New and Delete Operators

C++ program integrates the new and delete operators to dynamically allocate the memory. The **new** operator followed by the data type specifier dynamically allocates the memory of a program.

If the user input has a sequence of more than one element, then the **new[]** operator is need to allocate a block of memory.

Syntax

```
Pointer = new return-type
or
Pointer = new return-type [size]
```

The **new** operator allocates memory for a single element on the memory heap.

The **new []** operator allocates memory to an array/block of elements with the size being an integer value that represents the objects returned.

Syntax

```
    int *mem;
    mem = new int [4];
```

When you run the program, the system dynamically allocates memory space of the 4 elements of integer type and returns an array of elements assigned to pointer mem. Therefore, mem points directly to a memory block with four elements of integer (int) type.

You can access the first element in the array by calling mem [0], while the second element is accessed by mem [1].

You can also initialize the memory with the new operator, as seen below.

Syntax

```
Pointer-variable= new return-type (value);
```

Example:

```
   int *ptr = new int (30);
   float *r = new float (15)
```

There exists a difference between a normal array and a block of memory allocated dynamically using the **new** operator. In a normal array, the array size is a **constant** expression which is determined during variable declaration (before running the program), whereas the dynamic memory allocation is performed using the **new** operator that assigns memory space to a program during run time. It uses any variable value as the size for the block of elements.

The system dynamically allocates memory to a program from the memory **heap**. Non-static and local variables are allocated memory on **stack.**

For any dynamically allocated memory **(int *mem= new int[4])** the programmer has to deallocate the memory after the program execution. Otherwise, if the memory space is not deallocated, it will result in a memory leak. The memory should be deallocated after the program execution terminates.

Delete operator

In C++, the operator **delete** deallocates the already allocated memory space to a program. This makes the memory available for the next request to dynamically allocate space.

Syntax

```
delete pointer-variable;
or
delete [] pointer-variable;
```

If you dynamically allocated space to a single element using the **new** operator, then use **delete** pointer-variable to free the memory. To free a memory allocated to a block of elements, you use **delete []**. The arguments passed to the delete operator should be either a **pointer** that points to a block of elements or a **null pointer**. Passing a **null pointer** has no effect to the **delete** operator.

For example, delete [] ptr; or delete ptr;

```
#include <iostream>
#include <new>
using namespace std;

int main ()
{
  int l,m;
  int * ptr;
  cout << "Enter the numbers you want to print:";
  cin >> l;
  ptr= new (nothrow) int[l];
  if (ptr == nullpointer)
    cout << "Error: Unsuccessful memory allocation";
  else
  {
    for (m=0; m<l; m++)
    {
    cout << "Enter number: ";
    cin >> ptr[m];
    }
    cout << "The numbers entered are: ";
    for (m=0; m<l; m++)
    cout << ptr[m] << ", ";
    delete[] ptr;
  }
  return 0;
}
```

// output

```
Enter the numbers you want to print: 3
Enter number: 25
Enter number: 50
Enter number: 72
The numbers entered are: 25, 50, 72
```

If the system could not allocate the memory space requested for example, requesting a large memory allocation then the system will return an error message. **Error: Unsuccessful memory allocation.** The new request will throw a standard **bad_alloc** exception, unless you use the **nothrow** with the new operator. This exception type handle errors by checking the pointer value or through catching exceptions.

Handling Errors with Try and Catch

Computer memory is a limited resource and sometimes it's not a guarantee whether the request to dynamically allocated memory to a program using the new operator will be successful. The memory gets exhausted sometimes.

C++ uses two standard mechanisms to determine if the memory allocation was successful or not. If memory allocation fails, an exception is thrown. The **nothrow** exception is used to handle the errors in the program instead of throwing **bad_alloc** exception which terminates the program after an error occurred. These will be discussed later in detail.

Syntax

```
ptr= new (nothrow) int[1];
```

To know whether the block of memory allocation fails, you can detect the failure through checking whether the pointer variable is null.

Avoiding Memory Leaks

When a programmer creates a memory in the heap and forgets to delete it, it creates a memory leak. To avoid having a memory leak, you should free the memory allocated on the heap when no longer needed. Always make sure to use the right operator (delete or delete []) to deallocate the memory.

If there is a memory leak, then the memory usage increases. This makes the limited memory resource very costly thus creating more problems later. The example below is a program to show a memory leak.

Syntax

```
#include <iostream.h>
using namespace std;

void memory_leak()
{
   int *p = new int(4);

   return; // return method without deallocating the pointer variable p
}

int main()
{

   // Calling the function
   // function to get the memory leak
```

```
    memory_leak();

    return 0;
}
```

Smart pointers can also be used to free the memory. You don't have to manually manage the memory. Instead of declaring **char*** you can use **std::string** which manages the internal memory. This makes it faster and well-optimized compared to when managing memory manually.

You can also reduce memory leaks by reducing the new/delete calls.

Chapter Summary

Inheritance is one of the important features of object oriented programming. It allows programmers to reuse code instead of rewriting the same code again. In this, one class inherits the properties and methods of another class (base class). In this chapter, you have learned:

- How to derive new classes from existing classes so as to promote code reusability.
- How to use inheritance to support overriding methods as well as learn how to work with both base and derived classes.
- How you can specify what properties are to be inherited by the subclass using the access mode. This requires you to define the base class first before defining the subclass.
- About different types of inheritance and how to use each type in creating objects.
- How to use constructors and destructors in deriving objects.
- How to access a class using the base and derived constructors.
- How you can call a base class constructor in a derived class constructor. When you create a derived class object from an existing base class, the base class becomes a constructor by default, and it is executed first then followed by the derived class.
- How to make a call of the base class inside the derived class constructor that has parameters like the base class constructor.
- How to use upcasting feature in C++ to allow you to reference your base class.
- How to use a pointer to point directly to a subclass.
- How to dynamically allocate memory space for your program during run-time.
- How to use new and delete operators to allocate and deallocate memory when not needed.
- How to use delete or delete [] operators to help you avoid memory leaks in your program.
- How to use try catch exceptions to test whether memory allocation is successful or has failed.

In the next chapter you will learn about polymorphism. At the end of the chapter you will know what polymorphism is and how to apply different types of polymorphism during compile and runtime. You will also learn how to create abstract classes and virtual functions.

CHAPTER FIVE

Polymorphism

Polymorphism is an OOP feature that allows an object to have more than one form. If you have multiple classes that relate to each other by inheritance, the classes are using the polymorphism concept. When using inheritance, polymorphism is executed by use of overriding function. That is, both the superclass and subclass have same declared member function but different function definition.

In our previous chapter, the inheritance feature allowed us to create a new derived class that inherited attributes and properties of another class. Polymorphism uses similar methods to perform different tasks. It allows you to perform a single task using different forms. For example, a woman can have different characteristics depending on the situation, like being a wife, a mother, and an employee.

Polymorphism is divided in two:

- Runtime polymorphism
- Compile time polymorphism

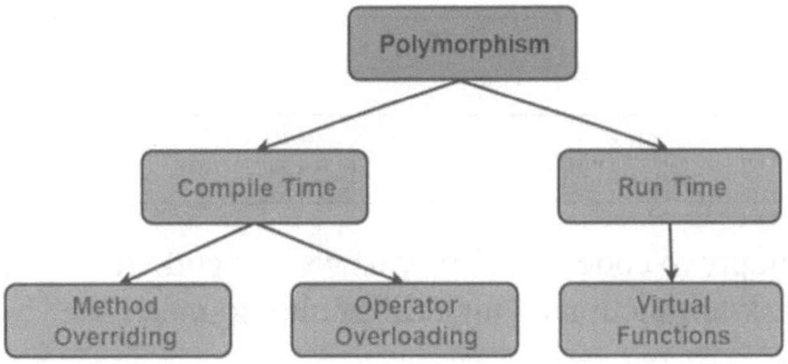

Compile Time Polymorphism

Compile time polymorphism is also known as static polymorphism, and it indicates the existence of an entity in more than one physical form. In static polymorphism, functions are bound based on their signature (data type and the number of parameters present). The function calls represent an early binding because they're made on the basis of data type and the sequence of parameters passed.

Compile time polymorphism is implemented using overriding function and operator overloading.

Overloading Function

Function overloading is a situation where you have multiple functions with the same name but different parameters. These functions have parameters with different data types or changes in the number of parameters being passed.

Syntax

```
int area (int x);
int area (int x, int y);
```

See example below.

```
#include <iostream.h>
using namespace std;
class Addition {
public:  float sum(float x, float y){
    return x+y;
  }
  float sum(float x, float y, float z){
    return x+y+z;
  }
};
int main() {
  Addition obj;
  // A call to sum function with two parameters
  cout<<"Total Sum: "<<obj.sum(8.80, 15.20)<<endl;
  //call to the second function with three parameters
  cout<<"Total Sum: "<<obj.sum(18.5, 26.4, 30.0);
  return 0;
}
```

// output

```
Total sum: 24.0
Total sum: 74.9
```

Overloading functions improve code readability as well as code reusability as shown above. You can perform the same task to functions with a different parameter list.

Operator Overloading

Operator overloading allows you to overload operators. For example, you can use operator (+)

to join two strings together. If you use the addition operator between two integers, it adds them but when the operator is placed between strings, it concatenates or joins them.

To overload an operator, you have to declare a class member function whose name is operator and then follow with the operator sign you want to use.

```
Type operator-sign (parameters)
```

For example: xyz operator + (xyz) / using operator overloading

Syntax

```
#include<iostream.h>
using namespace std;
class xyz
{
private:
    int a,b;
public:
    xyz()
    void getvalues()
    {
        cout<<"Enter value of a and b";
        cin>>a>>b;
    }
    void setvalues(float x, float y)
    {
        x=a;
        y=b;
    }
    void setvalues(double num1, double num2)
    {
        num1=a;
       num2=b;
    }
    void display()
    {
        cout<<"The value for a is:"<<a<<"The value for b
is:"<<b<<endl;
    }
    Double addition()
    xyz operator + (xyz)

};
xyz xyz::operator +(xyz)
{
    return (a+b)
}
int main()
{
    xyz x1,x2,x3;
    x1.getvalues(10,15);
    x2.setvalues(6,8);
```

```
    x3.setvalues(12,8);
    cout<<x1.addition();
    cout<<x2.addition();
    cout<<x3.addition();
    return 0;
}
```

Run-time Polymorphism

Run time polymorphism is also dynamic polymorphism. In this type of polymorphism, functions change their form depending on the situation. If a function exists in different forms and responds to different function calls made dynamically during running time, then it forms dynamic polymorphisms.

Runtime polymorphism supports dynamic binding and makes programs more flexible when being executed.

In dynamic binding, a function call is made at run-time and it depends on the function pointer content at run-time. If you change the contents of the function pointer, you will end up with different functions that share the same name but have different function body.

A dynamic polymorphism changes an entity based on the situation. A function exhibits dynamic polymorphism if it exists in different forms. The function calls to these types of polymorphism are made dynamically during the execution time.

Dynamic binding is also known as late binding, and it improves the flexibility of a program being executed. The calls to the function are made on the basis of content of function pointer. All polymorphic functions have the same name but with different data types or sequence of parameters.

Static binding is more efficient than dynamic binding in some cases. If you have a static function you don't need a run-time search, while dynamic functions calls for run-time search. Most function calls in dynamic binding are resolved at execution time.

Dynamic polymorphism is implemented using overriding functions and virtual functions.

Overriding Function

Function overriding allows you to have the same function name in the superclass and subclass. The subclass inherits the data members and member functions in the superclass. You can create an overriding function in the subclass by creating the same member functions with the same argument list.

Function overriding is done only in the derived class, and it is achieved during run time. Overriding function is redefining a base class inside the derived class with the same return type and parameters.

Syntax

```
class Super
{
    public:
    void print()
    {
          cout << "This is a base class";
    }
};

class Subclass: public Super
{
    public:
    void print()
    {
          cout << "This is a Derived Class";
    }
};
```

The print () in the base class is overridden in the derived class.

How to call overriding function

You can make a call to the overriding function in the **main ()** function. The function call and the function body connects through the binding process. If the connections occur before run time it is called early binding, static or compile-time binding.

Syntax

```
class Super
{
    public:
    void print()
    {
          cout << "This is a base class";
    }
};

class Subclass: public Super
{
    public:
    void print()
    {
          cout << "This is a Derived Class";
    }
};
int main ()
 {
   Super b; //creating object for base class
   Subclass d; // creating object for derived class
   b.print(); // static binding
   d.print();
```

```
    return 0;
 }
```

//output

```
This is a base class
This is a derived class
```

See below for an example of calling the above base function using pointers.

```
int main ()
 {
    Super *b; //creating object pointer for base class
    Subclass d; // creating object for derived class
    b = &d;
    b -> print (); // static binding
 }
```

In the above example, we have made a call to the overridden function using base object and derived object. The **b.print ()** object will call the base function while **d.print ()** object will call the derived class function.

Virtual Functions

A virtual function is a base class member function which is overridden in the derived class. The function call results in **late binding.** That is, it instructs the compiler to perform late binding on the overridden function.

To make member functions of the base class virtual, a **virtual** keyword is used when declaring the function. A late binding call is made at run time. Therefore, the compiler determines the object type during run time and makes the function call.

```
Virtual void function-name()
{//function body}
```

Example:

```
#include <iostream.h>

    class car
    {
    public:
        virtual void make()
        {
            cout<<"member function of the car base class is accessed";
        }
    };
    class 4wheel: public car
    {
    public:
        void make()
        {
```

```
            cout<<"Accessing virtual member function of the 4wheel
derived class";
        }
    };

    void main()
    {
        car *a, *b;
        a = new car();
        a -> make(); //an object pointer which is equivalent to
*a.make();
        b = new car();
        b -> make();
    }
```

If a member of the class is redefined inside the derived class, it is called a virtual member. In the above example, function **make()** is a virtual function inside the base class. A 4wheeler is a derived class of the base class car.

If the member function is not declared as virtual then it will result in static binding where the function call is bound during compile time. But if the function is declared as virtual, the function address is bound during run-time making it a dynamic binding.

To achieve dynamic binding concept, the compiler creates a **v-table** every time a virtual function is declared. The v-table contains information about the function pointers from each of the objects in the derived class and other function class information. This information is made available whenever a call is made to the virtual function.

How to Access Private Member Functions in a Derived Class Using Virtual Keyword

Using virtual keyword, you can easily call the private member function in a derived class with a pointer that points to the base class. In this case, the compiler will look at the access specifier mode during compile time.

During late binding when the program is running, the compiler doesn't check the access specifier of the function being called.

Syntax

```
class Super
{
    public:
    virtual void print()
    {
          cout << "This is a base class";
    }
};

class Subclass: public Super
{
    public:
    virtual void print()
```

```
    {
           cout << "This is a Derived Class";
    }
};
int main ()
 {
   Super *b;
   Subclass d;
   b = &d;
   b -> print ();
 }
```

// output

```
This is a derived class
```

Notes:

1. Only the base class function is declared with a virtual keyword.
2. If you declare a function as virtual in the base class, then the function will automatically be virtual in all of the derived classes.

Abstract Classes

An abstract class is a type of class which consists of at least a pure virtual function. Abstract class provides an interface to a derived class. If a class inherits properties of an abstract class, then you must define the pure virtual function, otherwise, the derived class will become an abstract class.

Characteristics of abstract class:

1. Even though you can create pointers and references in an abstract class, it cannot be instantiated.
2. Abstract class has both variables, functions and a pure virtual function.
3. Abstract classes are suitable in performing upcasting so as to allow the subclass to use its interface.
4. All classes that inherit the properties of an abstract class must implement the pure virtual function, to avoid becoming abstract too.

Pure Virtual Function

A virtual function with no definition is known as the pure virtual function. A pure virtual function has no function body and it uses the **virtual** keyword at the beginning and ends with a notation **=0** since it has no body.

Virtual void function-name () =0;

Both virtual and pure functions works the same way except that the pure virtual function has no function definition.

The example below demonstrates an abstract class.

```
class BPolygon
{
protected:
    float width, height;
public:
    void setvalues(float x, float y)
    {
          width=x; height=y;
    }
    virtual float area()=0;
};
class BRectangle:public BPolygon
{
public:
    float area()
    {
          return (width*height);
    }
};
class BTriangle:public BPolygon
{
public:
    float area()
    {
          return ((width*height)/2);
    }
};
int main()
{
    BRectangle rect;
    BTriangle tri;
    BPolygon *p1=&rect;
    BPolygon *p2=&tri;
    p1 -> setvalues(8,6);
    *p2.setvalues(8,6);
    cout<<p1 ->area()<<endl;
    cout<<p2 ->area()<<endl;
    return 0;
}
```

Chapter Summary

In this chapter you have learned what polymorphism is and the different types of polymorphisms. You're now able to:

- Differentiate between the compile time polymorphism and run time polymorphism using examples.
- Use static binding or early binding to make system calls to the member function and how to use dynamic binding to make a function call during program execution.
- Use function overloading and operator overloading to increase program efficiency.

- Make function calls using overriding functions and virtual functions as well as override a function inside a derived class.
- Declare virtual functions in your program and know how to use abstract classes.
- Access the private member functions using the virtual keyword as well as differentiate between a virtual function and a pure virtual function.

In the next chapter you will learn about constructors and destructors. By the end of the chapter, you will be able to declare class constructor and destructor and know how to use different types of constructors.

CHAPTER SIX

Constructors and Destructors

Overview

A **constructor** is a member function which initializes the objects of a class type and has the same name as the class name. The constructor class can accept arguments or not accept arguments, and it allocates memory space to class objects.

Constructor's member function performs construction work. That is, building values in an object through automatic initialization. A constructor is automatically invoked whenever a new instance of a class is created. You can define the arguments of the class manually or leave it without any arguments.

The name of the constructor is always the same as the name of the class and the constructor has no return type.

```
Class ConstructorName
{// class body};
```

On the other hand, a **destructor** is a member function that is complementary to the constructor. A destructor de-initializes an object after it has been destroyed. The destructor function call is made when an object within a class has gone out of scope, or when its memory space is de-allocated with the use of **delete** operator.

The destructor de-allocates memory space for the object. A destructor doesn't have any parameters, therefore it cannot be overloaded. It is usually called in reverse to constructor. If a class (derived class) inherits properties of another class (base class) and both classes have destructor, then the destructor in the derived class is called first.

A destructor has the same name as the class and the tilde (~) operator precedes it.

```
~ Class Name
{// class body
};
```

Definition and Declaration of a Constructor

A constructor definition is just like the other member functions in a class. The definition is either inside the class or outside the class using the class name followed by the scope resolution :: operator.

Syntax

```
Class Base
 {
        double a, b;
        Protected:
        Base (double, double); // constructor
        Void print ()
 };
```

The class base has a member function constructor **Base ()** which has the same name as the class Base. This member function is the constructor of the class and it can be utilized in order to create values for the object class. When making a call to the function, you can pass values to the function by declaring the object.

```
Base b; // object declaration
B= Base (35, 58);
```

In this case, an object b is created from the Base class and a constructor call is prompted.

See below for an example of a constructor demonstration.

```
#include <iostream>
#include <conio.h>
Class Triangle
{
private:
   double length, height;
public:
   length = 15.2;
   height = 20.5;
   double area()
   {
         return (length*height/2);
   }

};
 int main()
 {
   clrscr();
   Triangle tri;
```

```
    cout<<"The area of triangle is:" <<tri.area()<<"sq.units\n";
    getch();
}
```

// output

```
The area of triangle is: 155.8 sq.units
```

Characteristics of Constructors

1. They should always be declared under the public access specifier.
2. Constructors don't have a return type, not even a null (void) return type.
3. Creating a new object results in an automatic call to the constructor function.
4. A derived class can't inherit a constructor function but it can make a call to the base class constructor.
5. A constructor can have default parameters just like other functions.
6. Constructors can never work as virtual functions.
7. You can't refer to the address of a constructor.

Types of Constructors

C++ programming language has various types of constructors which extend its functionality. These constructors include: default, parameterized, overloaded and copy.

Default constructors

A default constructor doesn't have any arguments or parameters. See example below.

```
Class Cube
{
   Public:
         int x;
         Cube()
         {
               X= 5;
         }
};
int main ()
  {
         Cube c;
         Cout<< c.x;
  }
```

Once the object is created, a call to the constructor is made immediately, thus initializing the data member. The default constructor initializes the object members. If you don't define a constructor, the compiler implicitly assigns a default constructor to the class.

If a compiler returns a default constructor, it will initialize the object data members with a default value which is initially 0 or any random integer value.

Parameterized constructors

This is a constructor which has arguments. You can supply different parameters or values to the data members of different objects.

The initial values to the constructor are passed as arguments when the constructor is declared. This is done by:

- Calling the constructor explicitly.
- Calling the constructor implicitly.

See example below.

```
Class Cube
{
   Public:
          int val;
          Cube( int x)
          {
                val= x;
          }
};
int main ()
  {
          Cube c (5);
          Cube c1 (10);
          Cube c2 (15);
          cout<< c.val;
          cout<< c1.val;
          cout<< c2.val;
  }
```

Overloaded constructor

Constructors not only initialize data members, they're not different from other member functions. They also perform function overloading just like in polymorphism. The default and parameterized constructors can act as an overloaded constructor where one of them has no parameters while the other one has parameters.

Overloaded constructor allows you to have multiple constructors in a class with each having different parameter list.

See example below.

```
#include <iostream>
using namespace std;
class overload
{
 public:
    double area;
    overload()
    {
          area = 0;
```

```
    }
    overload(float num1, float num2)
    {
        area = num1 * num2;
    }
    void display()
    {
        cout<< area<< endl;
    }
};
int main()
 {
   // constructor overloading with same class name and different
arguments
   overload c1;
   overload c2(8.6, 6.2);

   c1.display();
   c2.display();
 }
```

// output

```
0
53.32
```

Copy constructors

C++ offers a special type of constructor which passes an object as a parameter to the function and copy data member values from one object to another. Copy constructor declares and initializes object values from another object.

Copy constructor creates new objects with exact features as the existing object, hence the name copy constructor. A copy constructor acts as overloaded constructor because it declares and initializes an object from another object.

There are two types of copy constructors:

- Default copy constructor: The compiler automatically defines this type of copy constructor if the user or programmer doesn't define the copy constructor.
- User defined constructor: It is a copy constructor defined by the programmer.

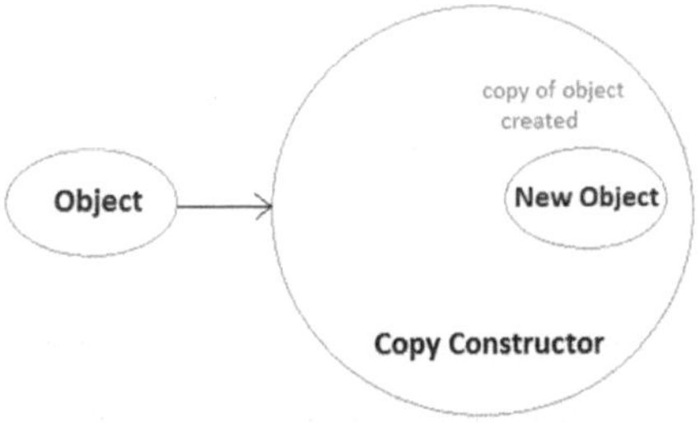

Syntax

```
Class_name (const class_name & object_name);
```

Example 1:

```
Class Copy
 {
   Copy (Copy &y) // copy constructor
   { // function body of copy constructor }
 };
```

To call the copy constructor in the above example, you have to initialize the object. This can be done in any of the following ways:

```
 Copy c2 (c1);
   or
 Copy c2=c1
```

Where,

c1 initializes the c2 object.

Example 2:

```
#include <iostream>
using namespace std;
class Copy
{
public:
float i;
Copy(float x) //parameterized constructor.
{
i=x;
}
Copy(Copy &y)  // copy constructor definition
{
i = y.i;
}
};
int main()
{
Copy c1(35);  // Call to parameterized constructor.
Copy c2(c1);   //  Call to copy constructor.
cout<<c2.i;
return 0;
}
```

// output

```
35
```

When a call is made to the constructor, two copies are produced:

- Shallow copy
- Deep copy

Shallow copy

The default copy constructor created by the compiler can only produce a shallow copy. It is a shallow copy since the objects are created by copying all data variables of an object to another object.

See the example below:

```
class Example
{
    int num1;
    int num2;
    int *ptr;
    public:
    Example()
    {
          ptr=new int;
    }
    void setdata(int a,int b,int c)
    {
          num1=a;
          num2=b;
          *ptr=c;
    }
    void printdata()
    {
          std::cout << "Num1 value is : " <<num1<< std::endl;
          std::cout << "Num2 value is : " <<num2<< std::endl;
          std::cout << "*ptr value is : " <<*ptr<< std::endl;
    }
};
int main()
{
   Example e1;
   e1.setdata (8, 9, 12);
   Example e2 = e1;
   e2.printdata();
     return 0;
}
```

// output

```
Num1 value is: 8
Num2 value is: 9
*ptr value is: 12
```

In the above example, the constructor is not defined, therefore the compiler assigns example **e2= e1** by calling the default copy constructor. In this case, the compiler creates a similar copy of the existing object. The pointer **ptr** points to the same memory location on both objects.

If the memory of one of the objects is freed, the other memory is automatically freed since both fields point to the same memory. To avoid this problem, you can define the copy constructor (user-defined constructor) that uses deep copy technique.

Deep copy

Deep copy is a technique where memory is dynamically allocated to a copy and then it copies the actual values. The source and the copy have distinct characteristics and won't share the same memory location.

In deep copy, the programmer has to write a user-defined constructor.

Syntax

```
class Example
{
Public:
int num1;
int num2;
int *ptr;
Example()
{
ptr=new int;
}
Example (Example &y)
{
num1=y.num1;
num2=y.num2;
ptr=new int;
*ptr=*(y.ptr);
}
void setdata(int a,int b,int c)
{
num1=a;
num2=b;
*ptr=c;
}
void printdata()
{
std::cout << "Num1 value is : " <<num1<< std::endl;
std::cout << "Num2 value is : " <<num2<< std::endl;
std::cout << "*ptr value is : " <<*ptr<< std::endl;
}
};
int main()
{
Example e1;
e1.setdata (5, 7, 9);
Example e2 = e1;
e2.printdata();
return 0;
```

```
}
```

// output

```
Num1 value is: 5
Num2 value is: 7
*ptr value is: 9
```

Since the programmer defined the constructor, then **e2=e1** calls for an already user-defined copy constructor. This result to an exact copy of the object which is pointed by ***ptr** and all the values on the type data members.

Class Destructor

A destructor has a special member function which executes when the delete operation is invoked in the object of that class or when an object in the class gets out of scope.

A destructor will have the same name as the class with a prefix of the tilde operator. It has no return values, and you can't pass any parameters to it. Destructor is an important C++ feature which frees memory space when it's no longer needed.

Example: The following example explains how to use constructors and destructors in a program.

Syntax

```
// constructor & destructor
Class CRectangle
{
int *len, *wid;
public:
   CRectangle (int, int)// constructor
   ~CRectangle ()//destructor
   int area()
   {
        return (len*wid);
   }
};
CRectangle:: CRectangle (int c, int d)
{
   *len=c;
   *wid=d;
};
//destructor to free the memory
CRectangle :: CRectangle ()
{
   delete len;
   delete wid;
};
 int main()
 {
   CRectangle.rect a (c,d);
   CRectangle.rect b (c,d);
   cout << Area of a rectangle is: <<rect a.area();
```

```
    cout << Area of a rectangle is: <<rect b.area();
    cout << endl;

}
```

Special Characteristics of Destructors

1. When an object is destroyed, a constructor is called automatic.
2. Just like other member functions, destructors follow the same access rules.
3. A destructor de-initializes an object before it gets out of scope.
4. Destructors don't have a return type and do not even support void.
5. Destructor functions can never be inherited.
6. A destructor doesn't allow the use of static destructors.
7. A destructor can make calls to member functions of it's class.
8. If an object in a class has a destructor, then that object can't be a member of the union.

Chapter Summary

In this chapter, you have learned about constructor, destructor and functions overload. Constructors are very essential in C++ language since they help build values in objects through automatic initialization. Specifically, you learned:

- How to declare and initialize constructors.
- How a constructor initializes an object of the class type.
- How a destructor de-initializes the object after execution. A destructor helps free the memory space by de-initializing the object after it has been destroyed.
- About parameterized constructors with parameters. You will be able to pass different parameters and values to the data members on different objects. You also learned how to make calls to the constructor.
- How to use the overloaded constructor and copy constructor.
- To understand the two types of copy constructors: shallow and deep.
- How to create a project with both types of copy constructors and how to make calls to the objects created.

In the next chapter you will learn how to use templates. At the end of the chapter you will be able to create class templates, function temples and how to create templates with multiple parameters.

CHAPTER SEVEN

Templates

Introduction to Templates

Templates are an important feature in C++ programming language, as it allows functions and classes to use generic types. They play an essential role on how functions and classes work by allowing them to define different data types without rewriting each other.

Using templates, you can write a generic code that can be used with any data type. All you need is to pass the data types as parameters. Templates promote code reusability and improve the flexibility of the program. You can create a simple class or a function and pass data types as parameters and implement the code to be used by any data type. Whenever you want to use the function, you make a call to the function and specify the return type.

For example, if you use **sort()** function to sort data in a warehouse, you can pass different data types as parameters to the function. You don't have to write and maintain multiple file codes to sort data. Based on the data type passed to the sorting algorithm, your data in the warehouse is sorted irrespective of that particular data type. Therefore, templates are used in situations where you need a code to be reusable with more than one data type.

Templates are of great importance when dealing with multiple inheritance and operator overloading. It is widely applied where code reusability is of prime importance.

Types of Templates

Templates are implemented in two ways:

- Using function templates
- Using class templates

A template can be defined as a macro. That is, when you define an object of a specific type, the template definition of that type of class substitutes it with the appropriate data type. Templates are often referred to as parameterized class or functions since a specified data type will replace the defined parameter during execution time.

Class Templates

Class templates offer the specifications for creating a class based on the parameters. A class template accepts members with parameter type. That is, you can instantiate a class template by passing a given set of data type to its parameter list. Class templates are mostly used in implementing containers.

Syntax

```
Template <class identifier>
Class class-name
{
...
//class member specifications
...
};
```

Example:

```
Template <class M>
Class vector
{
  M*v; //type M vector
  int size, sum;

  public:
   vector(int n )
   {
     v=new M [size = n];
     for(int j=0; j<size; j++) v[j] =0;
   }

  vector (M* a)
   {
     for(int j=0;j<size; j++)
     v[j]=a[j];
   }

   M operator*( vector &y)
    {
      M sum =0;
      for(int j=0;j<size;j++)
      sum+= -> v[j]*y-v[j];
      return sum;
    }
};
```

A class template definition is similar to normal class definition except that in templates, you add a prefix template **<class M>** where, M is the type. The template prefix tells the compiler that a class template is declared which uses M as the type name in the declaration. In this case, the class vector is a parameterized class that uses type M as its arguments. Type M can be replaced by any data type or by using a user-defined data type.

If a class is derived from a class template, then it's called a **template class**. The objects of the template class are defined as follows:

```
Classname<type> objectname (arglist);
```

Creating a derived class from class template is known as **instantiation process.** Before creating a template class, you have to debug the class template before converting it to a template class. The compiler checks for errors in a template class after instantiation has taken place.

Example: class template

```
template <Class TT>
Class Rectangle
{
    TT width;
    TT height;
public:
    void setvalues(TT num1,TT num2)
    TT area()
    {
        TT A;
        A=width*height;
        return A;
    }
};
void Rectangle <TT> ::setvalues (TT num1,TT num2)
  {
    width=num1;
    height=num2;
  }
int main()
{
    Rectangle obj1;
    Rectangle <int> obj1(5,6);
    Rectangle obj2;
    Rectangle <float> obj2(5.6,4);
    cout<< obj1.setvalues()
    cout<<obj2.setvalues()
    return 0;

}
```

//output

```
obj1=30
obj2=22.4
```

The above program creates a class of type TT. The <TT> in the (void Rectangle <TT> ::setvalues (TT num1,TT num2)) statement specifies that the function parameter is also a class template parameter and should always be included when calling a class.

Class Templates with Multiple Parameters

You can also have more than one generic data type in a class. You can declare the generic type class with a comma-separated list inside the template specification.

Syntax

```
Template <Class xy, Class xyz, …>
Class class-name
{
    //function body;
 };
```

Example: class with two generic types

```
template<class f1,class f2>
class numbers
{
    f1 j; f2 k;
public:
    numbers (f1 x, f2 y)
    { j=x; k=y;
    }
    void print()
     {
        cout<<j<<"and"<<k<<"\n";
     }
};
int main()
{
Numbers <float, int> numbers1 (2.53, 253);
Numbers <int, char> numbers2 (50,'Z');
numbers1.print();
numbers2.print();
return 0;
};
```

// output

```
1.53  and 253
50 and Z
```

Function Templates

Function templates work like a normal function except that the normal function works with only a single data type, while templates accommodate multiple data types. With templates, you can overload a normal function so as to work with different data types.

This makes function templates more useful since you only have to write a single program that works on all data types.

Templates are always expanded during compile time.

Just like class template, you can create a function template with different argument types.

Syntax

```
Template <class type>
Return-type function-name (arguments)
{
Function body;
};
```

When defining function templates, you must include the template type in both the function body and parameter list when necessary.

Example1: Function to swap values

```
Template <Class T1>
Void swap (T1&num1, T1&num2)
{T1 val= num1; num1=num2; num2=val;};
```

Calling a template function works the same way as the normal function call.

Example 2: Implementation of function template

```
template <class test>
test max (test x, test y);
{
    test results;
    results=x>y? x:y;
    return results;
};
int main()
{
    int a=5, b=6, c;
    double l=4, m=6, n;
    c= max <int> (a,b);
    n=max <double> (l,m);
    cout<< c<<endl;
    cout<<n<<endl;
    return 0;
}
```

In this example, test is the template parameter. The function max is called twice with different argument types (int and double). When the compiler instantiates, it calls the function each time by its type.

The output object produced (after instantiation of the template with specific type) will be of the same type with the parameters x and y.

The above program will sort values based on which is higher. If using an array of numbers, the sorting algorithm will be applied to sort the numbers from the smallest to highest.

Function Template with Multiple Parameters

Just like in class templates, you can have more than one generic data type separated by commas.

```
template<class T1 , class T2, …..>
returntype functionname(arguments of types T1, T2, …)
{
……
……
……
}
```

Example: Temple class with multiple parameters

```
template<class Temp1,class Temp2>
void display( Temp1 j, Temp2 k)
{
cout<<j<<" "<<k<<"\n";
}
int main()
{
j=display1(2019, "EDGE");
K=display2(18.54, "1854);
 return 0;
}
```

// output

```
2019      EDGE
18.54     1854
```

Overloading Template Functions

You can overload a template function using its template function or using the ordinary function from its name. Overloading can be done through:

1. Calling an ordinary function that matches the template function.
2. Calling a template function which is built with the exact function.
3. Use normal overloading function on an ordinary function and make a function call to the one that matches the template function.

If there is no match found, an error message is generated by the system.

Example: Overloaded template using an explicit function

```
template <class M>
 void display(M n)
{
cout<<"Display template function:" << n<< "\n";
}
void display ( int n)
{
cout<<"Explicit template display: "<< n<<"\n";
}
int main()
```

```
{
  display (80);   display (15.20);
  return 0;
}
```

//output

```
Explicit template display: 80 Display template function: 15.20
```

The function call **display (80)** calls the ordinary version of a **display ()** function and not its template version.

Member Function Templates

When creating class templates, all member functions can be defined outside the class since the member functions in a template class are parameterized using type argument. Therefore, the function template should define the member functions.

Member functions (whether inline or non-inline) declared inside a class template are implicitly a function template. If a template class is declared, it inherits all the template functions defined in a class template.

Member function templates are defined in three ways:

1. Explicit definition in a file scope for each return-type used to instantiate a template class.
2. During file scope within the template parameters.
3. Inclined within the class.

A member function template can instantiate functions not explicitly generated. If a class has both a member function and an explicit function, then the explicit definition is given more priority.

Syntax

```
Template <class T>
returntype classname <T> :: functionname(arglist)
{
……
……..
…….
}
```

Example: Class vector with member function template

```
template<class T>
class vector
{ T*v;
int size; public: vector(int m); vector(T* a);
T operator*(vector & y);
};
//member function templates template<class T>
vector<T> :: vector (int m );
{
v=new T[size=m]; for(int i=0; i<size ; i++) v[i]= 0;
}

template<class T>
vector <T>::vector(t*a)
{
for(int i=0; i<size ; i++)
v[i]=a[i];
}
template< class T >
T vector < T > :: operator*(vector & y)
{
T sum =0;
for ( int i=0; i< size ; i++)
sum += this -> v[i]*y.v[i];
return sum;
}
```

Non-type Template Arguments

Templates can have single or multiple type arguments. You can also use a non-type argument template in addition to the type T argument. You can create a template argument using strings, constants, built-in types and function names.

```
Template<class T, int size> Class array
{
T a[size];                    //automatic array initialization
//...........
//..........
};
```

The above template passes the size of an array as an argument. The compiler will only know the size of the array during the execution time. The arguments are specified during the creation of template class.

Chapter Summary

C++ programming language supports the use of templates concept in order to support generic programming. In this chapter, we are able to learn how templates allow us to create a family of classes or functions which can handle different data types. Other functions of templates you have learned include:

- Use of templates to avoid duplication of codes by just making a call to the template function argument return-type. This also makes it easy to manage the program as well as make the program development process easier.
- Creating templates by use of multiple parameters for both class templates and function templates.

- How to create a derived class from a class template which is called a template class. The process used in the creation of the template class is known as instantiation.
- Template functions and how you can overload the template function by either calling the ordinary function that matches the template name or by calling the template function which has an exact match to the function template.
- How to use arguments in class templates. All member functions of the class should be defined as a function template by using the arguments in a class template.
- How to instantiate member functions which are explicitly generated.
- How to use non-type arguments to define and declare function templates.

In the next chapter you will learn about the input and output streams and various file operation methods. At the end of the chapter, you will be able to use ios formatting functions, manage output with manipulators, design your own manipulators, carry out file operations, determine end of file, file opening modes, use put (), get () functions and using file stream classes.

CHAPTER EIGHT

C++ Input and Output Streams

Introduction

C++ programming language comes with a lot of libraries which helps in performing input output functions. The input output concept is performed through a series of bytes which are commonly known as streams. It supports two types of input/output streams with one stream inherited from the C programming language and the other from the object oriented input/output system. Just like the I/O streams in the C programming language, the I/O system in C++ language are fully integrated.

Every developed program takes in data as input, the data is processed then displayed out as an output. This is based on the input output processing cycle or fetch and execute cycle. C++ supports all the I/O function found in C language. The I/O methods in C++ supports object oriented programming concept and user defined data types.

Implementation of I/O operations in C++ is by use of streams concept and stream classes are achieved through the console and disk files.

Both input stream and output streams are used in class definition.

C++ Streams

A stream acts as a logical device which accepts input data and generates information. It is linked to a physical device via the I/O system. Even though the devices connected to the streams work the same, the devices may differ from one another.

Since streams behave in the same manner, their I/O functions can operate in any device. For example, you can use the same function to write to a file, printer, scanner, and display unit.

The stream is both the source and the destination. The source stream supplies data to the program and is commonly known as the **input stream.** On the other hand, a destination stream receives information as output and it is called an **output stream.**

Input stream: This involves flow of bytes from an input device like keyword into the main memory for processing.

Output stream: This is the flow of bytes or processed data from the main memory into an output device like the display screen.

C++ has both **cin** and **cout** as the predefined streams in its standard library. These streams are automatically triggered when a program begins to execute. **Cin** stream is an input stream that is connected to the standard input device and allows the user to enter new data into the system memory, while the **cout** represents the output stream which is connected to an output device to display information.

C++ Stream Classes

I/O system in C++ consists of a hierarchy of classes which define streams for handling the system console unit and disk files. Stream class hierarchy performs both input and output operations within the console unit. The I/O stream classes are declared in the header file of iostream. The header file should be inserted in every program that communicates with the console.

The ios acts as the base class for input stream (**istream**) and **ostream** (output stream) acts as the base class for **iostream** (input/output stream). The **ios class** is declared as a virtual base class and as a result, only a single copy of its data members will be inherited by the **iostream** (input/output stream.)

The ios class offers basic support for I/O operations on both formatted and unformatted streams. It supports handling of both input and output stream. The istream class is responsible for formatted and unformatted input while the ostream class is responsible for formatted output through inheritance concept.

Console Operation Using Stream Classes

Class Name	Properties
ios (basic input/output stream)	Has basic properties that can be used by other input and output classes. Has pointers for buffering objects. Declare functions and constants essential for performing formatted input and output operations.
istrcam (input strcam)	It inherits ios properties. Used to declare get (), getline(), and read () input functions. Consists of overloaded extraction operator >>
ostream (output stream)	It inherits ios properties. Allows you to declare output functions like put() and write().

	Uses overloaded insertion operator <<
iostream (input/output stream)	Inherits all characteristics of ios stream and ostream through the use of multiple inheritance. It has both input and output functions of both classes.
streambuf	Provides interface to all physical devices via the buffer. It works as the base class of filebuf available in ios files.

Unformatted Input/Output Operations

Overloaded Operators >> and <<

C++ **cin** and **cout** standard library functions for input and output uses overloaded operators >> and << respectively. The >> operator is overloaded in the istream class while << operator is overloaded in the ostream class.

To read input data from the keyword, you use the >> operator.

```
cin>> variable 1….>>variable n;
```

The input variable 1 up to variable n is a variable name which has already been declared inside the class. The cin standard tells the computer to search for the input data from the input devices like keyboard.

The data is read character by character and assigned to the indicated location by the >> operator. Data inputs are separated by white spaces and if the compiler encounters the white spaces when reading a variable or encounters a character that doesn't match the destination data type, it terminates.

Suppose you have a class with a variable declared as an integer, you can use the input data device to input the data.

```
int num;
cin>> num;
```

The **cin** statement followed by >> operator will prompt you to enter any value of integer type from the keyboard like 520. When you enter the input data, the operator reads the value 520 assigned to the num variable.

To display the data on the screen, you use the **cout** statement.

```
cout<< data1<< data 2…. <<data n;
```

The data1 all the way to data n can be a variable or a constant of any data type.

Put () and Get () Functions

The istream and ostream classes defines two types of member functions **get()**, and **put()** to handle input/ output operations of a single character.

The **get()** functions is represented into two forms of function prototype. That is, the **get(char*)** and the **get(void)**. These function prototypes fetch a new character, a blank space, newline and even a tab in the input data. The **get(char*)** prototype assigns input character to the function arguments while **get(void)** only returns the input character.

The function prototypes represent member functions of input/output stream and they should be invoked using an appropriate object.

Example:

```
Char i;
cin.get(i) // this allows you to get a character from the keyboard and
assign to variable i.
{
Cout<<i  // display the variable on the screen
}
```

The above code reads and displays a line of text statements. The >> operator in the cout statement reads a character by character and skips any white spaces or new line character in the statement.

```
cin>>i; can be used instead of cin.get(i)
```

Where,

```
i=cin.get();
```

In this, the value of the member function **get()** is assigned to the variable i.

Put() is a member function of ostream class and it outputs a single line of statements or a character by character. For example:

```
cout.put(i);
```

This code displays a single character **i** while **cout.put(ch)** displays the value to the **ch** variable. You pass any number variable as argument to the **put()** member function.

Example:

```
char x; cin.get (x); while(x!=\n)
 {
     cout.put(x);
     cin.get(x);
 }
```

A program using get() and put () to represent I/O data.

```
# include<iostream>
using namespace std;

int main()
  {
          int m=0;
          char n;
```

```
        cout<<"enter input text"
        cin.get(n);

        while (n1=\n)
        {
                cout.put(n);
                m++;cin.get(n);
        }

        cout<<\n Number of characters="<m<< "\n";
        return 0;
}
```

Input

```
C++ programming language.
```

Output

```
C++ programming language.
Number of characters = 22
```

Getline() and Write() Function

The **getline()** and **write()** functions are responsible for reading or displaying a line of text in an effective manner. The **getline()** reads a whole line of text which has a new line character "**\n**". When the compiler encounters the new line character, the program is executed. A call to the function is made through:

```
cin.getline (line, size);
```

The function call invokes getline() function which reads the characters entered to the system via the keyboard. Once the **size-1** or **\n** character is encountered, the reading is terminated.

Example:

```
char EmpName [30];
cin.getline(EmpName, 30);
```

Example:

```
#include <iostream>
using namespace std;
int main()
 {
        int size=30;
        char country[30];
        cout<<"enter the name of the country:\n ";
        cin>>country;
        cout<<"country name is:"<<country<<"\n\n"; cout<<"enter
another country name again: \n";
        cin.getline(country,size);
        cout<<"The current country name is:"<<country<<"\n\n";
```

```
        return 0;
}
```

//output

```
enter the name of the country: Kenya
enter another country name again: Uganda
the current country name is: Uganda
```

The write() function display the whole line and uses the following form:

```
cout.write(line, size)
```

The line argument indicates the string's name displayed and the size argument shows the number of characters. If the variable size is greater than the program line, then beyond the bound of the line is displayed.

Formatted Console I/O Operations

There are various features supported by C++ to help format the output. These features include:

- ios class function and flags.
- User-defined output functions.
- Manipulators.

ios Format Functions

The ios class has a large number of functions for formatting the output in a number of ways. These member functions include:

Member Function	Manipulators	Action
Width()	Setw()	This function indicates the required field size needed to display an output value.
fill()	Setfill()	It specifies the characters essential for filling unused portion of the field.
Precision()	Setprecision()	Indicates the number of digits which are to be displayed after the decimal point of float value.
Setf()	Setioflags()	It specifies the format flag used to control what form of output is to be displayed.

Unsetf()	Resetiosflags()	It clears any specified flag

When included in the I/O statements, these manipulators change the parameter format of a stream. To access manipulator functions in a program, you have to include **iomanip** file.

Defining Field Width

The **width()** function determines the width field needed for the output of an object. You can invoke the function through:

```
cout.width(w);
```

Where,

w is the width field and it is printed in a field of w characters wide. The function specifies the field width for a single object. After printing the output details of the single object, it reverts back to default settings.

For example, cout.width(7);

```
cout<<6543<<12<<"\n"; // printing in the format of 6, 5, 4, 3 and 1, 2
```

This will produce the following output:

	6	5	4	3	1	2

Setting Precision (Precision ())

When working with floating point numbers, they're printed six digits after the decimal point. To avoid printing all these six digits, you can specify the number of digits to be printed after the decimal point. This can easily be achieved by the use of **precision ()** member function.

```
cout.precision (d);
```

Where,

d is the number of digits after the decimal point are to be printed. The function retains its setting until they're reset, unlike the width ().

Example:

```
cout.precision (3)
```

Filling and Padding

The unused part of field width is always filled up with white spaces. The **fill()** function is used to fill these unused white spaces with any desired character.

```
cout.fill (ch);
```

Where,

ch is the character used in filling up the unused white spaces.

Example:

```
Count.fill ('*')
```

In this case, the white spaces will be filled with '*' operator. For example, some institutions like banks use this form of filling blank spaces, especially when printing a cheque.

Formatting Flags, Bit fields and Setf()

The **setf ()** is ios class member function for justifying answers.

```
cout.setf (arg1, arg2)
```

Where,

arg 1 is the already formatting flag in ios class. The flag indicates the formatting requirements of an output. Arg2 is an ios constant which specifies the formatting group to which the formatting flag belongs to.

Example:

```
cout.setf (ios::left, ios::adjustfield);
cout.setf (ios::scientific, ios::floatfield);
```

The first statement in the above example should have a group member to the second statement.

Example:

```
cout.fill (*);
cout.setf (ios::left, ios::adjustified);
cout.width (8);
cout<<"flag"<<"\n";
```

// output

F	L	A	G		*	*	*

Using Manipulator to Manage Output

The **iomanip** header file has a set of manipulator functions which manipulates the output format. These manipulators work the same way as ios member functions and flags. You can use more than one manipulator in a single statement.

Example:

```
Cout<<manip a<< manip b<< manip c<<item;
Cout<<manip a <<item1 <<manip b <<item2;
```

The above concatenation is great when you want to display data in column forms.

There are different types of manipulators you can use to alter fields. These manipulators include:

Manipulator	Set of Actions Performed	Alternative Member Function
Setw (int w)	Function for setting field with to w	Width()
Setprecision (int d)	Essential for setting the floating point numbers precision to d	Precision()
Setfill (int c)	Used to set the fill element with character c	Fill()
Setiosflags (long f)	Used for setting the format flag	Setf()
Resetiosflags (long f)	Used to clear any format flag specified by f	Unserf()
	Helps you insert a new line or to flush a stream.	"\n"

Example:

```
cout<<setw(8)<< 1234;
```

The above statement will print values 1, 2, 3,4 in a right justified field of 8 characters. The output of this statement can be altered to be left-justified. You can do this in the following way:

```
Cout<<setw (8) <<setiosflags (ios::left) <<1234;
```

File Operations

The I/O system handles file operations similar to the I/O operations. In this case, file streams are used as an interface between the specific files and the programs. Files have both input and output streams.

An input stream is a stream in which data is supplied to the program while an output stream is a stream that receives data from the program. The input stream extracts data from the file while the output stream enters data into the file. Any input operation used on the data acts as a link between the program and the input file. Similarly, output file operations consists of an output stream that links the program with the output file.

File Stream Classes

The input/output system in C++ programming language provides a set of stream classes essential for handling file methods and operations. Some of these methods include the use of **ifstream**,

ofstream, and **fstream**.

File stream classes are derived from fstream base class which corresponds to the iostream class. The class for managing disk files should be declared in the fstream and the file should be included in every program that needs the use of the file.

Steps to File Operation

When using disk files you have to:

1. Select a suitable name for the file.
2. Define the data type and structure of the files.
3. Define the file purpose.
4. Define method for opening the files.

File Stream Classes

Class	**Class contents**
filebuf	This class sets the file buffers for read and write operation. The class has **Openprot** constant used in opening the file through the **open()** function. It also has both **open ()** and **close ()** member functions.
fstreambase	Fstreambase class offers various file operations common to the file streams. The fstreambase act as the base or super class for fstream, ifstream, and ofstream file operations. It also contains both **open()** and **close()** functions.
ifstream	It is responsible for input operations and has **open ()** as the default input mode. Ifstream inherits **get(), getline(),read(), tellg()**,and **seekg()** functions from the istream I/O system.
ofstream	Ofstream is responsible for output operation and it uses the **open()** with the default output mode. The class inherits function properties like **put(),write(), seekp(),** and **tellp()** from the ostream.

fstream	It is responsible for offering support for simultaneous I/O operations. It uses **open()** with its default input mode. Fstream inherits properties from istream and ostream classes via the iostream.

A filename consists of a string of characters making it a valid file name. A filename is divided into two parts: the primary name and an extension. For example, **file.doc, test.txt,** and **input.cpp** among other extensions.

To open any file, you have to create a file stream first and then link it to the filename. The file stream is declared using the ifstream, ofstream and fstream classes which are included in the **fstream** header file.

The file class created depends on the purpose for creation. That is, whether to read data or write data into the file.

After creation of the file, you can open it using:

1. The constructor function in the class.
2. The member function **open()** in the class.

Opening a file using constructor function is only applied when one file is being used in the stream, while the **open()** function method is used when opening multiple files using a single stream.

Opening Files Using Constructor

If a constructor is used to open a file, the filename initializes the file stream object. This can be achieved through:

1. Creating a file stream object in order to manage the stream using an appropriate class. In this case, you can use ofstream class to create output stream while the ifstream class creates an input stream.
2. Using a desired filename so as to initialize the file object. For example, the following code is used to open a file named **performance** as an output:

ofstream outfile("performance"); // to display an output.

The outfile is created as an ofstream object whose main purpose is to manage the output stream.

You can also create an infile as an ifstream object and associate it with the file data for reading file inputs.

ifstream infile ("data"); // an input file

You can use the same file name to read or write data into a file.

When an object terminates, it automatically closes the connection to that file. In the above example on performance file, when the program is terminated, the performance file will be disconnected from the outfile stream. This also happens to the infile stream.

A filename consists of a string of characters making it a valid file name. A filename is divided into two parts: the primary name and an extension. For example, **file.doc, test.txt,** and **input.cpp** among other extensions.

To open any file, you have to create a file stream first and then link it to the filename. The file stream is declared using the ifstream, ofstream and fstream classes which are included in the **fstream** header file.

The file class created depends on the purpose for creation. That is, whether to read data or write data into the file.

After creation of the file, you can open it using:

1. The constructor function in the class.
2. The member function **open()** in the class.

Opening a file using constructor function is only applied when one file is being used in the stream while the **open()** function method is used when opening multiple file using a single stream.

Example: A program to write and read data from a file

```
#include <iostream.h>
#include <fstream.h>
int main()
{
char Prodname[20];
float price;
ofstream outfile("product");

cout <<"enter product's name:"
cin >>Prodname; outfile <<Prodname<<"\n";
cout <<"enter the product's price:";
cin >>price; outfile <<price <<"\n";
 outfile.close();

ifstream infile("product");
infile >>Prodname;
infile >>price;
cout <<"\n";
cout <<"Product name is : " << Prodname <<"\n";
cout <<"Product price: " << price <<"\n";
infile.close();
return 0;
}
```

// output

```
Product name is: Mango
Product price: 25
```

This program gets data via the input device like keyword and writes it to a file. After completion of the writing process, the file is closed. The file is then opened to read the information already written in the file and later displayed on the screen for the user to view.

Example 2: Writing to a file.

```
#include <iostream>
#include <fstream>
using namespace std;
int main () {
  ofstream samplefile;
  samplefile.open ("sample.doc");
  samplefile << "Writing data to the sample.doc file.\n";
  samplefile.close();
  return 0;
}
```

Opening Files Using Open() Function

The **open()** function opens multiple files that use the same object stream. If a set of files are to be processed sequentially, then a single object stream is created to enable opening of each file.

Syntax

```
Void open (const char* filename, ios:: openmode mode);
or
open (filename, mode);
```

The first argument indicates the name of the file and file format together with its address, while the second part of the argument indicates the access mode of the file.

There are different access modes for opening a file, and they include:

File Mode	**Description**
in	It is the default mode for ifstream files. It opens the file for reading purposes.
Out	This mode is responsible for writing into a file. It is the default mode for ofstream.
binary	It is used to open a file in a binary form or mode.
App	The app mode is suitable for opening the file and appends the file outputs at the end.
Ate	This mode is responsible for opening the file and transferring the control to the end of the file.

Trunc	It is used to delete data from an existing file.
Nocreate	It tests the existence of a file and opens it if it exists.
Noreplace	If a file doesn't exist, noreplace opens a new file.

Example:

```
Fstream example_file;
Example_file.open(example.txt", ios::out);
```

In order to access the member function of fstream class, you have to create that class. **Example_file** is an object of type fstream. Calling the open() function allows you to open the file and write data into it.

The default open mode for the files are:

- ifstream ios::in
- ofstream ios::out
- fstream ios::in | ios::out

The symbol | is used to combine different modes. For example:

```
Example_file.open(example.txt", ios::out  | ios::ate);
```

The input mode and control mode are combined to ensure the file is opened for writing then transfers the control to the end of the file.

When a program terminates, the allocated memory is freed up and all opened files are closed. Using the **close()** function ensures all the files are closed as soon as execution is complete.

With the stream insertion operator <<, you can write information into a file and use the stream extraction operator >> to read the information from the file.

Example: Opening a file using the open () and writing to the file

```
#include<iostream>
#include <fstream>
using namespace std;
int main()
{
fstream example_file;
example_file.open("example.doc", ios::out);
if(!example_file)
{
cout<<" File creation has failed";
}
else
```

```
{
cout<<"The new file was successfully created";
example_file<< “This is a new file created”; // writing to the file
example_file.close(); // close the file to free memory
}
return 0;
}
```

//output

```
C:\users\Faith\Documents>notepad++ example.cpp -o example.exe
C:\users\Faith\Documents\example.doc
The new file was successfully created
C:\users\Faith\Documents>
```

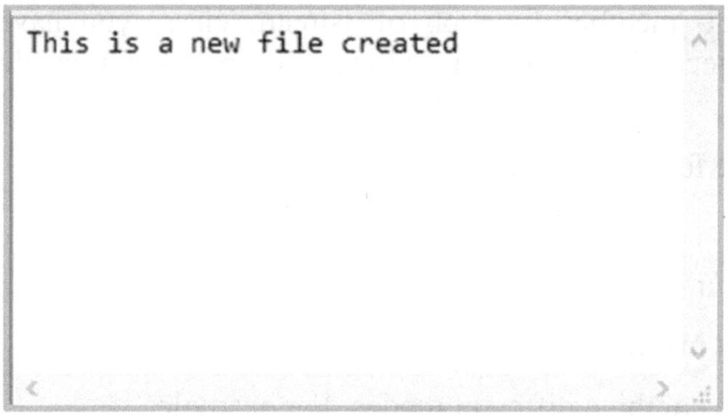
This is a new file created

In the above program, we have created an object example_file to be used in the fstream class. Then we open the object using the open() function and create a new file named example where to write data into. The file is assigned to out mode which allows writing into the file. If statement test whether the file exists or not if the file is unavailable “file creation has failed” statement is displayed, otherwise “The new file was successfully created” message will be displayed on the screen.

Example 2: Reading information from file

```
#include<iostream>
#include <fstream>
using namespace std;
int main()
{
fstream example_file;
example_file.open("example.doc", ios::in);
if(!example_file)
{
cout<<" The file doesn’t exist";
}
else
{
Char ch;
While (!example.eof())
{example-file>>ch;
cout<<ch;}
example_file.close(); // close the file to free memory
```

```
}
return 0;
}
```

The above program reads the example.doc file we had already created in the previous example. To read a file, the '**in**' mode is used (ios::in). The extraction operator >> is used to print the file content of the file.

Finding End of File

When reading a file, it's important to determine the end of file, otherwise the program will be in an infinite loop if it doesn't detect the end of file. The programmer should provide appropriate instructions to the program so as to be able to detect the end of file.

When the end of file is determined, the reading data process can easily be terminated after all the data has been read. If the end-of-file is determined, the **fin** ifstream object will return a zero value if an error occurs in the file operation.

When the **fin** returns 0 after reaching the end-of-the-file, the while loop will terminate. You can also detect the end of file using the eof() function.

```
 if(example.eof()!=0)
  {exit file}
```

If the end-of-file is detected, a non-zero value is returned, otherwise if the end-of-file is not detected, a 0 value is returned. The program will automatically terminate after reaching the end-of-file.

File Pointers and Manipulators

Each C++ file has two pointers: input pointer and output pointer. The input pointer reads the content of a particular file location while the output pointer writes data to a given file location. Whenever an input or output file operation takes place, an appropriate pointer is updated automatically.

Default File Actions

When you open a file in a read-only mode, the input pointer is set at the start of the file so as to enable reading from the start of that file. If the file is opened in a write-only mode, all the file content is deleted and the output pointer is placed at the start of the file. This ensures that you write the file from the beginning point.

To add more data to an existing file, the file should be opened in an 'append' mode. This automatically moves the pointer to the end of the file.

Functions and Manipulations of File Pointer

All the actions and file operations using pointers take place by default. In order to control file pointer movement operations, there are various file stream classes you can use. Some of these file stream class member functions include:

- **seekg()** This function moves the (input) get pointer to a specific location.
- **Seekp()** The function moves the (output) put pointer to a specific location.
- **Tellg()** This function indicates the get pointer current position.
- **Tellp()** It indicates the put pointer current position.

Example:

```
infile.seekg(5);
```

This function will move the pointer to a number byte labelled 5 since the file bytes are numbered from 0. The pointer then points to the 6th byte which is the current location of the file.

Example 2:

```
ofstream myfile;
myfile.open("Welcome", ios::app);
int ppt=myfile.tellp();
```

When the above statements are executed, the output pointer moves up to the end of file "welcome" and the ppt value indicates the number of bytes in the file.

Specifying Offset Functions

The seek functions **(seekg()** and **seekp())** take two arguments:

- **Seekg** (offset, refposition)
- **Seekp** (offset,refposition)

The offset argument indicates the number of bytes to move the file pointer from the specified location by the refposition argument.

The refposition takes the form of:

- **ios::beg** this indicates the start of file.
- **ios::cur** indicates the current position of the pointer.
- **ios::end** this indicates the end of a file.

The **seekg()** function moves all the associated files with the get pointer. The **seekp()** moves the file and its associated files using the put pointer.

Pointer offset calls

Seek call	Action
fout.seekg(o,ios::beg)	Go to start
fout.seekg(o,ios::cur)	Stay at the current position
fout.seekg(o,ios::end)	Go to the end of file
fout.seekg(m,ios::beg)	Move to (m+1)th byte in the file
fout.seekg(m,ios::cur)	Go forward by m byte from current position
fout.seekg(-m,ios::cur)	Go backward by m bytes from current position.
fout.seekg(-m,ios::end)	Go backward by m bytes from the end

Sequential Input and Output Operations

There are a number of member functions for performing input and output file operations supported by file stream classes. The member functions **put()** and **get()** handle single character operations at a time. The **write()** and **read()** functions write into and read to a block of binary data.

Put() and get() functions

You can write a single character into an associated stream using the **put()** function. The **get ()** function reads a single character from the associated stream. Let's write a program to illustrate how the functions works on a program.

```
#include <iostream.h>
#include <fstream.h>
#include<string.h>
int main()
{
char string[80]; cout<<"enter a string \n"; cin>>string;
int len =strlen(string);
fstream file;
file.open("TEXT". ios::in | ios::out); for (int i=o;i<len;i++) file.put(string[i]);
file .seekg(0); char ch; while(file)
{
file.get(ch);
cout<<ch;
}
return 0;
}
```

The above program requests for a string and once it receives the string, it writes on the file a character by character using the put () function with for loop. When the string length ends, the for loop is terminated.

After the execution, the program is displayed on the screen using the get() function. The get() function fetches a character by character data from the file until it reaches the end of file condition. The data read from the file is displayed on the screen for users to view using the << operator.

Write() and Read() Functions

The write () and read() function can handle binary forms of data. The data values are stored in the disk file using the same format used when they're being stored in an internal memory. For example, and int character can store 2 bytes of its data value into a binary form regardless of its size, while a 4 digit integer value can store 4 bytes in character form.

Binary input and output takes the form of:

```
infile.read (( char * ) & Var, sizeof (Var));

outfile.write (( char *) & Var, sizeof (Var));
```

The function receives two arguments: the address of the variable Var, and the length of the variable in the form of bytes. The address of the variable is represented with type char* (a pointer to a character data type).

Example:

```
#include <iostream.h>
#include <fstream.h>
#include <iomanip.h>
const char * filename ="Binary";
int main()
{

float weight[4] ={ 175.5,153.0,167.25,160.70};
ofstream outfile;
outfile.open(myfile);
outfile.write((char *) & weight, sizeof(weight));
outfile.close();
for (int j=0;j<4;j++)
weight[j]=0; ifstream infile; infile.open(myfile);
infile.read ((char *) & weight, sizeof (weight));
for (j=0;j<4;j++)
{
cout.setf(ios::showpoint);
cout<<setw(10)<<setprecision(2)<<weight[j];
} infile.close(); return 0;
}
```

Error Handling During File Operation

When carrying out various file operations, there are various errors encountered. Some of these problems encountered include:

- Non-existence of the file you are trying to access.
- The file name being used to create a new file already exists.
- Attempting an invalid file operation like trying to read data past the end of file condition.
- Not enough memory in the disk drive to store more data.
- Dealing with an invalid file name.

These are some of the common file operation problems you may face when handling and manipulating files. File operation stream in C++ language inherits the '**stream-state**' member from the ios class.

The stream-state member keeps information on the status of the current opened file. The ios class support a number of member functions for reading the file status recorded on the stream.

Error handling functions

Function	Meaning and its Return Value
Eof()	Eof() returns a true value or a non-zero value if the end of file is successfully detected while reading the file, otherwise, it will return a zero value.
Fail()	This functions returns true after the failure of both input and output operations.
Bad()	If an attempt of an invalid operation is encountered or unrecoverable error, it returns true. If the error can be recovered and file operation continues, then it returns false value
Good()	If no error has been encountered, it will return true. If the file.good() function returns true, then you can continue with other I/O operations. If it returns false, there are no further operations are carried out.

Chapter Summary

Input/output streams are an important feature in C++ programming language. The streams help in class definition and provide a set of library functions that perform a series of functions. In this chapter, you learned about the C++ streams concept and how to use input and output stream to execute programs. You also learned the various devices you can use when working with various stream input and outputs. C++ stream classes will enable you to:

- Define a hierarchy of classes that defines the use of streams console unit and the disk files.
- Learn how to declare the I/O stream classes in the header file as well as learn the various console operations using the stream classes.
- Learn different types of class names and their properties and functionalities.
- Learn how ios class provide basic support for I/O operations on both unformatted i/o operation and formatted i/o operations.
- Use the overloaded operators (>>&<<) used for data inputs and outputs. The **cin** standard library functions use the overloaded operators >> to read data from an input device. While **cout** standard library function operator << is used to display data on the screen or output device.
- Use unformatted I/O operations like **put()** and **get()** functions. The **put()** function is a member of ostream class which is used to output data character by character, while the **get()** function works as input stream.
- Learn how to use getline () and write() functions.
- Learn various formatted console I/O operations supported by C++ language to format the output.
- Use ios class functions and flags to format data inputs.
- How to use user-defined output functions or the use of output manipulators and other formatting features of ios class functions to format the output.
- Learn how to use user-defined functions to format output.
- Learn how to manage output with manipulators.
- Perform various file operations and know how to handle stream classes.
- Know how to open files using constructors and using **open ()** function, create new files and how to write into a file.
- Use C++ to write a code on how to open a file, write a code of how to write into an existing file or creating a new file, as well as write a code of reading information from a file.
- Use the close () member function which is added in every file code to close the file.
- Learn how to control input output streams through the use of classes. Both istream and ostream control the input and output functions.
- Using working examples, derive an iostream class from the istream and ostream classes. Other classes derived in I/O streams include: **istream_withassigh.ostream_withassign** and **iostream_withassign**. These classes are derived from the properties of istream, ostream, and iostream classes respectively.
- Use **eof ()** function to test whether the end of file is reached and it returns value 1 if it's detected. You're able to write a code that determines the end-of-file, how to use the close() function to terminate a program, and use of pointers to manipulate files.

- Use **seekg()** function links to the associated file pointer (both input and output file pointer).
- Write codes using the put() and get() functions which reads and writes a single character in a file while the write() and read() are used for writing and reading a block of binary data.
- Know how to how to handle errors during file operations.

In the next chapter you will learn about exception handling. By the end of the chapter, you will understand the concept and principles of exception handling, mechanisms of exception handling, and the use of throw and catch exceptions mechanisms.

CHAPTER NINE:

Exception Handling

Introduction

Exception handling provides you with a way to create and deal with the errors that occur during the program development process, such as run time errors. This is achieved by transferring the control of the program to a special function called **handlers.**

During the program development process, there are cases where the programmer is uncertain whether a piece of code will run successfully or not due to run time errors like limited resource allocation or out of range errors.

To solve this problem, you have to place the piece of code under the exception inspection. This is achieved by enclosing the piece of code in a try block. When an exceptional circumstance arises within that block of code, then an exception is thrown that transfers the control to the exception handler.

If there are no exception detected or thrown, then the program code continues to execute normally and the handlers created are ignored.

When the program code encounters an exceptional condition, it's important to identify the exception and deal with it effectively. An exception is that part of an object that occurs whenever an error is encountered on that part of the program.

Principles of Exception Handling

Exception handling is a mechanism for detecting and reporting exceptional circumstances in a program to ensure an appropriate action is implemented. Exception handling mechanism involves:

1. Detecting the exceptions (problem).
2. Throwing the exception (acknowledge the error has occurred).

3. Catching the exception (Receive detail information on the error).
4. Handling the exceptions (Taking corrective actions to solve the problem).

An exception handling mechanism should have two segments: one segment to detect the error and throw exceptions while the other segment will catch the exceptions and take up appropriate measures to handle the errors.

There are two types of exceptions; **Synchronous** and **asynchronous** exceptions. **Synchronous** exceptions are encountered during program run-time due to program anomalies, and they include out of range index error and overflow error. Occurrence of events beyond the program control results in **asynchronous** exceptions. An example of **asynchronous** exceptions is keyboard interrupts.

Exception Handling Mechanisms

Exception handling is built on three keyword operators:

1. Try.
2. Throw.
3. Catch.

The try keyword prefaces a block of statements in order to generate exceptions. The block of statements is known as the try block. Once an exception is detected it is thrown using the throw keyword inside the try block statements. Exception handlers are defined by the use of the catch keyword that catches an exception thrown using the throw statement in the try block. The catch block statements must appear immediately after the try block.

Syntax

```
Try
{
//block of statements to be tried
Throw exception
}
Catch (type arguments)
{
Code to be executed in case of exception
}
```

When an exception is thrown in the try block, the program control is transferred from the try block into the catch statement. If the thrown object type matches the arguments type in the catch block, then the catch statements to handle exceptions is executed.

If the object arguments don’t match, the program is aborted using abort () function. if no exception is detected or thrown, then the control is taken back immediately using the catch block.

Example:

```
#include <iostream.h>
using namespace std;
int main()
{
    try
    {
        throw 15;
    }
    catch(int a)
    {
        cout<< "An exception has occurred"; <<endl;
    }
    return 0;
}
```

If there is no exception thrown, the catch statements will not be executed.

Example:

```
# include <iostream>
using namespace std;
void divide (int x,int y,int z)
 {
   cout<<"we are outside the function";
   if ( ( x-y) != 0)
    {
     int r=z/(x-y);
     cout<<"result = "<<r;
    }
    else
     {
      throw(x-y);
     }
 }
int main()
{
try

cout<<"we are inside the try block";
divide(10,20,30);
divide(10,10,20);
}

catch (int i)
{
cout<<"caught the exception";
}
return 0;
}
```

// output

```
We are outside the try block We are inside the function Result =-3

We are inside the function

Caught the exception
```

Throw Mechanism

When an exception is detected, it is thrown using the following command:

```
throw (exception); throw exception; throw;
```

The exception object thrown may be of any form, even constants. Other objects not intended for error handling can also be thrown. If an exception is thrown, a catch statement will be able to catch it. The program control will be transferred from the try block into the catch block.

Catching Mechanisms

The exception handler will have a code in the catch block. The catch block is a function on its own and it's used to manage exceptions.

```
Catch(type  arg)
{   statements for managing exceptions
}
```

The type is used to indicate the type of exception handled by the catch block. The arguments are optional. The catch statement catches exceptions with type that matches the catch parameter. After the exception is caught, the block code inside the catch block is executed. When the handler is executed, the control is passed immediately. If the catch statements doesn't catch the exception then the catch block statements will be skipped.

Chapter Summary

Exceptions are various errors a program may encounter during its running time. C++ programming language has a built-in language function for trapping all program errors and control exceptions. The latest C++ compiler supports this feature making it easy for the user to debug a program.

- An exception acts as an object which is sent from the part of the program where an error has occurred to the part of the program where the error will be controlled.
- Exception method is done via the use of three keywords: try, throw and catch. The try keyword is for detecting an exception in the file and the exception statements known as try block is enclosed within curly braces.
- The catch block receives the exception sent by the throwing block inside the try block.
- You can create multiple catch blocks within a program or even pass the exception to another exception handler.
- Specified exceptions are great for binding functions to throw only condition for a specified exception.

FINAL WORDS

C++ programming language is a competitive general purpose program which borrows some features of imperative programming paradigm and can run on any platform. It is referred to as an imperative programming language because it uses step by step processes in order to achieve its goals. The program uses the concept of object oriented program to design and implement complex programs.

The program revolves around data which is created using objects. These objects communicate with each other by passing messages. The objects don't have to know the detail information of another object so as to exchange data between them. They only need to establish a connection between themselves and exchange information.

C++ programming language utilizes the features of OOP paradigms to develop and execute a program. Some of these features include: use of objects, classes, data abstractions and encapsulation, inheritance and polymorphism.

The program focuses on the use of data rather than procedures to solve real world problems. The program tries to eliminate the shortcomings of other conventional programming languages by improving the data security of programs, promoting code reusability and its ability to use inheritance feature to make an effective program.

Just like many other OOP languages, C++ supports various building blocks. In this tutorial, you have learned how to use various built-in data types when handling simple to complex programs. The data types are divided into primitive data types, derived data types, and abstract data types. You not only learned how to use the primitive or standard data types, but also how to declare your own user-defined datatypes.

You learned how to create arrays for storing values, and how you can access variables created using arrays. You also learned how to initialize arrays and how to work with different types of arrays.

Pointers play an important role in the allocation of memory space to the user programs. When declaring variables, a memory space is allocated for the variable. Each variable has a defined memory address for accessing the variable. Therefore, in this tutorial, you learned how to create programs that assign the memory address to the pointer variable. You also learned how to use dynamic free store operators like new and delete operator to allocate and deallocate memory space. The computer memory is a limited resource, therefore, you have to free the memory when a program no longer needs it and allocate that memory space to another program that needs it.

You also learned how to use library functions and user-defined functions in developing programs. The library functions are pre-defined or built-in C++ functions which perform a number of tasks. C++ also allow users to define their own functions and write a block of statements to be executed once the function is invoked. In this tutorial, you learned how to create your own function, function definition and declaration. You are also able to learn how to call functions and pass parameters to a function. You're able to know how to use function prototype, and use inline functions in a program.

Another important feature you learned about is how to organize different data elements and variables into a single unit using structures. You learned how to initialize a structure element, how to access the structure memory and how to use references.

In chapters two and three, you learned the basic concepts in OOP and how to work with classes and objects. You're now able to define a class and declare class members either private, public, or protected. Defining the class header files will allow you to reuse the code in various files. The class definition is put in a header file with the same name as the class. The member functions are stored outside the class and stored with the same name as the class.

You are now able to create class objects and define both private and public access specifiers, define data members and member functions, and use protected data members. C++ presents different types of class member functions which can be utilized to manipulate data. Learning how to use each of the data members will make it easy to modify data files and make calls to the member functions.

Classes can be created in two forms in C++ programming language: using a base class or using a derived class. The base class allows you to build other classes from it while a derived class inherits the properties and characteristics of the base class. You're now able to create a base class and derived class and extend the class functionality using overriding members.

In chapter 4, we discussed inheritance. That is, how to derive a new class from an existing class. In inheritance, a class borrows the members of other classes so as to avoid any repetitions. When inheriting members, the public members of the base class will remain public while the protected members will remain protected, while the private members will remain private in the derived class.

There are different types of inheritance users can define and these include: single inheritance, multiple inheritance, hierarchical inheritance, multi-level inheritance, and hybrid inheritance.

You are now able to create objects using constructors and destructors of derived objects. The constructors will help in initializing member variables while the destructor will destroy the object and free up memory space.

During a program execution, the compiler automatically calls for the constructor and destructor variables. Constructors and destructors can be used in the base class and also in the derived class. When the constructor is used in the derived class, the arguments will be passed to the base class.

Upcasting is another feature which utilizes the use of base class reference or a pointer to point directly to a subclass. In this chapter, you are able to learn how to use upcasting and downcasting features to create a base class.

C++ allows you to dynamically allocate memory space to programs. You can allocate the memory space to a program by initially defining the program variables before the program executes. In such a case, the memory is determined during run-time or based on the user inputs. Dynamically, allocation is achieved through the use of new and delete operators.

The new operator followed by the data type specifier automatically allocates memory space to the file. It allows you to allocate memory to an array of elements using the new[] operator. The delete operator deallocates the memory thus making the memory available for other programs When dealing with multiple elements the delete [] operator is used to deallocate memory space. If you create a memory and forget to delete it, it creates a memory leak. therefore, any memory created on the heap should be freed when no longer in use to avoid creating a memory leak.

Polymorphism is an OOP feature that enables you to have an object with more than one form. Creating multiple inheritance in a class results in polymorphism. Polymorphism is divided into two: run-time polymorphism and compile time polymorphism. Run-time polymorphism is achieved by use of overloading functions and virtual functions, while compile time polymorphism is achieved via overriding function and operator overloading. You now have practical knowledge about how to create virtual functions, overloading functions, and overriding functions. You also learned how to access the private member function in a derived class using virtual keyword and how to create abstract classes and pure virtual functions.

In chapter six, we discussed how constructors and destructors work, characteristics of constructors, how to define and declare a constructor class, and working with different types of constructors. We also discussed in class destructor and how to declare a class destructor.

Templates allows functions and classes to use generic type. This plays an important role on how functions and classes work by allowing users to define different data types without the need of rewriting the code. A template allows you to create a generic class which supports any data type. There are two main types of templates: function templates and class templates.

A class template works like a normal class with a prefix 'template' followed by the class identifier. Class templates accept members with any type of arguments. These templates are mostly used in implementing containers.

You can also create a derived class from the class template through a process known as instantiation. The derived class is known as template class. You can also pass multiple parameters to a class template. A multiple parameter class template supports more than one generic data type. The generic type classes are separated by commas.

Function templates accommodate multiple data types compared to the normal function which only accommodates a single data type. Templates allow you to overload a normal function with different data types. This makes them more useful since you only have to write a single program that can work with all data types. In this tutorial, you learned to create templates with multiple parameters, how to use overloading template functions and how to create member function templates.

This programming language supports a lot of libraries which are used in performing the input and output functions. The input output operations are performed using a series of bytes known as streams. This chapter discusses the input output streams used in running the program effectively. A stream acts as a sequence of bytes forming the source and destination of input output data. The source stream supplies data to a program through the use of an input device while the destination stream is used to receive an output from the program.

Input/output operations are implemented through the use of streams concepts and stream classes. These stream classes are declared in the header file of the iostream. C++ stream classes act as a logical device that accepts data inputs and displays output. Streams are I/O operations which can work in any device. The streams acts as both the source and the destination.

Stream classes consists of a hierarchy of classes which define streams for handling the system console unit and the disk files. Stream classes perform both input and output operations. The ios class is the base class for the input stream while ostream acts as the output stream. There are different class streams you can use to manipulate your files.

Overloaded operators >> and << are used for both input and output operations. The input operator >> uses the standard cin library to access input data. The output operator << is used together with cout to display the content. The >> operator is overloaded in an istream while << is overloaded in an ostream.

You can define the put () and get() functions to handle input/output operations on a single character. Other functions which can be used to handle class streams include the use of getline() and write () functions. Line oriented I/O functions like getline() and write() helps you to easily read and write into a line of text.

The header file iomanip provides a wide set of standard function manipulators which manipulate an output format. There are also various format consoles you can use to format data output. These formatted consoles include the use of ios class function and flags or the use of user-defined functions. You also learned about various file operations and using file stream classes.

The file operations work similarly to the console I/O operations. Some of the file operations you now understand are how to open files, write files, read from files, and close a file. When opening files, you can use constructors or use open () function. The file open() function works within a set of file stream classes like fstreambase, ifstream, and ofstream. The eof() function is used to detect the end of the file. When the end of file is detected the program is terminated.

Each file created has two types of pointers: the input pointer and the output pointer. The input file pointer reads the contents of the file while the output pointer is used to write into the file. whenever an I/O operation takes places, the specific file pointer is activated automatically. There are also various functions you can use to manipulate file pointers like the seekg() function. Other functions used to manipulate files include write() and read() function which write and read a block of binary data while put() and get() functions are used to read and write a single character.

Lastly, you learned how to handle errors during file operations and how to handle exceptions in a program. The exception handling mechanism involves use of three keywords: try, throw and catch exceptions to allow to detect anomalies, throw exceptions, and come up with appropriate measures to handle the exceptions.

REFERENCES

http://www.cplusplus.com/doc/tutorial/dynamic/

https://codescracker.com/cpp/cpp-data-structures.htm

https://www.edureka.co/blog/dynamic-memory-allocation-cpp/

https://www.edureka.co/blog/inline-function-in-cpp/

https://www.geeksforgeeks.org/c-classes-and-objects/

https://www.geeksforgeeks.org/object-oriented-programming-in-cpp/

https://www.programiz.com/cpp-programming/function

https://www.softwaretestinghelp.com/data-structures-in-cpp/

https://www.studytonight.com/cpp/function-overriding.php

https://www.studytonight.com/cpp/order-of-constructor-call.php

https://www.studytonight.com/cpp/types-of-member-function.php

https://www.tutorialspoint.com/cplusplus/cpp_arrays.htm

https://www.w3schools.in/cplusplus-tutorial/constructors-destructors/

Image Credit: geeksforgeeks.com

Image Credit: studytonight.com

C#

The Ultimate Beginners Guide to Learn C# Programming Step-by-Step

INTRODUCTION

If you are taking up programming, learning C# is one of the best decisions you will make. Knowledge of C# helps you lay the right foundation for your career in programming. With this knowledge, it is easier to advance into modern programming languages. You will also find it easier to learn some software development technologies, too. The principles, concepts, and knowledge learned in this book are useful even for programmers who do not wish to venture deeper into C# programming. You will realize that most of the concepts are cross-platform in that you can still apply and implement them in other languages.

An important point of note when reading this book is that the basic concepts and principles of writing computer programs have remained unchanged for more than a decade. Even as new programming languages enter the fray and technologies advance, the principles of programming have remained the same. Therefore, as a beginner, you should learn to think instinctively from the start. While learning about C# programming, you should also start thinking about algorithms and solving problems. Programming is essentially about making the world better, one line of code at a time.

This book is ideal not just for beginners, but also for anyone who has already ventured into programming, but is looking to go further. It is written in a manner such that you will start from scratch and grow into C#, mastering the fundamentals along the way. While it might not turn you into a software developer or software engineer overnight, it will help you lay the foundation upon which you can scale up your knowledge in programming and technology, which you can then use to map the way forward for your career.

For readers who can already write some simple lines of code, programs, or even if you just started a programming course in school, do not assume anything. This is the best attitude to get you through the world of programming. Never underestimate anything you come across, or its potential. While this book is written for beginners, you will learn important skills and concepts that many expert programmers do not have.

If you have some programming experience, you can also read this book in-depth and remind yourself of the concepts you have learned. This will help you advance into object-oriented programming and working with algorithms. Computer science and knowledge in other information technologies is not mandatory prior to reading this book, but will help you comprehend the content better.

One of the most important skills you need in programming is the desire to learn. This is what makes the difference between successful and failed programmers. There are many lawyers, engineers, and experts in other fields who have since advanced into programming because of their desire. You will encounter several challenges in your programming career, and without the desire, you might lack the motivation to push through them. This also explains why these days you come across many good programmers and developers in the industry without a degree in computer science. Basic computer literacy is, however, a must have.

Using variables, working with data structures, organizing logical statements, writing conditional statements, loops, and arrays are some of the fundamental programming skills you will learn in this book. This knowledge underpins other complex concepts you will learn later on in your programming career, such as exception handling and string processing.

C# is your gateway to object-oriented programming, which is a prerequisite for modern programming and software development. Over time you will go on to write high-quality programs and write code to solve complex problems in the real world. This is the ultimate call for any programmer: algorithms and solving problems.

Learning C#, you will also need to familiarize yourself with Microsoft's .NET platform. C# is a Microsoft project which has since been used as a platform for most of the successful Microsoft projects we are accustomed to, including websites, desktop applications, web applications, and office and mobile applications. As a high level language, C# features in the same league as the likes of C++ and Java.

Over the years, C# has grown to become one of the leading languages preferred by programmers and developers all over the world. This is partly due to its versatility in the development ecosystem, and also because of Microsoft's backing as their go-to platform for developing and program execution. This means that if you ever plan to work in any of the companies that are backed by Microsoft, learning C# will give you a competitive edge over your peers. Considering Microsoft's position in the world of technology, you can also take pride knowing that C# will continue to receive backing from one of the powerhouses in the industry for years to come.

Compared to C and C++, C# is one of the easiest modern programming languages you can learn. Millions of programmers all over the world code in C#. As an object-oriented programming language, you will be learning how to work with real world issues. Check any job listing website and you will find C# and .NET among the most requested skills by clients and employers, rivaling the likes of Java and PHP.

As you venture into programming, remember that knowing how to program is more important than the language you use. Whatever technology or language you need, you will master it faster if you know how to program, which means mastery of the basics. You will also realize that programming is essentially built around specific principles that evolve gradually with time. It is such principles that will make up the core of this book.

When reading this book, prepare yourself for lots of practice. You will never learn programming by reading alone. You must apply the knowledge learned to sharpen your skills. The more programming challenges you attempt, the faster you will learn and acquaint yourself. Write code all the time. There is no better way to learn C# or any other programming language.

CHAPTER 1:

C# An Overview

From the onset, programming is about working with computers at different levels. You are getting into a world of issuing commands and orders that your computer will execute through compilers. In the programming world, this is referred to as issuing instructions. Programming, therefore, is an act of organizing assignments issued to a computer through instruction sequences. This is where algorithms come in. At a later stage in your programming career, you will delve deeper into algorithms. An algorithm is simply a sequence of steps the computer follows to accomplish an assignment.

There are different programming languages in the market today, which are responsible for the programs we use on our computers, smartphones, and other devices. Everything you use online is written in some programming language. Programming languages are written to control computers at different levels. We have languages that are written to instruct computers at the lowest levels. An example of these is an assembler. We also have languages that are written to interact with computers at system level. Such languages instruct the computer through the operating system running. A good example is C. Beyond this we have programming languages that are used to interact with computers through programs and applications. These are the languages in which the programs are written. Such languages are known as high level languages, and in this category we have the likes of C#, PHP, Python, C++, Ruby, Java, and Visual Basic among many others.

Programming in a high level language like C# involves having access to, and controlling, most computer services, either through the operating system or by directly assigning computing resources to the services. Before we jump into C# programming, this overview will give you a glimpse of different aspects of software development, helping you understand the programming process better.

Any programmer you come across might tell you how time-conscious and complex their assignments are. There are times when you have to work with other programmers from different departments, or even collaborate online with programmers in different locations. To meet the collaboration needs, programmers use different practices and methods to make their work easier. In any of the methods applicable, you will go through the following steps:

Step 1: Understanding the assignment and gathering all the information and resources necessary

At the onset, you only have an idea of the project you are about to write. The idea includes a list of instructions, requirements, or the kind of interaction expected between the computer and the user. This information is properly defined. At this point in time, there is no programming expected of you. It is about identifying and clearly defining the problem at hand.

Step 2: Preparation and planning the structure and design of your program

Having understood the requirements, your next step is to prepare and plan the program design. You come up with a technical plan that will guide the implementation of your project. In this case, the technologies, platform, and architecture of the program are designed. This is the first point in the development process where your creativity comes in.

In this stage, some of the decisions you make will include the type of application, for example a client-server, desktop application, or web application. Today a lot of clients seek mobile applications to bring their products closer to the target audience.

You also have to think about the development architecture, whether you plan on using single, double, or multiple layer architecture and so on. You will also think about the programming language within which you will write the program, including the likes of C#, Python, Ruby, or Java.

Having settled on the programming language, you also have to think about the technologies and development frameworks. In terms of technologies, you will be looking at platforms like .NET, a database server such as MySQL or Oracle, and user interface technologies like ASP.NET and Flash. There are lots of other technologies you can consider for your project, depending on your implementation process and the parts of the software system you wish to build.

On the technical front, you will also have to consider the development framework for your project. Say you are writing a program in Python; you might want to consider Django, or Rails if you are programming in Ruby.

Away from the technical aspects of the project, think about the composition of your development team. How many developers are part of the project, and how confident are you that their skills will suit the project development requirements?

Step 3: The implementation stage (writing the program)

This is the programming stage. You write the program in line with the architecture, design, and client instructions. You will write the source code for the program. Most of this book is written with a view of helping you master this important stage in creating your project.

Step 4: Product testing and trials

Testing and trials is an important stage once you have written the program. The idea here is to ascertain whether all the program requirements are met accordingly. While you can test your program manually, it is always advisable to automate tests. Automated tests are small programs written to make the trial process seamless and efficient.

Quality assurance engineers often work with programmers in this stage to identify and fix bugs in the program. Note that in this stage, the objective is to identify defects in your code, and for the most part, you will not write new code.

Step 5: Deployment

After passing the testing and trials stage, the program moves to deployment. In this stage, the product goes into exploitation. The complexity of the program and number of people it serves determine how fast this process will be, and the costs involved. In most cases, you will create a small program known as an installer. Installers ensure easy and fast installation of the program.

Once the program is deployed successfully, the next step is to train users on how to use it effectively. This is where deployment experts come in. Deployment experts include system administrators, system engineers, and database administrators. While you don't need to write new code at this stage, you can tweak and configure the existing code accordingly to ensure it meets the client requirements for successful deployment.

Step 6: Maintenance and support

It is prudent to expect errors and problems at deployment. Such problems arise from different factors, especially at configuration and software errors. More often, problems arise because user requirements change, making it almost impossible for the program to meet the client needs because as currently constituted, the program can no longer perform the tasks for which it was created.

It does not matter how good the project is, maintenance and support are needed throughout the life of the project. The nature of support often depends on the kind and extent of changes made to the project, and the number of people involved in the maintenance and support process.

The development cycle of every program involves the six steps above. Beyond that, you have the documentation stage which basically sums up all the stages above. Documentation is important in that it connects all the steps, and is useful in development and program support. This stage is performed by developers and other experts involved in building the program.

At this point, you can already see that there is more to programming than writing code. Let's move on and write our first C# program. From here, we can delve deeper and learn more along the way. A typical C# program looks like this:

```
class Hello World
{
static void Main(string[] args)
{
System.Console.WriteLine("Hello World");
}
}
```

This is a simple instruction to print "`Hello World`" at output. It is still too early in the development cycle to execute the program, but we will use this excerpt to help you understand the program structure.

From the instruction above, you can deduce the following three important logical parts of the program:

- **Class definition `Hello World`;**

This is the first line of the program, defining the class `Hello World`. The simplest class definition will always include the keyword *class*, followed by the name of the class. The class in our example is `Hello World`, whose contents are enclosed in a block of code within curly brackets {}.

- **Method definition `Main()`;**

The third line of this program defines the method with the name `Main()`. This is where the program begins. All programs written in C# must start from this method, followed by the signature (title) below:

```
static void Main(string[] args)
```

This is how we declare methods in C#. Methods should be static and void, and include `Main` and in the list of parameters, have only one parameter of the type `array`. In the example above, we have the parameter `args`, though we can omit it since it is not mandatory. We can, therefore, simplify the code above as follows:

```
static void Main()
```

Take note of the instructions above because if any of them are not met, your program will never execute. The program might still compile, but since the starting point is not properly defined, it will not execute.

- **Method contents `Main()` .**

When writing programs in C#, you include the content of every method after the signature, enclosed within the curly brackets. As you can see above, we have used the system object `System.Console` and the method `WriteLine()` to print the message `"Hello World"`. In this method, you can write any manner of expressions, and they will be compiled and executed in the sequence order you assign to them. We will discuss more of these concepts as we go deeper into the book.

Going forward, you must also keep in mind that C# is a case-sensitive language. Therefore, when writing code in C#, be careful with your upper and lower case code. In C#, `static` and `Static` do not mean the same thing. This rule applies to all aspects of your program, including class names, variable names, and keywords.

This brings us to formatting rules. There are a few simple guidelines you should always remember when formatting code in C#:

1. All method names must begin with a capital letter
2. All variable names must begin with a lowercase letter
3. All class names must begin with a capital letter
4. Methods must be indented within class definitions using the Tab character on your keyboard.
5. The method contents must be indented within the method definition
6. You must place the opening curly bracket { on its own line, and under the class or method to which it refers.
7. You must place the closing curly bracket } on its own line, and directly under the relevant opening bracket, using the same indentation.

Code indentation, as used in the point above is another important rule you must adhere to when writing code in C#. When writing some new code inside another set of code, you must indent it to the right using a single Tab. For example, if you are nesting a method within a class, the method indents further to the right from the class.

When coding in C#, each program must have at least one class definition. Every class is further defined in a different file, with the file name corresponding to the class name. They must also have a **.cs** extension. From the example we used above, we have the class `HelloWorld`, and for that reason, the file is saved in a file named `HelloWorld.cs`.

C# and The .NET Platform

Microsoft released the first version of C# under the .NET platform. This platform was built to enhance the software development platform for the Windows ecosystem through managed code and the virtual machine concept. C# is a high-level object-oriented, general purpose programming language. While the C# syntax is similar to C++ and C, most of their features are not supported in C#. The idea behind this is to make programming in C# cleaner and easier.

Programs written in C# are compiled through the C# compiler, in the process creating assemblies. Assemblies are files that share similar names with the program, but have a different extension. You can identify assemblies with the extensions **.dll** or **.exe**. For example, if we create a `Hello World` program and compile `HelloWorld.cs`, you will see a file name `HelloWorld.exe` or `HelloWorld.dll`. There are lots of other files that can be created in the process.

Why is the .NET framework important? You get an error message when you try to run C# code on a computer without the .NET framework installed. Other than that, one of the benefits of the .NET framework is its automatic memory management. This is useful to programmers because without it, you would have to manually allocate memory to objects, and determine the appropriate time to release the memory from objects that no longer require such resources. It is safe to say that with the automatic memory management feature, .NET helps to improve the quality of programs and at the same time, enhance your productivity.

The .NET framework has a unique component known as the garbage collector. This is an automated memory cleaning system that checks when memory apportioned to different variables is not in use, and releases it, making it available for other objects that might need that memory.

Another benefit of the .NET framework is that you can easily exchange code with other programmers, as long as they code in any of the .NET supported languages. Therefore, given that you are coding in C#, you can use code written by other programmers who write in F#, Managed C++ or VB.NET. All this is possible because all .NET languages use similar infrastructure for execution, data types, and assemblies.

The .NET framework runs effortlessly because of the common language runtime (CLR). This is the environment within which managed code is executed in C#. It is because of the CLR that you can execute .NET programs on different operating systems and hardware systems. The CLR is essentially a virtual machine. It therefore supports memory access, instructions, registries and input-output operations. Through the CLR, you are able to execute .NET programs using the competencies of the operating system and processor.

What we refer to as the .NET platform, therefore, is a combination of the CLR, C# programming language, and a host of libraries and auxiliary instruments.

CHAPTER 2:

Types and Variables

When coding in C#, data types and variables are important concepts you must understand. Understanding their characteristics makes it easier to discern the appropriate instances where you can use them without your program yielding unsavory results. When it comes to variables, you need to know the unique features and how to declare each variable correctly in your code. Other than that, you must also know how to assign values to variables.

In programming, you will often use random values whose properties can change while in execution. You can, for example, create a program that measures the body mass index (BMI). Obviously, since the calculations depend on the individual's mass and height, you can expect different entries from each user. Therefore, when writing the program, you do not know the values that each user will introduce at input, so the best option is to write a program that can process all possible values users can enter.

Each time someone enters either the mass or height values to determine their BMI, they are temporarily stored in the computer's RAM. It is such values that change at execution depending on the user's input that we collectively refer to as variables.

Data Types

Data types refer to a range of values that share similar characteristics. For example, the ***byte*** data type refers to integers within the range of 0 and 255. Data types are identified according to their names, size (memory allocation) and default values. In C#, the basic data types are also known as primitive data types because they are built-in. They are hard-coded into the C# language at the fundamental levels. Let's look at the primitive data types below:

Integer Types

These types refer to integer values and are as follows:

- **sbyte**

These are signed 8-bit integers, meaning that they can only handle up to 256 values (2^8), including negative and positive values. From the default value 0, the minimum and maximum values stored by sbyte can be expressed as follows:

```
SByte.MinValue = -128 (-2^7)
SByte.MaxValue = 127 (2^7-1)
```

- **byte**

Unlike sbyte, these are unsigned 8-bit integers. They can also handle up to 256 integer values. However, bytes cannot be negative values. The default byte value is 0, and the minimum and maximum values stored in bytes can be expressed as follows:

```
Byte.MinValue = 0
Byte.MaxValue = 255 (2^8-1)
```

- **short**

These are signed 16-bit integer values. The default value for the short type is 0, while the minimum and maximum values stored can be expressed as follows:

```
Int16.MinValue = -32768 (-2^15)
Int16.MaxValue = 32767 (2^15-1)
```

- **ushort**

These are unsigned 16-bit integer values. The default value for ushort is 0, while the minimum and maximum values stored can be expressed as follows:

```
UInt16.MinValue = 0
UInt16.MaxValue = 65535 (2^16-1)
```

- **int**

These are 32-bit signed integer values. By now you can see that as the bits grow, the number of possible values that can be stored in the data type also grows. The default value for int is 0, while the minimum and maximum values stored can be expressed as follows:

```
Int32.MinValue = -2,147,483,648 (-2^31)
Int32.MaxValue = 2,147,483,647 (2^31-1)
```

Of all the data types, int is the most commonly used in most programming languages. This is because it naturally fits a 32-bit microprocessor, and the fact that it is large enough to handle most of the calculations performed in normal life.

- **uint**

These are 32-bit unsigned integer values. The default value for uint is `0u`, which can also be written as `0U`. This is one of the few exceptions in C# programming where upper or lower case mean the same thing. When using this data type, you must be careful to include the letter U, otherwise the compiler will interpret it as an int data type. The minimum and maximum values stored can be expressed as follows:

```
UInt32.MinValue = 0
UInt32.MaxValue = 4,294,967,295 (2^32-1)
```

- **long**

These are 64-bit signed integer types whose default value is `0l`, which can also be written as `0L`. When using this data type, it is often advisable to use the upper case L because the alternative can be misconstrued for 1. Another common mistake people make is to forget the L, in which case the compiler interprets the values as int, yet we know the number of values held within cannot match.

The minimum and maximum values stored can be expressed as follows:

```
LInt64.MinValue = -9,223,372,036,854,775,808 (-2^63)
LInt64.MaxValue = 9,223,372,036,854,775,807 (2^63-1)
```

- **ulong**

This is by far the largest integer type in C# programming. The 64-bit unsigned type has the default value as `0U` or `0u`. Without the U, compilers will interpret the data type as long values, so you must also be careful with that. The minimum and maximum values stored can be expressed as follows:

```
UInt64.MinValue = 0
UInt64.MaxValue = 18,446,744,073,709,551,615 (2^64-1)
```

Let's use an example to explain how you can declare several variables of the integer data types mentioned above.

```
// To declare loan repayment variables
byte years = 20;
ushort weeks = 1042;
uint days = 7300;
ulong hours = 175200;
// Print output to console
Console.WriteLine(years + " years are " + weeks + " weeks, or " + days +
" days, or " + hours + " hours.");
// output:
// 20 years are 1042 weeks, or 7300 days, or 175200 hours.
ulong maxIntValue = UInt64.MaxValue;
Console.WriteLine(maxIntValue); // 18446744073709551615
```

Real Floating Point Types

These data types refer to the real numbers you use every day. They are real numbers you use in mathematics all the time. Such data types are identified by floating points as per the IEEE 754 standard, and can either be a float or a double.

- **Real type floats**

This is a 32-bit float, also referred to as a single precision real number. The default value for this data type is `0.0f`, or `0.0F`. The 'f' character at the end of the value denotes the float type. This is important because all real numbers are often considered doubles by default.

When using this data type, you can express accuracy up to seven decimal points, rounding off all values accordingly. For example, the value 3.323588725723 when stored as a float is rounded off to 3.3235887.

We also have real type float values that are not necessarily real numbers, but they still fit mathematical concepts. These include negative infinity, positive infinity, and uncertainty (**`Single.NaN`**), which occurs when you perform an invalid operation using real numbers (for example when you try to calculate the square root of negative values).

- **Real type doubles**

These data types are also known as double precision real numbers, and are 64-bit data types whose default value is expressed as `0.0d` or `0.0D`. Unlike other data types, you can omit the 'd' because in C#, all real numbers are considered doubles by default.

When using real type doubles, you can express values up to 15 or 16 decimal points. Bearing this in mind, the minimum and maximum real type double values can be expressed as follows:

```
Double.MinValue = -1.79769e+308
Double.MaxValue = 1.79769e+308
```

We also have the `Double.Epsilon = 4.94066e-324`, which is the closest positive double type to zero. As we saw in real type floats, we can also have unique values in real type doubles, like `Double.Nan`, `Double.NegativeInfinity`, and `Double.PositiveInfinity`. Let's use an example below to show the difference between these two, and the accuracy levels:

```
// To declare random variables
float floatPI = 4.24827375472674328785f;
double doublePI = 4.24827375472674328785;
// Print output to console
Console.WriteLine("Float PI is: " + floatPI);
Console.WriteLine("Double PI is: " + doublePI);
// Console output:
// Float PI is: 4.248274
// Double PI is: 4.24827375472674
```

As you can see above, we declared a random float value to the 7th digit, but when declaring the same value as a double, we declare it to the 15th digit. This is proof that the real type doubles allow more precision than floats, so if you are writing a program that demands specificity beyond the decimal point, it makes sense to use real type doubles.

Real Decimal Precision Types

The decimal floating point method is commonly used in C#, where the decimal numbering system is used instead of the binary system. Using the decimal precision points, real numbers are expressed as 128-bit decimal types, allowing up to 28 or 29 decimal places. The default values using this system are **0m** or **0M**. The 'm' in the number is an explicit indicator for decimal types. This is important because by default, all values are considered of the double type as discussed earlier. Let's look at an example below:

```
decimal declaration = 6.38628428462492847264m;
Console.WriteLine(declaration); // 6.38628428462492847264
```

In the example above, the number used has not been rounded because it falls within a 21-digit precision, which naturally fits the decimal without rounding off. The decimal type is ideal for calculations that require a high level of accuracy, for example in financial calculations.

Boolean Types

This data type is declared using the keyword `bool`. Boolean types only return two possible values, true or false, false being the default Boolean value. Boolean types are ideal when storing calculations involving logical expressions. Let's explain this with an example below:

```
int x = 5;
int y = 10;
// which one is greater?
bool greaterXY = (x > y);
// Is 'x' equal to 5?
bool equalX5 = (x == 5);
// Print the results on the console
if (greaterXY)
{
Console.WriteLine("X > Y");
}
else
{
Console.WriteLine("X <= Y");
}
Console.WriteLine("greaterXY = " + greaterXY);
Console.WriteLine("equalX5 = " + equalX5);

// Console output:
// X <= Y
// greaterXY = False
// equalX5 = True
```

In the example above, we declared two variables of the type **int**, and by comparison, we assign the resulting value using the **bool** type, and variable **greaterXY**. In the same manner, we also declare for the variable **equalX5**. If the variable **greaterXY** returns **true**, then the console will print **X > Y**. If that is not the case, it prints **X <= Y**.

Character Types

These are single 16-bit characters. They are declared using the keyword **char**. The smallest possible char variable is 0, while the largest value is 65535. This data type represents values in the form of letters and other characters, and are always enclosed within an apostrophe.

In the next example, we will declare a variable of the type char, initializing it with the value ‘x’, then ‘y’ and finally ‘X’, printing the outcome to the console.

```
// Declare a variable
char ch = 'x';
// Print the results on the Console.WriteLine(
"The code of '" + ch + "'is: " + (int)ch);
ch = 'y';
Console.WriteLine(
"The code of '" + ch + "'is: " + (int)ch);
ch = 'X';
Console.WriteLine(
"The code of '" + ch + "'is: " + (int)ch);
```

```
// Console output:
// The code of 'x' is: 76
// The code of 'y' is: 77
// The code of 'X' is: 43
```

String Types

String characters are declared in C# using the keyword **`string`**, and their default value is **`null`**. They are always expressed within quotation marks, and can be used to process different text functions. For example, two strings can be joined together, a process known as concatenation, or split using a separator, and so on.

In the example below, we declare variables of different string types, and print the outcome to the console:

```
// Declare variables
string firstName = "Mazda";
string lastName = "Demio";
string fullName = firstName + " " + lastName;
// Print output to the console
Console.WriteLine("Welcome to, " + firstName + "!");
Console.WriteLine("You are currently viewing a " + fullName + ".");
// Console output:
// Welcome to, Mazda!
// You are currently viewing a Mazda Demio.
```

Object Types

These are special data types which house all the data types within the .NET framework. They are declared using the keyword **`object`**, and can assume values from any of the data types we have discussed above.

Object types are basically reference types, used to identify memory areas where actual data types are stored. In the example below, we will declare different variables of the **`object`** type, and print the outcome to the console:

```
// Declare variables
object containerX = 10;
object containerY = "Ten";
// Print the output on the console
Console.WriteLine("The value of containerX is: " + containerX);
Console.WriteLine("The value of containerY is: " + containerY);
// Console output:
// The value of containerX is: 10
// The value of containerY is: Ten.
```

From the example above, you can see that the **object** type can be used to store any other data types. Therefore, **object** types are universal data containers.

Variables, Value and Reference Types

A variable in C# refers to a container with some information. The information in question is not static, so its value can change from time to time, with respect to information storage, and retrieving the stored information. You can also use variables to modify the information.

Any variable is identifiable and distinguished from others by the following features:

1. The name of the variable (its unique identifier), such as color
2. The type of variable (the kind of information held in the variable), such as string
3. The value (information stored in the variable), such as 3.124

Since variables are a specific area in the memory, they store data values in a specific memory area only accessible by the name of the variable. Primitive data types like **bool, char** and **numbers** are value types because their value is stored within the program. On the other hand, reference data types like **arrays**, **objects**, and **strings** point to the dynamic memory where their value is stored. Such data types can be released or allocated, meaning that their size is not fixed as is the case with the primitive data types.

When naming variables, there are specific rules that you must adhere to. This is important to avoid unnecessary errors when you pass some information to the compiler. While you have freedom of naming choice with variables, they must follow the following rules in C#:

1. Variables can only be named using the characters **A-Z**, **a-z**, digits **0-9**, and the character'_'.
2. You cannot start a variable name with a digit
3. While you are free to name variables as you wish, the names should never be similar to the innate C# keywords. For example, your variables cannot have any of the following names: **null, this, int, default, object, char, base**, or any of the other keywords you will come across in C#.

That being said, the proper way of naming a variable can be any of the following:

```
1. name
2. name_name
3. _name37
```

If you write the variable name in any manner that contravenes the instructions above, you will get a compilation error.

Literals

Earlier on we mentioned primitive types, as unique data types that come prebuilt into C#. The values of such data types are specified within the program's source code. Here are some examples to explain this:

```
bool result = false;
char capitalD = 'D';
byte b = 600;
short s = 15000;
int i = 820000;
```

In the example above, the literals are **`false`**, `D`, `600`, `15000`, and `820000`. Their values are set within the program's code. The following are literal types you will use in C#:

1. **String**

These literals are used to represent the **`string`** data type. A string can be preceded by the character `@`, which denotes a verbatim string (quoted string).

2. **Character**

These literals are single characters which are enclosed within an apostrophe. They are used to represent **`char`** value types.

3. **Integer**

These are digit sequences, including the signs `+` and `-`, used as prefixes or suffixes.

4. **Real**

These are digit sequences, the signs `+` and `-`, suffixes and the decimal point. They are used with the decimal, double, and float value types.

5. **Boolean**

They return true or false, for example, **`bool result = false;`**

CHAPTER 3:

Operators and Expressions

Having learned about the different data types used in C#, the next step is to understand operators, expressions, and more importantly, when to use them on data. Primarily, you need to know the priorities assigned to different operators, their types, and arguments within which they can be used in programming. Another important aspect we will look at later on is how to convert different data types where necessary.

Operators

In programming, operators are used in every programming language to perform specific actions on data. The role of operators is to enable you to process objects and primitive data types. Operators are applied to one or more operands, returning a result.

Other than their indigenous roles, operators can also be classified based on the number of arguments that you can pass through them. According to this, we have the following operator types:

- Unary operators - they take one operand
- Binary operators - they take two operands
- Ternary operators - they take three operands

In C# programming, we calculate operations from left to right, a system referred to as left-associative. The only exception to this rule is for the assignment operators. Assignment and conditional operators in C# are right-associative. It is also important to note that unary operators are not associative, meaning that you can calculate them from either side.

Another point you will learn about operators is that they perform different tasks depending on the data types to which they are applied. Take the operator +, for example. When used on strings, it joins the relevant strings together to return a new string (concatenation). On the other hand, if you use the operator on numeric data types, it performs an arithmetic addition, yielding a new result. Let's explain this in an example below:

```
int x = 5 + 10;
Console.WriteLine(x); // 15
string firstName = "Mazda";
string lastName = "Demio";
// Do not forget the space between them
string fullName = firstName + " " + lastName;
Console.WriteLine(fullName); // Mazda Demio
```

From the example above, you can see how the operator performs a different role depending on the operation in question.

Another important point you will need to learn about operators is the precedence. Operator precedence is purely about priorities. This refers to the order in which operations are carried out, depending on the operators applicable. For example, when carrying out arithmetic operations, the multiplication operator takes precedence over addition. Building on this information, operators that have a higher precedence are always calculated ahead of those with a lower precedence. While you're at it, you can use the operator `()` to change the precedence of an operation just as you do in math.

If you write an expression that must use more than one operator, or is naturally complex, it is advisable to introduce parentheses into the expression. This makes it easier to understand, and reduces difficulties for anyone who might use the code later. Let's look at an example below:

```
// The expression below is ambiguous
a + b / 25
// You can write it better
a + (b / 25)
```

Always remember that parentheses are useful when you need to change the operator precedence. Let's have a look at the different types of operators below:

- **Arithmetic Operators**

In C# programming, arithmetic operators are similar to those you use in math. Arithmetic operators are used to perform addition, subtraction, division, and multiplication operations on integer values to return a numeric output.

The division operator does not have the same effect on real numbers and integers as other arithmetic operators. For example, when dividing two integers, the result must be an integer. If the result has a decimal point, you ignore the decimal. It is also by convention that you do not round off the value to the nearest whole integer. This is referred to as integer division, and you can see an example of this below:

```
9 / 4 = 2
```

On the same note, you cannot perform an integer division by zero. This would return the runtime exception **DivideByZeroException**. You can, however, divide two real numbers, a process known as real division. In this case, the result can be an integer or a real number with a fraction. Using the example above, we have the following:

```
9 / 4 = 2.25
```

In this concept, you can divide real numbers by zero, returning any of the following infinity values, depending on the operand used: **NaN** (Invalid value), -Infinity (− ∞), or Infinity (∞).

You will also come across the increment operator (++), that adds one unit to the variable value, and the decrement operator (--) that subtracts one unit from the variable value. The effect of these operators depends on their placement in the expression. When used as prefixes to the variable, you calculate the new value, then return the result. However, when used after the variable, you return the original value of the operand first, then perform the decrement or increment.

- **Logical Operators**

These operators take and return Boolean values and results (**True** or **False**). The basic operators here are **logical negation** (!), **OR** (||), **exclusive OR** (^), and **AND** (&&). In the table below, we look at how the operators can be used and the logical results:

a	b	!a	a && b	a || b	a ^ b
true	true	fasle	true	true	false
true	false	false	false	true	true
false	true	true	false	true	true
false	false	true	false	false	false

From the table above, we can see that the logical AND, &&, can only return a true when both variables are true, while the logical OR, ||, can only return a true when either of the operands are true.

Building on that, you can change the argument value using the logical negation operator, !. If, for example, your operand has a true value followed by the negation operator, the operation returns a false.

The exclusive OR, ^ can only return a true if one of the operands is true. If the operands do not have the same values, the exclusive OR returns a true output, or a false if the values are similar. Let's explain these statements in the example below:

```
bool x = true;
bool y = false;
Console.WriteLine(x && y);                    // False
Console.WriteLine(x || y);                    // True
Console.WriteLine(!y);                              // True
Console.WriteLine(y || true);                       // True
Console.WriteLine((3 > 5) ^ (x == y))   // False
```

- **Concatenation Operators**

In programming, the operator + can be used to join different strings, returning a new string as the result. Assuming that at least one of the arguments within the expression is of the string type, while other operands in the expression are of different data types other than string, the operator automatically converts them into the string type, hence string concatenation. Let's explain this using an example below:

```
string csharp = "C#";
string dotnet = ".NET";
string csharpDotNet = csharp + dotnet;
Console.WriteLine(csharpDotNet); // C#.NET
string csharpDotNet4 = csharpDotNet + " " + 5;
Console.WriteLine(csharpDotNet4); // C#.NET 5
```

In the example above, two string variables are declared and assigned values, which are eventually converted to string types and printed in the last row.

- **Bitwise Operators**

These operators are applied to numeric binary representatives. In computer language, most data is represented in binary language, hence the binary numeral system. For example, in the binary numeral system, Hello World is represented as follows:

```
01001000 01100101 01101100 01101100 01101111 00100000 01010111 01101111
01110010 01101100 01100100
```

Bitwise operators and logical operators are almost alike. They both perform the same roles, the only difference is that they act on different data types. While logical operators return **`True`** or **`False`** for Boolean values, Bitwise operators are applied to numeral values. We can represent this in the table below:

a	b	~a	a & b	a | b	a ^ b
1	1	0	1	1	0
1	0	0	0	1	1
0	1	1	0	1	1
0	0	1	0	0	0

From the table above, you can see the similarity between bitwise operators and logical operators. You will also come across the operators bit shift right >> and bit shift left <<. You can use these operators with numeral values to move bits to whichever side you want them. Note that when you use them, any bits outside the number are eliminated, and replaced with a zero.

- **Comparison Operators**

These operators are for operand comparisons. You can understand the term from basic English. In C# programming, you will come across the following comparison operators:

```
>   greater than
<   less than
>=  greater than or equal to
<=  less than or equal to
==  equality
!=  difference
```

Note that when using comparison operators in C#, the operators act on Binary operands, but return Boolean values as the outcome. They are, however, lower in priority to arithmetic operators. Let's look at an example below:

```
int a = 12, y = 6;
Console.WriteLine("a > b : " + (a > b)); // True
Console.WriteLine("a < b : " + (a < b)); // False
Console.WriteLine("a >= b : " + (a >= b)); // True
Console.WriteLine("a <= b : " + (a <= b)); // False
Console.WriteLine("a == b : " + (a == b)); // False
Console.WriteLine("a != b : " + (a != b)); // True
```

From the example above, you can see different forms of comparison between the variables a and b, and the Boolean outcomes. Note that while the comparison operators are lower in priority to arithmetic operators, they are higher than assignment operators which we will look at shortly.

- **Assignment Operators**

These operators are used to assign values to variables, using the character =. Here is an example:

```
int a = 10;
string helloWorld = "Hello World.";
int b = a;
```

You can also use the assignment operator more than once in one expression, a process known as cascading. Let's see an example of this below:

```
int a, b, c;
a = b = c = 55;
```

Be careful not to confuse the assignment operator = and the comparison operator ==. This is one of the most common errors people make when writing code in C#.

Instead of writing voluminous code, you can reduce the work by using compound assignment operators. This is possible by shortening two operations using an operator. The syntax for compound operators is as follows:

```
operand1 operator = operand2;
```

The expression above can be expanded as follows:

```
operand1 = operand1 operator operand2;
```

In an example, this is as follows:

```
int a = 3;
int b = 5;
a *= b; // Same as a = a * b;
Console.WriteLine(a); // 15
```

You will come across the following compound operators in C#:

```
+=
-=
*=
/=
%=
```

- **Conditional Operators**

This operator applies an expression's Boolean values to select one or more expressions whose result is needed. It is a ternary operator because it is applied to three operands. In application, the syntax for this expression would be as follows:

```
operand1 ? operand2 : operand3
```

The compiler is instructed to calculate the value of the first argument. If the first argument is true, it returns the result. However, if the first argument is false, the compiler calculates the value of the third argument, and sends back its result.

Type Conversion

Operators are written for arguments of the same data type. As you have seen so far, there are several data types in C#, and from time to time you will have to choose one that is most appropriate for your program. If you write a program whose variables are of different data types, you must convert them to one data type (type conversion). Writing an expression with different types can result in a compilation error.

While type conversion is a brilliant idea, there are only a few data types that can be converted. For ease of understanding, type conversions fall into the following three categories:

- **Implicit Type Conversion**

This is a hidden type conversion without the risk of data loss. An example is when converting a low range data type to a high range data type, like an `int` to a `long`. This type of conversion is implicit because you do not need to use an operator. The computer automatically converts types when you assign lower range values to larger range variables. This also happens if you write an expression with different data types within different ranges.

Let's look at an example of this below:

```
int myInt = 7;
Console.WriteLine(myInt); // 7
long myLong = myInt;
Console.WriteLine(myLong); // 7
Console.WriteLine(myLong + myInt); // 14
```

In the example above, the compiler has converted the **int** value to a **long** value, printing the outcome to the console. In C# programming, you can perform the following implicit conversions:

```
byte to short , ushort , int , uint , long , ulong , float , double ,
decimal;
float to double;
int to long, float , double , decimal;
long to float , double , decimal;
uint to long, ulong , float , double , decimal;
ulong to float , double , decimal;
ushort to int , uint , long , ulong , float , double , decimal;
sbyte to short , int , long , float , double , decimal;
short to int , long , float , double , decimal;
```

Note that after conversion from a small range to a large range, the numerical value generally remains unchanged, hence no data loss at conversion. There are, however, a few exceptions to this rule, like conversion from an **int** to a **float**, or converting to a **64-bit double** from a **64-bit long**. This happens because of a difference in the number of bits used, and the possibility of rounding off the fraction parts of the data types.

- **Explicit Type Conversion**

This conversion type is recommended in situations where data loss is possible upon successful conversion. Let's say you need to convert data from an **integer** to a **floating point**; you have to discard the fraction part of the data type, hence the need for an explicit conversion.

You might also experience data loss when converting from a large range to a lower range, for example, **long** to **int**. Let's look at an example of this below:

```
double myDouble = 7.1d;
Console.WriteLine(myDouble); // 7.1
long myLong = (long)myDouble;
Console.WriteLine(myLong); // 7
myDouble = 7e7d; // 7 * 10^7
Console.WriteLine(myDouble); // 50000000
```

Let's look at a different scenario below:

```
int myInt = (int)myDouble;
Console.WriteLine(myInt); // -2343576879
Console.WriteLine(int.MinValue); // -2343576879
```

In the example above, there is no change after conversion to **int**, because the value held in the variable **myDouble** is larger than the data range of **int**.

Given the difficulty in determining the variable value after conversion, it is advisable to use large data types to allow enough room for flexibility. At the same time, avoid, or be careful when converting to smaller data types.

- **String Conversion**

Where necessary, you can convert any data type to strings. String conversions happen automatically as long as you use the operator + for concatenation, alongside an argument that is not of the string type. If all these conditions are met, the compiler converts the argument and returns a string outcome. You can also achieve the same result using the method **`ToString()`** on the variables.

For example:

```
24.ToString() returns "24"
```

Using this information, let's look at some dimensions of a rectangle below:

```
int x = 3;
int y = 6 ;
string SUMMARY: = "SUMMARY: = " + (x + y);
Console.WriteLine(SUMMARY:);
Console.WriteLine("Perimeter = " + 2 * (x + y) + ". Area = " + (x * y) +
".");
```

From the arguments above, you will get the following output:

```
SUMMARY: = 9
Perimeter = 18
Area = 27
```

Note that if you need to change the operation priority, you must introduce brackets. Otherwise, arguments are executed from left to right by default.

Expressions

When you write a program, you are basically tasking it with calculating expressions. An expression loosely refers to a sequence of variables, literals, and operators, which return a value. You must be careful when writing expressions because some of them usually contain embedded assignment operators. The outcome can either increase or reduce. Let's look at an example to explain this:

```
int x = 19;
int y = ++x;
Console.WriteLine(x); // 20
Console.WriteLine(y); // 20
```

Make sure you consider the data type and the relationship between the operators when writing expressions. Ignoring this can lead to unpleasant outcomes. Many programmers assume that division by zero is impossible, because it is mathematically not doable. However, in C# programming, this concept will only be true with integer divisions. In other cases, fractional division by zero returns a **`NaN (Infinity)`**.

We mentioned this before, but we can highlight it again – the role of parentheses in programming. If you are in doubt about the priority of your operations, you can introduce parentheses for clarity.

CHAPTER 4:

Console Input and Output

The console in C# is a data input and output tool. It is the operating system window through which users interact with different programs in the operating system or other applications installed into the console. For this interaction, you will have text input from the standard input (keyboard) and the text display (computer screen). This is what we refer to as an input-output operation. Any console application through the operating system is connected through input and output devices. Generally, the default input and output devices are the keyboard and the screen, though you can also redirect either of the two to a unique file or device.

Modern user interfaces are more intuitive and convenient for users, making the console less desirable. However, there are many cases where you will still find the console coming in handy, especially for communication between users and the system. For example, if you need to write a simple computer program, you will have to use the console. This is because the console allows you to isolate the problem and focus on it, instead of the graphical representation of the solution to the user.

Another situation where the console will always come in handy is when you need to debug or test a subsection of code for a large program. You will simply isolate the section you need, address it, and solve the problem instead of having to go through the complexities of searching through the larger program.

Each operating system has a unique way of launching the console. Using Windows, for example, you can access the console in the following steps:

`Start > All > Programs > Accessories > Command Prompt`

The Windows console is also referred to as the **`Command Prompt`** or **`Shell`**. It is a command interpreter, a console-based program within the operating system through which you can access the system commands and any other programs you might need access to. There are two types of shells, depending on the kind of interface they provide your operating system. These are as follows:

- Command Line Interface (CLI) - This is the go-to console for commands, for example, **`bash`** if you are using a Linux environment, or **`cmd.exe`** if you are using a Windows environment.
- Graphic User Interface (GUI) - This is the environment in which you can see the graphics, for example, Windows Explorer

In each of these instances, the core role of the shell is to run all the programs you run. However, you will also realize that you can do the same with most interpreters, especially those that are built in such a way that you can inspect and examine content within the files and directories.

Understanding the Console

For the purpose of this book, we will primarily use Windows as the programming environment. We will also look at some of the basic console commands built into the command prompt, which come in handy whenever you need to run a new program.

The command interpreter that runs in the Windows console was initially referred to as **`MS-DOS Prompt`** in the earlier Windows releases, though in modern versions it is known as **`Command Prompt`**. The following are some of the basic commands you can access using this interpreter:

```
dir - Shows all content in the current directory
cd <directory name> - Will change the current directory
mkdir <directory name> - Will create a new directory within the current
directory
rmdir <directory name> - Will delete an existing directory
type <file name> - Will print content on the selected file
copy <src file> <destination file> - Will copy one file into the
selected file
```

You will also come across Standard I/O, which refers to a system input-output mechanism that has been in use since the creation of the UNIX operating system module. It uses special peripheral input and output devices to process data. In this mode, you will notice a blinking cursor whenever the console is processing or waiting for the user to input a command for processing.

You will realize that most programming languages read and print information from the console in the same manner. For this reason, the solutions returned are mostly under the standard input and standard output concept.

By default, every operating system defines its standard input-output mechanism for normal operation. When you start a program, it runs some code at initialization which allows it to automatically read your instructions from the standard input stream (**`Console.In`**) and print the outcome to the standard output stream (**`Console.Out`**). If the system detects an error, this is reported under (**`Console.Error`**).

We mentioned earlier that you input to the console through the keyboard. However, it is not the only input source. The console can receive input from many other sources, including barcode readers, microphones, and files. Below is an example of printing text to the console through a standard input-output operation:

```
Console.Out.WriteLine("Welcome Home");
```

When you execute the code above, you should have the following output

```
Welcome Home
```

This brings us to the **`Console.Out`** stream. With time, you will realize that there are different methods and properties used in **`System.Console`** not just to read and display text within the console, but also read and display the formatting correctly. The most important of these are as follows:

```
Console.Out
Console.In
Console.Error
```

Their role is to grant access to the basic streams you need when printing, reading on the console, and reporting errors identified. You can also replace these streams at runtime using the respective methods below:

```
Console.SetOut
Console.SetIn
Console.SetError
```

Console.WriteLine() vs Console.Write()

Earlier on we discussed different data types. It is easier to use different console properties because, by default, they allow you to print any of the basic data types, primitive, numeric, and string. Let's explain this using an example below:

```
// Print String
Console.WriteLine ("Welcome Home");
// Print Int
Console.WriteLine (7);
// Print double
Console.WriteLine (2.635542798664338);
The outcome when you print this code will be as follows:
Welcome Home
7
2.635542798664338
```

Using **Console.WriteLine()**, you can print any kind of data type because, for each type you use, you will find a predetermined version for the method **WriteLine()** within the console class.

While **Write()** and **WriteLine()** might seem alike, **Write()** prints all the contents of the parentheses to the console but does not perform any execution. On the other hand, **WriteLine()** is a direct instruction to print what is on that line. Essentially, it will not only perform everything **Write()** does, it will also proceed to the next line. However, note that it will not print the new line, but instead, it inserts a moving command cursor where the new line should begin. Let's look at an explicit difference between these two:

```
Console.WriteLine("I am");
Console.Write("missing");
Console.Write("Home!");
```

From the code snippet above, you will have the following feedback at output:

```
I am
missing Home!
```

Now if you pay attention, you will realize that the console prints the output on two separate lines yet the original code was written on three lines. This is because we use **WriteLine()** in the first line, which prints and jumps to the next line by default. The next two lines of the code use the **Write()** method that prints but does not jump to the next line, hence "**missing**" and "**Home!**" end up on the same line.

String Concatenation

By default, you cannot use operators over string objects in C#. The only instance where this is allowed is when using the (+) operation to concatenate two strings and return a new string as a result. Here is an example to explain this:

```
string students = “thirty five”;
string text = “There are” + students + “in the class.”;
Console.WriteLine(text);
```

When you execute the code, you get the following output:

```
There are thirty five students in the class.
```

The example above is a simple one. What if we encounter something slightly complex, with more than one type? So far, we have only worked with **`WriteLine()`** versions of one type. Assuming that you have to print different types at once using **`WriteLine()`**, you don't have to use different versions of the **`WriteLine()`** method. Note that in the next example, the number of students is of the integer type:

```
int students = “thirty five”;
string text = “There are” + students + “in the class.”;
Console.WriteLine(text);
```

We will still have the same output as shown below:

```
There are thirty five students in the class.
```

You can see the concatenation in the second line of the string "**`There are`**" and the integer type "**`students`**". We are able to combine these two types because the result of concatenation between a string and any other type will always result in a string.

That being said, you have to be keen when performing string concatenation, lest you run into errors. The order of execution is an important aspect of string concatenation that many programmers fail to get right. Let's explain this with an example:

```
string x = "Four: " + 1 + 3;
Console.WriteLine(x);
// Four: 13
string y = "Four: " + (1 + 3);
Console.WriteLine(y);
// Four: 4
```

In both instances, we perform a concatenation of **`Four`**. In the first instance, we end up with a string result. A second concatenation is performed but the result, **`Four`**`: 13` is not right. The reason for this is because the console performs the operation from left to right, returning a string in each of the operations.

You can, however, avoid such a scenario by introducing parentheses in the operation. Parentheses help you change the order of execution, giving you the correct result. The reason for this is because, in C# programming, parentheses are operators with the highest priority. Therefore, the addition will take place, followed by the concatenation.

The lesson here, therefore, is that if you are performing a concatenation that involves sum numbers and strings, always introduce parentheses to bring order into the flow of operations. Without that, the console will execute code from left to right.

Console.ReadLine() vs. Console.Read()

By now you know that the console input is the most ideal when working with small applications in console communication because of its ease of implementation. Every programming language has a unique method of reading and writing to the console. In C#, the standard input stream is controlled by **Console.In**, from which you can read text data or any other type of data available after the console parses the text.

You will also realize that in most cases, **Console.In** is rarely used. Instead, you will use **Console.Read()** and **Console.ReadLine()** to read from the **Console** class. The easiest way to read from the class is **Console.ReadLine()**. Using this method, you key in the input and press **Enter** when ready in order for the console to read the string as per the instructions issued. Let's explain this with an example below:

```
class UsingReadLine
{
static void Main()
{
Console.Write("Enter car model: ");
string firstName = Console.ReadLine();
Console.Write("Enter car name: ");
string lastName = Console.ReadLine();
Console.WriteLine("You are viewing, {0} {1}!", carModel, carName);
}
}
// Output: Enter car model: Mazda
// Enter car name: Axela
// You are viewing, Mazda Axela!
```

As you can see, reading text from the console using the **Console.ReadLine()** method is simple. When using this method, the console blocks the program from performing any operation until you key in some text, and press **Enter**.

We switch things up a bit when using the **Console.Read()** method. In this method, the console will first read one character at a time, instead of the entire line as we did in **`Console.ReadLine()`**. Another difference between the two methods is that instead of returning the result as a character, **`Console.Read()`** returns the character's code. Therefore, you must convert the code back into the character to use it, using the **`Convert.ToChar()`** method.

As long as the **`Console.ReadLine()`** method is in use, the **`Console.Read()`** method is rarely used. This is because of its propensity for errors, and to avoid unnecessary complications.

CHAPTER 5:

Conditional Statements

Conditional statements are used in programming to instruct the console to perform different actions if a given condition is true. To learn how to use conditional statements, you must also recall how to use comparison operators. Comparison operators help us describe the appropriate conditions that make conditional statements relevant.

There are many comparison operators you can use in C# to compare integers, strings, characters, and other types. Here are the most commonly used comparison operators, which we will also use throughout this chapter:

```
== Equal to
!= Not equal to
> Greater than
>= greater than, or equal to
< Less than
<= Less than, or equal to
```

You use comparison operators to compare different expressions, for example, numbers and variables, or even a set of numerical operations. The result of the comparison will always be a Boolean true or false. Let's explain this using an example below:

```
int weight = 800;
Console.WriteLine(weight >= 400); // True

char gender = 'f';
Console.WriteLine(gender <= 'm'); // False

double colorWaveLength = 2.360;
```

```
Console.WriteLine(colorWaveLength > 2.301); // True

int x = 7;
int y = 9;
bool condition = (y > x) && (x + y < x * y);
Console.WriteLine(condition); // True

Console.WriteLine('Y' == 'X' + 1); // True
```

From the code snippet above, we can compare characters and numbers. It is also evident that the **char** type in this example assumes the characteristics of a number, and for that reason, you can add, subtract, or compare it to other numbers. While this is possible, it is also advisable to use this approach sparingly because you can easily end up with complex code that is difficult to read or comprehend.

If we run the code snippets above, we should have the following results:

```
True
False
True
True
True
```

When programming in C#, you can compare object references or pointers, Booleans, numbers, and characters. Note that anytime you use comparisons, the iteration can affect two object references, two Boolean values, or two numbers. It is also possible to compare expressions that do not have the same types. For example, you can compare a floating-point number with an integer. Note, however, that you cannot always compare data types freely, for example, it is impossible to directly compare numbers with strings.

Role of Comparison Operators in Conditional Statements

In any comparison illustration, for example between characters and integers, what gets compared is their memory binary representation. Instead of comparing the types themselves, the console compares their values. Let's say we want to compare two integer variables; what is compared is their 4-byte series representation. Let's explain this with an example below:

```
Console.WriteLine("char 'x' == 'x'? " + ('x' == 'x')); // True
Console.WriteLine("char 'x' == 'y'? " + ('x' == 'y')); // False
Console.WriteLine("4 != 5? " + (4 != 5)); // True
Console.WriteLine("6.0 == 6L? " + (6.0 == 6L)); // True
Console.WriteLine("true == false? " + (true == false)); // False
```

We get the following result if we run the code above:

```
char 'x' == 'x'? True
char 'x' == 'y'? False
4 != 5? True
6.0 == 6L? True
true == false? False
```

When programming in C#, you will realize that not all reference data types contain their values. In some cases, the reference type will contain a memory address to which you can find the desired values. This is common with arrays, classes, and strings. In such cases, the reference data type has a null value, but instead, will act as a pointer to another object whose value you will infer. For such cases, instead of comparing the underlying value of the data type, you compare the address they point to.

It is also possible to have two references that point to the same or different objects. You can also have one of the references pointing nowhere, hence having a null value assigned. In the example below, we have two variables that point to the same object:

```
string str = "soda";
string anotherStr = str;
```

If we run the code, you will have both variables (**str** and **anotherStr**) pointing to the object with the value **soda**. If you want to find out whether two variables point to the same object, you use the comparison operator (==). Most of the time, the comparison operator will not actually compare the content of the objects, but instead, it verifies whether they point to the same memory location. In this way, it verifies whether they refer to the same object. Note that when using object type variables, you cannot use size comparisons (**>, <, >=, or <=**). Using this knowledge, let's look at an example below:

```
string str = "soda";
string anotherStr = str;
string thirdStr = "sod";
thirdStr = thirdStr + 'a';
Console.WriteLine("str = {0}", str);
Console.WriteLine("anotherStr = {0}", anotherStr);
Console.WriteLine("thirdStr = {0}", thirdStr);
Console.WriteLine(str == anotherStr); // True - same object
Console.WriteLine(str == thirdStr); // True - equal objects
Console.WriteLine((object)str == (object)anotherStr); // True
Console.WriteLine((object)str == (object)thirdStr); // False
```

If you run the code, you should get the following outcome:

```
Console.WriteLine(
str = soda
anotherStr = soda
```

```
thirdStr = soda
True
True
True
False
```

From the example above, the strings we used, which you can identify with the keyword **string**, have their values set as objects because they are reference type strings. You will also notice that while they are different objects, the objects **str** and **thirdStr** have equal values. They can, therefore, be found at different locations in the memory.

Take a look at the variables **str** and **anotherStr**. You will notice that they are equal, and are one, and are pretty much the same object. If we compare **str** and **thirdStr**, you end up with an equality. This happens because when we introduce the comparison operator ==, we compare the variables of the strings by their underlying value, and not their address. From the examples above, we can thus conclude that using the comparison operator == assumes different behaviors when comparing strings. However, when you use the comparison operator on other reference types like classes and arrays, the comparison is done by addresses.

In C#, we use logical operators in expressions to arrive at Boolean (logical) conclusions. The logical operators used in this case are `||, &&, ^, and !.` Let's have a look at how to introduce logical operators in conditional statements below.

You can only use the logical AND, and the logical OR on Boolean expressions. The result can only return true if all the operands are true. Let's see an example of this below:

```
bool result = (5 < 7) && (7 < 9);
```

The expression above will return true because the value in all the operands is true. As you delve into C#, you will come across the logical AND operator referred to as the short-circuit in some texts. This is true because of its nature. Using this operator, the compiler skips all the unnecessary computations. It first examines the first operand, and if the result is false, it does not proceed to the second operand. This is because as long as the first operand is false, by convention, the result of the entire operation cannot be true.

The operator will also result in true if at least one of the two operands is true. Let's see an example of this below:

```
bool result = (5 < 7) || (3 == 5);
```

This result will be true because the first operand is true. The compiler ignores the second operand because it already knows the first part is true.

The logical comparison operators **|** and **&** are similar in application to **||** and **&&**. The only difference is that in the application, these operators must be calculated in consequence, even though you know the outcome beforehand. For this reason, the operators are referred to as full-circuit logical operators, though they are rarely used.

If you compare an illustration where the two operands are in use, the second part is still executed even if the first one returns false. The same applies when the first operand is true. Take note, however, that as much as the Boolean operators and bitwise operators are written in the same manner, their actions and results are not the same.

Another example of a full circuit operator is the exclusive OR (^). The operator result returns true if only one of the operands is true. However, if both operands are simultaneously true, the result is false. Let's explain this in an example below:

```
Console.WriteLine ( "Exclusive OR: "+ ((5 < 7) ^ (6 > 7)));
```

If we run the code above, we get the following result:

```
Exclusive OR: False
```

In the example above, each of the operands (**5 < 7**) and (**6 > 7**) is true, hence the compiler returns a false.

"if "and "if-else"

Having learned how to perform comparisons, the next step is to look at implementing logic in C# programming. The conditional statements if and if-else are useful in conditional control. When in use, the compiler first checks for a predetermined condition before executing the statement. The default conditional if statement follows the syntax below:

```
if (Boolean expression)
{
Body of the conditional statement;
}
```

In the syntax above, the Boolean expression can only be either a Boolean logical expression or a Boolean variable. Also, note that a Boolean expression can never be an integer. This rule, however, does not apply in other programming languages like C or C++.

The body of the conditional statement can contain more than one statement. The expression that comes after the **if** keyword will only return a **true** or a **false**. If the expression returns true, the compiler executes the rest of the body of the conditional statement. However, if the expression returns a **false**, it skips the other operators within the body of the conditional statement. Let's explain this with an example:

```
static void Main()
{
Console.WriteLine("Input two digits.");
Console.Write("Input first digit: ");
int firstDigit = int.Parse(Console.ReadLine());
Console.Write("Input second digit: ");
int secondDigit = int.Parse(Console.ReadLine());
int largerDigit = firstDigit;
if (secondDigit > firstDigit)
{
largerDigit = secondDigit;
}
Console.WriteLine("The larger digit is: {0}", largerDigit);
}
```

If we run this code using the numbers 7 and 9, we should get the following output:

```
Enter two digits.
Enter first digit: 7
Enter second digit: 9
The larger digit is: 9
```

Next, let's see how to handle conditional **if-else** statements. The syntax for an **if-else** statement is as shown below:

```
if (Boolean expression)
{
Body of the conditional statement;
}
else
{
Body of the else statement;
}
```

In this case, the compiler will calculate the Boolean expression, whose result must be a Boolean true or false. If the result returns true, the compiler executes the body of the conditional statement. However, if it returns false, the compiler ignores the **else** statement, thereby preventing its operators from executing.

On the other hand, if the Boolean expression returns false, the body of the statement in the **else** statement executes. If this happens, the compiler will neither execute the main body of the conditional statement or its operators. Let's explain this with an example:

```
static void Main()
{
int a = 7;
if (a > 9)
{
Console.WriteLine("a is greater than 9");
}
else
{
Console.WriteLine("a is not greater than 9");
}
}
```

From the statement above, a = 7. The compiler will execute the Boolean expression of the else structure, returning the following result:

```
a is not greater than 9
```

When using **if** and **if-else** statements, you can easily run into complications. To avoid that, use the following tips:

First, many beginners struggle with ambiguous code from time to time. To make your code clearer, write in code blocks, and enclose your code in curly brackets after **if** and **else**.

Secondly, you should also make an effort to keep your code neat and cleanly formatted. For this purpose, offset the code inwards by one tab after the **if** and **else**. This makes your code easy to read.

CHAPTER 6:

Loops

In C# programming, you will often come across code or code snippets that must be executed repeatedly. This is what we refer to as a loop. A loop is a programming convention whereby the compiler is instructed to execute a given code segment repeatedly. There are different types of loops. Usually, the code snippet is repeated in a loop either until a preset condition is met, or up to a preset number of times. You can also have an infinite loop, that which never ends. Considering the memory consumption, you will hardly ever use an infinite loop. However, in cases where an infinite loop is necessary, you must introduce a break operator in the body to prematurely terminate the infinite loop.

While Loops

The easiest and most common loop in C# is the **while loop**. The syntax for this type is as shown below:

```
while (condition)
{
loop body;
}
```

This loop describes an expression that will return a Boolean true or false as the result. The loop condition describes how long the body will be repeated. This is the body of code that is executed each time the code snipped is in a loop (when the predetermined input condition returns true).

A while loop will first evaluate the Boolean expression. If it returns true, the compiler loops the body of code. This process will repeat until a point where the conditional expression returns a false. At this point, the compiler terminates the loop, and the immediate line after the loop body is executed.

Note that the loop body will only execute if the Boolean expression returns a true. If it returns false, the while loop will not execute. At the same time, if the underlying condition that perpetuates the cycle does not break, the loop will persist indefinitely. Let's look at a simple while loop example that prints cycles in ascending order below:

```
// Start the count
int count = 63;
// Keep the loop running while the loop condition remains true
while (count <= 68)
{
// Display the cycle value
Console.WriteLine("Cycle : " + count);
// Increase the count
count++;
}
```

If we execute the code above, we should get the following outcome:

```
Cycle : 63
Cycle : 64
Cycle : 65
Cycle : 66
Cycle : 67
Cycle : 68
```

Now, let's build on this example and see what else we can do with a while loop. The first step is to learn how to add numbers in a sequence as shown below:

```
Console.Write("x = ");
int x = int.Parse(Console.ReadLine());
int num = 1;
int sum = 1;
Console.Write("The sum 1");
while (num < x)
{
num++;
sum += num;
Console.Write(" + " + num);
}
Console.WriteLine(" = " + sum);
```

The compiler will begin with the variables **num** and **sum** at 1. In essence, we instruct the compiler to start with 1 and add 1 to each of the preceding numbers. Therefore, this is a simple loop where we add 1 to the previous number to get the next number.

In this part of the code **while (num < x)**, we instruct the compiler to keep adding 1 to the numbers, as long as it is within the range of 1 to x. This will persist until the final result when the **num** value is x. If we run the code above and enter the value of x as 6, we will have the following output:

```
while (num < x)
X = 6
The sum 1 + 2 + 3 + 4 + 5 + 6 = 21
```

As you can see, the program will keep running and adding 1 to the next value, until the value of x is 6.

Do-While Loops

The while loop is the basic foundation of loops. From there, we build on to the **do-while** loop. It works in the same way the while loop does, but with a twist. It must check after each loop execution to determine whether the condition is true or false. The syntax for a **do-while** loop is as shown below:

```
do
{
executable code;
} while (condition);
```

In the beginning, the compiler will execute the loop body. After that, it checks the condition of the loop. The loop repeats if the condition is true. However, if the condition is false, the loop terminates. If the condition of the loop never changes and is always true, this loop will run infinitely. It is an important loop that you can use when you are certain the code sequence will be run repeatedly at least once at the beginning of the loop. Let's look at an example to explain this:

```
Console.Write("x = ");
int x = int.Parse(Console.ReadLine());
decimal factorial = 1;
do
{
factorial *= x;
n--;
} while (x > 0);
Console.WriteLine("x! = " + factorial);
```

In this code, we begin with a result of 1 and keep multiplying the result at each loop with x, and at the same time, reducing x by one value until the value of x is 0. This is a simple example of mathematical factorial expressions, in the format **x*(x-1)*...*1**. You will realize that this sequence will not yield when the value of x is equal to or less than 0. This is because the sequence must perform at least one multiplication. In the example above, we should have the following output:

```
x = 7
x! = 5040
```

Note that this will work flawlessly for small numbers. However, if you input larger numbers for the value of x, for example, x = 143, the decimal type overflows, and you end up with an exception as shown below:

```
Unhandled Exception: System.OverflowException: Value was either
too large or too small for a Decimal.
```

To avoid this problem, you will use the **BigInteger** data type. This data type allows you to use large integers. Provided your computer has sufficient memory, there is no limit on the size of numbers you can use with the **BigInteger** data type.

It might take a while to calculate the factorial using this data type, but you will not run into **OverflowException** errors. Unfortunately, while this data type is powerful and allows you to do so much, it is heavy on memory consumption, thus slower than **long** and **int** data types.

For Loops

These loops build on the knowledge we have learned about the while and do-while loops. However, they are slightly more complex but are useful in that they reduce the amount of work you perform by writing less code than you would have with the while and do-while loops. The general structure of for loops is as shown below:

```
for (X; Y; Z)
{
N;
}
for (int i=0; i<10; i++)
{
/* loop body */
}
```

In the structure above, there are four parts, **N, X, Y,** and **Z**. The code initializes at **X**, the loop condition is prescribed at **Y**, while the body of the loop condition is outlined at **N**. At **Z**, we update the commands the loop variables will use. Based on these instructions, the syntax for this kind of loop is as shown below:

```
for (initialization; condition; update)
{
loop's body;
}
```

Explaining this further, the initialization applies to the counter (**int i=0**). We also have a Boolean condition where **i** must be less than **10 (i<10)**, and finally an instruction that updates the counter (**i++**). This counter is one of the distinct features between for loops and other loops. The number of iterations needed in a for loop is always predetermined before you execute the first line of code.

Note that any elements used in for loops are not usually mandatory. Because of this reason, you can create an infinite loop by omitting them. The initialization stage should look like this:

```
for (int num = 0; ...; ...)
{
// You can use the num variables at this point
}
// You cannot use num variables at this point
```

The initialization code block runs once before the loop begins. At this stage, you declare the loop variables and set the initial values. Note that at this point, more than one variable can be declared.

Next, we declare the condition for the loop. The loop condition looks like this:

```
for (int num = 0; num < 10; ...)
{
// Body of the loop
}
```

Like we mentioned earlier, the compiler will evaluate the condition of this loop each time before it iterates as we saw in while loops. If the evaluation returns true, the compiler executes the code block. If it returns false, the compiler skips this code block, effectively ending the loop.

In the loop body, you have all the variables declared in the initialization block. For example, if we run the following code,

```
for (int i = 0; i <= 6; i++)
{
Console.Write(i + " ");
}
```

We will get the following output:

```
0 1 2 3 4 5 6
```

We can now introduce the **continue** operator. This operator terminates the loop by stopping the most recent loop iteration. Let's use an example to show how it works:

```
int x = int.Parse(Console.ReadLine());
int sum = 0;
for (int i = 1; i <= x; i += 2)
{
if (i % 5 == 0)
{
continue;
}
sum += i;
}
Console.WriteLine("sum = " + sum);
```

In the example above, the code determines the sum of odd integers in the range of **1-x**, which are not divisible by 5 using the for loop. Using **x=13,** we are looking at the following odd integers: (1, 3, 5, 7, 9, 11, 13).

The code initializes with 1 (the first odd integer in our range **x=13**). At each iteration, the code confirms whether the value of **x** has exceeded **(i<=x)**. Since we are only looking at odd numbers, the update instruction is to increase the integers by 2.

Within the loop body, the compiler checks to determine whether the current odd integer is divisible by 5. If it is divisible, the operator **continue** is called into action, skipping the rest of the loop body. If the odd integer is divisible by 5, the code updates the sum with the current odd integer. Using **x=13**, we should have the following output:

```
13
sum = 44
```

Nested Loops

A nested loop is a set of programming instructions where loops are housed within other loops. When using nested loops, the outermost loops are iterated fewer times than the innermost loops. The general syntax for nested loops is as follows:

```
for ( initialization, verification, update)
{
for ( initialization, verification, update)
{
executable code
}
...
}
```

Immediately after the first for loop is initialized, the body, which houses the nested loop, is executed. The compiler initializes its variables, checks the condition, and executes the code within that loop body. If the condition is true, it is updated and the loop continues until the condition returns false. If we have a false, the second code snippet of the for loop begins, performing the same process as above.

Basically, when implementing a nested loop, you are essentially implementing a for-loop internally and another for-loop externally.

CHAPTER 7:

Arrays

Arrays are useful when programming a sequence of elements from the same data type. An array is a collection of variables. In C#, the elements of an array are known as indices and are numbered as 0, 1, 2, …, N-1. The length of an array refers to the total number of elements found in the array.

An array can contain different elements. That being said, you will either have reference type elements or primitive type elements. In C# programming, all the elements that make up either of the types mentioned must be of the same type. This way, it is easier to identify a group with similar elements and work on the sequence as one unit.

While arrays can exist in different dimensions, for the purpose of this discussion, and most of the arrays you will come across in C#, we will use one-dimensional and two-dimensional arrays. One-dimensional arrays are known as vectors, while two-dimensional arrays are known as matrices.

Array Declaration

Arrays length is assigned when you instantiate the array, and it also defines the number of elements contained in the array. Note that the array length is fixed, and once it is set, you cannot change it. The syntax for declaring an array is as follows:

```
int[] myArray;
```

In the syntax above, the name of the array is captured in **myArray**. The array must be of the integer type, hence **int[]**. You should also note that by enclosing the integer numbers in the brackets, we are simply highlighting that we have declared a variable that is not a single element, but an array of elements.

If you declare an array type variable, we have a reference. A reference has no value, hence it will direct us to null. Reference points directly to null because they do not have any memory allocated in lieu of the elements.

Moving on from references, we create arrays in C# using the keyword **new**. In doing so, the console assigns memory to the array. An example of this is shown below:

```
int[] myArray = new int[8];
```

From the example above, we create an integer type array with 8 elements. What this means is that in the console's dynamic memory, we just created room for 8 integer numbers, but when they initialize, they will all have their values set at zero. The dynamic memory is the point at which array elements are stored, also known as the heap. Each time you create a new array and allocate memory to the **myArray** variable, its reference point is in the dynamic memory.

As you allocate memory to the array created, you must also indicate the number of elements that will be present in the array. This must be a non-negative integer number, enclosed in brackets, which describes the length of the array. After the keyword **new**, you indicate the type of elements used in the array, to which memory will be allocated.

Elements within an array are initially set at zero values. To use the elements, you must either set them to a default value or initialize them to a different value. Note the difference between C# and other programming languages in that all variables must always have a default value. This is not the case in other programming languages. If you try to access a variable in C# that does not have a default value, you get an error.

The default initial value for variables in C# is **0** when using numeral data types. If you are coding with non-primitive data types, the default initial value can be any relevant equivalent. For example, if you are using the **bool** type, the default initial value can be **true**, or **null** for a reference type. Let's look at an example of this below:

```
int[] myArray = { 1, 2, 3, 4, 5, 6, 7, 8 };
```

What we have done in the instruction above is to initialize the array elements immediately after the array is declared. Using the syntax above, instead of the keyword new, you will use curly brackets. Enclosed within the brackets, you will find a list of all the initial values used in the array. Let's use another example below:

```
string[] EPLTop10GameWeek14 =
{ "Liverpool", "Leicester", "Everton","ManUtd", "Chelsea",
"Arsenal", "Tottenham", "Southampton","Wolves", "ManCity" };
```

In the example above, we have created an array of ten elements of the string type. The string type is the reference type, whose values are initialized in the dynamic memory. In the stack memory, we have allocated a variable **EPLTop10GameWeek14**, which directs us to a section in the dynamic memory where the array elements can be found.

By default, arrays are zero-based, meaning that we start counting from zero. The first array element is always 0, while the next, in an array of **n** elements, is derived as **N-1**.

Elements of an Array

In C#, you can directly access an array using its indicative index. Each element in an array can be identified using the array name and the index number corresponding to the element. In this manner, we can treat elements in the same manner that we treat variables. Let's look at an example below of how to access an element in an array:

```
myArray[index] = 73;
```

In the example above, the element is given a value of 73, which is its index position in the array. Each time you try to access an element, the .NET Framework automatically checks the elements to verify the validity of its index. This also helps you tell whether the element is outside the array range. If you try to access an element that is not within the range of the array (an invalid element), you get the following error:

```
System.IndexOutOfRangeException
```

This automated check is useful in that it will help you identify errors when coding with arrays. Unfortunately, such checks will always cause a performance lag, given that memory is committed to the check. However, what's a bit of memory lag compared to the magnitude of errors you would run into when trying to run code that references arrays which are impossible to reach?

CHAPTER 8:

Numeral Systems

Decimal, hexadecimal, and binary are the most commonly used numeral systems in computer programming. To get a better grip of C# programming, you must understand how these numeral systems work, and more importantly, how computers encode different numeral data. Numeral systems have been around for years, dating as far back as ancient times. There are many kinds of numeral systems that have been in use since then. In the modern world, the decimal system is widely used, especially since you can easily count the base numbers on your fingers.

In the realm of computer programming, numeral systems are simply a method through which we can represent finite digits. While many numeral systems have been used in the past, the Arabic numeral system gained more popularity over the years, with digits ranging from 0 to 9.

Each numeral system must have a base. The base is a unique number that is equal to the number of digits used in the system. For example, in the Arabic numeral system, we have 10 digits. This is a decimal system, and we can select any number to act as the base. The base in the Arabic numeral system must have an absolute value, which is neither 1 nor 0. The base can also be a complex number with a sign or a real number.

Non-Positional Numeral Systems

A positional numeral system is a numbering system where the position of digits is significant to the value of the number. What this means is that the digit's number does not have a distinct value. Therefore, since it is not strictly defined, the value depends on the position assigned to the digit. Let's look at an example to explain this below:

```
532, 25364
```

In the example above, the digit `2` has a value of 2 in 532, while it has a value of 20,000 in 25364.

For computing purposes, systems with bases of 2, 8, 10 and 16 are more prevalent than any other numeral system you will come across. Below, let's look at brief notation for different numbering systems as used in computer programming:

```
Binary     Octal     Decimal  Hexadecimal
0000        0           0           0
0001              1           1           1
0010              2           2           2
0011              3           3           3
0100              4           4           4
0101              5           5           5
0110              6           6           6
0111              7           7           7
1000              10          8           8
1001              11          9           9
1010              12          10          A
1011              13          11          B
1100              14          12          C
1101              15          13          D
1110              16          14          E
1111              17          15          F
```

Away from positional numeral systems, we also have non-positional numeral systems. In this system, digits have permanent and consistent values. Such values are not dependent on the position in the number as we saw in the earlier example of 2 in `532` and `25364`. In this category, we have the Greek and Roman numeral systems.

While non-positional numeral systems are used in many instances, they all face an inefficiency challenge in large number notation. For this reason, they are often limited to a few use cases. Because of this inefficiency, they are prone to inaccuracies, especially when determining the values. Let's take a closer look at each of these numeral systems:

The Roman numeral system sequence is as shown below:

```
Roman Number: I V X L C D M
Decimal Value: 1 5 10 50 100 500 1000
```

We already mentioned that the digit position holds no significance over the value of the number. Therefore, to determine the value, you consider the following rules:

First, you add the values if two consecutively represented digits are aligned in such a way that the first value is larger or equal to the second value. Here's an example:

```
MMC (2100) = 1000 + 1000 + 100
III (3) = 1 + 1 + 1
```

Second, if two values are aligned in increasing order of their values, you subtract them from right to left. Here are some examples:

```
MXL (1040) = 1000 - 10 + 50
IX (9) = -1 + 10
MXXIV (1024) = 1000 + 10 + 10 -1 + 5
```

The Greek numeral system, on the other hand, is a decimal system that groups digits in fives as shown below:

```
Greek Number: I Γ Δ H X M
Decimal Value: 1 5 10 100 1000 10000
```

Going by the examples above, the following are some numbering examples used in the Greek numeral system:

```
ΓΔ = 50 = 5 x 10
ΓH = 500 = 5 x 100
ΓX = 5000 = 5 x 1,000
ΓM = 50,000 = 5 x 10,000
```

The binary numeral system is the basis of computing. It is widely used because the cost of producing binary numeral devices is lower compared to other systems. Other than that, it is easy to implement for devices with two stable states. That being said, numbers expressed using binary systems are generally too long, which means that they consume a lot of memory for those with large bit numbers. This is, however, only a challenge for human application. We circumvent that problem by using systems programmed with large bases.

Number Conversion

Binary and decimal numbers are the most commonly used numeral systems in programming. From time to time, you will need to convert one to the other, using a conversion system applicable to each of the systems. The binary system is made up of digits ordered to the power of 2. This means that each binary digit is raised to the power of the position it holds. Let's look at an example below:

```
Convert the binary number to decimal: 10101_2
= (1 x 2^4) + (0 x 2^3) + (1 x 2^2) + (0 x 2^1) + (1 x 2^0)
= (16_10) + (0) + (4_10) + (0) + (0)
```

```
= 20₁₀
```

From the example above, you can see the multiplication by 2, raised to the power of the position the digit is located. This is how we convert from binary to decimal.

You can also perform the conversion from decimal to binary numeral systems. To do this, you divide the number by two, leaving a remainder. This is how to arrive at the remainder and quotient. You continue the same routine until you end up with a zero quotient. You will notice that from the remainders, you either have a 1 or 0. Let's work on an example of this, using the number 158:

```
158/2 = 79 remainder 0
79/2 = 39 remainder 1
39/2 = 19 remainder 1
19/2 = 9 remainder 1
9/2 = 4 remainder 1
4/2 = 2 remainder 0
2/2 = 1 remainder 0
½ = 0 remainder 1
```

After the division, you take the remainders and represent them in reverse order as shown below:

```
10011110
```

Therefore, the conversion of 158_{10} to binary is 10011110_2.

Binary Numeral Operations

The next process you will learn is how to perform normal arithmetic operations using binary numbers. However, you will notice a few differences when computing binary numbers. Let's look at some examples below:

```
Addition
0 + 0 = 0
1 + 0 = 1
0 + 1 = 1
1 + 1 = 10
Subtraction
0 - 0 = 0
1 - 0 = 1
1 - 1 = 0
10 - 1 = 1
Multiplication
0 x 0 = 0
1 x 0 = 0
0 x 1 = 0
1 x 1 = 1
```

You can use the bitwise operators AND, and OR to check the values of different numbers. Let's say we want to confirm whether a number is odd or even. To do this, you try to confirm whether the lowest bit in that order is 1. The number is odd if the lowest order bit is 1, and even if it is 0. When programming in C#, you can represent the bitwise AND using the & sign as shown below:

```
int result = integer1 & integer2;
```

You can also use the bitwise operator OR to raise the value of a given digit to 1. This is represented in code as shown below:

```
int result = integer1 | integer2;
```

Next, you can also use the bitwise XOR operator. When used in your code, the compiler processes every binary digit independently. Assuming the operand contains a 0, the compiler will copy the value of the bit in the first operand. In each position with a value of 1 in the second operand, the value is reversed as was displayed in the first operand. This is represented in code as shown below:

```
int result = integer1 ^ integer2;
```

Hexadecimal numbers have a base of 16. This means that they use 16 digits to represent all the digits between 0 and 15. Note, however, that in the hexadecimal system, digits are represented from 0 – 9, and then from A – F. In an earlier table, we outlined the corresponding numeral values for the Latin numbers A – F (10 – 15).

Based on this understanding, you can also have hexadecimal numbers like D3 and 2F1F3. To convert numbers from hexadecimal to the decimal numeral system, you first multiply the value of the digit to the furthermost right by 16^0, the one after it by 16^1, and so on until the last one, then you calculate the €. Let's look at an example of this below:

```
D1E (16) = E*16 0 + 1*16 1 + D*16 2 = 14*1 + 1*16 + 13*256 = 3358 (10)
```

On the other hand, if you are to convert from hexadecimal to a decimal numeral system, you divide the decimal numeral by 16 then use the remainders in the reverse order as we saw earlier in decimal to binary.

Remember, however, that the remainders are expressed in hexadecimal numeral systems wherever applicable. For example, we have the following:

```
3358 / 16 = 209 + remainder 14 €
209 / 16 = 13 + remainder 1 (1)
13 / 16 = 0 + remainder 13 (D)
```

The outcome of the remainders, in reverse order, gives us $D1E_{16}$.

If this process seems tedious or too long, you can also perform the conversion by dividing the binary number into four-bit groups. In some cases, the digits will not be divisible by four, in which case, you do not add the leading zeros for the highest orders in the sequence. After that, you replace each of the groups with their corresponding digits. Let's look at an example of this below:

```
11100111110₂
```

For this value, we will first divide into groups of four as shown below:

```
0011 1001 1110
```

When we replace each of the half-bytes with the corresponding hexadecimal digits, you end up with $39E_{16}$.

Binary code is useful to programmers because it allows you to store data in the operating memory. The manner in which information is stored is always determined by the data type. It is, therefore, imperative that you learn how to present and process different types of data. Note that computing devices can only process data when it is presented according to the number of bytes, thereby forming a machine word.

When using numeral systems, integers can always be presented either with or without a sign. If you use an integer with a sign, you implicitly introduce a signed order. This becomes the highest order in the sequence, with positive numbers having 0 and 1 as the highest value for negative numbers. All the other orders are used for information purposes only, and for this reason, they can only represent the value of the number assigned to them. If you use an unsigned number, its value can be represented by any or all of the bits.

CHAPTER 9:

C# Methods

Methods refer to the simple parts of a computer program that solve problems and can use parameters to return a result. A method simply outlines all the data conversion processes involved in returning a result. This is also referred to as the logic of the program. Think of a method in the context of the steps you follow when solving a calculus problem. Once you understand the method, you can use that knowledge to code bigger, more complex programs that can solve complicated problems.

Let's say we want to write a program that calculates the area of a rectangle. That code will be as shown below:

```
static double GetRectangleArea(double width, double height)
{
double area = width * height;
return area;
}
```

The concept of methods in programming follows the rule of divide and conquer. Most problems can be solved by breaking them down into smaller sub-problems. It is easier to define, understand, and solve such smaller problems than to try to resolve complex problems as a whole.

Based on the same principle, computer programs are written to solve problems. First divide the problem into smaller tasks, and by finding solutions to the small tasks you can put them together into one solution for the entire program. These small solutions are referred to as subroutines, which in some programming languages, can allude to procedures or functions. In C#, however, we call them methods.

Granted, there are many reasons why you should consider using methods in programming. Let's have a look at some of the reasons why methods are an important aspect of programming that you must learn.

First, you have a better chance of writing code that is easily readable and properly structured using methods. This is good practice because it makes it easier for someone else to read and maintain your code. Once you write a program, maintenance consumes a lot of time and resources. It gets even more complicated when adding new features and updates to the program. Once you write and release a program, other developers who have access to it will also invest their time and resources into maintenance to suit their needs.

Second, methods are a good way to prevent repetitive code. This is also related to code reuse. Code reuse refers to lines of code that are used several times in a program. If you have such code, you can highlight it in the method so that you don't have to rewrite it all the time. Code reuse will also help you avoid repeating code.

The challenge of repeating code is that it slows down the program and increases the risk of errors. Besides, when developers are fixing errors in code blocks, there's a good chance they will only fix some of the errors present in repeating code. Therefore, as long as some of the code still has errors, the program will still be buggy.

Declaring Methods

There are three kinds of actions you can perform to an existing method:

1. **Declaring a method** - This is a process where you call the method's identity so that the rest of the program can recognize it.
2. **Implementing a method** - This refers to creating a method. You enter code that eventually solves a given problem. Since the code already exists within the method, we can look at this as the logic of the method.
3. **Calling a method** - This is where you invoke the declared method from the section of the code where a problem is to be solved.

Before you learn how to declare a method, you should know where you can call methods in C#. Methods only exist when they are declared and enclosed within brackets of a class. On the same note, you cannot declare a method within the body of another method. Let's look at a simple example of declaring a method below:

```
public class HelloCSharp
{ // new class starts here
// declare the method here
static void Main(string[] args)
{
Console.WriteLine("Hello C#!");
}
} // new class ends here
```

To declare a method, you use the syntax below:

```
[static] <return_type> <method_name>([<param_list>])
```

From the syntax above, the type of result the method will return is identified by **`<return_type>`**. The name of the method is listed as **`<method_name>`**, while inside **`<param_list>`**, you list all the parameters that will be used in the method. Note that you can also have an empty list.

We can also use **`Main()`** to identify the elements present in the method declaration. An example of this is as shown below:

```
static void Main(string[] args)
```

In the example above, the method does not return any result, hence the returned value is **`void`**. The parameter in this example is the **`string[] args`** array. If you have an empty parameter list, all you have to do is key in `()` after the name of the method.

Method Implementation

Once you declare a method, the next step is to implement it. The implementation of a method will include the body of the code, which is executed when you call the method. Note that to represent the logic of the method, the code has to be within the body of the method in question. The body of the method refers to the code enclosed within the curly brackets as shown in the example below, which follows the declaration.

```
Static <return_type> <method_name>(<parameters_list>)
{
// The code in this segment is the body of the method
}
```

The method encapsulates the real programming work expected of the code. Therefore, if you are writing an algorithm to solve some problem, this is where it is included. Note that you can never declare a method within the body of another method.

Each time you declare a variable within the body of a method, the variable becomes a local variable with respect to the called method. The extent of a local variable starts at the line where you declare the variable and ends at the closing curly bracket of the method body. This extent is referred to as the variable scope or area of visibility of the variable. Assuming you try to declare another local variable after declaring a variable using a similar name, the compiler returns an error. Let's explain this with an example below:

```
static void Main()
{
int m = 82;
int m = 13;
}
```

You get an error when you try to run the code above. This is because the compiler cannot allow you to use the name **m** for two local variables. As a result, you will get the following error message:

```
A local variable named 'm' is already defined in this scope.
```

If we declare a local variable in a given block of code, it becomes a local variable for that block of code. Therefore, the area of visibility for that code will also start from the beginning of the variable declaration to the end, where you have the closing bracket.

Next, we look at what it means to invoke or call a method. This refers to executing the method code found in the method body. Invoking a method is quite easy, given that all you have to do is write the name of the method, the round brackets, and a semicolon as shown below:

```
<method_name>();
```

Immediately after you execute a method, it takes charge and initiates a sequence of events that will run your program. However, if you call the method and call another method within the active method, the original method relinquishes control to the newly called method. It will only return control back once it terminates execution. After that, the original caller method continues from the line it paused before calling the new method.

CHAPTER 10:

Recursion

Recursion refers to an instance where an object can be defined by itself or contains itself. It is a technique where a method can call itself to solve problems. If this happens, the method is said to be recursive. One of the reasons why recursion is an important technique in programming is because it helps make code easily readable.

The simplest example of recursion is the Fibonacci numbers sequence. In this sequence, the next number is arrived at by adding the previous two numbers. Let's look at an example of the sequence below:

```
1, 1, 2, 3, 5, 8, 13, 21, 34, 55, 89, 144, ...
```

Recursive functions are useful in simplifying complex problems. However, you must also be attentive when using recursive functions in programming.

A direct recursive is an instance where a call to a method arises within the body of the same method. Assuming you have three methods, X, Y, and Z, if X calls Y, Y calls Z, and Z calls X, we have a mutually recursive or indirectly recursive function.

Before you start a recursive function, you must first make sure that you will get a definite result after a given number of recursive calls. As a precautionary measure, it is wise to have at least one scenario where you can arrive at a solution directly without invoking a recursive call. Such scenarios are referred to as the bottom of recursion.

In the Fibonacci numbers example we used earlier, the bottom of recursion is a situation where n is equal to or less than 2. You don't need to run a recursive function to arrive at this, because by default, the first two elements in the Fibonacci sequence must always be equal to 1. In an instance where the recursive method used does not have a bottom of recursion or base, we end up with an infinite, hence the outcome **`StackOverflowException`**.

Recursive tasks are generally complex in nature. For this reason, you must create smaller tasks (subtasks), solve them, and use the successful algorithm in a recursive function. By recursively using the algorithm, you arrive at solutions to the subtasks, and in the long run, you find a solution to the initial problem.

Recursive Calculations

To understand recursive calculations, we will use a simple factorial example. The factorial of x, written as (**`x!`**) should give us the product of all the integers between 1 and x inclusive. This can also be defined as `0! = 1`, and expressed as follows:

```
x! = 1.2.3...x
```

To create the definition above, it is easier to use the corresponding factorial definition as shown below:

```
x! = 1, for x = 0
x! = x.(x-1)!, for x > 0
```

In many cases, you have to analyze a problem and work out the values before you can identify the first integers. The simplest case is always found at the bottom of the recursion. In our case, that is **`x = 0`**, where the factorial value = 1. For other instances, you must first solve **`x - 1`** and then multiply the result by **`x`**. Since there are a definite number of integers between 0 and x, you will arrive at the bottom of the recursion after a definite number of steps. From here, you can then write the recursion method to compute factorials as shown below:

```
static decimal Factorial(int x)
{
// The bottom of the recursion
if (x == 0)
{
return 1;
}
// The method will call itself (a recursive call)
else
{
return x * Factorial(x - 1);
}
```

```
}
```

Using the method above, you can easily write an application to read integer values from the console, compute the factorials, and print the result. Let's look at an example of this below:

```
using System;
class RecursiveFactorial
{
static void Main()
{
Console.Write("x = ");
int x = int.Parse(Console.ReadLine());
decimal factorial = Factorial(x);
Console.WriteLine("{0}! = {1}", x, factorial);
}
static decimal Factorial(int x)
{
// The bottom of the recursion
if (x == 0)
{
return 1;
}
// The method will call itself (a recursive call)
else
{
return x * Factorial(x - 1);
}
}
}
```

Assuming that we are looking for the factorial of x = 6, we will have the following outcome:

```
x = 6
x! = 720
```

Recursion vs. Iteration

To explain the concept of recursion, factorial calculations are the most natural example. As simple as they are, there are many other instances where a recursion might not be the best solution. Naturally, a recurrent solution fits a recurrent problem definition. You will hardly encounter difficulties using that approach. However, iterative solutions might actually be a better option, and more efficient than recursive solutions. Here is an example of an iterative syntax:

```
static decimal Factorial(int x)
{
decimal result = 1;
for (int i = 1; i <= x; i++)
{
result = result * i;
}
return result;
}
```

The lesson here is that before you rush to a recursive solution for your problems, you should also consider the possibility of an iterative solution, then choose the most viable of the two.

This brings us to the question, which is the better alternative between recursion and iteration? Granted, the first thing you have to consider is the nature of the algorithm. If you have a recursive algorithm, it makes sense to implement a recursive solution. Compared to an iterative solution, this would be more elegant and easy to read.

There are some instances where it might be difficult to define the algorithm, or prove the difference between a recursive and iterative one. Recursion is generally recommended for shorter, simpler problems.

At the same time, it is worth noting that recursion is generally resource-intensive. The computer must set aside some new memory for each recursive call. If your program makes a lot of such calls, you will end up with a stack overflow as you run out of memory. There are also instances where a simple recursion solution might be more challenging to implement than a relevant iterative solution.

The bottom line is that regardless of its resource-intensive nature, recursion is still one of the most powerful techniques you will come across in C# programming. However, you must weigh your options before you use it. More often, using an unnecessary recursion solution where an iteration would be more efficient leads to maintenance problems. You might also end up with an inefficient program that is difficult to understand.

We mentioned the Fibonacci sequence earlier, as the simplest and most fitting example of recursion. We will build on that and show why recursion might not be the best idea. Let's look at an example below, where we use recursion to find the xth Fibonacci number in the sequence:

```
static long Fib(int x)
{
if (x <= 2)
{
return 1;
}
return Fib(x - 1) + Fib(x - 2);
}
```

This syntax is simple and easy to understand. At a glance, it looks like the best solution. Unfortunately, this is not the case. Let's say the xth value is set at 141. The program will take a very long time to compute the value, and waiting would be pointless. Besides, implementing the solution would be equally inefficient, given that each recursive call creates two more calls, which further create two more and so on. Bearing this in mind, the Fibonacci tree will grow to exponential lengths, which is cumbersome.

You can overcome this problem through memoization. Memoization helps you optimize recursive methods by saving the numbers already calculated in arrays. This way, it will only call the array if the calculation you are about to perform has not been done yet.

```
using System;
class RecursiveFibonacciMemoization
{
static long[] numbers;
static void Main()
{
Console.Write("x = ");
int x = int.Parse(Console.ReadLine());
numbers = new long[x + 2];
numbers[1] = 1;
numbers[2] = 1;
long result = Fib(x);
Console.WriteLine("fib({0}) = {1}", x, result);
}
static long Fib(int x)
{
if (0 == numbers[x])
{
numbers[x] = Fib(x - 1) + Fib(x - 2);
}
return numbers[x];
}
}
```

By optimizing this new computation, you get the answer almost instantly because it performs a linear computation. Running the code above, you should have the following output:

```
n = 141
fib(141) = 131151201344081895336534324866
```

An iterative solution for calculating the next number in the Fibonacci sequence means you calculate the numbers consecutively. In this case, you use only the last two elements calculated in the sequence to determine the next element in the sequence. An example of this is as shown below:

```
using System;
class IterativeFibonacci
{
static void Main()
{
Console.Write("n = ");
int n = int.Parse(Console.ReadLine());
long result = Fib(n);
Console.WriteLine("fib({0}) = {1}", n, result);
}
static long Fib(int n)
{
long fn = 0;
long fnMinus1 = 1;
long fnMinus2 = 1;
for (int i = 2; i < n; i++)
{
fn = fnMinus1 + fnMinus2;
fnMinus2 = fnMinus1;
fnMinus1 = fn;
}
return fn;
}
}
```

This method will return the solution faster. It is elegant and shorter than a recursive solution. Other than that, it does not hog memory. From our discussion, it is safe to recommend you avoid recursion unless you are certain about what runs under the hood in your code. While it is a powerful programming tool in C#, it could be just as lethal when used in the wrong place.

In principle, you do not need to use recursion if the computational process is linear. Iteration is simpler, and performs efficient computations, for example when performing factorial computations. In such computations, you determine the elements in a sequence wherein each of the next elements in the sequence depend on the previous ones only, and not any other.

The main difference between a linear computation and an exponential computation process as used in a recursion solution is that the recursion is called only once in each step, and only in one direction. Below is an example of a linear computation syntax:

```
void Recursion(parameters)
{
Perform computations;
Recursion(some parameters);
Perform computations;
}
```

As you can see, if the body of the recursive method only features one recursion call, the iteration is obvious and you do not need to use recursion. However, in the event of a branched computation, for example when using N nested loops, you cannot replace the process with an iteration. Restrict the use of recursion to situations where it is the simplest, easiest to comprehend, and most efficient solution to your problems, and more importantly, where an obvious iterative solution does not exist.

CHAPTER 11:

Exception Handling

An exception refers to an instance where the normal operation of a computer program is interrupted. Most exceptions are often unexpected, so you should have a way to detect and react to them when they happen. In the unfortunate event of an exception, the normal flow of the program is interrupted. That being said, the state of the program is saved, and the control process is moved along to the exception handler.

Exceptions are raised by the program when an error arises, or if the program encounters an unusual situation. Let's say you are trying to open a file that was deleted from the hard drive. Since the file no longer exists, the path leading to it is inaccurate. In this case, the code instructions for opening the file will raise an exception and display the relevant error message.

From what we have explained so far, exception handling is an important part of object-oriented programming. By now you can already relate to the number of times your computer will raise exceptions when you try to process something out of the ordinary.

An exception in .NET refers to an object that identifies an unexpected event or an error that interrupts the normal flow of your program. When this happens, the method being executed sends a special object with unique information about the error, the program, or operation where the error was identified, and its state at the moment the error occurred. All the relevant information about the error can be found in the stack trace.

You have to understand the construct of a stack trace in order to use it effectively. You can read the following information from the stack trace:

1. Information on the call stack
2. Name of the exception class
3. A message with any additional information about the error

When you read the call stack dump, you will notice that each line has the following information, or something similar:

```
at <namespace>.<class>.<method> in <source file>.cs:line <line>
```

Let's look at an example of an exception:

```
class ExceptionsDemo
{
static void Main()
{
string fileName = "MissingTextFile.txt";
ReadFile(fileName);
}
static void ReadFile(string fileName)
{
TextReader reader = new StreamReader(fileName);
string line = reader.ReadLine();
Console.WriteLine(line);
reader.Close();
}
}
```

In the example above, we are trying to open a text file that is missing. The method throws an exception in the first lines, **`ReadFile()`**. This code will still compile successfully. However, at runtime, we will receive an exception if we did not have the **`MissingTextFile.txt`** file. An error message is displayed on the console, complete with information on how and where the error was identified.

Building on this, exception handling refers to the process wherein exceptions are identified. The process runs through the common language runtime (CLR), wherein each exception is passed on to the kind of code that can handle the issues arising.

When an error is triggered, the local variables do not initialize, and instead, return `null` as the default value. In this case, the CLR will not process any of the lines of code that come after the method where the error happened. Thus, the program stays interrupted until the exception is processed by the relevant handlers.

Exception handling is an important part of object-oriented programming because errors can be processed centrally. This is a significant improvement from procedure-oriented programming where every function can return an error code.

An exception will generally arise when a problem is encountered such that it becomes impossible to successfully complete an operation. The method supporting the said operation can catch and handle the error, or move it along to the method calling the operation. This process makes it easier to run the program because error handling can be designated to different levels in the program call stack. In this way, you write programs in such a way that error management is efficient and flexible, and this also makes it easier to handle unusual situations when they arise.

Hierarchy of Exceptions

You will learn about two types of exceptions in the .NET Framework as shown below:

1. **ApplicationException** - These are raised by applications running on the system. They are defined by different app developers and are used by unique programs.
2. **SystemException** - These are raised by the runtime. They are defined within the .NET libraries and can only be used by the .NET Framework.

Each of the two types of exceptions has a different exception class hierarchy, with unique characteristics. When programming an app, it is always wise to inherit exceptions from the **ApplicationException**. It is good practice only to inherit the **SystemException** within the .NET Framework.

In the .NET Framework, every exception must have an exception class. The two types of exceptions mentioned above can directly inherit from the exception classes. You will also realize that for most of the exceptions you come across when running a program, **ApplicationException** and **SystemException** are the recognized base classes.

Within the exception class, you will find a copy of the call stack at the precise moment the exception was raised. You should also find in this class, a short message that describes the error raised by the method. In some cases, you might also find within the exception an internal exception, also known as a nested, wrapped, or inner exception. This is an important concept that saves time and resources. Instead of each exception appearing in isolation, you can have an exception chain that links all the relevant exceptions together.

CHAPTER 12:

Strings and Text Processing

Think about your computing activity for a moment. It almost always revolves around reading some text files, searching online for some keywords, keying in user data, and so on. All this data is stored in the form of text, which makes up strings. The strings are then processed in C#.

A string is simply a sequence of characters stored in memory in a specific address on your computer. In the Unicode table, all characters have a unique serial number in the .NET Framework. In C# programming, strings are handled through the class **System.String**. Strings allow you to work on computers for most of the tasks you need to process. Below is an example of a string in C#:

```
string greeting = "Good Morning!";
```

In the example above, we have created a string type variable known as **greeting**, with the context of **Good Morning**. This is simply a character array. Instead of declaring the class, you can also declare the variable **char[]**, and enter each character of the rest of the details. There are, however, a few problems with this. First, it is time and resource consuming to key in the characters one by one. Second, the fact that you must key in the characters one by one means that you do not know the text length beforehand. This means that you are unsure whether the text will fit into the preassigned space in your array. Finally, manual text processing is cumbersome.

It is worth noting that **System.String** is not always the best method. Therefore, it is wise to learn a few other ways of representing characters. Compared to other data types, the **string** class meets the threshold for object-oriented programming principles. Values used in this class are stored in the computer's dynamic memory, while its variables maintain a reference to any objects stored in the dynamic memory.

An important feature that defines strings is that they are immutable. This means that the sequence of characters stored within the string cannot be changed directly. If you have to change the content of a variable once it has been assigned, it can only be saved to a different location within the dynamic memory. From here, the variable can point to it.

You will also realize that strings and char arrays (**char[]**) share similarities, but they are not immutable. Just as you would expect with arrays, strings have identities through which you can tell how unique each string is. This way, you can access strings using their indices. To access the character of a given position in the string, you must use the indexer operator **[]**. Note, however, that using the indexer, you can only enjoy read properties for the characters, not read and write. Let's look at an example below:

```
string str = "wxyz";
char ch = str[1]; // ch == 'x'
str[1] = 'w'; // Compilation error!
ch = str[73]; // IndexOutOfRangeException
```

When using strings, you must be careful about how to use punctuation marks. For example, you identify the quoted character by assigning a forward slash before it. Here is an example:

```
string quote = "Her flight arrives \"on Tuesday\"";
// Her flight arrives "on Tuesday"
```

The quotation marks used in the example above are actually part of the text. You add them to the variable after the backslash. By doing this, you instruct the compiler that they are part of the content, and not used to mark the beginning or end of the string. This process where you use special characters within the code is referred to as escaping.

When declaring a string, you are essentially declaring the data type **string**. Note that at the point of declaration, you have not assigned any variables to the string, neither have you allocated memory on the computer for it. All you have done so far is to instruct the compiler that you are creating variable **str**, and when it is used, it should process it as a **string** type. Therefore, no variable has been created at the point of declaration yet, and for that reason, no memory allocated either. The value for the declared string so far is **null**. Note, however, that the value null does not mean the string contains an empty value. Null is a special value, and if you try to manipulate a string of this value, the compiler returns the following error **NullReferenceException**.

Once you declare a string, the next step is to create and initialize it. This process is known as instantiation. At this point, a section of the dynamic memory is assigned to the string. You can instantiate a variable in any of the following methods:

1. **Passing an operation value which will return a string**

You can instantiate a string by passing the value of the operation or expression, thereby returning a string result. The result can be anything from a method that results in values of different variables depending on the instructions passed. Let's look at an example below:

```
string blog = "http://blog.gardens.me";
string info = "I have a blog at: " + blog;
// I have a blog at: http://blog.gardens.me
```

From the example above, we have created the `info` variable by concatenating a variable and a literal.

2. **Assigning the value of a different string**

By assigning the value of a different string, you are essentially redirecting the string variables or value to another string. In this case, you first instantiate the source variable. The assigned variable will then assume the value of the source. The string class in this case acts as a reference to a different address as defined in the first variable.

Since the variables are all directed to the same place, they both receive the same dynamic memory address, and for that reason, they hold the same value. In such an instance, altering the values of either of the variables only affects the altered variable, and not the redirected one. The reason for this is because of string immutability.

3. **Assigning a string literal to it**

This simply means assigning some text content to the string variable. This method of instantiation is recommended when you are already aware of the values expected to be stored in the variable. An example of this is as shown below:

```
string blog = "http://blog.gardens.me";
```

In the example above, you instantiated the variable `blog` with the string literal values referring to the online blog address.

The next step is learning how to read strings and print them to the console. Earlier in the book, we talked about the **`System.Console`** class. We will build on that for this section. Below is simple syntax for reading from strings:

```
string name = Console.ReadLine();
```

As we learned earlier, the **ReadLine()** method waits for you to key in some values and only responds with the variable name once you press Enter on the keyboard. The same class applies when printing data to the console. The syntax is as shown below:

```
Console.WriteLine("I have a blog at: " + blog);
```

Since we are using the **WriteLine()** method, the console will display the message (**I have a blog at**), and **blog** as the value of the name variable. You will also note that at the end of the name variable, the compiler adds the character for a new line. To avoid this and have the messages appearing on the same line, use **Write()** instead.

String Operations

Now that we already know how to create and print strings, our next step is how to perform different operations on them. We will look at some of the methods you use for string operations in C# below.

String Comparisons

While there are several parameters you can use to compare strings, most of the string class comparisons come down to the particular task you need to perform using that string. For example, let's say we want to compare two strings to determine whether or not their values are equal. To do this, we implement the **Equals()** method together with the **==** operator. For this operation, you will receive a Boolean result (**true** or **false**).

This method checks and compares each character in the strings under investigation. Let's look at an example below:

```
string grade1 = "A";
string grade2 = "a";
Console.WriteLine(grade1.Equals("A"));
Console.WriteLine(grade1.Equals(grade2));
Console.WriteLine(grade1 == "A");
Console.WriteLine(grade1 == grade2);
// Console output:
// True
// False
// True
// False
```

In the example above, the console has identified that we are comparing a small letter and a capital letter. Therefore, if we compare the grades "**A**" and "**a**" using the **Equals(0)** method, the compiler returns **false**.

Contrary to the simple example above, practically, the character casing rarely comes into focus when comparing two strings. You can circumvent the character casing and only focus on the content of the string using the **Equals()** method and introduce the **StringComparison.CurrentCultureIgnoreCase** parameter. Using this parameter in the code above, the compiler will return a true if we compare the grades "**A**" and "**a**". The expression should look like this:

```
Console.WriteLine(grade1.Equals(grade2,
StringComparison.CurrentCultureIgnoreCase));
// True
```

Lexicographical Comparisons

Apart from equality, you can also compare different strings in alphabetical order. Usually, when comparing numbers, you can use the operators **>** and **<**. This, however, is not possible when comparing strings. Instead, to compare strings in alphabetical order, you use the **CompareTo()** method.

Using the **CompareTo()** method, you can compare the values in two strings to identify the appropriate alphabetical order. For this comparison, you must ensure that both of the strings under review have the same number of characters, which must also match. For the purpose of this example, the strings "gear" and "rear" cannot be compared because while they might have the same length, they do not have the same first character.

In such string comparisons, the compiler will return either a negative, positive, or zero value. A negative value means that the first string comes before the second string. A zero value means that the strings are equal, while a positive value means that the second string comes before the first. Let's explain this with an example:

```
string grove = "gRove";
string gravy = "gravy";
Console.WriteLine(grove.CompareTo(gravy));
Console.WriteLine(gravy.CompareTo(grove));
Console.WriteLine(gravy.CompareTo(gravy));
// Console output:
// 1
// -1
// 0
```

In the example above, the **CompareTo()** method does not ignore character casing, so it identifies a mismatch between the "**R**" and "**r**" in the first and second strings. Because of this subtle difference, the compiler returns a positive 1.

If we swap the position of the first and second string, the compiler will return a negative 1 because the comparison now starts at **gravy** instead of **grove**. In the last comparison, the compiler returns a 0 because we perform a self-comparison.

We can also make an alphabetical comparison while ignoring the character casing. For this comparison, we use the **string.Compare(string strX, string strY, bool ignoreCase)** method. This method serves the same purpose as the **CompareTo()** method, but because of the **ignoreCase**, segment, it overlooks character casing. Let's look at an example of this below:

```
string beta = "beta";
string grade1 = "gRadE";
string grade2 = "grade";
Console.WriteLine(string.Compare(beta, grade1, false));
Console.WriteLine(string.Compare(grade1, grde2, false));
Console.WriteLine(string.Compare(grade1, grade2, true));
Console.WriteLine(string.Compare(grade1, grade2,
StringComparison.CurrentCultureIgnoreCase));
// Console output:
// -1
// 1
// 0
// 0
```

In the example above, we use **Compare()** and by introducing the **StringComparison.CurrentCultureIgnoreCase** parameter, the compiler does not consider the difference between the character cases. It is important to mention at this juncture that when using the **Compare()** and **CompareTo()** methods, small letters alphabetically come before capital letters.

Keep this in mind because the rule might not always apply in all programming languages. For example, in the Unicode table, small letters come before capital letters. This simple rule can be confusing depending on how you code. Therefore, always remember that in C#, the alphabetical string comparison contravenes the Unicode table arrangement.

Operator Comparisons

The **!=** and **==** operators can be used to make comparisons using the **Equals()** method. Let's look at a simple example to explain this concept:

```
string str1 = "Good Morning!";
string str2 = str1;
Console.WriteLine(str1 == str2);
// Console output:
// True
```

In the example above, we are comparing two matching strings, **str1** and **str2**, hence the compiler returns **true**. This happens because while the second string does not have any reservation in the dynamic memory, it references a reserved position for the variable in the first string. For this reason, the strings share a common address, and if we compare them for equality, the compiler returns true.

Let's look at another example to expand on this concept:

```
string beg = "Beg";
string begin = "Begin";
string copy = beg + "in";
Console.WriteLine(copy == begin);
// True
```

In this example, let's direct attention to the strings **begin** and **copy**. The first variable assumes the value **Begin**. The second variable, on the other hand, derives its value from combining a variable and a literal to return a value equal to the value of the first variable.

Up to this point, each of the variables is pointing towards a unique memory block. However, note that the content in each of the memory blocks is not the same. Using the operator **==**, the comparison returns a **true** result.

CHAPTER 13:

Defining Classes

In computer programming, one of your key objectives is to implement some ideas and solve problems. When tackling a big problem, it makes sense to create a simpler concept of it, which does not necessarily represent the entire problem but gives you a glimpse of the key facts useful towards achieving the end objective. Object-oriented programming languages are some of the most commonly used languages in the world at the moment. This is primarily because the language syntax is somewhat similar to the semantics of the normal human language.

Through this kind of programming, you have access to a lot of tools you can use to outline different object classes. Classes in this context refer to a definition or specification of a cluster of objects. By this definition, a class will represent identified patterns that describe different behavioral states of the cluster of objects.

Borrowing from this explanation, an object refers to a copy of the definition of a class, also referred to as an instance. If we create an object from the description of a class, say for example m, we can refer to it as an object of the type (m).

Let's say you have the class type **`Mazda`**. This class will describe some of the features you expect of cars in this category. Some of the objects you can find in this class include **`Axela, Demio,`** and **`Verisa`**.

A class essentially defines the objects and data types that describe it. The object in a class contains the data, while the data contains information about the state of the object. Other than the state, the class also defines the behavior of objects within it, by the actions you can expect of the objects.

In object-oriented programming, we describe the behavior of objects in a class by declaring **methods** within the body of the class.

Elements of a Class

There are several elements that make up a class. The following are the key elements:

1. **Class declaration** - this is where we declare the name of the class. An example of this is as shown below:

```
public class Mazda
```

2. **Body of the class** - The body of a class is outlined after the class declaration. The body must also be enclosed within the curly brackets. Below is an example:

```
public class Mazda
{
// The body of the class comes here
}
```

3. **Constructor** - You use the constructor to create a new object. Below is an example of a constructor:

```
public Mazda()
{
// Write some code here
}
```

4. **Fields** - This refers to the variables you declare within the class. The data represented by the variables tells you the state of the object. An example is as shown below:

```
// Define the field
private string name;
```

5. **Properties** - they are used to define the characteristics of a class. The values of such characteristics are stored in the fields of the objects. An example is shown below:

```
// Define the properties
private string Name { get; set; }
```

6. **Methods** - We discussed methods earlier in the book and realized they perform specific roles in any block of programming code. Objects, for example, derive their behavior from methods depending on the class type. It is through methods that we are able to implement algorithms and data handling protocols effectively.

Implementing Classes and Objects

To use classes, you must first learn how to create objects. This you can do using **new** and a set of other constructors within the class. This way, you create an object from the class type. For each object you want to iterate, you must assign a variable to the object of the underlying class type. This is how the variable retains its reference to the object. If done correctly, you should be able to call methods and object properties and access other variables, too.

In recent examples, we defined the class **Mazda** that describes the car Mazda, probably in a dealership. We further added the method **Main()** to the class. In the following example, we will learn how to use the elements discussed above to create some more objects, add properties to the objects, and call methods on the said objects.

```
static void Main()
{
string firstMazdaModel = null;
Console.Write("Enter first Mazda model: ");
firstMazdaModel = Console.ReadLine();
// Here we use a constructor to identify a specific Mazda model
Mazda firstMazda = new Mazda(firstMazdaModel);
// Here we use a constructor to identify a different Mazda model
Mazda secondMazda = new Mazda();
Console.Write("Enter second Mazda name: ");
string secondMazdaModel = Console.ReadLine();
// Here we use the properties to name the Mazda model
secondMazda.Model = secondMazdaModel;
// Here we identify a Mazda model
Mazda thirdMazda = new Mazda();
Mazda[] Mazda = new Mazda[] { firstMazda, secondMazda, thirdMazda };
foreach (Mazda Mazda in Mazda)
{
Mazda.Color();
}
}
```

If we run this code, we have the following output:

```
Enter first Mazda Model: Axela
Enter second Mazda Model: Demio
Axela color is: Black!
Demio color is: White!
[Unnamed Mazda] is White!
```

In the example above, we used **Console.ReadLine()** to derive the name of the objects of the type **Mazda**, which the user keys in. After that, the second string is entered using the variable **firstMazdaModel**. This is the variable we will also use to create the first object from the class type **Mazda - firstMazda**, by assigning it to the constructor's parameter.

The second **Mazda** object is created without using a string for the name of the car in the constructor. Instead, we also use **Console.ReadLine()** to derive the name of the car, and then from there, we assign the value to the property **Model**.

The third object is derived from the class type **Mazda**, which we used for the default car model, whose value is **null**. In the **Color()** method, any Mazda model whose name we don't know (**name==null**) will be printed as **[Unnamed Mazda]**.

At this juncture, we successfully created an array from the type **Mazda** by initializing three of the new objects we created. Finally, we created a loop that runs through the array of objects of type **Mazda**.

It is important to note that each time you create an object in the .NET Framework, it is built from two parts. The first part, the significant data, holds all the object's data and can be found in the dynamic memory of the operating system. The second part, the reference part to the created object, is found in a different part of the operating system memory. The reference part stores the parameters and local variables associated with the object's methods.

If, for example, we create a class **Mazda**, some of the properties we can assign to it include color and model. From the same class, you can also create a variable for the year of manufacture, which is pretty much a reference to the main object and is located within the dynamic memory. Note that the reference, in this case, is only a variable that you can use to access objects.

Using Namespaces in Classes

When programming in C#, one of the challenges you will encounter, especially when working with custom classes, is that you must save them using the file extension **.cs**. Using the **.cs** file, you can define different structures, classes, and data types. While it is not mandatory for the compiler to do this, it makes sense to store each class in a separate file that corresponds to its name. For example, you should store the class **Mazda** using the file **Mazda.cs**.

C# namespaces are generally a collection of classes that are connected logically, but without a strict illustration on how to store them in the file system. If you need to include a namespace in declared classes, you must use a directive. You don't always have to use them, but where necessary, you must show them on the first line of your class file before you declare the class or any other data type.

After inserting the namespace, you declare the namespace of the classes used in the file. Remember that it is not mandatory to declare classes within the namespace, but it is good practice because it helps to organize your code better, and will also be useful if you have some classes in your code that have the same name.

Note that within a namespace, you can find other namespaces, classes, interfaces, structure, and other kinds of data. For example, the nested namespace **`System`** will also hold the namespace **`Data`**. This can be written in full as **`System.Data`**, but it is still nested within the **`System`** namespace.

In the .NET Framework, the full name of a class is written as follows: the namespace to which the class is declared, followed by the class name as shown below:

```
<namespace_name>.<class_name>
```

This way, it is easier to use data types from different namespaces without necessarily writing their full names.

Modifiers and Visibility

Modifiers are reserved words in C# programming, which can be used to add more information to the compiler, and any necessary code relevant to the modifier. There are four access modifiers used in C#:

1. Public
2. Private
3. Protected
4. Internal

These modifiers can only be used before the following class elements:

1. Class declaration
2. Fields
3. Properties
4. Methods

Through the access modifiers mentioned above, you can control visibility (access levels) to different class elements to which they are applied. The access levels used in the .NET Framework are as follows:

1. Public
2. Private

3. Protected
4. Internal
5. Protected internal

For the purpose of this discussion, we will only discuss internal, public, and private. Using the public access level before an element, you instruct the compiler that the element can be accessed from any class, regardless of its assembly, from the namespace in use. Using the public access level also means that there are no restrictions to it in terms of visibility.

The private access level is that with the most restrictions to elements and class visibility. Using this modifier, you instruct the compiler that the element to which it is applied cannot be accessed from any other class other than the class to which it is defined. This restriction applies even if the separate class trying to access it exists within the same namespace as the class to which the element is defined. Note that the private access level is often set by default, such that it applies by default if you do not have any visibility modifier before an element in the class.

The internal access level limits access to class elements only to files located in the same assembly. This means that the elements can only be accessed by files that are used in the same project. Assemblies in the .NET Framework refer to collections of different resources and types that form a logical unit. Assemblies are found in `.dll` or `.exe` files, which are binary files. You must also have noticed this by now: all the files in the .NET Framework and C# exist within assemblies.

Let's explain class visibility using a simple illustration. We have two classes, `X` and `Y`. Class `X` can access all the elements of class `Y` if it can create an object from the class type `Y`. The same also applies if it can access the unique fields and methods used in class `Y`, as per the unique access levels applicable to the fields and methods under consideration.

Based on this illustration, as long as class `Y` is not visible to class `X`, the visibility levels of the fields and methods in class `Y` will not change a thing. Therefore, an outer class can only have public and internal access levels. Inner classes, however, can be defined using other access levels.

CHAPTER 14:

Working with Text Files

You work with text files all the time in programming. For this chapter, one of the most important aspects of text files you will learn about is a stream. It is an essential aspect of any input-output library you will come across in programming. Streams play an important role in programming because it is through them that your program learns how to read or write data to external sources like servers, other computers, or files.

Streams are essentially an order of byte sequences that are sent from an input device to an output device. This can also be from one application to another. Streams are written and read in sequence, such that the recipient receives them in the same manner they were sent. They are basically an abstract platform through which two applications or devices can communicate effectively.

In the computing world, streams are the primary means of communication. It is through them that we can create a communication network between two or more remote computers. Communication between computers, therefore, is simply reading and writing through a stream. Let's look at an example of printing a file. Essentially, you sent some byte sequences to the stream connected to the printing port. Each time you read or write to or from a file, you basically open a stream to the file where the reading or writing takes place, then close the stream when you are done.

Streaming Basics

Most computing devices in use today implement streaming for data access. Streams allow communication between remote computers, programs, and files. Note that the sequence of bytes must be in order. Streams must be ordered and organized. Any attempt at distorting or influencing the order or organization of information flow through a stream makes the information unusable.

When we mention that streams support sequential data access, we must once again stress the importance of sequence. Any data in a stream can only be handled or manipulated in the order in which it is received from the stream. Therefore, order and sequence are mandatory in a stream.

Building on that, you realize that you cannot randomly access data in a stream. The access must be sequential, and strictly so. Depending on the situation for which you need data access, there are different types of streams you can use. We have streams that work with text files, streams that use binary files, and others that only work with strings. For any form of communication across a network to be successfully established, you must use the appropriate stream. Knowledge of the types of streams will help you select the right one for each application. Without that, you can forget about effective communication.

Like any other task you perform on a computer, you must always ensure you close the stream once they serve the purpose for which you opened them. Without this, there is always a risk of data loss, file damage, and so on.

There are a number of operations you can perform using streams. Let's have a look at them below:

1. **Opening (creation)** - This is the point at which you connect a data source to the stream or another stream. Let's say you are working on a file stream. You pass the name of the file and the file mode to the compiler. The file mode is the action that will take place on the file, for example, writing, reading, or both.
2. **Reading data** - At this point, you extract data from the stream. Reading takes place in sequential order from the present position of the stream. Note that reading is a blocking operation. A blocking operation is one whereby you are unable to do anything until something that precedes the blocking operation happens. For example, you cannot read until the data you are supposed to read arrives.
3. **Writing data** - This is where you send data to the stream in an appropriate manner. Writing also takes place in sequential order from the present position of the stream. Unlike reading data, writing may or may not be a blocking operation depending on circumstances before the data is sent. For example, there are instances where you can still write to data before the sent data arrives.
4. **Positioning** - In a stream, positioning, also referred to as seeking, implies moving the current stream position. Positioning is always done relative to the current stream position. It is, however, not possible with all streams, so you can only do it with streams that support positioning. Network streams are an example of streams that do not support positioning.

Most file streams, on the other hand, are fully compliant.

5. **Disconnecting (closing)** - Once the stream has served its purpose, you disconnect it. This frees up all resources that were in use. It is always advisable to disconnect the stream as soon as you are through, for resource efficiency. Note that once some resources are committed to the stream, they cannot be used by any other users, including any program on the computer that might require the resources, but run parallel to it.

Types of Streams

When programming in .NET, you will find all classes relevant to working with streams in the `System.IO` namespace. Some important features of streams that you must understand include the hierarchy, functionality, and organization. The input-output stream class is the highest order in the hierarchy of streams. This stream class outlines the core functions of all the other streams, and for that matter, you cannot instantiate it.

Next, we have buffered streams. These do not have any extra functionalities, but are useful when writing or reading data by creating a buffer. The buffer created is purely for performance enhancement. We also have streams that introduce additional functionality to reading and writing data. In this case, you can have streams that convert data into any manner of files to allow easy access. You also have streams that compress or decompress data, encryption and decryption streams, and so on. Such streams are often attached to a different stream, for example, a network or file stream, such that by activating their role in the stream, they make it easier for the attached stream to process the data, hence enhancing functionality.

In the **`System.IO`** namespace, we have the following main classes:

- Stream
- FileStream
- BufferedStream
- GZipStream
- NetworkStream
- MemoryStream

Note that whichever of these streams you use, you must always close the stream once you finish what you are working on.

Streams are widely divided into two, binary and text streams. Binary streams usually work with raw or binary data. For this reason, they lack specificity and are universal. Therefore, you can use them to read information from any kind of file. You will primarily read or write from binary streams using the following classes:

- **FileStream**

The **FileStream** class offers different methods of reading and writing to a binary file. Other than that, it also allows you to perform other activities like confirming the number of bytes available, skipping some bytes, and closing the stream.

- **BinaryWriter**

The **BinaryWriter** allows you to write different binary values and primitive data types to the stream using a unique encoding. It only uses one method, **Write()**, whose role we had seen in earlier chapters. Through the method **Write()**, you can record any data type to the stream.

- **BinaryReader**

Through the **BinaryReader**, you can read binary values and primitive data types created by the **BinaryWriter** to the stream. It allows you to read data from any integers, character arrays, floating points, and so on.

Text streams are almost similar to binary streams, but they only support text data. They only work with strings (**string**) and character sequences (**char**). Since they are only ideal for text files, text streams are not ideal when working with other binaries.

In the .NET Framework, the primary classes for working with text streams are **TextWriter** and **TextReader**. These classes are abstract, and for that reason, you cannot instantiate them. They basically describe the underlying functionality for reading or writing to classes where they are used. The following methods are used in text streams:

- **ReadLine()** - This method will return a string after reading one line of text
- **ReadToEnd()** - This method returns a string, but will read the stream to the end
- **Write()** - We use this method to write a string to the stream
- **WriteLine()** - This method will only write one line of text to the stream

The classes **StreamWriter** and **StreamReader** naturally inherit the functionalities of the classes **TextWriter** and **TextReader**, thereby implementing their read and write roles on a file. Before you create an object of the type **StreamWriter** or **StreamReader**, you must first ensure you have a string complete with the file path. With those in place, you can implement any of the methods you are already aware of to read and write to the console.

Working with Text Streams

There are many ways of reading files in C#, but the simplest and easiest is to use the **System.IO.StreamReader** class. This is because it resembles reading from a console. Note that **StreamReader** can work with streams, but it is not a stream. It only gives us a comprehensively easy way to read from text files.

To read a file, create a **StreamReader** from the filename relevant to the path of the file. This is important because it will also reduce the chances of errors. An example of this is as shown below:

```
// We create a StreamReader for the relevant file
StreamReader reader = new StreamReader("testfile.txt");
// The compiler reads the file
// Once you are through, close the reader to free up resources
reader.Close();
```

It is always advisable to avoid using the full file path, and instead, work with relative paths. This reduces the amount of code and further reduces the risk of errors. It is also easier to install and maintain the program.

Let's look at an example to highlight the difference between full and relative paths below:

Example of a full path:

```
C:\Temp\Test\testfile.txt
```

Example of a relative path:

```
..\..\testfile.txt
```

If you have to use the full path, you must be careful to pass the full path to the file, without forgetting the backslash. The backslash helps to distinguish folders along the path to the file. An easier way of representing such files in C# is to use a quoted string or a double slash in front of the string literal. For example, our scenario above **C:\Temp\Test\testfile.txt can be represented as follows:**

```
string fileName = "C:\\Temp\\Test\\testfile.txt";
string theSamefileName = @"C:\Temp\Test\testfile.txt";
```

It is worth noting that while relative paths might seem difficult to use because you must consider the project directory signature, the project can change several times throughout its life, so it is always wise to avoid using full paths.

The other problem with using full paths when writing a program is because it ties down the project to the environment. This means that the program can only exist within the environment within which it was created. It also makes your program untransferable. Therefore, if you were to move the program to a different computer, you will have to verify all the file paths to ensure the program works correctly. Using a relative path, however, is effective regardless of the environment, and makes your program portable.

CHAPTER 15:

Data Structures

Lists and linear data structures are some of the most important forms of presentation you will use in programming. Learning about data structures is important because you will learn how to work with different aspects of classes in C#. When writing any program, you generally work with different kinds of data. You add and remove elements according to the requirements of your program. At the same time, you also have to find different methods of data storage relevant to the job at hand. This is where data structures come in.

Data structures are sets of data that are organized according to unique mathematical or logical laws. They are an important consideration in programming because your choice generally determines how efficient the program will be. Efficiency in this case is not only limited to resource and memory allocation at execution but also in terms of the amount of code you might have to write for the program. In programming, you will mostly write lots of code to build efficient solutions. It is only credible that you also learn how to code efficiently.

An abstract data type (ADT) defines different structures in terms of their properties and permitted operations, without necessarily focusing on their implementation. This way, ADTs can be implemented in different ways in a program, and perform at different efficiency levels. Below are the different data structures you will come across in programming:

1. Linear data structures
2. Tree-like data structures
3. Sets
4. Dictionaries

5. Other data structures, including graphs, bags, and multi-sets

For this discussion, we will focus on linear data structures. Knowledge of data structures is crucial for programming because it is almost impossible to efficiently write programs without them. Alongside data structures, another important aspect of programming is using algorithms.

Working with Lists

The most common data structures you will use in programming are lists. These are linear data structures that define all the series, sequences, and rows used in programming. A list is an ordered sequence of elements. Think of it as your to-do list. You can read each of the tasks on the list (elements), add or remove tasks as you see fit, or even reorganize their order of priorities.

A list must have a distinct length, and the elements on the list must be arranged in order. Elements on a list can be added at different positions and moved around accordingly. Every ADT used in programming must describe a specific interface. Below are some method definitions you can get from an ADT:

- **`int Add(object)`** - this method will add an element at the end of the list
- **`void Clear()`** - this method will delete all the elements on the list
- **`void Insert(int, object)`** - this method will add an element at a specific position on the list
- **`void Remove(object)`** - this method will remove an element from the list
- **`void RemoveAt(int)`** - this method will remove an element from the list, at a specific location
- **`int IndexOf(object)`** - this method will tell you the position of a called element

The methods mentioned above can be used in different instances especially when working with arrays. An array will generally perform most of the roles that the methods on the ADT list above can perform. However, the difference is that arrays practically are fixed in size, so you cannot add any new elements to an array.

That notwithstanding, you can still implement a list using an array by increasing its size automatically. Let's look at an example to explain the operations on a to-do list. We will work with a list of tasks, add, insert, and remove a few tasks, then print the list to the console. We will also try to ascertain whether some tasks are available on the list:

```
class CustomArrayListTest
{
static void Main()
{
CustomArrayList<string> todoList =
new CustomArrayList<string>();
todoList.Add("Cleaning");
todoList.Add("Painting");
todoList.Add("Repairs");
todoList.Add("Mowing");
todoList.Add("Cooking");
todoList.Remove("Repairs");
todoList.Insert(1, "Studying");
todoList.Insert(0, "Jogging");
todoList.Insert(6, "Relax");
todoList.RemoveAt(0);
todoList[3] = "I have to finish " + todoList[3];
Console.WriteLine("Complete the following tasks today:");
for (int i = 0; i < todoList.Count; i++)
{
Console.WriteLine(" - " + todoList[i]);
}
Console.WriteLine("Position of 'Cooking' = {0}",
todoList.IndexOf("Cooking"));
Console.WriteLine("Position of 'Mowing' = {0}",
todoList.IndexOf("Mowing"));
Console.WriteLine("Can I go Shopping? " +
todoList.Contains("Shopping"));
}
}
```

If we run the code above, we should have the output below:

```
Complete the following tasks today:
- Cleaning
- Studying
- Painting
- I have to finish Mowing
- Cooking
- Relax
Position of 'Cooking' = 4
Position of 'Mowing' = -1
Can I go Shopping? False
```

The list above is a static list, and while it might be effective, it has one major flaw. The operation to remove and insert new items from within the array will involve rearranging the elements. This is doable for a small list. However, if you are dealing with a large list, this will definitely slow down your performance. For this reason, you can consider using a linked list. Let's explain how this works:

Linked lists are dynamic. When using such a list, the compiler will first check if the index you need is available. If it is not available, it raises an exception. After the exception, the compiler considers one of three possibilities. First, the list can remain empty after removing the exception. This removes everything on the list. Second, if the element to be removed is found at the beginning of the list, the new list can begin from the element right after the removed element. If the element we removed was the last one, the new list can start at `null`.

Finally, if the element to be removed is found at the end of the list or in the middle, the element before the removed one is redirected to start at the element before it, or a `null` if it is the last one.

When you are done, always check to ensure that the tail of the list links to the last item on the list. If the element you removed was the tail element, ensure it links to the removed element's predecessor.

ArrayList Class

Once you learn how to work with different list implementations, you can look at classes used to pull data structure lists. The **`ArrayList`** is one such class, whose implementation is similar to the static list we discussed earlier. Using this list, you can add, remove, and search for elements. Below are some of the important members you will use in this class:

- **`Add(object)`** - You use this to add a new element to the list
- **`Remove(object)`** - You use this to remove an element from the list
- **`Count`** - This tells you the number of elements on the list
- **`Clear()`** - This will remove all the elements from your list
- **`this [int]`** - This is an indexer through which you can access any element according to its position

As we have already seen, one of the challenges you will experience with this array implementation is to resize the inner array, especially when you are adding or removing elements to it. This problem is easily solved by creating a buffer within the array. This allows you to add or remove items from the list without resizing the array at the point of addition or removal.

Since the **`ArrayList`** class is of the untyped category, you can use it to store any kind of element, including strings, numbers, or even other objects. Let's look at an example of this:

```
using System;
using System.Collections;
class ProgrArrayListExample
{
static void Main()
{
ArrayList list = new ArrayList();
list.Add("Welcome");
list.Add(7);
list.Add(2.46271);
list.Add(DateTime.Now);
for (int i = 0; i < list.Count; i++)
{
object value = list[i];
Console.WriteLine("Index={0}; Value={1}", i, value);
}
}
}
```

By running the code above, the compiler will give us the outcome below:

```
Index=0; Value=Welcome
Index=1; Value=7
Index=2; Value=2.46271
Index=3; Value=22.12.2020 19:12:16
```

In the example above, we created the **ArrayList** and then added different kinds of elements. In particular, the elements we added were of the types **string**, **int**, **double**, and **DateTime**.

One of the challenges that you will encounter using classes that use the **System.IList** system like the **ArrayList** class is that each time you add an object to that class, it is added as an object type. If you search for an element at a later date, the compiler returns it as an object. Given that all the elements on your list might not be of the same type, you need to find a solution to this problem. You also have to consider the fact that conversion from one type to the other might take a lot of time, and significantly reduce the performance of your program.

Generic classes are the easiest way to solve the problem above. These are unique classes that are meant to work with more than one type. When you create this type, you specify the types of objects that will be used in them. Let's look at a simple example of this below:

```
GenericType<M> instance = new GenericType<M>();
```

By indicating the type of element in question, we create a generic class, which in the example above, is **GenericType**. The data type **M** as used in the example above can refer to any member of the class **System.Object**. In the recent example, we could use the data type **M** to represent

DateTime. Here are some examples where this can be applied:

```
List<int> intList = new List<int>();
List<bool> boolList = new List<bool>();
List<double> realNumbersList = new List<double>();
```

Another important generic variant you can introduce into your work is the **List<T> class**. When using this class, you must also indicate the elements that will be used in the class. These are the elements that can be held, such that you can always replace the denoted element type with a real data type. By creating a list that only contains integer numbers, we implicitly cannot add other data types to the list. Therefore, if you try to add any other object type other than integer numbers to the **List<int>**, the compiler returns a compilation error. This is a useful application because the compiler automatically helps you avoid common mistakes when using data collections of different types.

The **List<T>** class comes in handy at different instances. Since it uses the inner array to keep elements, the array will simply resize if it is overfitted. Bearing that in mind, the following are possibilities when using this class:

It is incredibly fast when searching for elements using their index. The number of elements in your class does not matter; it will search through each of the elements with the same speed. It is also a faster way of adding a new element to the class. This makes sense because, by addition, you essentially increase the array's capacity. Increasing the capacity of an array is a really slow operation. However, by using the **List<T>** class, the insertion speed is not reliant on the number of elements in the class, hence it works faster.

Unfortunately, searching for an element in the class by its value is slow using this approach. The speed challenge comes in because the method performs as many comparisons as the number of elements in the class.

Another challenge you will encounter using this approach is that of adding or removing elements to the class. Each time you add or remove an element, you must shift the other elements that are not affected directly by the change. This procedure is slow, especially if the elements being moved around are not found at either end of the array.

Considering the factors above, it is only advisable to use the **List<T>** class if you are certain you won't need to add or remove elements to the class frequently. On the same note, it also makes sense only when the new elements will be added at the end of the list, or if you need to access them by their index and not element values.

CONCLUSION

You have carefully read the entire book and are certain to have gained valuable knowledge in programming that will work for you in many instances. One thing you learn about programming is that knowledge is always transferrable. Therefore, what you learn in C# will come in handy in any other programming language that you might come across in the near future. The beauty of learning C# is that it is one of the fundamental programming languages used in computing. Therefore, even as technology advances from time to time, the knowledge learned will always be useful.

An important lesson you learn when writing code is about sustainability. Your code should stand the test of time, and be usable by any other programmer who comes across it. There's no better way to do that than to program in a language whose premise is sustainability. C# is the undertone of Microsoft. Looking at the mammoth of a company and player in different fields of programming Microsoft is, you can rest assured that C# is here to stay. Microsoft is at the forefront of future programming projects, including machine learning. This gives you confidence knowing that the foundation of C# programming will always be aligned with future advancements. This takes care of the fear that many programmers have today, whether their preferred programming language will still be relevant over the coming years.

Whether you move on to other programming languages or not, C# offers the ideal foundation for programming. With time, you will work alongside other programmers on small and large projects alike. You will also come to learn the value of shared knowledge, such that you can all work on a project that needs different skill sets. This way, as each programmer plays their role, there is no disconnect regardless of the programming languages you use.

Like math, you can only get better at programming by practicing every day. This is especially true when you are just learning the fundamentals. Spare a few minutes to code every day. This puts you in a better position and gives you a firm grasp of the core of C# programming. Try your hand at different challenges. Create solutions to simple problems around you. This gives you a simpler knowledge of how programming works, and more importantly, forms the foundation on which you will continually learn and become a better programmer.

From time to time, you will encounter challenges you cannot solve. Some of these might be simple, others difficult, but they should not discourage you. Learning is a collective effort when it comes to computer programming. There are many communities out there from which you can learn, share ideas, and find solutions to your current code challenges. It might take you a while, but as long as you are committed to the cause, you will enjoy the world of C# programming.

Where do you go from here? After reading this book and learning the basics of C# programming, the next step is to cast your net further. Delve deeper into C# programming. Tackle harder challenges. Look for code camps and hackathons to learn more about C#. You will be amazed at how much there is to do out there. Besides, as the world evolves, so does programming. You will come across programmers out there who have combined different languages to build some amazing projects.

With the foundation you learned from this book, you can also take a leap of faith and learn another programming language. There is so much out there, so you might be spoilt for choice. Note that there is nothing wrong with learning other programming languages. They all borrow from each other in one way or the other. To become an all-around programmer, you should be able to code proficiently in more than one language. That being said, you should at least work towards being an expert in two or three languages.

The C# platform is closely related to other paradigms that should interest you, like PHP, Java, Ruby, and so on. When choosing any of these, try to dwell on languages and technologies that are supported by your native platform. This makes it easier to learn the new interest, given that most of the concepts flow easily across platforms.

Having learned C#, it is also advisable to look at databases. Tables and relations are an important part of database programming. When building an application, you must be able to carefully work with tables and the relations between the content therein. You will also learn how to build queries, to select and update data in different databases. There are several databases you can learn, including MySQL and Oracle.

It would be pointless to talk about programming without touching on the obvious question lingering in your mind; the Internet, and websites. Of course, you can also learn different techniques and technologies in use for building some of the most amazing websites. In a world as interconnected as ours is, everyone is learning how to work with websites, web apps, and mobile apps. Learning concepts like HTML, JavaScript, and CSS should be on your to-do list. Start by creating simple websites and graduate into dynamic websites with dynamic content. You can also learn how to create mobile applications.

Practicality is another point you should consider. As you learn C# programming, how practical are your skills? Put that knowledge to use. Look for, and challenge yourself to more serious projects. All the applications you see online today were once just an idea in someone's head. They probably started with simple illustrations, then built the programs. Programming using advanced software might be difficult, but you will get there someday. Start with simple programs and build your way up to the level of complexity that you desire.

One thing that I can guarantee you is that there is a whole world of opportunities out there that you should conquer. C# programming and programming, in general, will be your ladder to these opportunities. Get coding and grasp these opportunities. You should be at the forefront in programming, and positioning yourself for greater things that lie ahead.

Good luck in your programming journey.

REFERENCES

Mills, H. D. (1988). Principles of Computer Programming : A Mathematical Approach. Wm. C. Brown.

Ullman, L. E., & Signer, A. (2006). C++ Programming. Peachpit Press.

Zheng, L., Dong, Y., Yang, F., & De, W. (2019). C++ Programming. Berlin De Gruyter.

C#

The Ultimate Intermediate Guide To Learn C# Programming Step-By-Step

CHAPTER 1:

Introduction - Setup and History of C#

Microsoft announced C# in 2000 and launched the language in 2002. C# was supposed to be called "Cool," which stands for "C-like object-orientated programming." C# is a C-based programming language. It is pronounced C "sharp"; the hash symbol was meant to suggest that C# is the later iteration of C++.

Below is the timeline of C#, detailing what has been added to each version ("C# Introduction"):

Jan 2002

C# 1.0

- Typesafe programming language
- Modern
- OOP (Object Oriented Programming)

Nov 2005

C# 2005

- Generics
- Partial classes
- Anonymous types
- Iterators
- Nullable types

- Static classes

Nov 2007

C# 2007

- Improvements of previous additions
- Extensions methods
- Expression trees
- Partial methods

April 2010

C# 4.0.

- Dynamic binding techniques
- Unique naming and arguments (optional)

Aug 2012

C# 5.0

- Asynchronous Programming (A huge addition allowing programmers to create multithreaded applications)
- Attributes for caller info

July 2015

C# 6.0 (This includes this book includes this version and above)

- Exception filters
- String interpolation
- Namespaces including static type members
- Compiler as a service

August 2017

C# 7.0

- Out variables
- Tuples and deconstruction
- Pattern matching
- Local functions
- Expanded expression-bodied members
- Ref locals and returns

September 2019

C# 0.8

- Readonly members
- Default interface methods
- Pattern matching enhancements:
  - Switch expressions
  - Property patterns
  - Tuple patterns
  - Positional patterns
- Using declarations
- Static local functions
- Disposable ref structs
- Nullable reference types
- Asynchronous streams
- Indices and ranges
- Null-coalescing assignment
- Unmanaged constructed types
- Stackalloc in nested expressions
- Enhancement of interpolated verbatim strings

Running C# on Windows

You are probably familiar with all of the things we are going to cover in this chapter, but we have to go through them because going through the basics is always a good idea. Think of it as a much-needed refresher from those who have stepped away from programming for a bit. It's still a better idea to work with C# on Windows, as C# is a Microsoft language. The Windows operating system is optimized for it.

Mac Users:

You can work with C# on Mac. Microsoft has released a Visual Studio version for Mac, but the experience of working with C# on a Windows laptop is better. It helps that you can run virtual Windows Os on Mac using tools like Virtual Box by Oracle.

1. Object-Oriented Language

Everything in C# is an object except for primitive data types. Objects, as you may know, have properties and building functions. If you have worked with other object-oriented languages, you have seen this. We are going to see more of this in the upcoming chapters. C# is easily maintainable and modular because it is object-oriented.

2. Strongly Typed

As you would expect from a programming language based-off C, C# is strongly typed. Meaning, unlike Javascript, you have to specify data types in your program. This significantly reduces run-time error. This is referred to as type safety. The benefit of type safety becomes more apparent as you work with bigger applications.

3. Automatic Garbage Collection

C# regularly runs garbage collection, which removes unused objects and dangling pointers, refreshing memory. The .NET framework runs this task. You do not have to do these cumbersome tasks yourself; it saves you time and allows you to focus on your applications' functionality.

4. Easy to Learn

C# is a high-level programming language, which makes it easier to learn. Unlike low-level programming languages like C and C++, many of the tasks you would have to perform – like memory management and pointers – are done automatically. This makes your code a lot more concise and focused. Something that would take ten lines of code in C can take about three lines of code in C#.

5. Application Range

C# is at the crux of Microsoft's ecosystems. Many of its technologies run on it. Windows Phone used C#, ASP.NET used C# for its backend, and Windows Form and Windows Presentation Framework also run on C#. If you are building something to run on Windows and want it to run well, C# is the best choice. There are other ways you can write programs that will run on Windows, but performance won't be the same unless you go the extra mile to optimize your program. From web development, to applications, operating systems, and game engines, C# can do plenty.

6. Part of Visual Studio

Microsoft's Visual Studio is one of the most widely used IDEs globally, and C# is the part of Visual Studio languages that highlights the importance and power of the language.

7. Huge Developer Community

When working with a program, it is always a big help when the development community for it is larger. This means that if problems arise, it is more likely that someone has encountered that problem, logged it, and found a solution for it. As a result, you will not be stuck for long, and you always have free support available. C# has the 4th largest community on Stack Overflow. What's also interesting is that Stack Overflow is written in C#.

Environment Setup

Here is some of what we talked about in the first book. When working with C#, it is best to do it on a Windows machine with the latest .Net framework installed. When you install Visual Studio, all the files and frameworks you need to develop in C# will be loaded to your system. Visual Studio is the go-to IDE for C#. You can download the latest Visual Studio here. You should see this when you do.

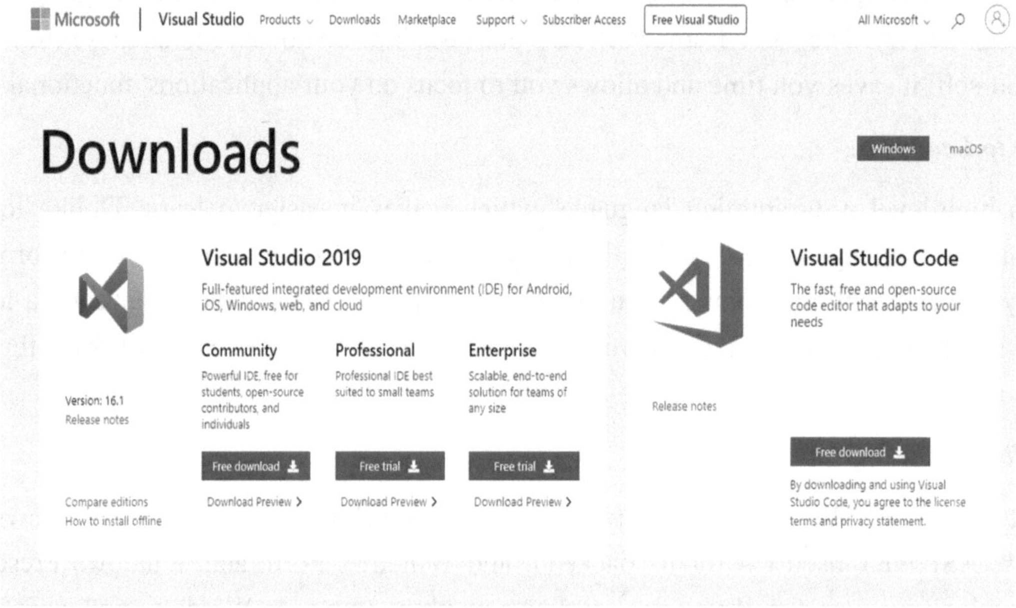

You will find Visual Studio in three versions: the Community version, which is free, Professional, and Enterprise versions, which are paid. The community version requires you to have a Microsoft account. If you are on a Windows machine, you probably have one already. If you don't have one, it is easy to create, and it is free. The installation process is just like downloading any other program. It does not do anything extra.

Running Your First Program

Follow these steps to run your first C# program.

1. Open Visual Studio on the start menu or search for it in the Windows search box ("Visual Studio"):

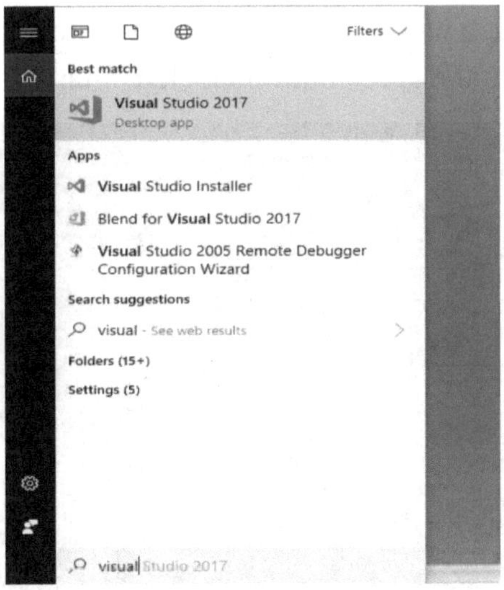

2. Create a new project by selecting File -> New -> Project as shown below.

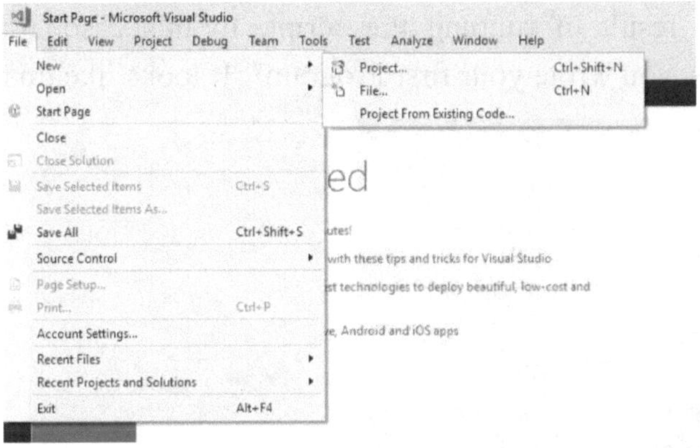

3. You will be faced with many C# program options. Select "Console App (.NET Framework)" and give it the application name you choose. I named it "MyProgram." Click OK.

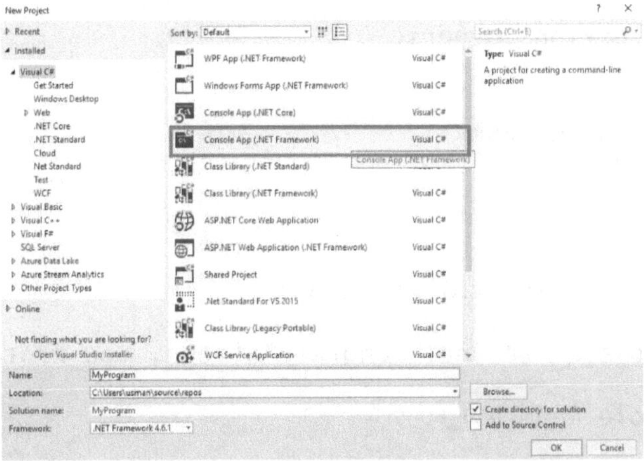

4. You will be navigated to a window where you can write C# code. Copy the following code in the window and press the green button labeled "Start" from the top menu.

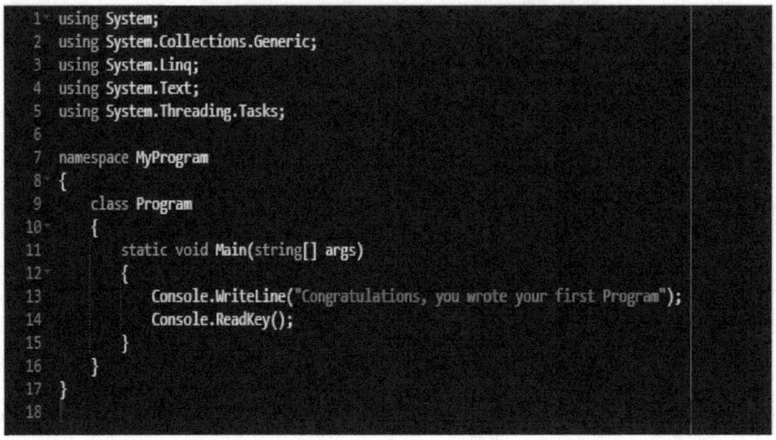

5. When you run the script, as you have by pressing the 'Start" button, the console window will display the result of running the script. In this case, it displays the message: "Congratulations, you wrote your first Program". It looks like this:

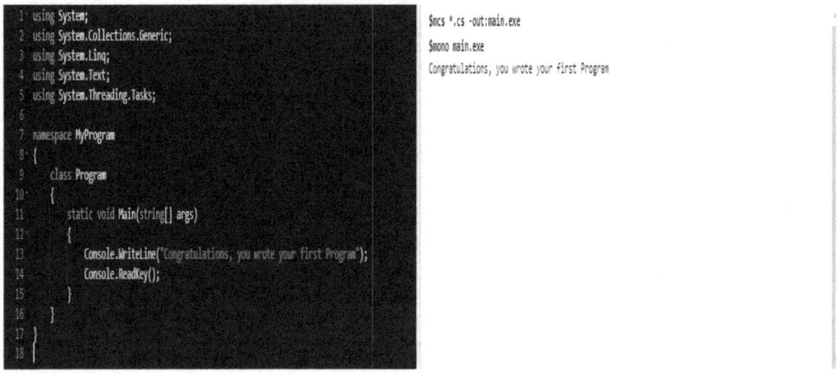

$mcs *.cs -out:main.exe
$mono main.exe
Congratulations, you wrote your first Program

To understand what happened, let's take a look at the code that we wrote:

```
using System;
using System.Collections.Generic;
using System.Linq;
using System.Text;
using System.Threading.Tasks;
namespace MyProgram
{
    class Program
    {
        static void Main(string[] args)
        {
            Console.WriteLine("Congratulations, you wrote your first
Program");
            Console.ReadKey();
        }
```

```
    }
}
```

Using statements, the ones on top, are declared to import libraries that contain pre-built functions called methods that we may need in our code. Any chunks of code in C# are placed within a class that is inside a namespace. This is to be expected, since the program is object-orientated. In the program we wrote, our class is Program, and our namespace is "MyProgram ".

Classes, as a type of object, contain methods within them. Our program class has the Main method whose return type is void, and method type is static. The Main method is where the C# code we will execute begins. To write the line, we used the WriteLine method, which is part of the Console class. We passed the text we want to see displayed in the console. Then we used the ReadKey method of the Console class to prevent the text from disappearing oncc it is printed on the screen.

That is pretty much all there was to our first program.

CHAPTER 2:

C# Interfaces

Interfaces are classes that contain declarations of functions that can be inherited by other classes. The classes that inherit the method define the method.

Interfaces are defined like this:

```
public interface interfacename
{
// interface methods declaration
}
```

The inheriting class then defines the methods like this:

```
class classname : interfacename
{
// interface method definition
}
```

Here is an application using interfaces.

```
using System;
namespace Demo
{
    // Defining the interface
    public interface Score
        {
        // Declaring the interface methods
        void DisplayScore();
        int Calculate();
    }
    public class Player : Score
```

```
    {
        public int PlayerID;
        public string PlayerName;
        public int score1,score2;

        // Defining the interface methods
        public void DisplayScore()
        {
            Console.WriteLine("The score for try  1 is " + score1);
            Console.WriteLine("The score for try 2 is " + score2);
        }
        public int Calculate()
        {
            return (score1 + score2);
        }
    }
    class Program
    {

        // The main function
        static void Main(string[] args)
        {
            Player  player1 = new Player();

            player1.playerID = 1;
            player1.PlayerName = "John";

            player1.score1 = 10;
            player1.score2 = 20;

            player1.DisplayScore();
            Console.WriteLine("The Total score is " +
player1.Calculate());

        Console.Read();
         }
    }
}
```

Here is what we see happen in the code above:

- We define an interface class called 'Score,' which has a 'Display' method and a 'Calculate' method.
- We then define the implementation of these functions in the 'Player' class.

This what we should see in the console:

The score for try 1 is 10

The score for try 2 is 20

The Total score is 30

We can also have a class inherit multiple interfaces at once. Let's look at an example of this.

Below is an application of multiple interfaces.

```
using System;
namespace Demo
{
    // Defining the interface
    public interface Score
        {
        // Declaring the interface methods
        void DisplayScore();
        int Calculate();
    }

    public interface location
    {
        // Declaring the interface methods
        void InputCity(string city);
        void DisplayCity();

    }

    public class Player : Score, location
    {
        public int PlayerID;
        public string PlayerName;
        public int score1, score2;
        private string city;

        // Defining the interface methods
        public void InputCity(string pcity)
        {
            city = pcity;
        }

        public void DisplayCity()
        {
            Console.WriteLine("The player is from" + city);
        }

        public void DisplayScore()
        {
            Console.WriteLine("The score for try 1 " + score1);
            Console.WriteLine("The score for try 2 " + score2);
        }

        public int Calculate()
        {
            return (score1 + score2);
```

```
        }
    }

    class Program
    {
        // The main function
        static void Main(string[] args)
        {

            Player player1 = new Player();

            player1.PlayerID = 1;
            player1.PlayertName = "John";

            player1.score1 = 10;
            Player1.score2 = 20;

            player1.DisplayScore();
            Console.WriteLine("The Total score " + player1.Calculate());

            player1.InputCity("New York");
            player1.DisplayCity();

        Console.Read();
        }
    }
}
```

With the above program:

- We have defined two interfaces: the ‘Score’ interface and the ‘Location’ interface.
- The ‘Player’ class takes both interfaces and defines the methods.

Here is what the program should display:

The score for try 1 is 10

The score for try 2 is 20

The Total score is 30

The player is from New York

Properties in Interfaces

It is possible to define properties in the interface. They can only have a “get” or “set” keyword, which tells us if they are read-only or read-write properties.

Below is the syntax.

```
public interface interfacename
        {
            // Property declaration:
            datatype propertyname
            {
                get;
                set;
            }
        }
```

If both the get and set methods are defined, it means that the property is a read-write property. Here is an example of how properties in interfaces work.

Using the properties in interfaces

```
using System;
namespace Demo
{
    // Defining the interface
    public interface Score
        {
            // Read write property
        int score
        {
            get;
            set;
        }
        // Read write property
        string Try
        {
            get;
            set;
        }
        // Read only property
        int PlayerID
        {
            get;
        }
    }

    public class Player : Score
    {
        public int PlayerID;
        public string PlayertName;

        public int score  // read-write instance property
        {
            get
            {
                return marks;
            }
```

```
            set
            {
                score = value;
            }
        }

        public string Try  // read-write instance property
        {
            get
            {
                return Try;
            }
            set
            {
                Try = value;
            }
        }

        public int PlayerID  // read-write instance property
        {
            get
            {
                return 1;
            }
        }
    }

    class Program
    {
        // The main function
        static void Main(string[] args)
        {
            Player player1 = new Playert();

            player1.PlayerID = 1;
            player1.PlayerName = "John";

            player1.score = 20;
            player1.try = "first try";

            Console.WriteLine("The score is " + player1.marks);
            Console.WriteLine("The try is the " + player1.try);
            Console.WriteLine("The PlayerID is " + player1.PlayerID);

        Console.Read();
        }
    }
}
```

In the above program:

- We have set 3 properties in the interface.

- The 'Try' and 'Score' properties are read-write properties because they have 'get' and 'set' methods.
- The 'PlayerID' only has the 'get' property, which means it is a read-only property.
- We then define the implementation of these properties in the class.

In regard to the program, the result should be in this format:

The score is 20

The try is the first try

The PlayerID is 1

CHAPTER 3:

Namespaces

Namespaces allow us to separate and use functions that have similar names and parameters but serve different purposes ("C# Namespaces"). It is not common for programming languages to allow it. Every function has to have a name that is unique.

Here's the syntax:

```
namespace namespaceName
{
Class definition
{
// Define the functions
}
}
```

All functions defined will belong to the 'namespaceName' namespace. In some programs, you will need the following definition.

```
using System;
```

It will result in using the functions defined in the 'System' namespace.

Example: The program below is used to showcase how to use namespaces.

```
using System;

// One namespace
namespace NameA{
    public class ClassA
    {
```

```
    public void FunctionA(){
        Console.WriteLine("This is from namespace A");
    }
    }
}

// Second namespace
namespace NameB{
    public class ClassB
    {
        public void FunctionA()
        {
            Console.WriteLine("This is from namespace B");
        }
    }
}

namespace Demo
{
        class Program
    {

        // The main function
        static void Main(string[] args)
        {
            // Using the namespaces
            NameA.ClassA clsA = new NameA.ClassA();
            clsA.FunctionA();

            NameB.ClassB clsB = new NameB.ClassB();
            clsB.FunctionA();

        Console.Read();
        }
    }
}
```

In the program above:

- We defined two namespaces: NameA and NameB. Both have classes with similar functions defined.
- We can call each function via its namespace in the main program.

The program gives us the following output:

This is from namespace A

This is from namespace B

We can call the functions with the "using" directive to avoid specifying the functions' specific namespace, like below:

This program is used to showcase the usage of the clause for namespaces.

```
using System;
using NameA;
using NameB;

// One namespace
namespace NameA{
    public class ClassA
    {
    public void FunctionA(){
        Console.WriteLine("This is from namespace A");
    }
    }
}

// Second namespace
namespace NameB{
    public class ClassB
    {
        public void FunctionA()
        {
            Console.WriteLine("This is from namespace B");
        }
    }
}

namespace Demo
{
        class Program
    {
        // The main function
        static void Main(string[] args)
        {
            // Using the namespaces
            ClassA clsA = new ClassA();
            clsA.FunctionA();

            ClassB clsB = new ClassB();
            clsB.FunctionA();

        Console.Read();
        }
    }
}
```

In regard to the program, the result should be in this format:

This is from namespace A

This is from namespace B

Nested Namespaces

Namespaces can also be nested, which means placing one namespace inside of another. Here's how the syntax looks:

```
namespace namespaceName1
{
      Class definition
       {
       // Define the functions
         }
      namespace namespaceName2
      {
             Class definition
             {
               // Define the functions
                }
          }
  }
```

I have highlighted the namespaces curly braces so you can see they are nested and for easy navigation. Below is how we would access function A.

```
namespaceName1.FunctionA
```

We would access function B this way.

```
namespaceName1.namespaceName2.FunctionB
```

You can see we are using dot notation, another sign that what we are essentially dealing with are objects.

Using the nested namespaces.

```
using System;

// One namespace
namespace NameA{
    public class ClassA
    {
    public void FunctionA(){
        Console.WriteLine("This is from namespace A which contains
namespace B");
    }
    }
    // inner namespace
    namespace NameB
    {
```

```
        public class ClassB
        {
            public void FunctionA()
            {
                Console.WriteLine("This is from namespace B inside
Namespace A");
            }
        }
    }
}

namespace Demo
{
        class Program
    {

        // The main function
        static void Main(string[] args)
        {
            // Using the namespaces
            NameA.ClassA clsA = new NameA.ClassA();
            clsA.FunctionA();

            NameA.NameB.ClassB clsB = new NameA.NameB.ClassB();
            clsB.FunctionA();

        Console.Read();
        }
    }
}
```

In the program above:

- We have nested namespace NameB inside namespace NameA. They both have a similar function defined despite NameB being inside NameA.
- We then access specific functions via dot notation.

We end up with the following result:

This is from namespace A which contains namespace B

This is from namespace B inside Namespace A

CHAPTER 4:

Advanced Decision Statements and Flow Control

The != Operator

The != operator is used to check if two given operands are NOT equal. The ! operator can also be used to negate conditions. It is used to execute code when the opposite of a condition is true.

The syntax would be like this:

```
bool levelComplete = (score >= pointsNeededToPass);
if(!levelComplete)
{
Console.WriteLine("You haven't won yet. Keep trying...");
}
```

You can use the ! operator with other operators, but you should keep in mind that the ! has higher precedence than relational operators. This means its condition is checked before the others. If you want a relational operator to be checked before negation, you will need to put the relational conditionals in parentheses just like you would in math, like this:

```
if(!(score > oldHighScore))
{
}

// that's the same as:
if(score <= oldHighScore)
{
```

```
}
```

In programming, there are many ways of doing the same thing. You just have to choose the most simple and appropriate. One shouldn't complicate code unnecessarily.

Conditional Operators: && and | |

Your conditional operators can be made to track more than one thing. Let's say you are making a game where a player controls an avatar through tough terrain. The player loses when the avatar's energy is gone, or food is gone. If they run out of energy, they can always have food as long as it's available. If they run out of food, they can live off their energy until they hit the next stash. The only way for them to lose is if they have no energy and no food. So, you will need to have a conditional that checks both conditions and only ends the game when both conditions are met.

To do this, you will need to use the AND operator (&&).

This is where we play with the conditional operators. We have the AND operator (&&), as mentioned, and the OR operator (||), and these are what we use to check several elements at a time:

```
int food = 20;
int energy = 40;

if(food <= 0 && energy <= 0)
{
Console.WriteLine("Game over");
}
```

This means if the food is less than or equal to zero and energy is less than or equal to zero, the game should end.

The || operator only needs one condition to be true. It would work better in a game where you can die in two ways. Let's imagine our avatar can die when their energy is zero or when they run out of time (in this instance, we don't have the food variable). Only one of these things needs to be true for the game to end, not both of them.

```
int energy = 50;
int time = 40;

if(time < 0 || energy < 0)
{
Console.WriteLine("You lost. Try again!")
}
```

You should know that by default, computers do "lazy evaluations," which means they will not check the second condition if the first one is met. The only time it will check the second condition (energy) is if the first one (time) is not met.

It is possible to put multiple conditional operations together. You can get very creative by using parentheses. But always, when you make these conditions, remember to make it simple for others to read and never make things too complicated for their purpose.

CHAPTER 5:

Reflection

The ability of C# to retrieve information from sections of code during runtime is called reflection. You would use reflection if you wanted to know more information about a method ("C# Reflection"). We can do more than that: we can also create objects and invoke methods during runtime through reflections

In the example below, we use "Type" datatype to get information about a class.

Using the Type to get information on a class

```
using System;
using System.IO;

namespace Demo
{
    class Player
    {         // Defining the members
        public int id;
        public string name;

        public void Display()
        {
            Console.WriteLine("The player ID is " + id);
            Console.WriteLine("The name of the player is " + name);
        }
    }

    class Program
    {
        // The main function
```

```
        static void Main(string[] args)
        {
            Player player1 = new Player();

            // Trying to get the type of object
            Type myTypeObj = player1.GetType();

            Console.WriteLine("The object is of Type " + myTypeObj);
            Console.Read();
        }
    }
}
```

Here's what we have done:

Using 'Type,' we got information about the 'player1' object.

We were able to get the class of the object.

Below is what we would see as the output:

The object is of Type Demo.Player

MethodInfo

The following reflection method is used to get information about a method from a class.

Below is an example:

The next program showcases the way to use MethodInfo.

```
using System;
using System.IO;
using System.Reflection;

namespace Demo
{
    class Player
    {
        // Defining the members
        public int id;
        public  string name;

        public void Display()
        {
            Console.WriteLine("The ID is " + id);
            Console.WriteLine("The player name is " + name);
        }
    }

    class Program
```

```
    {
        // The main function
        static void Main(string[] args)
        {

            Player player1 = new Player();

            // Trying to get the type of object
            Type myTypeObj = player1.GetType();

            Console.WriteLine("The object is of Type " + myTypeObj);

            // Using reflection to get information about the Display
method
            MethodInfo myMethodInfo = myTypeObj.GetMethod("Display");

            Console.WriteLine("Is the method a static method\? " +
myMethodInfo.IsStatic + "\.");
            Console.Read();
        }
    }
}
```

The program will give us the following results:

The object is of Type Demo.Player

Is the method a static method? False.

CHAPTER 6:

Collections

Collections are special classes that simplify working with special data classes ("Collection in C#").

For instance, collections have a size() method inside an ArrayList collection that can get an array's size without cumbersome code.

C# has the following collection classes:

- ArrayList - Array containers are used to store continuous values of the same data type.
- SortedList – These are sequence containers that permit the insertion of constant time and delete operations. Iterations can be done in both directions.
- Stacks - This is a type designed for a LIFO (last-in-first-out) situation, where items are inserted and extracted from one end of the container.
- Queues - This is a type designed for a FIFO (first-in-first-out) situation, where items are inserted into one side and then extracted on the other.

Let's look at these in more detail. It's important to have a clear understanding of these concepts.

Arrays are great because we can make them as small or as big as we need them to be. Because the memory used is contiguous, we know that arrays are efficient and frugal. But arrays are not dynamic. With the computing needs of today, programmers have to get creative to overcome this. This used to be a strength because it meant arrays wouldn't grow out of control and take over system memory. Computers back then did not have the sort of memory available for us today, so arrays played an important role in preventing processes from hogging memory.

These days, programmers can write ever more dynamic programs that can shrink and expand as the need arises because computers have more memory, and they are stronger. This is good for programmers because it means they write more exciting things as there is now room for them to do so (without being irresponsible, of course).

This is why lists have become more popular over arrays when programmers are looking for versatility and power. If you have worked with programming languages like Python, this is not new to you. A list is a flexible array.

Lists can go to whatever size is needed at any given time as things change. Lists don't have a defined length. They can always be added to. They are like fossils; there was a time when there weren't any. They have now developed over millions of years, and things that are alive today and those that will be alive in the future will be added to that list of fossils until there is no Earth anymore. How many fossils can be added to the list is not limited by any inherent size. The only limit is how low long the Earth will exist. If the Earth existed forever, and with it life, we would have fossils being added forever. The same principle applies to lists.

Lists also come with full-fledged built functions. To use lists and take advantage of all their features, you will need to import the Systems.Collections namespace.

When using lists, you will have to declare the list and its type, like this:

```
List<type> name = new List<type>();
```

You add items using the *Add* method, like this:

```
myList.add(2);
myList.add(5);
myList.add(8);
```

You can also add existing arrays to the lists using the *AddRange* method like this:

```
myList.addRange(arrayName);
```

You can remove items from a list in one of two ways: by the item's *value* or the item's index. The indices of lists work the same as array indices.

```
myList.remove(5); // will remove the 5, removing by value
myList.removeAt(0); // will remove the 2, removing by index
// only 8 is left within the list. Notice we are working on the list we
made in the previous example.
```

I hope this illustrated how flexible lists are.

ArrayList

The arrayList containers store values of the same data type. Let's look at an example of this.

You define ArrayLists the following way:

```
ArrayList variablename=new ArrayList():
```

"Variablename" is the variable we assign to the Arraylist so that we can use all kinds of methods on it. This is us using the *Add* method to add an item to the arrayList.

```
Variablename.Add(element)
```

We can access this element by its index if we need. The following examples illustrate an ArrayList.

Here is an application of array lists.

```
using System;
using System.Collections;

namespace Demo
{
    class Program
    {
        // The main function
        static void Main(string[] args)
        {
            // Defining the ArrayList
            ArrayList ar = new ArrayList();

            // Adding elements to the array list
            ar.Add(10);
            ar.Add(15);
            ar.Add(23);

            // Displaying the elements of the array
            Console.WriteLine(" The first element of the array is " +
ar[0]);
            Console.WriteLine(" The second element of the array is " +
ar[1]);
            Console.WriteLine(" The third element of the array is " +
ar[2]);

            Console.Read();
        }
    }
}
```

This is what we are going to see in the console:

The first element of the array is 10

The second element of the array is 15

The third element of the array is 23

We can add all kinds of data types to an ArrayList.

This program shows the way to use array lists of strings.

```
using System;
using System.Collections;

namespace Demo
{
    class Program
    {
        // The main function
        static void Main(string[] args)
        {
            // Defining the ArrayList
            ArrayList ar = new ArrayList();

            // Adding elements to the array list
            ar.Add("Hi");
            ar.Add("There");
            ar.Add("World");

            // Displaying the elements of the array
            Console.WriteLine(" The first element of the array is " +
ar[0]);
            Console.WriteLine(" The second element of the array is " +
ar[1]);
            Console.WriteLine(" The third element of the array is " +
ar[2]);

            Console.Read();
        }
    }
}
```

The output in the console will be:

The first element of the array is Hi

The second element of the array is There

The third element of the array is World

The ArrayList class has many methods that can be used to manipulate data.

ArrayList Operations

The section below summarizes the various operations available for ArrayList.

Function	Description
size	This property tells us the size of the ArrayList
Clear()	This function removes all elements in an ArrayList
Contains()	This method checks if an ArrayList contains a particular element then returns a Boolean value: True if it does and False if it doesn't.
IndexOf()	This returns the index of the specified element in the ArrayList.
InsertAt()	This method inserts a value/item in a particular index in the ArrayList
Remove()	This method removes an item from an arrayList.
RemoveAt()	This method will remove an item at a specified index
Reverse()	This method reverses elements in an ArrayList.
Sort()	This method sorts the elements in an array alphabetically or in ascending order if they're numbers.
GetRange()	This method is used to extract an array and add it to an ArrayList.

Let's look at how each method briefly defined above works.

Size Function

This property tells us the size of the ArrayList, as in the number of elements in it. We are going to use the intuitive *Count* method to do this.

Using count property

```
using System;
using System.Collections;

namespace Demo
{
    class Program
    {
        // The main function
        static void Main(string[] args)
        {
            // Defining the ArrayList
            ArrayList ar = new ArrayList();

            // Adding elements to the array list
            ar.Add(11);
            ar.Add(13);
            ar.Add(15);

            // Displaying the size of the array list
            Console.WriteLine(" The size of the array list is " +
ar.Count);

            Console.Read();
        }
    }
}
```

Below is what the console will print:

The size of the array list is 3

Clear Function

This function removes all elements in an ArrayList

Using the clear method

```
using System;
using System.Collections;

namespace Demo
{
    class Program
    {
        // The main function
        static void Main(string[] args)
        {
            // Defining the ArrayList
            ArrayList ar = new ArrayList();
```

```
            // Adding elements to the array list
            ar.Add(12);
            ar.Add(14);
            ar.Add(17);

            // Clearing all the elements of the array list
            ar.Clear();

            Console.WriteLine(" The size of the array list is " +
ar.Count);
            Console.Read();
        }
    }
}
```

It should tell us there is nothing in the array, like below:

The size of the array list is 0

Contains Function

This method checks if an ArrayList contains a particular element, then returns a Boolean value: True if it does and False if it doesn't.

The next program shows how to use the contains method.

```
using System;
using System.Collections;

namespace Demo
{
    class Program
    {
        // The main function
        static void Main(string[] args)
        {
            // Defining the ArrayList
            ArrayList ar = new ArrayList();

            // Adding elements to the array list
            ar.Add(13);
            ar.Add(27);
            ar.Add(30);

            Console.WriteLine("Does the array contain the value 3? " +
ar.Contains(30));
            Console.Read();
        }
    }
}
```

The program should return true, like this:

Does the array contain the value 3? True

IndexOf Function

This returns the index of a specified element in the ArrayList.

Here is an application of the IndexOf method.

```
using System;
using System.Collections;

namespace Demo
{
    class Program
    {
        // The main function
        static void Main(string[] args)
        {
            // Defining the ArrayList
            ArrayList ar = new ArrayList();

            // Adding elements to the array list
            ar.Add(50);
            ar.Add(2000);
            ar.Add(37);

            Console.WriteLine("The index of value 37 is  " +
ar.IndexOf(37));
            Console.Read();
        }
    }
}
```

The program should print this in the console:

The index of value 37 is 2

Insert Function

This method inserts a value/item in a particular index in the ArrayList.

The program below showcases the insert method.

```
using System;
using System.Collections;
```

```
namespace Demo
{
    class Program
    {
        // The main function
        static void Main(string[] args)
        {
            // Defining the ArrayList
            ArrayList ar = new ArrayList();
              // Adding elements to the array list
            ar.Add(100);
            ar.Add(22);
            ar.Add(37);

            Console.WriteLine("The index of value 37 is " +
ar.IndexOf(37));

            // Inserting the value 4 at Index position 2
            ar.Insert(2, 4);

            Console.WriteLine("The value at index 2 is " + ar[2]);
            Console.Read();
        }
    }
}
```

This is what we should see in the console:

The index of value 37 is 2

The index of value 2 is 4

Remove Function

This method removes an item from an arrayList.

Using the remove method

```
using System;
using System.Collections;
namespace Demo
{
    class Program
    {
        // The main function
        static void Main(string[] args)
        {
            // Defining the ArrayList
            ArrayList ar = new ArrayList();

            // Adding elements to the array list
            ar.Add(19);
```

```
            ar.Add(200);
            ar.Add(37);

            Console.WriteLine("The value at position 1 is " + ar[1]);

            // Removing a value
            ar.Remove(200);

            Console.WriteLine("The value at position 1 is " + ar[1]);
            Console.Read();
        }
    }
}
```

This is what we should see in the console:

The value at position 1 is 200

The value at position 1 is 37

RemoveAt Function

This method will remove an item at a specified index

This program shows the way to use the RemoveAt method.

```
using System;
using System.Collections;

namespace Demo
{
    class Program
    {
        // The main function
        static void Main(string[] args)
        {
            // Defining the ArrayList
            ArrayList ar = new ArrayList();

            // Adding elements to the array list
            ar.Add(89);
            ar.Add(202);
            ar.Add(303);

            Console.WriteLine("The value at position 1 is " + ar[1]);

            // Removing a value
            ar.RemoveAt(1);
            Console.WriteLine("The value at position 1 is " + ar[1]);
            Console.Read();
        }
    }
```

```
}
```

This is what we should see in the console:

The value at position 1 is 202

The value at position 1 is 302

Reverse Function

This method reverses elements in an ArrayList.

Using the reverse method

```
using System;
using System.Collections;

namespace Demo
{
    class Program
    {
        // The main function
        static void Main(string[] args)
        {
            // Defining the ArrayList
            ArrayList ar = new ArrayList();

            // Adding elements to the array list
            ar.Add(22);
            ar.Add(27);
            ar.Add(40);

            Console.WriteLine("The value at index 0 is " + ar[0]);
            Console.WriteLine("The value at index 1 is " + ar[1]);
            Console.WriteLine("The value at index 2 is " + ar[2]);

            // Reversing the list
            ar.Reverse();

            Console.WriteLine("The value at index 0 is " + ar[0]);
            Console.WriteLine("The value at index 1 is " + ar[1]);
            Console.WriteLine("The value at index 2 is " + ar[2]);

            Console.Read();
        }
    }
}
```

In regard to the program, the result should be in this format:

The value at index 0 is 22

The value at index 1 is 27

The value at index 2 is 40

The value at index 0 is 40

The value at index 1 is 27

The value at index 2 is 22

Sort Function

This method sorts the elements in an array

The program below is used to showcase the way to use the sort method.

```
using System;
using System.Collections;

namespace Demo
{
    class Program
    {
        // The main function
        static void Main(string[] args)
        {
            // Defining the ArrayList
            ArrayList ar = new ArrayList();

            // Adding elements to the array list
            ar.Add("c");
            ar.Add("a");
            ar.Add("b");

            Console.WriteLine("The value at index 0 is " + ar[0]);
            Console.WriteLine("The value at index 1 is " + ar[1]);
            Console.WriteLine("The value at index 2 is " + ar[2]);

            // Sorting the list
            ar.Sort();

            Console.WriteLine("The value at index 0 is " + ar[0]);
            Console.WriteLine("The value at index 1 is " + ar[1]);
            Console.WriteLine("The value at index 2 is " + ar[2]);

            Console.Read();
        }
    }
}
```

The console will print the following:

The value at index 0 is c

The value at index 1 is b

The value at index 2 is a

The value at index 0 is a

The value at index 1 is b

The value at index 2 is c

If the values were numbers, it would put them in ascending order.

GetRange Function

This method is used to extract an array and add it to an ArrayList

Using the GetRange method

```
using System;
using System.Collections;

namespace Demo
{
    class Program
    {
        // The main function
        static void Main(string[] args)
        {
            // Defining the ArrayList
            ArrayList ar = new ArrayList();

            // Adding elements to the array list
            ar.Add(10);
            ar.Add(20);
            ar.Add(3);
            ar.Add(4);

            // Creating the new arraylist
            ArrayList ar1 = new ArrayList();
            ar1 = ar.GetRange(0, 2);

            Console.WriteLine("The value at index 0 is " + ar1[0]);
            Console.WriteLine("The value at index 1 is " + ar1[1]);
            Console.Read();
        }
    }
}
```

We will see this in the console:

The value at index 0 is 10

The value at index 1 is 20

Stack

In computer programming, you are going to come across stacks a lot, whether they are in game development, writing algorithms, or caching. Stacks are preferable because they are very easy to keep track of. They make tracking processes easy since they use the last-one-first-out process of caching.

A stack functions the way it sounds like it would. It is a tower of things, with new items being added on top of the pile. It is not necessarily an organized way of doing things, but it can be very powerful. In a regular stack, as in a computer stack, it is dangerous to remove things that are in the middle of the bottom of the tower, so things that are added last are removed first, and you cannot remove things in the middle or the bottom.

Adding stuff to the stack is called pushing. You can perform this whenever you need it. Removing an item is called popping. When you pop something, it is removed from the stack, but you can do something with it. You can also throw it away completely.

Lists and stacks are important to computer programming. If you master them, you will see your skill improve overall as you will be able to manipulate data, keep logs, and run algorithms more efficiently.

Below is the syntax of the stack.

```
Stack variablename=new Stack ():
```

'Variablename' is the variable we give to the stack.

Below we are using the push method to add elements to the stack.

```
Variablename.Push(element)
```

The 'element' is the value being added to the stack.

Using stacks

```
using System;
using System.Collections;
namespace Demo
{
    class Program
    {
```

```
        // The main function
        static void Main(string[] args)
        {
            // Defining the Stack
            Stack ar = new Stack();

            // Adding elements to the Stack
            ar.Push(1);
            ar.Push(2);
            ar.Push(3);
            Console.Read();
        }
    }
}
```

The Stack class has many operations that can be performed on it. We will briefly go over them below:

Stack Operations

Below is a summary.

Function	Description
Count	It tells us how many elements are in the stack
Clear	It is used to remove all elements in the stack
Pop	It is used to remove the last element on the stack
Peek	It is used to look at the last element in the stack. It does not remove it.
ToArray	It is used to put all elements into an array
Contains	It is used to check if a stack contains a certain element.

Count Function

Below we are using the count operation to find out how many elements are in the stack

Using the count property

```
using System;
using System.Collections;

namespace Demo
{
    class Program
    {
        // The main function
        static void Main(string[] args)
        {
            // Defining the Stack
            Stack ar = new Stack();

            // Adding elements to the Stack
            ar.Push(11);
            ar.Push(22);
            ar.Push(33);

            Console.WriteLine("The number of elements on the stack is "
+ ar.Count);
            Console.Read();
        }
    }
}
```

The console will print the following answer for us:

The number of elements on the stack is 3

Clear Function

Below we use the clear function to remove all elements in the stack.

Using the clear function

```
using System;
using System.Collections;

namespace Demo
{
    class Program
    {
        // The main function
        static void Main(string[] args)
        {
            // Defining the Stack
            Stack ar = new Stack();

            // Adding elements to the Stack
            ar.Push(45);
            ar.Push(77);
            ar.Push(99);
```

```
            ar.Push(54);

            Console.WriteLine("The number of elements on the stack is "
+ ar.Count);
             // Clearing the stack
            ar.Clear();

            Console.WriteLine("The number of elements on the stack is "
+ ar.Count);
            Console.Read();
        }
    }
}
```

We should get the following result in the console:

The number of elements on the stack is 4

The number of elements on the stack is 0

Pop Function

Below we are using pop to remove the last element that was added.

Using the pop function

```
using System;
using System.Collections;

namespace Demo
{
    class Program
    {
        // The main function
        static void Main(string[] args)
        {
            // Defining the Stack
            Stack ar = new Stack();

            // Adding elements to the Stack
            ar.Push(87);
            ar.Push(90);
            ar.Push(15);

            Console.WriteLine("The number of elements in the stack is" +
ar.Count());
            Console.WriteLine("We have popped an element reducing the
number of elements to " + ar.Pop());
            Console.Read();
        }
    }
```

```
}
```

In regard to the program, the result should be in this format:

The number of elements in the stack is 3

We have popped an element reducing the number of elements to 2

Peek Function

We are going to use peek to look at the last element in the stack.

Here is an application of the peek function.

```
using System;
using System.Collections;

namespace Demo
{
    class Program
    {
        // The main function
        static void Main(string[] args)
        {
            // Defining the Stack
            Stack ar = new Stack();

            // Adding elements to the Stack
            ar.Push(11);
            ar.Push(22);
            ar.Push(333);

            Console.WriteLine("The element at the top of the stack is "
+ ar.Peek());
            Console.Read();
        }
    }
}
```

We should see this result in the console:

The element at the top of the stack is 333

ToArray Function

We are going to use the ToArray method to dump the content of a stack into an array.

The next program shows the way to use the ToArray function.

```
using System;
using System.Collections;
```

```
namespace Demo
{
    class Program
    {
        // The main function
        static void Main(string[] args)
        {
            // Defining the Stack
            Stack ar = new Stack();
            object[] ar1 = new object[3];

            // Adding elements to the Stack
            ar.Push(11);
            ar.Push(22);
            ar.Push(33);

            // Transfering the elements to an array
            ar1=ar.ToArray();

            Console.WriteLine("The first element is " +
ar1[0].ToString());
            Console.WriteLine("The second element is " +
ar1[1].ToString());
            Console.WriteLine("The third element is " +
ar1[2].ToString());

            Console.Read();
        }
    }
}
```

We should see this in the console:

The first element is 33

The second element is 22

The third element is 11

Contains Function

Below we use the function to find out if a stack contains a particular element.

This program is used to showcase the contains function.

```
using System;
using System.Collections;

namespace Demo
{
    class Program
```

```
    {
        // The main function
        static void Main(string[] args)
        {
            // Defining the Stack
            Stack ar = new Stack();

            // Adding elements to the Stack
            ar.Push(800);
            ar.Push(342);
            ar.Push(3);

            // Transfering the elements to an array
            Console.WriteLine("Does the stack contain the element 800?
True or False? " + ar.Contains(800));
            Console.Read();
        }
    }
}
```

Here is what we should get in the console:

Does the stack contain the element 800? True or False? True

Queue

The Queue collection is a first-in-first-out collection, the opposite of a stack collection. The syntax below is for defining a queue:

```
Queue variablename=new Queue ():
```

Just like before, "variablename" stands for whatever variable we assign to the Queue collection. The "Enqueue" method adds an element of the queue

```
Variablename.Enqueue (element)
```

In the example above, the element stands for the value being added to the queue.

Below, we illustrate how queues are used.

Here is an application of queues.

```
using System;
using System.Collections;

namespace Demo
{
    class Program
    {
        // The main function
```

```
        static void Main(string[] args)
        {
            // Defining the Queue
            Queue ar = new Queue();

            // Adding elements to the Queue
            ar.Enqueue("apples");
            ar.Enqueue("beans");
            ar.Enqueue("carrots");

            Console.Read();
        }
    }
}
```

Queues have a number of operations that can be performed on them. Below we will look at those operations.

Queue Operations

Function	**Description**
Count	It tells us the number of elements in the queue
Clear	Used to delete all element in the queue
ToArray	Used to deposit elements into an array
Dequeue	Used to remove elements from the queue (the first element)
Contains	Used to find out if a queue contains a certain element

Count Property

It is essential for obtaining the number of elements in the queue.

Using the count property

```
using System;
using System.Collections;

namespace Demo
{
    class Program
    {
        // The main function
        static void Main(string[] args)
```

```
        {
            // Defining the Queue
            Queue ar = new Queue();

            // Adding elements to the Queue
            ar.Enqueue(1);
            ar.Enqueue(2);
            ar.Enqueue(3);

            Console.WriteLine("There are " + ar.Count + " elements in
the queue.");
            Console.Read();
        }
    }
}
```

This is what we should expect to see in the console:

There are 3 elements in the queue.

DeQueue Function

Here is an example of dequeue.

Using the DeQueue function

```
using System;
using System.Collections;

namespace Demo
{
    class Program
    {
        // The main function
        static void Main(string[] args)
        {
            // Defining the Queue
            Queue ar = new Queue();

            // Adding elements to the Queue
            ar.Enqueue(1);
            ar.Enqueue(2);
            ar.Enqueue(3);

            Console.WriteLine("The first element out of the queue is " +
ar.Dequeue());
            Console.WriteLine("The second element out of the queue is "
+ ar.Dequeue());
            Console.WriteLine("The third element out of the queue is " +
ar.Dequeue());

            Console.Read();
```

```
        }
    }
}
```

In regard to the program, the result should be in this format:

The first element out of the queue is 1

The second element out of the queue is 2

The third element out of the queue is 3

Clear Function

This function is used to delete functions in the queue.

Using the clear function

```
using System;
using System.Collections;

namespace Demo
{
    class Program
    {
        // The main function
        static void Main(string[] args)
        {
            // Defining the Queue
            Queue ar = new Queue();

            // Adding elements to the Queue
            ar.Enqueue(1);
            ar.Enqueue(2);
            ar.Enqueue(3);

            Console.WriteLine("There are " + ar.Count + " elements in
the queue.");

            // Clearing the queue
            ar.Clear();
            Console.WriteLine("There are " + ar.Count + " elements in
the queue.");
            Console.Read();
        }
    }
}
```

This is what you should expect to see in the console:

There are 3 elements in the queue.

There are 0 elements in the queue.

Contains Function

Below we will use the contains method to check if the queue has a particular element in it.

The program below is used to showcase the contains function.

```
using System;
using System.Collections;

namespace Demo
{
    class Program
    {
        // The main function
        static void Main(string[] args)
        {
            // Defining the Queue
            Queue ar = new Queue();

            // Adding elements to the Queue
            ar.Enqueue("red");
            ar.Enqueue("roses");
            ar.Enqueue("wine");

            Console.WriteLine("Does the queue contain roses? True or
false? " + ar.Contains("roses"));
            Console.Read();
        }
    }
}
```

The program should output this in the console:

Does the queue contain roses? True or false? True.

ToArray Function

We are going to use the ToArray method to input all elements in the queue into an array.

Use the ToArray function.

```
using System;
using System.Collections;

namespace Demo
{
    class Program
    {
        // The main function
```

```
        static void Main(string[] args)
        {
            // Defining the Queue
            Queue ar = new Queue();
            Object[] ar1 = new Object[3];

            // Adding elements to the Queue
            ar.Enqueue("All");
            ar.Enqueue("Things");
            ar.Enqueue("End");

            ar1 = ar.ToArray();

            Console.WriteLine("The first element of the array is " +
ar1[0].ToString());
            Console.WriteLine("The second element of the array is " +
ar1[1].ToString());
            Console.WriteLine("The third element of the array is " +
ar1[2].ToString());

            Console.Read();
        }
    }
}
```

In regard to the program, the result should be in this format:

The first element of the array is All

The second element of the array is Things

The third element of the array is End

SortedList

SortedLists store data in key/value pairs. This data can be accessed by key or index. Below is the syntax we use to initiate a SortedList collection.

```
SortedList variablename=new SortedList ():
```

To add something to the collection, you need to use the Add() method in the following way.

```
Variablename.Add (key,value)
```

As you can see, items are added with their key and the value. Below is an example of how that might look in the real world.

The next program is used to show how to use SortedList.

```
using System;
```

```
using System.Collections;

namespace Demo
{
    class Program
    {
        // The main function
        static void Main(string[] args)
        {
            // Defining the SortedList
            SortedList ar = new SortedList();

            // Adding elements to the SortedList
            ar.Add(111,"Chicken");
            ar.Add(222,"Master");
            ar.Add(333,"Egg");

            // Displaying the values of each element in the SortedList
            Console.WriteLine("The first value of the SortedList is " +
ar[111].ToString());
            Console.WriteLine("The second value of the SortedList is " +
ar[222].ToString());
            Console.WriteLine("The third value of the SortedList is " +
ar[333].ToString());

            Console.Read();
        }
    }
}
```

From above:

- Each element consists of a key and value.
- We can access each element with its key

This is what we should see in the console when we run the code:

The first value of the SortedList is Chicken

The second value of the SortedList is Master

The third value of the SortedList is Egg

Like the collections we have looked at, SortedList collections have their own methods.

SortedList Operations

Below are brief descriptions of SortedList methods.

Function	Description
Count	It tells us how many items are in the SortedList
Clears()	Removes all elements in the SortedList
ContainsKey()	Checks if the collection contains a specific key
ContainsValue()	Checks if a SortedList contains a particular value
IndexOfKey()	It gives us the index of a particular key
IndexOfValue()	It gives us the index of a particular value
Remove()	Removes an item/location from the SortedList
RemoveAt()	Removes item/object at a particular location

Count Property

We are going to use the Count method to find out how many items are in the SortedList.

```
using System;
using System.Collections;

namespace Demo
{
    class Program
    {
        // The main function
        static void Main(string[] args)
        {
            // Defining the SortedList
            SortedList ar = new SortedList();

            // Adding elements to the SortedList
            ar.Add(1,"One");
            ar.Add(2,"Ring");
            ar.Add(3,"To Rule Them All");

      Console.WriteLine("There are " + ar.Count + " items in the
SortedList!");
            Console.Read();
        }
    }
}
```

We should get the following result in the console:

There are 3 items in the SortedList

Clears Function

We are going to use clear to remove all items in the SortedList.

```
using System;
using System.Collections;

namespace Demo
{
    class Program
    {
        // The main function
        static void Main(string[] args)
        {
            // Defining the SortedList
            SortedList ar = new SortedList();

            // Adding elements to the SortedList
            ar.Add(1, "One Ring");
            ar.Add(2, "To");
            ar.Add(3, "Rule Them All!");

            Console.WriteLine("There are " + ar.Count + " items in the
SortedList! :)");

            // Clearing all the elements of the list
            ar.Clear();
  Console.WriteLine("There are " + ar.Count + " items in the SortedList.
:(");
            Console.Read();
        }
    }
}
```

In regard to the program, the result should be in this format:

There are 3 items in the SortedList! :)

There are 0 items in the SortedList. :(

ContainsKey Function

We are going to use ContainsKey to find if the SortedList contains a specific key.

Here is an application of the ContainsKey function.

```
using System;
```

```
using System.Collections;

namespace Demo
{
    class Program
    {
        // The main function
        static void Main(string[] args)
        {
            // Defining the SortedList
            SortedList ar = new SortedList();

            // Adding elements to the SortedList
            ar.Add(767, "One");
            ar.Add(090, "Two");
            ar.Add(999, "Three");

            Console.WriteLine("True or false, does the SortedLIst
contain the key 999? " + ar.ContainsKey(999)+ ".");
            Console.Read();
        }
    }
}
```

We should see the following result in the console:

True or false, does the SortedList contain the key 999? True.

ContainsValue Function

Below we are going to use ContainsValue to find out if a SortedList contains a specific value.

The program below is used to showcase the ContainsValue function.

```
using System;
using System.Collections;

namespace Demo
{
    class Program
    {
        // The main function
        static void Main(string[] args)
        {
            // Defining the SortedList
            SortedList ar = new SortedList();

            // Adding elements to the SortedList
            ar.Add(1, "One Ring To Rule Them All");
            ar.Add(2, "Sam helped Frodo");
            ar.Add(3, "Sing along");
  Console.WriteLine("True or False, does the SortedList contain the
```

```
Value \"One Ring To Rule Them All\"? " + ar.ContainsValue("One Ring To
Rule Them All")+".");
            Console.WriteLine("True or False, does the SortedList
contain the Value \"Snowhite\"? " + ar.ContainsValue("Snow White")+
".");

            Console.Read();
        }
    }
}
```

The console should display the following results when you run the code:

True or False, does the SortedList contain the Value "One Ring To Rule Them All"? True.

True or False, does the SortedList contain the Value "Snowhite"? False.

IndexOfKey Function

We are going to use the IndexOfKey method to find out what the index of a key is.

The next program is used to show the way to use the IndexOfKey function.

```
using System;
using System.Collections;

namespace Demo
{
    class Program
    {
        // The main function
        static void Main(string[] args)
        {
            // Defining the SortedList
            SortedList ar = new SortedList();

            // Adding elements to the SortedList
          ar.Add(767, "One");
          ar.Add(090, "Two");
          ar.Add(999, "Three");
         Console.WriteLine("The index of the key 999 is " +
ar.IndexOfKey(999)+". :)");
            Console.Read();
        }
    }
}
```

We should observe the following result in the console:

The index of the key 999 is 2. :)

IndexOfValue Function

We will use the IndexOfValue method to find out the index of a value of our interest.

This program shows how to use the IndexOfValue function.

```
using System;
using System.Collections;
namespace Demo
{
    class Program
    {
        // The main function
        static void Main(string[] args)
        {
            // Defining the SortedList
            SortedList ar = new SortedList();

            // Adding elements to the SortedList
           ar.Add(1, "One Ring To Rule Them All");
            ar.Add(2, "Sam helped Frodo");
            ar.Add(3, "Snow White");

            Console.WriteLine("The Snow White value is at index " +
ar.IndexOfValue("Snow White")+ ". :)");

            Console.Read();
        }
    }
}
```

We should see the following result in the console:

The Snow White value is at index 2. :)

Remove Function

This function is used to remove an object from the SortedList.

Using the remove function

```
using System;
using System.Collections;

namespace Demo
{
    class Program
    {
        // The main function
        static void Main(string[] args)
        {
```

```
            // Defining the SortedList
            SortedList ar = new SortedList();

            // Adding elements to the SortedList
           ar.Add(1, "One Ring To Rule Them All");
            ar.Add(2, "Sam helped Frodo");
            ar.Add(3, "Snow White");

            Console.WriteLine("The Snow White value is at index " +
ar.IndexOfValue("Snow White")+ ". :)");
            // Removes element with key 3, aka Snow White
            ar.Remove( 3 );
            Console.WriteLine("Is Snow White still at index 2? True or
False? " + ar.ContainsValue("Snow White")+ ".");

            Console.Read();
        }
    }
}
```

We will see the following results in the console:

The Snow White value is at index 2. :)

Is Snow White still at index 2? True or False? False.

RemoveAt Function

We are going to use the RemoveAt method to remove an item at a particular index.

The program below is used to show how to use the RemoveAt function.

```
using System;
using System.Collections;

namespace Demo
{
    class Program
    {
        // The main function
        static void Main(string[] args)
        {
            // Defining the SortedList
            SortedList ar = new SortedList();

            // Adding elements to the SortedList
         ar.Add(1, "One Ring To Rule Them All");
         ar.Add(2, "Sam helped Frodo");
         ar.Add(3, "Snow White");

            Console.WriteLine("Snow White is at index " +
ar.IndexOfValue("Snow Wite");
```

```
        //Removes Snow White at index 2
            ar.RemoveAt(2);
            Console.WriteLine("Is Snow White Still at 2? True or False?
" + ar.ContainsValue("Snow White"));

            Console.Read();
        }
    }
}
```

You should expect to see this in the console:

The Snow White value is at index 2. :)

Is Snow White still at index 2? True or False? False.

CHAPTER 7:

Indexers

Indexers allow custom classes to be indexed like an array. Each member is accessed with the array access operator ([]) instead of properties (you would expect that since it is a class) ("C# Indexers").

Indexers are defined like this:

```
type this[int index]
{
            get
            {
                //returns values
            }
            set
            {
                //sets values
            }
}
```

Here is how you would access the class:

Example[2];

In the example below, we will use it as an album collection searcher, which tells us what year an album was released.

```
using System;
using System.Collections.Generic;

namespace ConsoleApplication1
```

```
{
    class Program
    {
        static void Main()
        {
            Album main_floor = new Album();

            //Adds Items
            main_floor.AddItem(new Item("The Crux", 2012));
            main_floor.AddItem(new Item("Chromatica", 2020));

            //Uses indexer to grab Year
            Console.WriteLine("The Crux by HURT was released in " +
main_floor["The Crux"] + " and Chromatica by Lady Gaga in " +
main_floor["Chromatica"] + ".");
            Console.ReadKey();
        }
    }

    class Album
    {
        List<Item> Items = new List<Item>();

        public void AddItem(Item item)
        {
            Items.Add(item);
        }

        public double this[string index]
        {
            get
            {
                foreach (Item item in Items)
                {
                    if (item.Name == index)
                    {
                        return item.Year;
                    }
                }

                //Used to signify that there is not item
                return -1;
            }
            set
            {
                //You can also use this to set a value much like setting
a value in
                //an attribute
            }

        }
    }
```

```
    //Simple class to hold item
    class Item
    {
        public Item(string name, double year)
        {
            Name = name;
            Year = year;
        }

        public string Name { get; }
        public double Year { get; }
    }
}
```

We should get this result in the console:

The Crux by HURT was released in 2012 and Chromatica by Lady Gaga in 2020.

If you have trouble seeing what I did there, copy and paste the code in your IDE. It will be highlighted properly, and the code will be easier to follow.

CHAPTER 8:

Generics

Generics allow us to declare lists, classes, and other elements without specifying their data type. In other words, you will be able to make methods and classes that can work with any data type. Parameters will function as placeholders for different data types. A compiler will use the methods according to the data types provided. Generics improve code reusability and flexibility. Let us look at the example below, so you can have a more vivid example of what generics do.

We will use the Display here and later to show how this works.

In this example, we use multiple methods to display integers.

```
using System;
using System.Collections;

namespace Demo
{
    class Program
    {
        // Display method for Integers
        public static void Add(int i)
    {
    Console.WriteLine("The value is " + i);
    }

    // Display method for double numbers
        public static void Add(double i)
    {
```

```
    Console.WriteLine("The value is " + i);
    }

        // The main function
        static void Main(string[] args)
        {
            Display(1);
            Display(1.1);
            Console.Read();
        }
    }
}
```

In regard to the program, the result should be in this format:

The value is 1

The value is 1.1

In the previous example, we were creating two methods that perform the same task. However, we need one for integers and another for double data type. We can make this program more generic with the 'Generic' data type.

Example: The next program shows how to use the generic data type.

```
using System;
using System.Collections.Generic;

namespace Demo
{
    class Program
    {
        // Generic Display method
        public static void Display<T>(T i)
    {
        Console.WriteLine(" This is value " + i);
    }

        // The main function
        static void Main(string[] args)
        {
            // Calling the generic with the data type
            Display<int>(1);
            Display<double>(1.1);

            Console.Read();
        }
    }
}
```

The program will print this in the console:

This is value 1

The is value 1.1

Generic Classes

Classes can also be generic. The syntax declaration of a generic class is given below.

```
public class classname<T>
```

In this code, 'classname' is the name of the class. Let's look at an example of a generic class.

Example: The program below showcases the way to use the generic class.

```
using System;
using System.Collections.Generic;

namespace Demo
{
    // Generic class
    public class GenericSet<T>
    {
        private T[] array;
        public GenericSet(int size)
        {
            array = new T[size + 1];
        }
        public T getItem(int index)
        {
            return array[index];
        }
        public void setItem(int index, T value)
        {
            array[index] = value;
        }
    }
    class Program
    {
        // The main function
        static void Main(string[] args)
        {

            GenericSet<int> gn=new GenericSet<int>(2);
            gn.setItem(1,1);
            gn.setItem(2,2);

            Console.WriteLine("Item number one is " + gn.getItem(1));
            Console.WriteLine("Item number two " + gn.getItem(2));
```

```
            Console.Read();
        }
    }
}
```

In regard to the program, the result should be in this format:

Item number one is 1

Item number two is 2

Generics List <T> Collection

Generic collections allow us to make data collections that have Array and ArrayList functionalities. So, they are more like arrays. You have to declare them and initialize them, just like below:

Example 1:

```
using System;
using System.Collections.Generic;
namespace MySampleApplication
{
    public class Program
    {
       public static void Main(string[] args)
        {

          List<int> myRows = new List <int> ();
             myRows.Add(11);
             myRows.Add(22);
             myRows.Add(33);


            foreach(int i in myRows)
                {
                Console.WriteLine("Number " + i + " in the house!");
                }

        }
    }
}
```

The type signature of List class is List<T> where T can be any data type: springs, char, int, double, and others. If you define a list of int, it will only hold int, and it's the same with any other data type. In the example above, the list will only contain integers because that is how we defined it. Furthermore, we can use the Add() method to add as many integers as we want. Lists allow us to use many methods on them, like Contains, Remove, Count, etc.

Below is the output of the example above:

Number 11 in the house!

Number 22 in the house!

Number 33 in the house!

This works because we have declared myRows, which stores int data types. We used the Add method to add integers and a foreach loop to print the values of those integers in the console.

Generic Methods

Generic methods and classes give us high code reusability in a variety of circumstances across data types. What's amazing about generic methods is that they can be used in spaces where the containing class is not generic or where a class has parameters that are not initially defined. The generic method always follows this pattern: "method name (type param syntax)". Let's take a look below.

Example 2:

```
namespace MySampleApplication
{
 public static class MathExp
{
  public static T Max<T>(T first, params T[] values)
      where T : IComparable
  {
      T max = first;
      foreach (T item in values)
      {
          if (item.CompareTo(max) > 0)
          {max = item;  }
      }
      return max;
  }
  public static T Min<T>(T first, params T[] values)
      where T : IComparable
  {
      T mini = first;
        foreach (T item in values)
     {
      if (item.CompareTo(mini) < 0)
            { mini = item; }
        }
      return mini;
   }
```

```
}
```

The sample class “MathExp" has two generic methods: “Min <T> and Max <T>.” The function of these is straightforward. Min<T> finds and returns the smallest value in a list. Max<T> finds the greatest value in a list. The <T> is the placeholder for any kind of data type like int, strings, floats, etc.

Here is an example of both methods:

```
Console.WriteLine (MathEx.Max<int> (63, 800, 700))
Console.WriteLine (MathEx.Max<string> (“Almonds,” “Walnuts,”
“Pistachios”))
Our output will be:
800
Pistachios
```

In the example, we had to specify the data type in the list in the “<>.” What is interesting is that even if we don’t specify the data type, the C# compiler would still be able to run the method because it can find out what data type is in the list. This is known as type interfacing. To see it in action, we have to try the code again, like this:

Here is an example of both methods:

```
Console.WriteLine (MathEx.Max(63, 800, 700))
Console.WriteLine (MathEx.Max(“Almonds,” “Walnuts,” “Pistachios”))
Our output will be:
800
Pistachios
```

Our output is the same as before, even when we didn’t specify the data type in the list. The only time that this method would fail is if we mixed different data types in one list. So, you can’t run it on a list of integers and floats, for example.

CHAPTER 9:

Garbage Collection

When you create an object, CLR allocates memory from the Heap. This process repeats each time new objects form and are made. But it cannot go on forever, because memory is limited. Now and then, the system has to purge unused objects and make space for new ones. Garbage Collection, or GC, manages memory. It allocates and reclaims memory. It allocates memory for new objects and then goes to the heap to remove objects that are not in use by the program. This means enough memory is still available.

Memory Facts

When the process is triggered, it is given a piece of virtual space that stems from your physical memory. Physical memory is the actual memory that your computer uses, RAM. Programs deal with virtual space - that's their working memory. Machines deal with physical space.

Virtual memory has free-blocks that are called holes. When an object asks for memory, GC looks for an empty block and assigns it to the objects. Virtual memory is the memory that the computer has given to the program or code to work within.

Below are the three types of blocks in virtual memory:

There are three blocks in virtual memory:

- Free, which is empty space
- Reserved, which is already allocated
- Committed, which is reserved for physical memory and cannot be allocated

How Does GC Work?

The Heap is a memory block that is used for storing objects. When GC happens in the Heap, it looks for inactive objects and removes them, and then it compacts the remaining objects to free up more memory.

The Heap is managed by a group of generations. These generations store and handle short-term and long-term objects. These generations are:

- 0 Generation – it holds short-term, temporary objects that don't last long. GC is activated frequently.
- 1 Generation – is the buffer existing between short-term and long-term objects
- 2 Generation – holds long-term objects, such as static and global variables, that need to last longer, and that the program may depend on. When an object is not collected in 0 generation, it is moved up to 1 Generation. That object is called a survivor. If it is not collected again in 1 generation it is moved up to 2 Generation because it must be important if it is still active.

How Does GC Determine the Live Objects?

To determine if an object is live or not, GC will check the information below:

- All object handles that are not allocated by CLR or by user code are collected
- Static objects which are referenced by another object are tracked
- GC uses the Stack Walker and JIT Stack.

When Does GC Get Triggered?

There is no set time when GC gets triggered. It is triggered when the conditions below are met:

- When virtual memory space is low
- When the memory is repressed past a certain threshold. If GC discovers a high level of living objects, it increases the allocation
- It is also triggered and is called specifically using the GC.Collect() method. This is rare because GC is always active and performs actions when needed.

What are the Managed/Unmanaged Objects or Resources?

In a nutshell:

- Any object created, managed, and within the CLR scope is a managed object. It is managed if it is impure .Net code, runtime-managed, and within the .NET scope. So any classes within the .NET framework would count as managed objects.
- Any project that is not CLR managed is created externally to the .NET library and is not

a managed object. These include COM objects, connect objects, interop objects, and all third party library objects even when they are referenced within the .NET framework.

Cleaning up all the Resources that are Unmanaged

GC cannot clean unmanaged objects. It is the programmer's responsibility to explicitly get rid of them when a task is completed. Unmanaged objects are hidden around operating system resources like database connections, file streams, class handles, pointer, registries, etc. GC can track the life cycle of managed and unmanaged resources, but the responsibility of removing unmanaged objects lies with the programmer.

Here are a few ways you can do this:

- Implementing the Dispose method and the IDisposable interface
- By the "using" code block

You can implement the Dispose method in two ways:

- By using the SafeHandle class, a built-in abstract class containing the IDisposable interface and CriticalFinalizerObject. You will need to implement both
- By overriding the Object.Finalize method, which cleans the unmanaged resource used by an object before the object is destroyed.

Let's look at the code which allows us to do this:

The 'using' Statement

The 'using' statement ensures that the object is removed. If the object falls outside of scope, the Dispose method is called. It acts the same way as the Try. I will show you how it works by creating a class with IDisposable implementation. The 'using' statement will call Dispose no matter what:

```
class testClass : IDisposable
{
    public void Dispose()
    {
        // Dispose of the objects here
 // clean resources
 Console.WriteLine(00);
    }
}

//call class
class Program
{
    static void Main()
    {
        // Use the using statement with the class that implements
```

```
Dispose.
 using (testClass objClass = new testClass())
 {
     Console.WriteLine(01);
}
 Console.WriteLine(02);
     }
}
```

```
//output
01
00
02
```

```
//it is exactly the same as the TRY...Finally code below
{
   clsDispose_Fin objClass = new clsDispose_Fin();
   try
   {
      //the code goes here
   }
   finally
   {
      if (objClass != null)
      ((IDisposable)objClass).Dispose();
   }
}
```

In a set up like this, once the 01 is printed, the 'using' code block calls the Dispose method, followed by the statement after the 'using' block

Quick Primer

- Object-oriented programming, or OOP, is programming that makes code that reflects real-world objects
- C# classes describe what a category of objects does, the data type it will hold, functions, and uses
- Creating new objects is as easy as Random random = new Random(). This will create a Random object which generates random numbers
- Destructors are generally not needed in C# because Garbage Collection disposes of an object when it is not in use
- Stack and Heap help manage memory
- Garbage Collector allocates and deallocates memory

- GC manages the Heap - a memory block used for storing objects
- GC is not scheduled; it is triggered when certain conditions are met.
- CLR creates and manages managed objects
- Unmanaged objects are hidden or wrapped around the resources of the operating system
- We can use the Dispose method and/or the 'using' statement to remove unmanaged objects

CHAPTER 10:

Lambda Expressions and Expression Trees

In this section, we are going to discuss Lambda expressions and expression trees. We are going to learn how they are created and how to use them to simplify and enhance our code. Understanding delegates, which we discussed in the first book, is essential.

Lambda Expressions

Lambda Expressions are anonymous, unspecified functions that create delegates or expression trees. They provide fast and easy ways of defining delegates. They are methods without declaration-like access modifiers. They will make your code more compact, reducing lines of code and making it easy to maintain and reuse.

With Lambda Expressions, we can write our methods at the same place we are going to use them. They are like anonymous methods, but they have a smarter syntax.

Lambdas are critical in method-based LINQ queries that can be fed in the standard query operator methods like the "Where."

Below is the basic structure of Lambda Expressions :

```
Parameters => Executed code
```

Example 1:

```
x =>           x*x;
```

The input parameter is 'x,' and 'x*x' is the expression. The x value is returned after it has been multiplied by itself.

Lambda expressions can be assigned to delegate as show below:

```
delegate int del(int i);
 static void Main(string[] args){
 del myDelegate = x => x * x;
  int resultVariable= myDelegate(8);
}
```

We have assigned the Lambda Expression "x => x * x" to a delegate called "myDelegate". Then we called myDelegate and passed "8". The result is stored in an integer variable named "resultVariable" which gave us 64.

Example 2:

```
Class LambdaExpression{
static void Main(string[] args){
List<string> names=new List<string>();
 names.Add('Mark');
 names.Add('Jeff');
 names.Add('Johnson');
 string resultString=names.Find(name=>name.Equals('Jeff'));
}
}
```

Above we have declared a list of String values "names". Then we added names to that list with the list.Add method. Then we use the list.Find, passing the Lambda Expression "name=>name.Equals('Jeff')" which then saves our result in a string literal called "resultString"

Example 3:

```
namespace lambdaexample
{
  class QueryOperator
  {
     static void Main(string[] args)
     {
        int[] numbers = { 1, 1, 2, 3, 5, 8, 13, 21, 34 };
        double averageNumber = numbers.Where(num => num % 2 ==
1).Average();
        Console.WriteLine(averageNumber);
        Console.ReadLine();
     }
  }
}
```

In the previous example, we have declared an array of integers called numbers. The array holds Fibonacci numbers. Then we used a Lambda Expression next to the where clause like this:

numbers.Where(num => num % 2 == 1).Average(). This expression finds odd numbers in the list and gets their average with the "Average()" method, saving the result in the "averageNumber" variable. The result is then printed using a console statement: Console.WriteLine(averageNumber).

Expression Trees

Expression trees are data structures that contain expressions like Lambda Expressions. At their core, expressions are pieces of code that have a tree structure. You can use them to run Lambda Expressions on data sets. They are like a binary tree because binary trees can quickly find data. They give us the ability to translate executable code into data. For example, you can change the LINQ query expression to function on another SQL database process.

Example 4:

Func <int, int, int> function = (a, b) => a + b;

The above statement has three parts:

- The declaration: Func<int,int,int> function
- An equals sign operator: =
- A Lambda Expression: (a,b) => a+b;

The executable code is located in the "function" variable which can house the result from the Lambda Expression((a,b) => a+b). The Lambda Expression looks like this:

```
int d = function(12, 8);
```

When we call it, the variable 'd' will be equal to 20.

Because Expression trees are data structures, the code can be converted into a data structure by using LINQ syntax. To do this, you will have to add the Linq.Expressions namespace:

```
using System.Linq.Expressions;
```

Then you would create the Expression tree like this:

```
Expression<Func<int, int, int>> expression = (a,b) => a + b;
```

The Lambda Expression is now changed into an Expression Tree, which looks like this: "Expression<X>." You won't be able to execute the identifier expression because it now counts as a data structure.

In Visual Studio (IDE), you can use the "ExpressionTreeVisualizer" to see the expression tree of the expression statement.

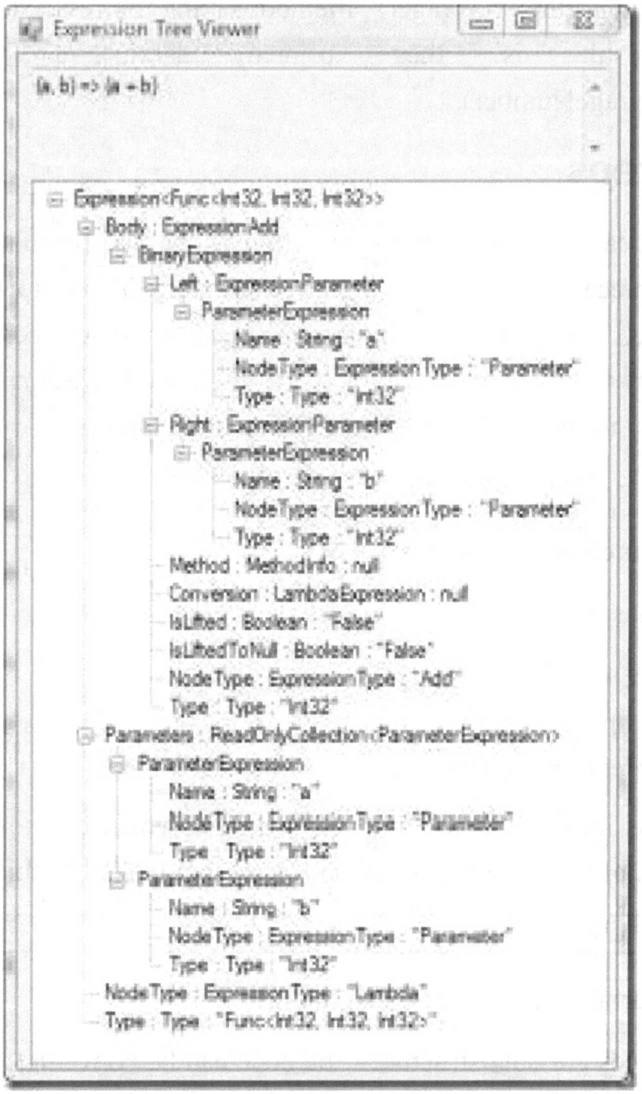

The diagram above shows us the Lambda Expression and its integral parts in the TreeView Control.

The Expression<x> class contains four properties:

- Body
- Parameters
- NodeType
- Type

These are clearly visible when we make the tree collapse, as shown below.

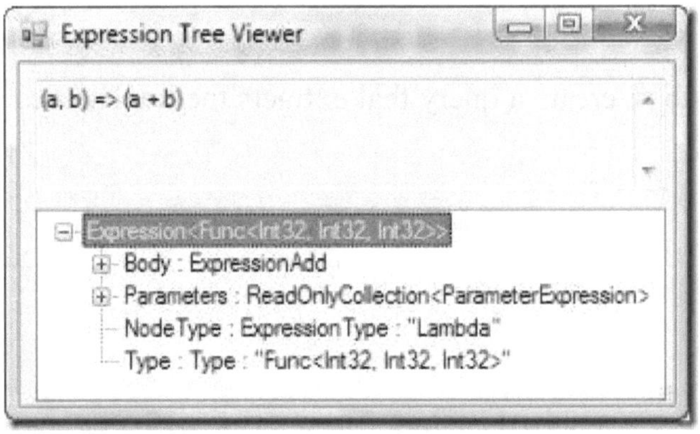


```
BinaryExpression body = (BinaryExpression)expression.Body;
ParameterExpression left = (ParameterExpression)body.Left;
ParameterExpression right = (ParameterExpression)body.Right;
Console.WriteLine(expression.Body);
Console.WriteLine(' The expression's left section: ' +
'{0}{4} The NodeType: {1}{4} The right part: {2}{4} The Type: {3}{4}',
left.Name, body.NodeType, right.Name, body.Type, Environment.NewLine);
```

The code above helps us explore the expression tree. We start by declaring the "body" variable of the "BinaryExpressions" type. This holds the body of the expressions, which is (a+b). We access the parameter on the left with "(ParameterExpression)body.Left" which is the "left" variable of the "parameterExpression" type. This is the variable "a". Then we use the "(ParameterExpression)body.Right" in the "right" variable of the "parameterExpression" type to access the variable "b." Then we print the body of the expression in the console with its NodeType, the left & right, and the expression type with built-in methods.

Exercise

Task 1:

Write a Lambda Expression, which calculates the total number of scores greater than 57 in this series (31-, 23, 64, 40, 85, 55, 50, and 99).

Solution

```
class SampleLambda
{
    static void Main()
    {
        int[] scores = { 31-, 23, 64, 40, 85, 55, 50, 99};
    int highScores = scores.Where(n => n > 57).Count();
        Console.WriteLine('{0} scores are greater than 57', highScores);
    }
}
```

Task 2:

Using Lambda Expressions, create a query that extracts the total scores for first grade students, second grade, and so on.

Solution

```
private static void StudentsByGrade()
{
    var categ =
    from student in students
    group student by student.grade into studentGroup
    select new { GradeLevel = studentGroup.Key, TotalScore =
studentGroup.Sum(s => s.ExamScores.Sum()) };
    foreach (var cat in categ)
    {
        Console.WriteLine ('Key = {0} Sum = {1}', cat.GradeLevel,
cat.TotalScore);
    }
}
```

CHAPTER 11:

Nullable Types

C# provides a special null value data type with its own range. An int32 data type has a range of -2147483648 to 2147483647, while nullable int32 can store a null value of all numbers in the int data type range. A Nullable of a Boolean value is able to store a true, false, or a null value.

In this chapter, we are going to look at:

Contents

- **Structures of Nullable types**
- **Syntax of Nullable types**
- **The HasValue and Has Property**
- **The Null Coalescing operator**

Structures of Nullable types in C#

The table below shows us Nullable type structures of primitive data types along with their range. As we have illustrated, Nullable types have an extra null value.

Type	Range
Nullable Boolean	True or False or Null
Nullable byte	0 to 255 or Null
Nullable decimal	(-7.9 x 1028 to 7.9 x 1028) / 100 to 28 or Null

Nullable double	(+/-)5.0 x 10-324 to (+/-)1.7 x 10308 or Null
Nullable DateTime	Represents an instant in Time or Null
Nullable Int16	-32,768 to +32,767 or Null
Nullable Int32	-2,147,483,648 to 2,147,483,647 or Null
Nullable Int64	-9,223,372,036,854,775,808 to +9,223,372,036,854,775,807 0r Null
Nullable Single	Single value or Null
Nullable char	U+0000 to U+FFFF or Null

Syntax for Nullable types in C#

There are two main ways of declaring the Nullable type. The first one is as follows:

```
System.Nullable<data_type> <variable_name>;
```

It opens with a System.Nullable keyword (which is called the relevant object), followed by the specification of the data type — int, double — and the variable name.

The other way of declaring a Nullable type looks like this:

```
< data_type> ? <variable_name> = null;
```

It opens with the data type specification, a question mark, and then variable name.

Let's look at some examples.

Example 1:

```
Namespace nullable
{
    Class program
    {
      static void Main ()
    {
      int? x= null;
      int? y=11;
      if(x==null)
     {System.Console.WriteLine(y.Value)}
      else {System.Console.WriteLine('Undefined');}

      }
   }
}
```

In the example above, we declared nullable integers y and x. int? x has a null value and int? y has the value of 11. If the if-else statement says x is a null value, the program should print out the value of y. If not, it should print "undefined."

Output 1:

```
11
```

In the next example, we illustrate Nullable types in Booleans and DateTime types.

Example 2:

```
Namespace nullable
{
    Class program
    {
      static void Main ()
    {
      int? a= null;
      int? b=7;
      Double? c=null;
      Double? d=4
      bool? Val= new bool?();
      DateTime? Start= DateTime.today;
      DateTime? End= null;
Console.Writeline('Showing values of Nullables: {0}, {1}, {2},
{3}',a,b,c,d);
Console.Writeline('A Nullable Boolean Variable: {0}',Val);
Console.Writeline(Start);
Console.Writeline('We don't know yet:', End);
      }
   }
}
```

In the examples above, we have defined Nullables of int, double, Boolean, and DateTime. The program will display the following in the console. You can begin to see the use of Nullable.

Output 2:

```
Showing values of Nullables:, 7, , 4
A Nullable Boolean Variable:
12/25/2020 12:00:00 AM
```

We don't know yet:

The HasValue and Value Property

Nullables have properties that are public and read-only.

- HasValue Property:

The HasValue tests a condition and returns a Boolean value. If the type in question is a non-null value, the HasValue property will return true. If the type has no value or null, it will return false.

- **Has Property:**

The Has property only has value when the HasValue property is true. If the HasValue property is false, the Has property throws an Exception. Let's look at an example to illustrate this:

Example 3:

```
using System;
Namespace nullable
{
    Class program
    {
      static void Main ()
    {
      int? a= null;
      Console.WriteLine(a.HasValue); // HasValue property is false
      Console.WriteLine(a.Value);    // will cause an exception
      Console.readKey();
      }
   }
```

A has a null value, so the HasValue property returns false. When we try to display a via the "Value," we get an exception.

Output 3:

```
False
```

Example 4:

```
using System;
namespace nullable
{
    class program
    {
      static void Main ()
    {
      int? a= null;
      Console.WriteLine(a.HasValue); // HasValue property is false

      a=6; //assigning value to variable
```

```
      Console.WriteLine(a.HasValue); // hasvalue Property is true
because a has non-null value
      Console.WriteLine(a.Value);    // returns value of a
      Console.WriteLine(a);
      }
   }
```

Output 4:

```
False
True
6
6
```

The Null Coalescing Operator

C# gives us an operator that can check Null values. Upon finding Null value variables, it assigns a value to that variable. The operand is a double question. It can be used on both Nullable and reference types. Where implicit conversion can be performed, it changes the operant to reflect another value type operand. Let's have a look at this:

Example 5:

```
using System;
namespace nullable
{
    class program
    {
      static void Main ()
    {
      int? a= null;
      int? b=4;
      int c=a ?? 8;
      System.Console.WriteLine($"Value of c is: {c}");
      c=b ?? 8;
      System.Console.WriteLine($"Value of c is: {c}");

      }
   }
}
```

Output 5:

```
Value of c is: 8
Value of c is: 4
```

CHAPTER 12:

Anonymous Types

C# allows us to create new data types called anonymous data types. We can create them without defining them. They are created at instantiation, and they are both compiler generation and reference types. The compiler will define them based on their properties. Anonymous types are an important feature used in SQL, and are useful in LINQ queries. Anonymous types are read-only.

In this chapter, we will study "Anonymous" types:

Contents

- **The Var Statement**
- **Creating and Using Anonymous Types**
- **Comparing Two Anonymous Instances**

Var Statement

Vars were introduced in C# 3.0. As the name suggests, they are used to declare local variables implicitly, meaning you don't have to specify the data type it will hold. Let's have a look at the example below:

```
var str='name';
var num='89';
var array=new[]{1,2,3};
```

The compiler will compile all that code like this:

```
var str='name';      // string str='name';
var num='89'         // int num='5';
var array=new[]{1,2,3}; // int array=new[]{1,2,3};
```

Let's have a look at the example below:

Example 1:

```
using System;
using System.Collections.Generic;
using System.Linq;
using System.Text;
using System.Threading.Tasks;
namespace anonymous
{
    class Program
    {
        static void Main(string[] args)
        {
            var name = "Jonathan Davis";
            var number = 25;
            string s = "USA";
            var s2 = s;
            s2 = null;
            string s3 = null;
            var s4 = s3;
            Console.WriteLine(name);
            Console.WriteLine(number);
            Console.WriteLine(s);
            Console.WriteLine(s2);
            Console.WriteLine(s3);
            Console.WriteLine(s4);

        }
    }
}
```

Output 1:

```
Jonathan Davis
25
USA
```

The values of variables var s2, var s3, and var s4 are null, and that's why they create empty spaces. A value of the var variable cannot be null at compile time but can be at run time.

Vars are not anonymous types.

Other Invalid var statements:

```
var a; // invalid because it needs to be initialized
var num=null  // cannot be Null at compile time
var v='Lord of the Rings'
v=15 // an integer cannot be assigned to a string variable declared
implicitly
```

Creating and Using Anonymous Types in C#

Anonymous types are reference types that can be created using the var statement. If we needed to create an Anonymous type to represent a point, we would do this:

```
 var point = new {x=18,y=10};
```

Var statements need us to initialize from the beginning, so values cannot be initialized to a null value. The following would be wrong:

```
var point = new {x=18,y=null};  //wrong statement, cannot be null at
compile time
```

Example 2:

```
using System;
namespace anonymous
{
    class Program
    {
        static void Main(string[] args)
        {
            var Name = new { FirstName = "Phillip", LastName = "Glass"
};
            Console.WriteLine(Name.FirstName);
            Console.WriteLine(Name.LastName);
        }
    }
}
```

Output 2:

```
Phillip
Glass
```

Here's how a compiler creates an anonymous type:

```
using System;
namespace anonymous
{
    class Program
    {
```

```
        static void Main(string[] args)
        {
            var Employee = new { EmpName = "Cain", EmpAddress =
"Florida" , Empsalary="28,000"};

        }
    }
}
```

The compiler then creates the type as follows::

```
namespace anonymous
{
    class Program
    {
 private string Name;
 private string Address;
 int salary;
public string EmpName
{get {return EmpName;}
 Set {EmpName=value;}
}
Public string EmpAddress
{
Get{return EmpAddress;}
Set{EmpAddress=value;}
}
Public int Empsalary
{
Get{return Empsalary;}
set{Empsalary=value;}
} }
}
```

In all the examples, we are naming properties explicitly. We can also do that implicitly if they are set on the basis of property, field, or variable.

Example 3:

```
using System;
namespace anonymous
{
    class Program
    {
        static void Main(string[] args)
        {
            int variable = 88;
            var implicitProperties = new { variable, DateTime.Now };
            var explicitProperties = new { variable = variable, Now =
DateTime.Now }; //same as above
```

```
            Console.WriteLine("Time is "+implicitProperties.Now+" and
implicit Variable is " + implicitProperties.variable);
            Console.WriteLine( "Time is "+ explicitProperties.Now+" and
explicit Variable is " + explicitProperties.variable);

        }
    }
}
```

Output 3:

```
Time is 12/27/2020 2:30:24 PM and implicit Variable is 88
Time is 12/27/2020 2:30:24 PM and explicit Variable is 88
```

Comparing Two Anonymous Instances

Based on underlying properties, Anonymous types can create overrides of "Equals()" to compare two Anonymous variables. We can retrieve their Hash Codes using "GetHashCode()." Here's an example of how we would do that.

Anonymous types create overrides of "Equals()" based on the underlying properties, so we can compare two anonymous variables. We can also get their Hash Codes using "GetHashCode()." For example, if we had the following 3 points:

Example 4:

```
namespace anonymous
{
    class Program
   {
        static void Main(string[] args)
        {
             var point1 = new { A = 1, B = 2 };
             var point2 = new { A = 1, B = 2 };
             var point3 = new { b = 2, A = 1 };
    Console.WriteLine(point1.Equals(point2));
           // true, equal anonymous type instances always have same hash
code
    Console.WriteLine(point1.GetHashCode() == point2.GetHashCode());
    Console.WriteLine(point2.Equals(point3));
         // quite possibly false
    Console.WriteLine(point2.GetHashCode() ==
point3.GetHashCode());
        }
    }
}
```

Output 4:

```
True
True
False
False
```

CHAPTER 13:

LINQ

LINQ stands for "Language Integrated Query" ("LINQ Tutorials from Basics to Advanced"). If you have worked with databases, you will know what a query is. In a nutshell, it is how programmers interact with a database to manipulate data. Programmers use them to access the database — to insert, edit, retrieve, or delete data. LINQ gives C# developers a fresh way of accessing and working with multiple data types like XML field, databases, lists, and dynamic data.

LINQ functions are composed of two fundamental units: sequences and elements. LINQ sequences are a set of items that implement the Ienumerable<T>. Interface where each item in the set is referred to as an element. A typical example of an Ienumerable<T> interface is an array, like below:

```
string[] cities = {"Frankfurt", "New York", "Cardiff", "Sydney",
"Toronto" };
```

The string type array contains the names of cities. A collection like this is called a local sequence because all the items in it are in the local memory of the system.

Query Operators

Query operators take LINQ sequences as input, transform, and return the transformed sequence as output. The Enumerable class of the System.Linq namespace has about 40 query operators. Let's look at the most used LINQ operators.

Where Operator

The “where” operator filters a sequence based on a set of conditions. For instance, you want to get a list of cities in the array where the length of characters is equal to or greater than 8. Here is an example of that below.

Example 1:

```
using System;
using System.Collections;
using System.Collections.Generic;
using System.Linq;
namespace MyCSharpApplication
{
    class Program
    {
        public static void Main()
        {
            string[] cities ={"Frankfurt", "New York", "Cardiff",
"Sydney", "Toronto" };
;
            List<string> citiesendingwiths = (from c in cities
                                              where c.Length >=8
                                              select c).ToList();
            foreach(string c in citiesendingwiths)
            {
                Console.WriteLine(c);
            }
            Console.Read();
        }
    }
}
```

Output:

```
Frankfurt
New York
```

The LINQ query sequence is similar to an SQL query. We have illustrated this above by fetching cities from the lists that are eight characters long or longer. “New York" makes the cut because spaces count as characters.

This LINQ syntax is often referred to as the query syntax because of its similarity to an SQL query syntax. There is another way of executing LINQ queries using Lambda Expressions. It is called fluent syntax. The example below illustrates it:

Example 2:

```
using System;
using System.Collections;
using System.Collections.Generic;
using System.Linq;
namespace MyCSharpApplication
{
    class Program
    {
        public static void Main()
        {
            string[] cities = {"Frankfurt", "New York", "Cardiff",
"Sydney", "Toronto" };
            List<string> citiesendingwiths = cities.Where(c => c.Length
>= 8).ToList();
            foreach(string c in citiesendingwiths)
            {
                Console.WriteLine(c);
            }
            Console.Read();
        }
    }
}
```

Just like in SQL, you can use logical operators with comparison operators in LINQ. For instance, you might want to get a list of cities that have more than six characters and have the letter "o" in their names. The AND operators will help you achieve this, as shown below.

Example 3:

```
using System;
using System.Collections;
using System.Collections.Generic;
using System.Linq;
namespace MyCSharpApplication
{
    class Program
    {
        public static void Main()
        {
            string[] cities = {"Frankfurt", "New York", "Cardiff",
"Sydney", "Toronto" };
            List<string> citiesendingwiths = cities.Where(c => c.Length
>= 6 && c.Contains("o")).ToList();
            foreach(string c in citiesendingwiths)
            {
                Console.WriteLine(c);
            }
            Console.Read();
        }
```

```
    }
}
```

We are only going to get Toronto and New York printed in the console because they are the only cities that meet both conditions of being more than six characters long and containing the letter o.

Select

The select query is often used with objects that have multiple members. It is used to extract a specific member of an object collection; it can also be used by any object. The example below illustrates the Select query.

Example 4:

```
using System;
using System.Collections;
using System.Collections.Generic;
using System.Linq;
namespace MyCSharpApplication
{
    public class Person
    {
        public int age;
        public string name;
        public Person(int age, string name)
        {
            this.age = age;
            this.name = name;
        }
    }
    class Program
    {
        public static void Main()
        {
            Person p1 = new Person(9, "James");
            Person p2 = new Person(8, "Carrie");
            Person p3 = new Person(13, "Mark");
            Person p4 = new Person(15, "Evelyn");
            Person p5 = new Person(6, "Max");
            List<Person> plist = new List<Person>();
            plist.Add(p1);
            plist.Add(p2);
            plist.Add(p3);
            plist.Add(p4);
            plist.Add(p5);
            List<string> personnames = plist.Where(p => p.age <=
12).Select(per => per.name).ToList();
            foreach(string pname in personnames)
            {
                Console.WriteLine(pname);
```

```
            }
            Console.Read();
        }
    }
}
```

We made a Person class that has two member variables: age and name. They are initialized through the constructor. Then we created 5 Person Objects and stored them in a Person list collection we named plist. We then used a LINQ query with the Where and Select operator to extract persons whose age is younger than 12. Without the select operator, the whole object would be extracted, but that is not what we want. We want the names of people who meet those conditions. This is why we used a Select operator and passed a Lambda Expression that got the name.

LINQs are vast topics that can fill an entire book. We will end the discussion of the operators here.

Working with Other Data Types

What makes LINQ an attractive technology to work with is its compatibility with many data types. You can use the same syntax to handle data coming from an external source, while other query languages will require a different syntax for each source. For instance, SQL queries for interacting with SQL server and Xquery for XML data types.

In this section, we will look at the relationship between:

Contents

- **LINQ and SQL**
- **LINQ and Lambda Expressions**

LINQ and SQL

LINQ is the smarter alternative to working with SQL data. You will hear the term "LINQ to SQL," which demands accessing an SQL database with LINQ. The way to do that is to map the target SQL database to LINQ.

Mapping LINQ to SQL

Mapping LINQ to SQL is when .NET recognizes a database as Objects(Classes). It is easy to do. You open Visual Studio, target project in solution explorer. Click Add, then select New Item. Select "Data" from listed "Categories" options, and select "LINQ to SQL Classes" from the

Templates on the left. You end up with a ".dbml" file that produces a Graphic User Interface. The GUI has a part that allows you to drag and drop tables and another where you can drop stored procedures. Select, drag, and drop all essential tables and procedures.

Selecting Data:

As soon as we have our ".dbml" file and its "DataContext," LINQ queries can use objects to communicate with the databases. Here's an example below.

Example 1:

```
public bool checkValidUser(string Name, string passcode)
{
DBToysDataContext sampleDB = new DBToysDataContext();
var getter = from u in sampleDB.Users
                        where u.Username == Name
                        && u.Password == passcode
                        select u;
return Enumerable.Count(getter) > 0;
}
```

When we mapped the "DBToys.dml" file, a "DBToywDataCOnectc" class file was created by the .NET framework. We then passed the strings "Name" and "Passcode" through the "checkValidUser" function, which validates the user's entered name and password against the table "User" in the Toys database.

In the first line of the function, we instantiate the "sampleDB" object to access our Toys database using the "DBToysDataContext" class file. The "u" from the "from u in sampleDB.Users is read as an object of the "Users" class, which refers to our "Users" table in the Toys database. Then we passed the incoming column/field values as an object of the "var" type. The various data types denoted dynamic data. Whatever data we get from a LINQ query can be stored in a "getter" variable. In this example, we are extracting and storing a username and password from the "Users" table. The "Enumerable.Count" function returns the number of data rows returned by the LINQ query.

There's a way to access the data without using a syntax similar to SQL in LINQ.

Example 2:

```
public bool checkValidUser(string Name, string passcode)
{
      DBToysDataContext sampleDB = new DBToysDataContext();
      List<Users> getter = sampleDB.Users.Where(u => u.Username == Name
&& u.Password==passcode);
      if(users.Count>0)
```

```
        {
                return true;
        }
        return false;
}
```

As you can see, we had used the "where" method to directly access data from the "Users" table of the Toys database instead of using traditional SQL syntax. Everything works the same as before, except we used the "List" data type to store values returned by the LINQ query.

Example 3:

```
public User bringUser(string name)
{
      DBToysDataContext sampleDB = new DBToysDataContext();
      User use = sampleDB.Users.Single(u, u.UserName=>name);
      return use;
}
```

LINQ expressions also allow us to extract or send a single row. The "bringUser" function takes a name as input and matches it against objects in the Users table. The "Single" method in "SampleDB.Users.Single()" looks for a match and returns a single row.

LINQ and Lambda Expressions

While we have already discussed Lambda Expressions earlier, LINQ queries mostly imply Lambda Expressions in dealing with collections or lists of data to filter list items based on some specific criteria. Let's see how:

Example 4:

```
IEnumerable <SelectListItem> toys = database.Toys
        .Where(toy => toy.Tag == curTag.ID)
        .Select(toy => new SelectListItem { Value = toy.Name, Text =
toy.ID });
 ViewBag.toySelector = toys;
```

In the code above, we have declared the variable "toys" and are casting it to type "SelectListItem" to save the resultant row from our LINQ query. We have used two methods, "Where" and "Select," to find the target toy that matches our query. The line '"toy => toy.Tag == curTag.ID" selects a toy based on a passed tag, whereas the line "toy => new SelectListItem {Value = toy.Name, Text = toy.ID" selects a particular toy based on a passed ID and name. The resultant toy that meets this criterion is saved in the "toys" variable.

Working with XML

Let's look at how we can use LIN to work with XML data. XML stands for Extensible Markup Language. The data type is widely used on the World Wide Web because of its compatibility with different systems. It is often referred to as self-describing or self-defining data. XML is highly standardized, and its customizable tags are used in sharing, accessing, and manipulating data.

We will see how we can use LINQ to:

Contents

- **Retrieve and delete XML data**
- **Insert and update XML data**

Retrieve and Delete XML Data

XML data files have a root/parent tag or element that encapsulates, defines the type of child record and its attributes. The child records (elements) contain the data. Look at the XML code below. We will be using it to test our LINQ queries.

Sample XML Data

```
<? xml version='1.0' encoding='utf-8'?>
<Toys>
  <Toy ID='1'>
    <Name>Batman</Name>
    <Price>$0.45</Price>
  </Toy>
  <Toy ID='2'>
    <Name>Snowhite</Name>
    <Price>$0.40</Price>
  </Toy>
  <Toy ID='3'>
    <Name>Hulk</Name>
    <Price>$0.55</Price>
  </Toy>
</Toys>
```

Toys is the root element with multiple Tot elements inside. Every child toy element has an ID attribute and "Price" and "Name" as inner elements.

Now let's extract data from the table using LINQ queries.

Example 1:

```
private string file = 'SampleData.xml';
        private void GetData()
        {
            try
            {
```

```
                  XDocument doc = XDocument.Load(file);
                  var comingToys = from toy in doc.Descendants('Toy')
         select new
                  {
   ID= Convert.ToInt32(toy.Attribute('ID').Value),
   Name = toy.Element('Name').Value ,
Price = toy.Element('Price').Value
                                };
                  foreach (var x in toys)
                  {
      Console.WriteLine('Toy ID', x[ID]);
Console.WriteLine('Toy Name', x[Name]);
Console.WriteLine('Toy Price', x[Price]);                    }
              }
              catch (Exception err)
              {
                  MessageBox.Show(err.Message);
              }
      }
```

The opening line points to our XML data file is called "SampleData.xml." In the function, we load the xml file using the "Load(file)" function. After the file is loaded, extract child "toy" elements using the "Doc.descendant()" method. Then we go over each "toy," and retrieve the ID attribute and its inner elements, and store them in the dynamic variable.

Output 1:

```
Toy ID 1 Toy Name Batman Toy Price $0.45
Toy ID 1 Toy Name Snowhite Toy Price $0.40
Toy ID 1 Toy Name Hulk Toy Price $0.55
```

If you want to remove a name from the data file you would do the following:

Example 2:

```
private string file = 'SampleData.xml';
Private void DeleteData (int id)
      {
          try
          {
              XDocument sampleXML = XDocument.Load(file);
              XElement cToy = sampleXML.Descendants('Toy').Where(c =>
c.Attribute('ID').Value.Equals(id);
              cToy.Remove();
              sampleXML.Save(file);
          }
          catch (Exception e)
          {
              MessageBox.Show(e.Message);
          }
```

```
        }
```

After the file is loaded, the code goes over the child elements looking for a match and, when it finds it, removes that child with the "Remove()" method, saving the resulting file.

Insert and Update XML data

There isn't a big difference between inserting data and extracting data from an XML file. We will only need an "Xelement: object" that has the same signature as existing elements in the target XML file. Then we insert the "XElement" object into the file using "XDocument" object.

Example 3:

```
private string file = 'SampleData.xml';
private void InsertData(string name, string price)
        {
            try
            {
  XDocument doc = XDocument.Load(file);
           XElement newToy = new XElement('Toy',  new XElement('Name',
name), new XElement('Price', price));
  Var lastToy = doc.Descendants('Toy').Last();
  Int newID = Convert.ToInt32 (lastToy.Attribute ('ID').Value);
  newToy.SetAttributeValue('ID',++newID);
     doc.Element ('Toys').Add (newToy);
         doc.Save (file);
            }
            catch (Exception err)
            {
                MessageBox.Show (err.Message);
            }
        }
```

After creating "Xdocument" object, we created an "Xelement" type with the same signature as the "Toy" element. We did this in this line: XElement newToy = new XElement('Toy', new XElement('Name', name), new XElement('Price', price). We then select the last toy element with the var lastToyusing the "doc.Descendants("Toy").Last()" method. We accessed its "ID" value and then incremented it while we set that as an attribute for our new toy element. We did this at this line: "newToy.SetAttributeValue('ID',++newID)." Lastly, we inserted the new "toy" object with the "Add()" method, then saved our changes.

Output 3:

The XML file will now contain a fourth child. If we had passed "Thor" as the name and "$0.65" as the price, we would get the following as the fourth element.

```
<Toy ID='4'>
    <Name>Thor</Name>
    <Price>$0.65</Price>
  </Toy>
```

To make changes to the XML file, we have to locate our target element first. The following line does that:

```
"XElementcToy=doc.Descendants('Toy').Where(c=>c.Attribute('ID').Value.Eq
uals(id)";
```

It looks for an element that matches an ID we provided, allowing the "XElement" object, "cToy", to point at it. Once that is done, we can update its inner values using:

```
"cToy.Element('Price').Value = price"
```

Then we save the changes we have made. All this is shown below.

Example 4:

```
private string file = 'SampleData.xml';
private void UpdateData(string name, string price, int id)
        {
            try
            {
    XDocument doc = XDocument.Load(file);
  XElement cToy = doc.Descendants('Toy').Where
(c=>c.Attribute('ID').Value.Equals(id);
 cToy.Element('Name').Value = name;
 cToy.Element('Price').Value = price;
        doc.Save(file);
            }
            catch (Exception err)
            {
                MessageBox.Show(err.Message);
            }
        }
```

Output 4:

If we had passed the following arguments: id= 1, name= "Black Widows," price="$0.90" we would have replaced Batman with the following toy:

```
<Toy ID='1'>
    <Name>Black Widow</Name>
    <Price>$0.90</Price>
  </Toy>
```

CHAPTER 14:

The Factory and Composite Pattern

Factory Pattern

Factory patterns allow you to create multiple objects with ease using a boilerplate object making pattern.

How it essentially works:

You start by creating a class interface that standardizes data object creation. You would use subclasses to create the data objects. The subclass allows for flexibility in what you are able to create. If the programming language you use does not have interfaces or abstract classes, you will need to create a factory interface class and have subclasses extending it.

Imagine you were charged with creating a wide range of sports balls at any given time. We are talking basketballs, cricket balls, volleyballs, footballs, and more. You would always know how you should make each one when requested. What should your code look like for each? This is why you need to create an interface that outlines the construction of the ball objects.

We will call the interface the "BallMaker." For each ball type, we would create a subclass that extends "BallMaker." The subclasses will create the ball objects, each one doing so according to its own specifications. This means a FootballMaker would make footballs, and BasketballMaker would make basketballs.

The implementation pseudocode is available in the Archive. It should help you create the pattern for the language of your choosing.

The Factory Pattern, in C#

```
==== ==== ==== ==== ====
```

This is how the factory pattern looks in C#:

```
// Factory is implemented by any subclasses that need to use it
    interface Factory {
        // INPUT: your choice
            // OUTPUT: your choice (set to Void by default)
        // Constructor for Classes that implement this interface
        void createObject();
    }

    // SubFactory1:
    // creates distinct objects based on Factory Interface
    class SubFactory1 : Factory {

        // This implements the same function outlined in the interface
         void Factory .createObject() {
        // include ANY unique distinctions for this creator class
        // any other code here
        }
    }


    // SubFactory2:
    // creates distinct objects based on Factory Interface
    class SubFactory2 : Factory {

        // This implements the same function outlined in the interface
         void Factory.createObject() {
        // include ANY unique distinctions for this creator class
        // any other code here
        }
    }
```

Implementing the Factory Pattern

Use an IDE of your choice to implement the code. You can use online ones like codechef.com, rextester.com, ideone.com, or codepad.org.

```
========================== ======
```

Now let's see the factory pattern first-hand with an example. There will also be a workshop that allows you to continue with the pattern.

Sports Ball Creator

Imagine you had a build-to-order web app for creating sports balls of different kinds.

Below is how a general ball class would look:

```
/*
// A Sports Ball has:
// - the Type of ball it is
// - an array of materials used to manufacture it
// - its size, as a radius (inches)
// - any additional comments required
// - the company brand that made it
// - a product name
*/
class SportsBall {
       public String type;
       public String[] materialsUsed;
       public float radius;
       public String comments;
       public String make;
       public String modelName;
}
```

As you can see, a lot of small details are involved in creating sports ball objects. For instance, if you had to create a football, the process would be different than creating a tennis ball. They use different materials, come in different sizes, and have different styles. In the real world, they are probably made by different companies that give them different features.

If you wanted to create the ball easily, with much less code, you would use the factory pattern method.

However, as you can see, there are far too many small details involved when creating data objects for sports balls. So if you had to create, let's say, a certain basketball, the process would be far different compared to creating a soccer ball. They both would have different types, materials, and sizes. They also would probably be created by different brands and would have different features, too.

Let's go through the steps involved in setting up a design pattern.

You will then practice by extending the work.

Step 1: The Factory Interface

We start by creating the interface that all ball creating factory classes will implement.

It has one method, creating and returning instances of sports balls.

```
// the BallFactory interface:
// - interface for how a ball will be created
```

```
interface BallFactory {
    /*
    // INPUT: none
    // OUTPUT: a Sports Ball object
    // EFFECT: Creates a Sports Ball;
    // Classes that implement this will have their own distinctions in
making one
    */
    SportsBall createBall();
}
```

Step 2: The First Factory Class

Now we create a factory class that implements the BallFactory interface. Right now, it only creates basketballs.

```
// The Basketball Maker:
// - creates basketball objects with distinct fields
class BasketballMaker : BallFactory {

    // (method implements the Interface Version)
    // EFFECT: Creates a sports ball as a Basketball
    SportsBall BallFactory.createBall() {
        SportsBall b = new SportsBall();
        b.type = "Basketball";
        b.materialsUsed = new String[3];
        b.materialsUsed[0] = "rubber";
        b.materialsUsed[1] = "fiber";
        b.materialsUsed[2] = "synthetic composite";
        b.radius = 4.8f;
        b.make = "Spalding";
        b.modelName = "Series Basketball";
        return b;
    }
}
```

Step 3: Design any additional Factory Classes you need

We can create as many different factory classes as we need. All of them implement the Ball Factory interface and create sports ball objects that have distinct features and qualities.

Below is one that makes baseballs.

```
// The Baseball Maker:
// - creates baseball objects with distinct fields
class BaseballMaker : BallFactory {

    // (method implements the Interface Version)
    // EFFECT: Creates a sports ball as a Basketball
    SportsBall BallFactory.createBall() {
        SportsBall b = new SportsBall();
```

```
        b.type = "Baseball";
        b.materialsUsed = new String[6];
        b.materialsUsed[0] = "cork";
        b.materialsUsed[1] = "wool";
        b.materialsUsed[2] = "poly/cotton";
        b.materialsUsed[3] = "cowhide";
        b.materialsUsed[4] = "yarn";
        b.materialsUsed[5] = "composite rubber";
        b.radius = 1.45f;
        b.make = "Rawlings";
        b.modelName = "MLB Official Baseball";
        return b;
    }
}
```

Step 4: Run Some Code

After they are created, you can run the code. Create a main function for each factory class you've designed. We are referring to the main class that has the public-static-void-main method. You are going to call these factories to make balls.

In our example, we made two factories: basketball and baseball factories. We'll be using them to make basketball and baseball objects.

```
// Creating the Factories
        BallFactory f1 = new BasketballMaker();
        BallFactory f2 = new BaseballMaker();

        // Creating a basketball object:
        // Use the Basketball Factory to make Basketballs
        SportsBall bb1 = f1.createBall();


        // Creating a baseball object:
        // Use the Baseball Factory to make Baseballs
        SportsBall bb2 = f2.createBall();

        // TESTING:
        // This line should print out "Basketball"
        Console.WriteLine(bb1.type);

        // This line should print out "Baseball"
        Console.WriteLine(bb2.type);
```

Composite Pattern

Imagine you had organized data in a hierarchical manner, and all this data looked like 'files' and 'folders.' As you know, files can go into folders, and folders can go into other folders and so on. You will want to have something similar without replicating unnecessary code. A composite pattern can help with that.

How it essentially works:

There are two classes: a File class and a Folder class. Think of them as an item and group, toys and box, or clothing and bag. It is a combination of two classes in which one is made of both types.

Both might have similar traits, methods, and fields, so you might need to write twice the code you would normally: one for the items and the other for groupings. To solve this, you need them to extend a common superclass or abstract class. In other words, a component. There needs to be one important distinction: the Group should contain the collection of the superclass. Because they emanate from a common superclass, the Group class can house a collection of groups or items.

So if you have two classes, Clothing and Bag, a Bag contains clothes, but it can also contain bags inside. They share similar qualities, like the name and description. It would be unwise to write separate code for each instance if they share so many similarities. You can apply a Composite Pattern where both clothing and bags extend a superclass. The bag class would be tweaked so it can accept either bags or clothes.

The important thing is that item/container classes extend a common superclass or component. The container class will contain a list of components, which can either be items or containers.

Depending on your language, the superclass can be an abstract class, interface, or other kinds of abstractions available to the language. The pseudocode of the composite pattern is included in the Archive, so if you need to use it in a different language, it will help you.

Now, let's look at the Composite Pattern below.

The Composite Pattern, in C#

```
==== ==== ==== ==== ====
```

Here is how the Composite Pattern looks in C#:

```
/*
// Component is the superclass which File and Folder classes extend
// You may define any fields and methods shared by both subclasses
*/
abstract class Component {
    // insert any amount of fields and methods
    // where necessary
    String someField;
    void someMethod() {};
```

```
}

// General Item Class (as File):
// contains all fields and methods defined at Component
class File: Component {

}

// General Group Class (as Folder):
// contains all fields and methods defined at Component
// Also has:
// - a List of Components, which can contain either Items or Groups
class Folder : Component {
    List<Component> contents = new List<Component>();
}
```

Implementing the Composite Pattern

Use an IDE of your choice to implement the code. You can use online ones like codechef.com, rextester.com, ideone.com, or codepad.org.

```
========================== ======
```

We are going to consider a situation where having a Composite Pattern is a great solution and construct the Composite Pattern.

File Manager

Imagine you are a web developer for a popular social media site, and you are tasked with adding a feature that allows users to upload and organize their data in files. In other words, you have to make File and Folder classes. From the beginning, you realize these share many characteristics, like name, date created, date modified, icons, and thumbnails. You know you need to implement a Composite pattern, as it would be a simpler way to do this.

Step 1: The Component Superclass

The first thing we do is create the superclass that the File and Folders will emanate from. Since we are working with C#, we have the Abstract class available to us.

So we will make a superclass that accepts the name, date created, and date last modified.

```
/*
// Component is the superclass which File and Folder classes extend
// It has:
// - Name, as a String
// - the Date Created
```

```
// - the Date Last Modified
// It can:
// - rename itself
// - update the Last Modified date
*/
abstract class Component {
    String name;
    DateTime dateCreated;
    DateTime dateLastModified;
}
```

Step 2: Customizing the Component Constructor

Then we code a slightly different version of our component/superclass. So when a new component is made, a name will be set and dates will be set to the current date.

All the files and Folders will use the same component as a constructor.

```
abstract class Component {
    public String name;
    public DateTime dateCreated;
    public DateTime dateLastModified;
        /*
    // INPUT: a String
    // Custom Constructor for the Component Class,
    // Upon creation, the dates created and last modified
    // are set to the current date an object would be created
    */
    public Component(String n) {
        this.name = n;
        this.dateCreated = new DateTime();
        this.dateLastModified = new DateTime();
    }
}
```

You can see how a setup like this can shrink the lines you write, preventing bugs and other undesirable outcomes. All important fields and methods will be available to both classes, so they don't need to code the same thing twice because they share so many similarities. It would be receptive to do so, and also mundane. All objects that emanate from the superclass will be treated the same.

Step 3: Creating the File Class

The File class will share many similarities with the folder class, but it will include other fields that indicate the file's type, like document, picture, video, PDF, epub, and others. So the File constructor has to be modified to reflect these attributes.

```
/*
```

```
// General Item Class (a.k.a. File):
// contains all fields and methods defined at Component
// Also has:
// - a file type, as a string
*/

class File : Component {
    public String fileType;

    /*
    // INPUT: a String
    // Custom Constructor for the File Class,
    // Follows the same procedure as the superclass,
    // Then sets the file type
    */
    public File(String n, String f) : base(n) {
        this.fileType = f;
    }
}
```

Step 3: Creating the Folder Class

When making the Folder class, the process will be the same, except you add a key field that can accept either Files or SubFolders.

```
// General Group Class (a.k.a. Folder):
// contains all fields and methods defined at Component
// Also has:
// - a List of Components, which can contain either Items or Groups
class Folder : Component {
    public List<Component> contents = new List<Component>();
    public Folder(String n) : base(n){
    }
}
```

Step 4: Running and Testing the Code

The next step is to test the code by creating files and folders and then sorting them. So run the code in the Main Class or the place where this code will run.

```
Folder top = new Folder("Top Folder");
File a = new File("A", "Spreadsheet");
File b = new File("B", "Picture");
Folder mid = new Folder("Mid Folder");
top.contents.Add(a);
top.contents.Add(b);
top.contents.Add(mid);
File c = new File("C", "Video");
File d = new File("D", "Letter Document");
Folder bot = new Folder("Bottom Folder");
mid.contents.Add(c);
```

```
mid.contents.Add(d);
mid.contents.Add(bot);
File e = new File("E", "PDF");
bot.contents.Add(e);
```

Afterward, put the following code after the code above and run it.

```
        Console.WriteLine(top.name);
        foreach (var Component in top.contents) {
            Console.WriteLine("    " + Component.name);
        }
        foreach (var Component in mid.contents) {
            Console.WriteLine("        " + Component.name);
        }
        foreach (var Component in bot.contents) {
            Console.WriteLine("            " + Component.name);
        }
```

After following these steps, the output should be like this:

```
Top Folder
  A
  B
  Mid Folder
    C
    D
    Bottom Folder
      E
```

If done correctly, we can create a hierarchical system of files, folders, and subfolders.

CHAPTER 15:

The Observer Pattern

In some cases, you will need to create two classes that have an observer and observed prelations. In other words, one object needs to observe or watch another object for its functions. For example, you can have a class that collects data about the environment around you: time, weather, locations, and more. You might also have another object that needs that data to alert a user of their friends nearby, of the weather, and remind them of events and plans. To be able to do this, you need an Observer Pattern because an object needs to observe other objects for its main functions.

How it essentially works:

Observe patterns are popular among developers because many of the applications we use function in the described way. There is the Subject and the Observer. Observing and being the object are descriptions of behavior, so we implement Observe and Subject interfaces. This will allow classes to apply Observer and Subject behaviors. All these classes have to apply their interfaces.

All classes implementing the Observer interface will have a slit of subjects to watch. They will need an update method, which updates their data based on the relevant changes in the subject objects.

All the classes that implement the Subject interface will have a list of observer objects to notify users of changes in data.

When there is a data change in the subject object, it calls the notify() method, which notifies a list of its observers. Once the observers are notified, they call the update() method, which updates their own data based on the subject's recent update.

When implementing the observer pattern, you only need to think about two things: the number of observers and number of subjects. We are going to be working with multi-observe and multi-subject scenarios to show dynamics.

The Observer Pattern, in C#

```
==== ==== ==== ==== ====
```

Below is how the observer pattern looks in C#. You will see two sets of class/interface pairs. We will start with the Observing pair.

```
/*
// All Observing Classes implement an Observer abstraction
// It can:
// - update object data based on subjects
// Observing Classes may need a List of Subjects to access
// (added on Observer Class)
*/
interface Observer {
    void update();
    // enter any other methods here
}

/*
// Observing Classes have:
// - working version of the update() method
// - any number of additional fields & methods
*/
class ObservingClass : Observer {
     // enter any key fields here;
    // INPUT: (optional)
    // OUTPUT: none
    // EFFECT: updates data in response to subject
    void Observer.update() {
    // make any changes to observer's key fields here
    }
}
```

Below is the subject class/interface pair.

```
/*
// All Subject Classes implement a Subject abstraction
// It can:
// - notify observers
// - add/remove observers in its update list
// Subject Classes also need a List of Observers to Update
// (added on Subject Class)
*/

interface Subject {
```

```
    public void notifyObservers();
    public void addObs(Observer o);
    public void deleteObs(Observer o);
    // enter any other methods here
}

/*
// Subject Classes have:
// - a List of Observers to notify
// - a working version of notifyObservers()
// - any number of additional fields & methods
// Subject Classes also need a List of Observers to Update
// (added on Subject Class)
*/
class SubjectClass : Subject {
     // enter any key fields here;
    private List<Observer> obs = new List<Observer>();

    // INPUT: (optional)
    // OUTPUT: none
    // EFFECT: updates all observers in list of any changes


    public void notifyObservers(){
        foreach (var o in obs) {
            o.update();
            }
        }

    // Add/Delete Methods:
    // INPUT: - an Observer
    // OUTPUT: none
    // EFFECT: updates data in response to subject
    public void addObs(Observer o) {
        obs.Add(o);
        }
    public void deleteObs(Observer o) {
        obs.Remove(o);
        }
    }
```

Now, we go through implementing an observer pattern in detail.

Implementing the Observer Pattern

Use an IDE of your choice to implement the code. You can use online ones like codechef.com, rextester.com, ideone.com, or codepad.org.

```
========================= ======
```

We will use an example you might encounter in the real world. For this example, you will be a hacking specialist.

Manhunt

Imagine you are recruited by the FBI to catch a terrorist group. You can easily track the terrorist group, but dozens of agents in the field need the information in real-time. This means you will have to change the software on their devices.

You will need to create a prototype that alerts the agents when terrorists are near.

Step 1: Identify the Observers & Subjects

In this context, who are your observers and who are your subjects?

The terrorists are the subjects. You will need to keep track of their location. That is the information your code will have. It will be a few lines:

```
// A single terrorist has:
// - a Location, as a String
// - a List of Observer Objects
class Terrorist{
public String location;
}
```

The FB devices are the Observers. We will need to modify the device Module, so it sends push notifications on critical developments. The device module looks like this:

```
// A Device module has:
// - an alert status (a Boolean)
// - notification updates (as string)
// - a Location, as a String
// It can:
// - push alerts
// - update alerts & notifications
class Module{
    public String location;
    public boolean alert;
    public String notifications;

//   EFFECT: if alerts is true, print an alert notice
    void sendAlerts(){
        if (alert) {
            Console.WriteLine("ALERT: "
                              + notifications
                              + "Agents in "
                              + this.location);
        }
    }
```

```
}
```

Step 2: Set up the Observer and Subject Abstractions

In C#, our abstraction for both will be interfaces.

They will look like this:

```
/*
// All Observing Classes implement an Observer abstraction
// It can:
// - update object data based on subjects
// Observing Classes may need a List of Subjects to access
// (added on Observer Class)
*/
interface Observer {
    void update();
}

/*
// All Subject Classes implement a Subject abstraction
// It can:
// - notify observers
// - add/remove observers in its update list
// Subject Classes also need a List of Observers to Update
// (added on Subject Class)
*/
interface Subject {
    void notifyObservers();
    void addObs(Observer o);
    void deleteObs(Observer o);
}
```

Step 3: Modify our Subject Class to Act as One

The data object which tells us where the terrorists are is the subject class. So, it will implement the Subject interface. This means you need to add and include methods specified in the Subject interface. This will also need to include a list of observer objects that need to be notified. This field should be kept private for protection against hackers.

```
// A single terrorist has:
// - a Location, as a String
// - a List of Observer Objects
// Also implements the Subject Interface;
// (will need to implement its methods)
class Terrorist : Subject{
public String location;
private List<Observer> obs = new List<Observer>();
// NEW: from Subject Interface
 public void notifyObservers() {};
```

```
 public void addObs(Observer o) {};
public void deleteObs(Observer o) {};
}
```

For the notifyObservers method we will need to iterate through our list of Observers and update them. So the method should be modified like this:

```
// NEW: from Subject Interface
 public void notifyObservers() {
foreach (var o in obs) {
o.update();
}
}
```

We will not need to implement addObs() and deleteObs() methods which will add and remove Observers as required.

```
 public void addObs(Observer o) {
        obs.Add(o);
    };
public void deleteObs(Observer o) {
        obs.Remove(o);
    };
```

After all the changes, your Terrorist class should look like this:

```
class Terrorist implements Subject{
String location;
private List<Observer> obs = new ArrayList<Observer>();

// NEW: from Subject Interface
 public void notifyObservers() {
for (Observer o: obs) {
o.update();
}
};
 public void addObs(Observer o) {
        obs.add(o);
    };
public void deleteObs(Observer o) {
        obs.remove(o);
    };
}
```

Step 4: Modify our Observer Class to Act as One

Our Module data class will act as an Observer, so it will include the observer method and all its methods.

```
// A Device module has:
```

```
// - an alert status (a Boolean)
// - notification updates (as string)
// - a Location, as a String

// It can:
// - push alerts
// - update alerts & notifications
// Also implements the Observer Interface;
// (will need to implement its methods)
class Module : Observer{
   public String location;
    public boolean alert;
    public String notifications;

    public void update() {};

    //  EFFECT: if alerts is true, print an alert notice
    void sendAlerts(){
        if (alert) {
            Console.WriteLine("ALERT: "
                                   + notifications
                                   + "Agents in "
                                   + this.location);
        }
    }
}
```

It's worth thinking about how the module is going to work before we add the update() method.

Step 5: Modify the Observing Class to update based on Subject Classes

The Module class has to send updates & alerts whenever Terrorists are nearby.

The Terrorists' local field is a Sting, same with the Module.

Whenever a Module's location matches Terrorists, an alert will be sent, but before it receives the data from the Terrorist class, the update method needs to have an input from the Terrorist objects.

```
    // INPUT: a Terrorist Object
    // OUTPUT: none
    // EFFECT: if Terrorist and this module's locations are the same,
    // set Alert to true and update the notification.
    // Afterwards, send the alerts
    public void update(Terrorist t) { };
```

You will need corresponding updates for any other code with this method. The observer interface will need to be modified to include the input like this:

```
interface Observer {
…
    public void update(Terrorist t);
```

```
...
```

The terrorist class's notifying method will also need to be modified with the input type. It needs to be able to notify observers in its Class. So the class itself will be the input.

```
class Terrorist : Subject{
...
public void notifyObservers() {
foreach (var o in obs) {
o.update(this);
}
};
...
```

Step 5: Implementing update()

The next step is to get the update() method to work. We will put the code in the update() method in the Module class.

```
    // INPUT: a Terrorist Object
    // OUTPUT: none
    // EFFECT: if Terrorist and this module's locations are the same,
    // set Alert to true and update the notification.
    // Afterwards, send the alerts
    public void update(Terrorist t) {
        if (this.location == t.location) {
            this.alert = true;
            this.notifications = "Terrorist Nearby ";
        }
        else {
            this.alert = false;
            this.notifications = "";
        }

        sendAlerts();
    };
```

Running the Code

We will run the code in two scenarios. In both, the observing class will signal an alert based on the information it gets from the subject class.

In this scenario, there are more observers than subjects.

(Copy and paste the code below inside your Main() method)

```
// Part 1: Create all Data Objects
            Terrorist t = new Terrorist();
            Module m1 = new Module();
            Module m2 = new Module();
```

```
        Module m3 = new Module();
        Module m4 = new Module();

        // Part 2: Add all Observers to Subject's List
        t.addObs(m1);
        t.addObs(m2);
        t.addObs(m3);
        t.addObs(m4);

        // Create all locations
        String[] locs = new String[10];
        locs[0] = "Los Angeles";
        locs[1] = "Chicago";
        locs[2] = "New York";
        locs[3] = "Seattle";
        locs[4] = "Cleveland";
        locs[5] = "Boston";
        locs[6] = "San Francisco";
        locs[7] = "Miami";
        locs[8] = "St. Louis";
        locs[9] = "Dallas";

        // Part 3: Set Observers to their locations
        m1.location = locs[1];
        m2.location = locs[4];
        m3.location = locs[5];
        m4.location = locs[9];

        // As the Terrorist relocates all over the US,
        // it will notify all Device Modules of its location.
        // Modules will trigger when a Terrorist is nearby.
        for(int i = 0; i < 10; i++) {
            t.location = locs[i];
            t.notifyObservers();
        }
```

This is what you will get in the console when the code runs:

```
ALERT: Terrorist Nearby Agents in Chicago
ALERT: Terrorist Nearby Agents in Cleveland
ALERT: Terrorist Nearby Agents in Boston
ALERT: Terrorist Nearby Agents in Dallas
```

In these scenarios, there are more subjects than observers.

(Copy and paste the code below inside your Main() method)

```
// Part 1: Create all Data Objects
            Terrorist t1 = new Terrorist();
            Terrorist t2 = new Terrorist();
            Terrorist t3 = new Terrorist();
            Terrorist t4 = new Terrorist();
```

```
        Terrorist t5 = new Terrorist();
        Module m = new Module();

        // Part 2: Add all Observers to Subject's List
        t1.addObs(m);
        t2.addObs(m);
        t3.addObs(m);
        t4.addObs(m);
        t5.addObs(m);

        // Create all locations
        String[] locs = new String[10];
        locs[0] = "Los Angeles";
        locs[1] = "Chicago";
        locs[2] = "New York";
        locs[3] = "Seattle";
        locs[4] = "Cleveland";
        locs[5] = "Boston";
        locs[6] = "San Francisco";
        locs[7] = "Miami";
        locs[8] = "St. Louis";
        locs[9] = "Dallas";

        // Part 3: Set Observers to their locations
        t1.location = locs[1];
        t2.location = locs[4];
        t3.location = locs[2];
        t4.location = locs[7];
        t5.location = locs[5];

        // The single agent with the Device Module will travel all
over the US,
        // All Terrorists will then notify the observing module.
        // The module will trigger when a Terrorist is nearby.
        for(int i = 0; i < 10; i++) {
            m.location = locs[i];
            t1.notifyObservers();
            t2.notifyObservers();
            t3.notifyObservers();
            t4.notifyObservers();
            t5.notifyObservers();           }
```

You will get the following in the console:

```
ALERT: Terrorist Nearby Agents in Chicago
ALERT: Terrorist Nearby Agents in New York
ALERT: Terrorist Nearby Agents in Cleveland
ALERT: Terrorist Nearby Agents in Boston
ALERT: Terrorist Nearby Agents in Miami
```

CHAPTER 16:

The Facade Pattern

Driving a car is easy. To start a car, you twist the keys in the ignition or press a button. To accelerate, you step on the gas pedal. To slow down or stop, you step on the brake pedal, and the steering wheel allows you to control the direction of the car.

However, a car is very complex. Starting a car requires a lot of energy. It requires gasoline. Your engine needs enough oil for the engine pistons and all the other parts. The spark plugs need to ignite the engine cylinders and create enough energy for the car to move. Functions like steering, acceleration, and braking require a system of different, complex components to work together.

From the driver's seat, we don't have access to all of this complexity. We can only see the simple tools in front of us. In a nutshell, a Facade.

How the Facade Pattern Works

A Facade Pattern Works the same way. It provides a top-level component that oversees the functionality of a complex system. This makes operating a complex system far simpler because all you have to control in the Facade is the simple system in front of you. Our car anomaly serves to show us this. The driver doesn't need to work every component himself, go inside the engine, or perform a billion operations to make the car move. He just needs to understand how to operate the gear stick, pedal, wheel, and know basic things—simplifying something that is complex. Each action the driver takes is setting off a complex chain of events.

Creating the Facade Pattern

When you want to implement a Facade Pattern, you need to first understand the core Procedures and/or Behaviors we would benefit from simplifying.

Using an interface, we would follow the steps below:

1) Create a Facade interface that includes the core procedures
2) Create a general client class that enacts the Facade interface
3) The general client should apply ALL the major procedures and contain as many component instances as necessary.
4) If necessary, create multiple Facade interfaces and client classes. When you do, repeat steps 1 to 3.
5) Create subclasses for general client classes when necessary; code that accesses the system does so as a client subclass.

Follow these steps if you're using an encompassing class:

1) Create the general "Facade" class. This class implements ALL the Major Procedures mentioned earlier. It should contain as many instances as needed.
2) Create a general client class. It should contain an instance of the Facade class.
3) If appropriate, create multiple Facade classes and repeat steps 1 & 2.
4) Create subclasses for the general client class if needed. Any code that accesses the system does it through the Facade class in the client subclasses.

The steps you take will depend on your situation. So decide if using one encompassing Facade wrapper class is appropriate.

The Facade Pattern, in C#

```
==== ==== ==== ==== ====
```

To have a full understanding of the Facade Pattern, we need to look at its environment. Pay attention to the collection of components that make the complex system.

Below is an example of a component class with multiple sub-components whose method may depend on its sub-components.

```
/*
// Component Class, with Sub-Components
// Methods:
// - one method which accesses the subcomponents
*/
class ComponentOne {
```

```
    SubcompOneOne sc11 = new SubcompOneOne();
    SubcompOneTwo sc12 = new SubcompOneTwo();
    // IN & OUT: (your choice)
    // EFFECT: (your choice)
    public void distinctMethodOne() {
        sc11.distinctMethodOneOne();
        sc12.distinctMethodOneTwo();
    }
}
class SubcompOneOne {
    // IN & OUT: (your choice)
    // EFFECT: (your choice)
    public void distinctMethodOneOne() {
     }
}

class SubcompOneTwo {
    // IN & OUT: (your choice)
    // EFFECT: (your choice)
    public void distinctMethodOneTwo() {

   }
}
```

This is an example of two other components in the environment:

```
class ComponentTwo {
    // IN & OUT: (your choice)
    // EFFECT: (your choice)
    public void distinctMethodTwo() {
        // (add implementation here)
    }
}
class ComponentN {
    // IN & OUT: (your choice)
    // EFFECT: (your choice)
    public void distinctMethodN() {
        // (add implementation here)
    }
}
```

All components need to be coordinated.

Below is how we would implement a Facade Pattern in C#. It would look like this:

```
/*
// Facade as an Interface
// (include all major procedures that utilize
// components within the environment)
*/
interface Facade{
```

```
    // MAJOR PROCEDURES:
    // IN & OUT: (your choice)
    // EFFECT: (your choice)
    //- calls methods from all system components
    void activateA();
    void activateB();
}

/*
// Client Classes
// (Implement all procedures defined within
// the Facade interface)
*/

class Client : Facade {
    ComponentOne c1 = new ComponentOne();
    ComponentTwo c2 = new ComponentTwo();
    ComponentN cN = new ComponentN();

    // Methods from Facade Interface:
    void Facade.activateA() {
        c1.distinctMethodOne();
    }
    void Facade.activateB() {
        c2.distinctMethodTwo();
        cN.distinctMethodN();
    }
}
```

The interface would be implemented by the Client class:

```
// Client Subclasses:
// (add whenever necessary)
class ClientA : Client {
}
class ClientB : Client {
}
```

If the Facade is implemented as a large superclass instead, it will look like this:

```
/*
// Facade as a major Class
// - include instances for each component
// in the environment
// - include all major procedures that utilize
// components within the environment
*/
class Facade{
    ComponentOne c1 = new ComponentOne();
    ComponentTwo c2 = new ComponentTwo();
...
    ComponentN cN = new ComponentN();
```

```
    // MAJOR PROCEDURES:
    // IN & OUT: (your choice)
    // EFFECT: (your choice)
    public void activateA() {
        c1.distinctMethodOne();
    }
    public void activateB() {
        c2.distinctMethodTwo();
        cN.distinctMethodN();
    }
}
```

Client classes have instances of the Facade class:

```
// Client Class:
// (rest of software accesses)
class Client {
    Facade f = new Facade();
}

// Client Subclasses:
// (add whenever necessary)
class ClientA extends Client{}
class ClientB extends Client{}
```

Applying the Facade Pattern

Use an IDE of your choice to implement the code. You can use online ones like codechef.com, rextester.com, ideone.com, or codepad.org.

```
========================= ======
```

Below is an example that requires a Facade Pattern.

Galactic Starship with Warp Drive

Here is a part of the code from the Galactic Starship system. Each part of the code manages the matching hardware component of the ship.

```
/*
// GALACTIC STARSHIP GSX2013-A4
// Components listed:
// - Positron Engine
// - Ignition Crystal
// - Dark Matter Drive
// - Energy Pre-Igniter
// - Matter Fusion Reactor
// - Warp Drive
// - Galactic Navigation
```

```
// - Co-ordinates
// - Warp Igniter
*/

class PositronEngine {
    IgnitionCrystal igc = new IgnitionCrystal();
    DarkMatterDrive dmd = new DarkMatterDrive();

    public void startEngine() {
        igc.lightUp();
        dmd.activate();
    }
}

class IgnitionCrystal {
    public void lightUp() {
        // (some hardware implementation here)
    }
}

class DarkMatterDrive {
    EnergyPreIgniter epi = new EnergyPreIgniter();
    MatterFusionReactor mfr = new MatterFusionReactor();

    public void activate() {
        epi.ignite();
        mfr.fuse();
    }
}

class EnergyPreIgniter {
    public void ignite(){
        // (some hardware implementation here)
    }
}

class MatterFusionReactor {
    public void fuse() {
        // (some hardware implementation here)
    }
}

class WarpDrive {
    WarpIgniter wi = new WarpIgniter();
    MatterFusionReactor mfr = new MatterFusionReactor();

    public void warpTo(Coordinates c) {
        wi.activate();
        mfr.fuse();
        // (warp Starship to given location)
    }
}
```

```
// NOTE:: make sure the line 'using System.Collections;'
// is near the top of your code
class GalacticNavigation {
    ArrayList points = new ArrayList();
}

class Coordinates {
    int x, y, z;
    public Coordinates(int x, int y, int z) {
        this.x = x;
        this.y = y;
        this.z = z;
    }
}
class WarpIgniter {
    public void activate() {
        // (some hardware implementation here)
    }
}
```

Although we only have a few lines, we can see that this is a complex system. Let's say we were told to coordinate the components for a task like starting the main engine and activating the warp drive. We would see that these tasks need to be handled under a common handler. That is why we apply the Facade pattern.

Identify the Major Procedures

Our major procedures are the following:

- starting the main engine
- activating the warp drive

We need to implement a Facade pattern for them. The approach we choose is using one encompassing Facade wrapper class.

1) **Create the general "Facade" class…**

We would begin by making the wrapper Facade class like so:

```
class Facade {
}
```

This class should implement ALL the Major Procedures mentioned earlier.

```
class Facade {
    // NEW LINES:
    // MAJOR PROCEDURES:
    public void startEngine(){
```

```
            pe.startEngine();
            // (rest of implementation)
        }
        public void activateWarpDrive(){
            wd.warpTo(new Coordinates(0, 0, 0));
            // (rest of implementation)
        }
        }
    }
```

It will include as many components as needed.

We need to include instances from the classes that contribute to the major procedure.

Looking closely at the code, we will notice that other components rely on others to function. If we mapped it, it would look like this:

```
PositronEngine relies on:
-> IgnitionCrystal
-> DarkMatterDrive (relies on:)
- -> EnergyPreIgniter
- -> MatterFusionReactor
WarpDrive relies on:
-> WarpIgniter
-> MatterFusionReactor
```

We can see that the PositronEngine and WarpDrive classes have relevant classes they rely on in some way.

This means we are going to need instances of both classes, and the rest would be linked to them in whatever way necessary.

```
    class Facade {
        // NEW LINES:
        PositronEngine pe = new PositronEngine();
        WarpDrive wd = new WarpDrive();

        // MAJOR PROCEDURES:
        public void startEngine(){
            pe.startEngine();
            // (rest of implementation)
        }
        public void activateWarpDrive(){
            wd.warpTo(new Coordinates(0, 0, 0));
            // (rest of implementation)
        }
    }
```

2) Create a general client class that contains an instance of the Facade class.

Generalizations for the client class is class with a Facade instance in it:

```
// Client Class:
// (rest of software accesses this)
class Client {
    Facade f = new Facade();
}
```

We would need to access the client class and its facade to access the system's functionality:

```
Client c = new Client();
// Starting Engine:
c.f.startEngine();
// Activating Warp Drive:
c.f.activateWarpDrive();
```

3) Create subclasses for the general client class as required.

One option for further developing your client classes is by creating a specialized subclass and more.

```
// Client Subclasses:
// (add whenever necessary)
class ClientA: Client {
}
class ClientB: Client {
}
```

You client subclass will access Facade procedures just like the general client:

```
Client ca = new ClientA();
Client cb = new ClientB();
// Starting Engine:
ca.f.startEngine();
cb.f.startEngine();
// Activating Warp Drive:
ca.f.activateWarpDrive();
cb.f.activateWarpDrive();
```

We can see how the Facade Pattern creates a simple crux or functionality. So when faced with a problem like this one, consider using the pattern.

IF MULTIPLE FACADES:

If the procedure needs you to create multiple facades, let's see how that would work. Let's use our example to show this:

```
class EngineFacade {
```

```
    PositronEngine pe = new PositronEngine();

    // MAJOR PROCEDURES:
    public void startEngine(){
        pe.startEngine();
        // (rest of implementation)
    }
}

class WarpDriveFacade {
    WarpDrive wd = new WarpDrive();

    // MAJOR PROCEDURES:
    public void activateWarpDrive(){
        wd.warpTo(new Coordinates(0, 0, 0));
        // (rest of implementation)
    }
}
```

Even the general Client class will reflect these changes:

```
// Client Class:
// (rest of software accesses this)
class Client {
    EngineFacade ef = new EngineFacade();
    WarpDriveFacade wdf = new WarpDriveFacade();
}
```

CHAPTER 17:

Asynchronous Programming

C# allows you to write asynchronous code. Suppose you were working on a Windows program that downloads images. Clicking the button and downloading the image would take more than 30 seconds, and your program would be unresponsive if you tried downloading the image synchronously. A better way would be asynchronous.

We are going to explore what this means and how we can use it in our applications.

Contents

- **Asynchronous Programming using async and await**

We can use asynchronous programming by using two keywords: async and await. Let's look at both.

Async

If we put the keyword before a function when we declare it, that function will become asynchronous. This keyword activates resources of the .NET framework that allow us to create an asynchronous framework. The function will be called asynchronous. Below is the syntax:

public async void MyProcess()

```
            { }
```

The function above will be called asynchronously.

Await

The function that has “async” before it must also have an “await” keyword inside. Its syntax is as follows:

```
public async void MyProcess()
{
// do the asynchronous work
 await Task.delay(5);
}
```

The function above will activate after waiting for 5 seconds.

The code below downloads images asynchronously from the web.

Example 1:

```
 private void button_Click(object sender, EventArgs e)
{
    WebClient image = new WebClient();
    byte[] imageData = image.DownloadData('http://urlOfTheImage');
    this.imageView.Image = Image.FromStream(new
MemoryStream(imageData));
}
```

Your application will become unresponsive while the code executes, and that is not desirable. We can fix this using async and await like this:

Example 2:

```
private async void button_Click(object sender, EventArgs e)
{
    WebClient image = new WebClient();
    byte[] imageData = await
image.DownloadDataTaskAsync('http://urlOfTheImage');
    this.imageView.Image = Image.FromStream(new
MemoryStream(imageData));
}
```

If you look at both blocks of code, you will find three differences:

- Adding the async keyword before the function.
- The await keyword precedes the image download method.
- DownloadDataAsync has replaced the DownloadData method.

The “DownloadData” method downloads data synchronously. When it's finished, it returns control to the caller which makes the program unresponsive. “DownloadDataAsync” returns the control and downloads asynchronously. The await method releases the UI thread unless the download is complete. When the await keyword is encountered, the function returns when a specified process completes, and the function continues executing from where it stopped.

NOTE: Asynchronous methods can return three types of values.

- Void: return nothing.
- Task: It will perform one operation.
- Task<T>: Will return a task with a T type parameter.

Task: A Task will return no value (given it is void), while Task<int> will return an int type element. We can call this a generic type.

Note: An async method will run synchronously if the await keyword is missing.

Example 3:

```
using System;
using System.IO;
using System.Threading.Tasks;
class Program
{
    static void Main()
    {

            Task task = new Task(ProcesstheDataAsync);
            task.Start();
            task.Wait();
            Console.ReadLine();
    }
    static async void ProcesstheDataAsync()
    {

            Task<int> task = HandleFileAsync('C:\\enable1.txt');

            Console.WriteLine('Wait ' +
                'while I carry out something vital.');

            int x = await task;
            Console.WriteLine('Count: ' + x);
    }
    static async Task<int> HandleFileAsync(string file)
    {
            Console.WriteLine('HandleFile enter');
            int count = 0;

            using (StreamReader reader = new StreamReader(file))
            {
                string v = await reader.ReadToEndAsync();

                count += v.Length;
```

```
                    for (int i = 0; i < 10000; i++)
                    {
                        int x = v.GetHashCode();
                        if (x == 0)
                        {
                            count--;
                        }
                    }
                }
                Console.WriteLine('HandleFile exit');
                return count;
        }
}
```

Output initial 3:

```
HandleFile enter
Please wait patiently while I do something important.
```

Output final 3:

```
HandleFile enter
Wait while I carry out something vital.
HandleFile exit
Count: 1916146
```

After the main method, we created an instance of the ProcesstheDataAsync task method as an argument. In the next line, we initiated the task with the "task.Start()," and then we waited for it to finish with the "task.Wait()." The "async" signature in the ProcesstheDataAsync tells us the method is asynchronous, which makes "await" mandatory.

The first line inside the method calls the "HandleFileAsync" method. This means control will be returned before the "HandleFileAsync" method returns. As the method performs the task, we display the following messages on the screen:

HandleFile enter

Please wait patiently while I do something important.

The first line is from HandleFileAsync. It gets printed to the screen, and then control returns back to the "ProcessDataAsync " method. Then the second line is printed on the screen. The total computed result is then assigned to the variable "x," which prints on the screen.

Let's turn our attention to the second HandleFileAsync method. After the first line prints, a dummy integer is initialized in the "count" variable, setting it to "0" when we pass the location of the file in the argument. To read the data from the file, "C:\\enable1.txt", we initialize the

"StreamReader" reader type and pass it the file location. An asynchronous built-in method, "reader.ReadToEndAsync();", reads the file, and we tell it to wait until it finishes with the "await" keyword. Afterward, we assign the result to a string type variable "v." We then add the total length of the string to the "count" dummy variable. We then use dummy code to count the value. Remember, dummy code is for your understanding. In the end, the method prints the line "HandleFile exit" and the dummy value.

CHAPTER 18:

Game Development

We are going to learn how we can use our C# skills in game development. We will explore the basic aspects of game development and how we can work with them in C# to develop video games.

Many people believe writing video games is one of the best ways to learn programming. Games will teach you many things that are related to programming as a whole. You get to encounter programming concepts you would not have any other way and it expands your thinking and logical reasoning.

In 2004, Microsoft announced a game development engine called XNA. Popular titles like *Terraria* were developed using this engine. XNA is now outdated. It has been integrated into another gaming engine called MonoGame, which is more popular and allows programmers to develop across platforms. XNA only allowed you to develop games for Microsoft. MonoGame has built games for Microsoft (Xbox), Sony (Playstation), Apple (iPhone), and Google (Android).

MonoGame is free and open-source. You can download it and make changes to the code, giving you greater autonomy over the software. You can find MonoGame easily online. There are many tutorials on MonoGame online. In this chapter, we are going to explain the core concepts in-depth, so you have an easier time following any tutorials.

Content Pipeline

All games need content. The content pipeline is the method you can use to feed your game content.

The MonoGame content pipeline runs parallel with Visual Studio, providing you with a simple way of creating and importing content. For example, if you need to create a font, you will need to create a new SpriteFont in your content pipeline. If you need to import character art, you will also use the content pipeline to do it.

The Structure of a MonoGame Program

The MonoGame project has few methods in the automatically created main class. You will find *Update*, *Initialize*, *LoadContent*, and *UnloadContent* classes among them. It's important that you know how these work.

All these classes are protected methods. This means you can override them with the new classes you create from the Game class. You can call Load Content and UnloadContent from your newly created Game classes. It makes sense because it might be useful to get rid of specific game assets to do something more appropriate for your project. For instance, if an enemy dies and it is the last time they will be seen in the game, you would use an overridden UnloadContent to unload the asset from the game, improving performance.

The default classes are the most important to understand, so we will explore them below.

Draw() is used to draw a frame on the screen. This is used to determine drawing logic. In some cases, you'll need to draw an independent draw function derived from the protected method and defined within the specifications of a relevant class. However, it's important to understand how it functions in the context of the game.

Initialize() initializes your content. It is called after the Game and the GraphicsDevice objects are created and before the LoadContent method is called. You use it to initialize game objects and more. It can also be called from a derived class if you want to initialize something after the game has begun.

LoadContet() loads all the game's *graphics resources*. These are your SpriteFonts, game sprites, and more. We will discuss it more later.

UnloadContent() unloads all the game's graphics resources. It can be used at any time, for example if you don't need a specific spirit anymore, as we talked about earlier. The method can be called within the Game class or in a derivative class. It is especially important to know this when working with bigger games.

Update() updates your game. This method runs constantly and contains your game's logic. This includes things like artificial intelligence, unit collision, and more. It contains anything in your game that is happening regularly. It is a very important part.

All these are the five primary methods that are created when starting a new instance of a Game class. There are more protected Game class methods. These are the ones you need to know at this point.

Textures

Textures refer to sprite images that are used by the game to represent data. They can be constantly updated. Nothing is final about them. Textures allow you to make character animations and graph representations of items in your game.

Textures can be imported through the content pipeline. They can then be imported into the LoadContent with appropriate methods. This is done after they are initialized with the Initialize method.

A 2D sprite is initialized below:

private Texture2D myTexture;

A SpriteBatch object has to be created in order to draw all your textures, so this should be made earlier. Usually, the standard template had already created a SpriteBatch when you started creating your game project.

You write the following code in the LoadContent method:

```
myTexture = Content.Load<Texture2D>("textureName");
```

When finished, you draw the sprite in the Draw() method.

You begin with the drawing process like this:

```
spriteBatch.Begin();
```

Then you draw the sprite:

```
spriteBatch.Draw(myTexture, new Vector2(0, 0), Color.White);
```

New Vector2 gives you the x and y coordinates to draw the sprite at. Drawing starts at the top left of the sprite. Numbers moving to the right and downwards are bigger; those to the left and up are lower.

Color. White gives your texture a basic tint. Your sprite is also loaded with the default coloration, as you have specified. Without it, your sprite would have a different coloration.

The spriteBatch process is ended like this:

```
spriteBatch.End();
```

You can run the game to see if your sprite has loaded correctly. It should load on top of your default Cornflower Blue background. If that was successful, congrats! You now understand how to load images into the game. It is an extremely useful skill to have.

Taking in Information from Keyboard and Mouse

We are going to look at how the keyboard and mouse input work. MonoGame has support for all kinds of input like gamepads and touchscreens, but for our purpose, it would be much simpler if we used the tools you already have access to. It is one of the better places to start.

XNA and MonoGame have simplified working with input. Input is based on the state of given peripherals: keyboards, mouse, and gamepads. The logic for this is in the update function after initialization. Assume all in this section occurs in the Update function.

To work with the keyboard, you need to create a keyboard state and get the information from the keyboard. Because the Update method runs continuously, the information will always be collected.

You will need to create a KeyboardState object. You can call it what you want, but to get the current state, you will need to use the Get.State method of the Keyboard class.

```
KeyboardState state = Keyboard.GetState();
```

Here's how you check if a certain key is pressed. Let's say every sprite has an X and Y coordinate stored as integrated inside a 2d vector, like this:

```
Vector2 spritePosition = Vector2.Zero;
```

The sprite position would be drawn using Draw(). Its position would be updated by the update() method. If we wanted to move the sprite to the corresponding position when a key is pressed, we would write isKeyDown checks. When the Key is down, the position gets changed. Keys are stored with an enumeration in the Keys namespace, so there isn't mapping to worry about.

We would put the following logic in the Update method:

```
if (state.IsKeyDown(Keys.W))
spritePosition.Y -= 5;
if (state.IsKeyDown(Keys.A))
spritePosition.Y += 5;
if (state.IsKeyDown(Keys.S))
```

```
spritePosition.X -= 5;
if (state.IsKeyDown(Keys.D))
spritePosition.X += 5;
```

In this example A moves sprite left, W moves it up, S moves it down, and D moves it to the right. Because the Update() method is always running, these conditions will be checked constantly, meaning the game will respond immediately when a key is pressed. We could implement an Escape check which closes the game when pressed.

```
if (state.IsKeyDown(Keys.Escape))
Exit();
```

Debug it and test it yourself. Run it and see if all the keys and texture you have imported move the way they should.

Let's look at handling input from the mouse. It has similarities with keyboard input, as everything is based on the current state of the mouse. Remove the keyboard logic and replace it with the following code.

MouseState state = Mouse.GetState();

Draw the position of your sprite, so it moves with your mouse by having it drawn to the vector SpritePostion. Move it using the vector returned by the mouse's state:

```
spritePosition.X = state.X;
spritePosition.Y = state.Y;
```

They will now correspond to one another. When you move your mouse, the sprite should also move. Test and debug the program yourself.

This is more than enough to get you started with inputs. Now you see how they work on a basic level. This knowledge can easily be extended to other input devices like gamepads.

Basic Unit Collision

Unit collision is one of the most important features of game programming. Everything in a game is presented as a texture. Even the game menu is a texture. If you want to check things like mouse hover events, you have to use unit collision.

Unit collisions come in many forms. The simplified form is called a bounding box collision. This is the one we are going to focus on. Bounding box is based on the idea that all sprites can be reduced to rectangles with width and height. So if the lines of one rectangle intersect with another we can conclude they are colliding.

Remember, this is the least resource-intensive unit collision; it's not always the best. For instance, if you have something fine in your game to check for collisions, like bullets, you will need a collision unit that is more refined. For our purposes, here is the best way to teach the basics of unit collision and detection.

Rectangles in XNA have an in-built collision detection property, which means you don't have to worry about writing it. If you prefer, you can try your hand at writing one. We are going to cover the catered XAN rectangle collision diction.

The first thing we do is define rectangles of the two entities:

Rectangle(X_position, Y_position, Width, Height);

You could create two:

Rectangle playerRect = new Rectangle(playerPosition.X, playerPosition.Y, playerTexture.Width, playerTexture.Height);

and do the same for the opponent:

Rectangle enemyRect = new Rectangle(enemyPosition.X, enemyPosition.Y, enemyTexture.Width, enemyTexture.Height);

Then write an if statement for the collision:

```
if (playerRect.collides(enemyRect)) {
// collision detection logic goes within
}
```

The logic behind this is simple. You will not have any problem with it. You need to get your hands dirty to see what I mean. As you improve, it will get a little harder, but the more you work at it the better you will be.

Artificial Intelligence

Artificial intelligence in video games is impressive. We will discuss that a bit before we work with it.

Let's say you are making an artificial intelligence system that should cause an entity in the game to follow the player. There are many ways to do it. It comes down to pathfinding, which refers to finding the shortest path between two points. It is important for gaming and many other applications.

There are different forms of pathfinding. The A* method and the MaxDxDy are the most popular.

The A* method is less accurate than the MaxDxDy algorithm. The MaxDxDys are popular for their high accuracy with a huge chunk of system resources. Games already demand a lot from our systems, so we are going to focus on the simpler, more frugal A* method. Other reasons for preserving the A* method are that it's simple and beginner-friendly, and it is also the most common pathfinding algorithm.

The A* method operates on system nodes, meaning we don't have to worry about rigid algorithmic structures. For instance, some pathfinding algorithms will only be appropriate for elements of a specific size. A* method is focused on how things relate to one another in the game and proximity, regardless of the setup. A* pathfinding is also the most efficient and fast. It predicts how much distance remains between two points and looks for the best path forward and favors those that it determines will work well.

The A* is a complete algorithm, meaning it can always find a solution to a problem if the problem is appropriate to its application.

Pathfinding algorithms work the assumption that maps are full of nodes. So it is best to practice them on a top-down tiled game because it will be easier to see the way the algorithm works before trying it on more complex applications.

A* algorithms search for the path that costs less; cost is defined by the distance and time to the goal and other factors.

The goals is to minimize this:

```
f(n) = g(n) + h(n)
```

N can be defined as a node on the path - the last to be chosen - while g(n) is the total expenditure so far from the first node of the program towards the given n, and the h(n) is a heuristic method that gives solid guesses about the expenditure of the current node to the goal.

The algorithm loops to minimize expenditure based on the previous and the current node to determine the next best node. The *f*(n) of the nodes is compared and the next with the last *f*(n) is taken. Things that are not nodes, obstacles, and difficult terrain, are not considered viable.

You can implement the algorithm by creating a tiled map, where your sprite must reach another destination on the map. You can even test different pathfinding algorithms by plotting the destination file at another.

There are two ways to apply the heuristic method: the Euclidean or the Manhattan method.

The simplest is the Manhattan method, but it doesn't give the best estimation. It is also the least mathematically complex, so it takes few resources.

The Manhattan distance can be applied this way:

```
| destination.X - node.X | + |destination.Y - node.Y |
```

The Euclidean distance can be applied this way:

```
sqrt( (destination.X - node.X)² + (destination.Y - node.Y)² )
```

They both will give *h(n)* for any given node *n*. This is the simplest form of artificial intelligence you can implement in games. There are more algorithms out there that can do more; we chose this one because it was easier to understand

These are the bare essentials. You have a strong understanding now to move on and to other foundational concepts of game development. Then you can begin building your own games. Game development will quickly improve your programming skills and reasoning. There is no reason why you shouldn't give it a shot. There is nothing that is wasted time in programming; every lesson will count for something. Also, you can make the game you have always wanted to make.

CONCLUSION

Your next step is to use all you have learned. To improve, challenge yourself. Programming challenges are a good way to improve your skills. If there is something you want to build, find out if there are other people who have done the same thing, and learn how they did it. Learn as much as you can about programming all the time and don't be afraid to experiment or ask questions.

I won't lie to you; programming is not easy. There is a long difficult journey ahead for you. If you choose to be a programmer, you just have to accept that you will never know all of it, and you have to be open to constantly learning. This is why I have decided to teach you the underlying concepts and methods. This is merely foundational, a bag of tools, that you will sharpen, grow, and learn to wield better. You are ready.

There will be times when you feel like banging your head on your desk and quitting. The imposter syndrome is real in tech; everyone feels like a fraud, but that is because programming is a vast field with so much to know. The only thing that matters is to be competent enough to fix problems when they occur and build things that are required of you. You will find most of the time that you have to devise plans or research. Very rarely are you just going to know what to do.

You can also try looking in opensource projects, or keep reading to improve. What you go away with here is a good foundation that you can extend into other C-style programming languages.

REFERENCES

C# Indexers. (n.d.). *www.tutorialspoint.com*. Retrieved 28 May 2019, from https://www.tutorialspoint.com/csharp/csharp_indexers.htm

C# Interface. (n.d.). *Tutorialsteacher.com*. Retrieved 28 May 2019, from https://www.tutorialsteacher.com/csharp/csharp-interface

C# Introduction - Tutlane. (n.d.). *Tutlane.com*. Retrieved 28 May 2019, from https://www.tutlane.com/tutorial/csharp/csharp-introduction

C# Logical Operators. (n.d.). *www.tutorialspoint.com*. Retrieved 28 May 2019, from https://www.tutorialspoint.com/csharp/csharp_logical_operators.htm

C# Namespaces. (n.d.). *www.tutorialspoint.com*. Retrieved 28 May 2019, from https://www.tutorialspoint.com/csharp/csharp_namespaces.htm

C# Reflection. (n.d.). *www.tutorialspoint.com*. Retrieved 28 May 2019, from https://www.tutorialspoint.com/csharp/csharp_reflection.htm

Chauhan, S. (2014). *Understanding Expression and Expression Trees. Dotnettricks.com*. Retrieved 28 May 2019, from https://www.dotnettricks.com/learn/linq/understanding-expression-and-expression-trees

Chiarelli, C. (n.d.). *Introduction to Game Development Using C# and Monogame Part 1 ... The Basics | Charlie Chiarelli | Skillshare. Skillshare*. Retrieved 28 May 2019, from https://www.skillshare.com/classes/Introduction-to-Game-Development-Using-C-and-Monogame-Part-1-...-The-Basics/1049146739

Collection in C#. (n.d.). *Tutorialsteacher.com*. Retrieved 28 May 2019, from https://www.tutorialsteacher.com/csharp/csharp-collection

Design patterns with real time example. (2015) *Stack Overflow*. Retrieved 28 May 2019, from https://stackoverflow.com/questions/11553804/design-patterns-with-real-time-example

Generics in C#. (n.d.). *Tutorialsteacher.com*. Retrieved 28 May 2019, from https://www.tutorialsteacher.com/csharp/csharp-generics

LINQ Tutorials from Basics to Advanced. (n.d.). *Tutorialsteacher.com*. Retrieved 28 May 2019, from https://www.tutorialsteacher.com/linq/linq-tutorials

Schults, C. (2019). *C# Garbage Collection Tutorial*. *Stackify*. Retrieved 28 May 2019, from https://stackify.com/c-garbage-collection/

C#

The Ultimate Advanced Guide To Master C# Programming

INTRODUCTION

In this book, we will study various advanced C# programming topics and the .NET framework. Our purpose is to provide you with the foundations you need to be an advanced programmer.

You will study various advanced topics like indexer methods and extension methods. We will cover how to create and configure custom class libraries. That will include topics like defining custom namespaces and creating nested namespaces. We will also learn attribute-based programming and low-level programming with CIL.

In the final chapters, we will explore new technologies that are part of today's development pipeline. We will look at the Windows Presentation Foundation, ASP.NET, and .NET Core.

You are at a point where you are ready to deal with some advanced techniques. You often manage on your own and read the documentation, and we expect you to continue to do this as we have a detailed discussion of the book's concepts.

CHAPTER 1:

Advanced C# Language Features

In this chapter, we are going to explore several complex C# programming concepts. We are going to look at the indexer method and its implementation. Indexer methods allow you to create custom types that enable you to access internal subitems with array-like syntax. Once you're done, you will be able to overload operators and create implicit and explicit conversion routines.

This chapter will also include information that is helpful when working with LINQ API. We will look at extension methods and anonymous types. While concepts like these help with LINQ APIs, they are also useful to understand on their own. Then we will explore pointer types and unmanaged pointers. Pointers are used rarely in C# development, but they are useful when dealing with situations with complex interoperability.

While pointers are rarely used when developing applications written in C#, they can sometimes come in handy when you encounter situations that include complex interoperability.

Indexer Methods

You know how to access an item from an array with an index operator, but let's look at it again:

```
static void Main (string[] args)
{
// Looping through the command line arguments
// with an index operator.
for (int i = 0; i < args.Length; i++)
Console.WriteLine("Args: {0}", args[i]);
          // Declaration of an array containing local integers
int[] myInts = { 12, 8, 101, 523, 8964};
```

```
        // Accessing every element with an index operator
for (int y = 0; y < myInts.Length; y++)
Console.WriteLine("Index {0}  = {1} ", y,  myInts[y]);
Console.ReadLine();
}
```

This is a textbook example of accessing items from an array with an indexer operator. Interestingly, C# allows us to create a customs class that can be indexed just like an array. To do this, we have to define an indexer method. This is helpful when developing generic and non-generic collection classes as well.

Before we implement a custom indexer, let's see how it works. Let's say we have support for the indexer method added to a custom collection type called "CarCollection". We haven't added the indexer yet, but pay attention to its usage below:

class myProgram

```
{
static void Main(string[] args)
{
Console.WriteLine ("++++ Indexers are awesome ++++\n");
                     CarCollection myCar = new CarCollection();
// Use the indexer syntax to introduce objects
myCar[0] = new Car ("Nissan", "Qashqai", 2018);
myCar[1] = new Car ("Renault", "Clio", 2016);
myCar[2] = new Car ("Ford", "Mustang", 1969);
myCar[3] = new Car ("Toyota", "Tacoma", 2019);
myCar[4] = new Car ("Mercedes", "C300", 2016);
// Using an indexer to retrieve and display the items.
for (int i = 0; i < myCar.Count; i++)
{
Console.WriteLine("Car number: {0}", i);
Console.WriteLine("Brand: {0} {1}",
myCar[i].BrandName, myCar[i].ModelName);
Console.WriteLine("Year: {0}", myCar[i].Year);
Console.WriteLine();
}
}
}
```

As you can see, indexers allow us to control a collection of subitems in a way similar to arrays. What we need to figure out is how we can configure our CarCollection class to exploit this functionality. When you think of an indexer type of a C# property definition, here's how we should modify the CartCollection class:

```
// Introduce the indexer in the definition of the class
public class CarCollection : IEnumerable
{
```

```
private ArrayList arCar = new ArrayList();
// The class' custom indexer
public Car this[int index]
{
get => (Car)arCar[index];
set => arCar.Insert(index, value);
}
}
```

As you can see, our indexer is the same as property declaration without the "this" keyword. We also have the "get" syntax used to return the right item. This means the request is delegated to the indexer, which belongs to the ArrayList item, the class that accepts our indexer. We also have the "set" syntax, in which we need to add new "Car" items with the insert method, which belongs to the ArrayList class. In this case, the indexer serves the same purpose as a regular public method, but indexer methods implemented into custom collections are easily integrated into any .NET library.

When creating custom collections, it is advisable to take advantage of indexer methods. However, you can also use generic types, as they offer the same kind of functionality. Imagine we have a method with basic "List<T>" or "Car" items, and you want to use an index of "List<T>." Here's how it would look:

```
static void UseGenericListOfCars()
{
List<Car> myCar = new List<Car>();
myCar.Add(new Car ("Ford", "Mustang", 1969));
myCar.Add(new Car ("Toyota", "Tacoma", 2019));
// Use the indexer to change the first car.
myCar[0] = new Car ("Mercedes", "C300", 2016);
// Acquire and display every single object with the indexer.
for (int i = 0; i < myCar.Count; i++)
{
Console.WriteLine("Car number: {0}", i);
Console.WriteLine("Brand: {0} {1}",
myCar[i].BrandName, myCar[i].ModelName);
Console.WriteLine("Year: {0}", myCar[i].Year);
Console.WriteLine();
}}
```

Data Indexing with String Values

The CarCollection class defines an indexer, which allows the caller to determine the subobjects through a numerical value. However, this is not something required in order to use an indexer method. You can replace the ArrayList with a system collections generic dictionary, for example. Dictionaries give access to all enclosed types with a key. Let's have a look below:

```
public class CarCollection : IEnumerable
{
private Dictionary <string, Car> listCar = new Dictionary <string, Car>
();
// Depending on the string index we will return a car object using the
indexer
public Car this[string name]
{
get => (Car)listCar[name];
set => listCar[name] = value;
}
public void ClearCar()
{ listCar.Clear(); }
public int Count => listCar.Count;
IEnumerator IEnumerable.GetEnumerator() => listCar.GetEnumerator();
}
Let's see how the caller can interact with the "Car" objects:
static void Main(string[] args)
{
Console.WriteLine ("++++ Indexers are awesome ++++\n");
CarCollection myCar = new CarCollection();
myCar["Nissan"] = new Car ("Nissan", "Qashqai", 2018);
myCar ["Renault"] = new Car("Renault", "Clio", 2016);
// Get "Nissan" and print data.
Car nissan = myCar["Nissan"];
Console.WriteLine(nissan.ToString());
Console.ReadLine();
}
```

In this case, a generics dictionary could also be used. We would have the same functionality without a custom class to support an indexer. Take note that the indexer's data type depends on the collection's type, which allows the callers to obtain the subobjects.

Indexer Overloading

You can overload the indexer method on one class. You can also define more than one indexer for one type to enable the caller to use a numerical or string index to access subobjects. For example, the .NET"s data access API (ADO.NET) has a DataSet class that supports the "Tables" property that returns the "DataTable Collection" type. This type gets and sets all data table items by defining three indexers, one of them after the ordinal position and the rest by string denomination with an option to contain a namespace. Below is an example:

```
public sealed class DataTableCollection : InternalDataCollectionBase
{
...
// These are overloaded indexers
public DataTable this [int index] { get; }
public DataTable this [string name] { get; }
```

```
public DataTable this [string name, string tableNamespace] { get; } }
```

Types from the base class library often support indexers. So, even if you don't need to create a custom indexer, there are several types that support the syntax.

Multidimensional Indexers

On top of that, you can have an indexer that accepts more than one parameter. Imagine we have a collection using a two-dimensional array to store subobjects. Here's how that would look:

```
public class SomeContainer
{
private int[,] my2DintArray = new int [10, 10];
public int this[int row, int column]
{
/* get or set value from the two-dimensional array */
}
}
```

If you don't create a custom collection, there's no need for a multidimensional indexer. However, this structure is still useful in ADO.NET. It is best to think of the "DataTable" as a table with rows and columns, like an Excel spreadsheet. A data adapter is used to fill the table with objects. Let's build a table with three columns that will contain vehicle details: brand, model, and year of manufacture. Look at how once we have one row, we can take advantage of a multidimensional indexer. Let's look at the code below to get a better understanding. You will need to import System.Data for the code to work.

```
static void MultiIndexerDataTable()
{
// Create a data table that has three columns.
DataTable myTable = new DataTable();
myTable.Columns.Add (new DataColumn("Brand"));
myTable.Columns.Add (new DataColumn("Model"));
myTable.Columns.Add (new DataColumn("Year"));
// Next, we are going to insert a row.
myTable.Rows.Add ("Ford", "Mustang", 1969);
// Now we can implement the indexer to learn about this row.
Console.WriteLine ("Brand: {0}", myTable.Rows[0][0]);
Console.WriteLine ("Model: {0}", myTable.Rows[0][1]);
Console.WriteLine ("Year : {0}", myTable.Rows[0][2]);
}
```

Even when you are not familiar with ADO.NET, the example above is made to show you how multiple dimensions are supported by indexers, meaning they can simplify how you access and manipulate subitems in a custom collection.

Operator Overloading

As you know, programming languages have symbols that are required to perform various tasks on specific data types. An example is the + operator, which is used to add floats or integers together.

```
// An example of the plus operator with integers.
int x = 100;
int y = 200;
int z = x + y;
// The value of z is now 300.
```

You learned this when you were just starting. But have you thought about how this operator can be used on other data types, like strings?

```
// An example of the plus operator with strings.
string x = "Hello";
string y = " world!";
string z = x + y;
// String z is now "Hello World!"
```

Again, you know this. Notice how the operators behave differently according to the data type they are working with. When used on numerical data types, we get a sum; when used on a string, the string is concatenated. C# allows you to create custom classes, meaning these operators will behave in a unique way to the operators you will use. Operator overloading allows you to do this.

In the beginner's guide, we briefly touched on this when we talked about Polymorphism. We will explore that on a deeper level here.

Operator overloading is all about defining the functionality of an operator, so it has a unique effect on your objects and classes. Below is the list of operators that can be overloaded:

6. Unary operators: +, -, !, ~, ++, --, true and false.
7. Binary operators: +, -, *, /, %, |, ^, <<, >>.
8. Comparison operators: ==, !=, <, >, <=, >=. Keep in mind that in C# you have to overload the "like" operators together.

Below is a list of operators you cannot overload:

1. Shorthand assignment operators: +=, -=, *=, /=, %=, &=, |=, ^=, <<=, >>=. Note that while these operators cannot be overloaded, they will be included when you overload a binary operator related to them.
2. The [] operator: You can't overload this operator; however, you can use an indexer construct in its stead to gain the same kind of functionality.

3. The () operator: This operator cannot be overloaded; however, if you need that type of functionality, you can use custom conversion methods.

Now that you have all the rules, let's start overloading some operators. We will begin with Unary operators.

Unary Operators Overload

When overloading a unary operator, it is required to use a static keyword with the operator's keyword. In the following example, we are going to have a single parameter of the same type as the class definition.

```
public class Line
{
...
// For the Line, we will add a value of 1 to its values X and Y.
public static Line operator ++(Line l1) => new Line (l1.X+1, l1.Y+1);
// Now let's do the same with a subtraction instead.
public static Line operator --(Line l1) => new Line (l1.X-1, l1.Y-1);
}
We can also decrement and increment the same values as in this example:
static void Main (string[] args)
{
...
// We will apply the ++ and -- operators to the Line.
Line lnFive = new Line (1, 1);
Console.WriteLine ("++lnFive = {0}", ++lnFive); // [2, 2]
Console.WriteLine ("--lnFive = {0}", --lnFive);  // [1, 1]
// We will do the same as a post-increment/decrement.
Line lnSix = new Line (20, 20);
Console.WriteLine ("lnSix++ = {0}", lnSix++);  // [20, 20]
Console.WriteLine ("lnSix-- = {0}", lnSix--);  // [21, 21]
Console.ReadLine();
}
```

Notice how we are using the same custom operators twice, but in different ways. If you have worked with C++, you know that you can independently overload the pre-increment/decrement and post-increment/decrement operators. C# doesn't allow you to that, as the return value is controlled automatically.

Binary Operators Overload

To illustrate how to overload binary operators, we will define our Line class into a console application that calls OverloadEx:

```
public class Line
{
```

```
public int x {get; set;}
public int y {get; set;}
public Line (int xPos, int yPos)
{
x = xPos;
y = yPos;
}
public override string ToString() => $"[{this.x}, {this.y}]";
}
```

The next step is adding Lines together. We do this by adding a two-line variable to get a new line value, which is the sum of x and y. If you want, you can subtract one Line from another. Let's look at the code below:

```
static void Main (string[] args)
{
Console.WriteLine ("***** Overloaded Operators are our friends
*****\n");
// Create the two Lines.
Line lnOne = new Line (100, 100);
Line lnTwo = new Line (40, 40);
Console.WriteLine ("lnOne = {0}", lnOne);
Console.WriteLine ("lnTwo = {0}", lnTwo);
// Create a larger Line by calculating the sum of the two Lines.
Console.WriteLine ("lnOne + lnTwo: {0} ", lnOne + lnTwo);
// Create a smaller line by subtracting.
Console.WriteLine ("lnOne - lnTwo: {0} ", lnOne - lnTwo);
Console.ReadLine();
}
```

The code we have so far will result in compile-time errors because the type of Line doesn't know how to treat the operators used. To allow a custom type to respond in a specified manner to operators, we use the operator keyword is with the static keyword. When a binary operator is overloaded, we'll have to pass through a couple or more arguments of the same type as the class (Line in this case). So let's update our code like below:

```
public class Line
{
...
// Using an overloaded + operator.
public static Line operator + (Line l1, Line l2) => new Line (l1.x +
l2.x, l1.y + l2.y);
// Using an overloaded - operator.
public static Line operator - (Line l1, Line l2) => new Line (l1.x -
l2.x, l1.y - l2.y);
}
```

The add operator returns the Line objects based on the sum of retrieved Line parameters. It means when we declare ln1 + ln2, the following hidden call takes place. Here's is the pseudo-code to illustrate:

```
Line l3 = Line.operator+ (l1, l2) Line l3 = l1 + l2;
Line l4 = Line.operator- (l1, l2) Line l4 = l1 - l2;
```

Our program should be able to compile properly without errors. Now, we can add and subtract linear objects like this:

```
lnOne = [100, 100]
lnTwo = [40, 40]
lnOne + lnTwo: [140, 140]
lnOne - lnTwo: [60, 60]
```

Note that when a binary operator is overloaded, you don't have to use pass parameters of the same type. If you think it's best, you can have different arguments. In the following example, we overloaded the plus operator, enabling the caller to retriever another Line object focused on a numerical arrangement:

```
public class Line
{
...
public static Line operator + (Line l1, int change) => new Line (l1.x +
change,  l1.y + change);
public static Line operator + (int change, Line l1) => new Line (l1.x +
change,  l1.y + change);
}
```

Know that both method variations are required to pass the arguments. Defining one of them is not enough because the compiler does not handle the other automatically. You can use either version of the operator like this:

```
// Print [110, 110].
Line largerLine = lnOne + 10;
Console.WriteLine ("lnOne + 10 = {0}", largerLine);
// Print [120, 120].
Console.WriteLine ("10 + largerLine = {0}", 10 + largerLine);
Console.WriteLine();
```

Now that we have looked at overloading binary operators, let's discuss the problem of shorthand assignment operators. Remember, you can't overload the += and -= operators as you would in C++. In C# the operators can be simulated automatically if you have a type overloading a binary operator related to it. In the previous examples, we overloaded the plus and minus operators. Now we can use shorthand operators:

```
static void Main (string[] args)
```

```
{
...
// +=
Line lnThree = new Line (90, 5);
Console.WriteLine ("lnThree = {0}", lnThree);
Console.WriteLine ("lnThree += lnTwo: {0}", lnThree += lnTwo);
// -=
Line lnFour = new Line (0, 500);
Console.WriteLine ("lnFour = {0}", lnFour);
Console.WriteLine ("lnFour -= lnThree: {0}", lnFour -= lnThree);
Console.ReadLine();
}
```

Comparison Operators Overload

You already know how to work with an IComparable interface to compare objects. However, we can overload comparison operators, as long as they are for the identical class. Remember, if you plan to overload the < operator, you have to overload the > operator, as well as with the <= and >= operators. Let's look at an example of our Lien type overloading these operators, so we can compare Lines:

```
static void Main (string[] args)
{
...
Console.WriteLine ("lnOne < lnTwo : {0}", lnOne < lnTwo);
Console.WriteLine ("lnOne > lnTwo : {0}", lnOne > lnTwo);
Console.ReadLine();
}
```

Overloading these operators is an easy task. Here's how the process looks:

```
// Line is now comparable.
public class Line: IComparable<Line>
{ ...
public int CompareTo (Line other)
{
if (this.X > other.X && this.Y > other.Y)
return 1;
if (this.X < other.X && this.Y < other.Y)
return -1;
else
return 0;
}
public static bool operator < (Line l1, Line l2) => l1.CompareTo(l2) <
0;
public static bool operator > (Line l1, Line l2) => l1.CompareTo(l2) >
0;
public static bool operator <= (Line l1, Line l2) => l1.CompareTo(l2) <=
0;
public static bool operator >= (Line l1, Point p2) => l1.CompareTo(l2)
```

```
>= 0;
}
```

Equality Operators Overload

To overload the equality operators, you need to be familiar with overriding "System.Object. Equals". Hence, it changes from reference-based comparisons to value-based comparisons. When we override "Equals," we find ourselves with the task of overloading == and the !== equality operators. Below is an example of doing this using an updated Line type:

```
public class Line
{
...
public override bool Equals (object o) => o.ToString() ==
this.ToString();
public override int GetHashCode() => this.ToString().GetHashCode();
// Next we are overloading the == and != operators.
public static bool operator == (Line l1, Line l2) => l1.Equals(l2);
public static bool operator != (Line l1, Line l2) => !l1.Equals(l2);
}
```

See how two operators call the "Equals" method that was overridden. This handles most of the workflow. We can use overloaded operators like this:

```
static void Main (string[] args)
{
...
Console.WriteLine ("lnOne == lnTwo : {0}", lnOne == lnTwo);
Console.WriteLine ("lnOne != lnTwo : {0}", lnOne != lnTwo);
Console.ReadLine ();
}
```

Comparing two objects with the equality operator is easier than calling "Equals." When you overload them, C# will ask you to override them. You shouldn't worry about forgetting this step because the compiler will remind you.

C# allows you to create custom types that act in more unique ways than the commonly used operators. You might be tempted to modify all your classes so they support this, but it all has to make sense when you look at it as a whole. You need to have a good reason for doing so. Imagine you have to do a multiplication operation for a "MyHorse" object. The danger of that is confusing everyone else looking at the code.

```
MyHorse newHorse = myHorse * yourHorse;
```

It isn't intuitive. Overloading operators makes sense when they are trying to create data styles that involve text, fractions, and hexagons. There isn't a need when your operators are dealing with people, cars, or websites. To decide with confidence, consider the user's ability to understand the type's functionality. If it makes things unnecessarily complex, avoid it. Only use overloading when it is necessary.

Extension Methods

Extension methods were introduced with .NET version 3.5. They enable us to implement methods and properties to a class without changing their original type directly. Imagine a class that is in development and suddenly needs to start supporting new members. If you change the definition, there's a chance you will ruin backward compatibility it has with previous codebases that rely on it. To ensure backward compatibility, you must determine a child class, but that means maintaining twice as many classes. While maintenance is boring, you always have to think about it when you develop. Assume you have a certain structure, and you need to add new members to it, so it behaves in a polymorphic manner. You can't extend a structure, but you can only add a member to its type. Even here, you are facing the problem of backward compatibility.

The extension method will allow you to change the types without having to use subclasses. You won't have to change the type. The functionality will be given to the type when we reference the extension method in our project.

You need to define extension methods within a static class, so you have to use the static keyword. Also, an extension method is recognized by the "this" keyword, which is applied to the first parameter belonging to the method. It determines if an object is extended or not.

To illustrate extension methods, we will build a new console application, and we will name it FunWithExtensions. We will define a class called "MyExtensions," which will contain the definition of two extension methods. The first will hold a method called "DisplayDefining Assembly." This method uses System types, and the "Reflection" namespace is needed to show the assembly containing such a type.

We'll call the second method "BackwardsDigits." It will enable integers to reverse themselves. So, a number like 45 will return 54. Now, let's apply all this. Remember to use System.Reflection namespace for this exercise.

```
static class MyExtensions
{
// The following method will enable all items to display
// the assembly in which it is defined.
public static void DisplayDefiningAssembly (this object obj)
{
Console.WriteLine ("{0} lives here: => {1}\n", obj.GetType().Name,
```

```
    Assembly.GetAssembly (obj.GetType()).GetName().Name);
}
// The next method is used to reverse the digits of an integer.
public static int BackwardsDigits(this int i)
{
// Retrieve all characters by translating the integer to a string.
char[] digits = i.ToString().ToCharArray();
// Next, we will reverse the array objects.
Array.Reverse(digits);
// And place them inside a string.
string newDigits = new string(digits);
// Lastly, we can return the string we changed in the form of an
integer.
return int.Parse(newDigits);}}
```

See how the "this" keyword marks the first parameter of every extension before definition. You need to do this consistently as the first parameter is the one that tells the program we are extending the type. In our example, we use the DisplayDefiningAssembly method to extend System.object, so all types contain it as a member. Remember, when it comes to the .NET framework, Object is the parent of all types inside it. On the other hand, the BackwardsDigits method is used to extend integers. So if another type calls this method, we will get an error.

Let's look at an example where the Main methods extend some types from the class libraries.

```
static void Main(string[] args)
{
Console.WriteLine ("++++ Extension Methods Rule! ++++\n");
 // The integer has been assimilated, resistance is futile!
int myInt = 123456789;  myInt.DisplayDefiningAssembly();
// The Dataset changes as well.
System.Data.DataSet d = new System.Data.DataSet();
d.DisplayDefiningAssembly();
// The Media Sound Player is the next to fall!
System.Media.SoundPlayer sp = new System.Media.SoundPlayer();
sp.DisplayDefiningAssembly();
Console.WriteLine ("Value of myInt: {0}", myInt);
Console.WriteLine("Reversed digits of myInt: {0}",
myInt.BackwardsDigits());
Console.ReadLine(); }
Our output should be:
++++ Extension Methods Rule! ++++
Int32 lives here: => mscorlib
DataSet lives here: => System.Data
SoundPlayer lives here: => System
Value of myInt: 123456789
Backwards digits of myInt: 987654321
```

All classes holding extension methods need to be defined through a .NET namespace. If you have a namespace that differs from those using extension methods, you will need to add them with the "using" keyword. It means your program will have access to all extension methods used for the types you're extending. If you don't use the right namespace, those methods will not be available for your program file. Also, remember that extension methods aren't global, they are restricted to namespaces, like if the class we defined is added to a namespace called "AwesomeExtensionMethods" as shown below:

```
namespace AwesomeExtensionMethods
{  static class MyExtensions  {  ...  } }
```

You would need to import this namespace in a project that required the class definition.

A best practice is restricting your extension methods to a specific .NET namespace and a class library. Following this workflow will help you create programs that can access extensions through references that point to the appropriate library and import the needed namespace.

Anonymous Types

You already know that defining several classes that represent the function of specific objects is one of the most important things to do when you model them. It's best to create a class when you know it will have functions that will be useful for future projects. Reusable code in the form of a method, events, and constructors significantly lowers the time and effort you put into your projects, allowing you to focus on more important things. However, there are cases where you need a class to build a collection of data points that don't have any adaptable functions or methods. In some cases, you might need a type that is only used by select methods inside a program. It might be a better idea to avoid developing a class definition if you only have a few places where you can implement it.

Let's look at a basic value-based schematic data type:

```
class MyClass {
// Determine all of the variables.
// Create a property for each one of them.
// Override ToString() clarify the key member variables.
// Override GetHashCode() and Equals() to function using a value-based
equality.
}
```

Notice how this requires several lines of code and the additional class you have to pay attention to. When working with short-term data, consider using a custom data type instead. Say you need a method to receive certain parameters; you would like to use them to build a new data type that would be used within the method. Also, you want to print the information with the ToString method. You can do this with anonymous types.

Definition

To define anonymous types, you use the "var" keyword and object initialization. This will tell the compiler to create a class definition during compilation. Object initialization also tells the compiler to build read-only properties for the type and private backing fields. To illustrate how anonymous types are defined, we will create an application called "Anonymous." Then we insert the next method inside our class. This will define a new type from the parameters.

```
static void BuildAnonType ( string make, string color, int currSp )
{
// Create the anonymous type with the incoming arguments.
var bird = new { Species = species, Size = size, Speed = currSp };
// Now, we can fetch property data by using this type.
Console.WriteLine ("I saw a {0} {1} flying {2} MPH", bird.Size,
bird.Species, bird.Speed);
// There are custom implementations for every virtual method in
System.Object.
Console.WriteLine ("ToString() == {0}", bird.ToString()); }
```

We can call the method from "Main", but can also make anonymous types with hard coded values, like this:

```
static void Main (string[] args)
{
Console.WriteLine("++++ Anonymous Types Meeting++++\n");
// Create an anonymous type that represents a bird.
var myBird = new { Color = "Black",  Species = "Raven", FlightSpeed = 50
};
// Display the color and species.
Console.WriteLine ("My bird is a {0} {1}.", myBird.Color,
myBird.Species);
// Next, we use the helper method to create the anonymous type through
arguments.
BuildAnonType ("Raven", "Black", 50);
Console.ReadLine(); }
```

Anonymous functions allow us to quickly come up with a data type that will allow basic encapsulation functionality through properties and value-based syntax. To see this, let's look at an example to see how anonymous types are created during compile time. Remember, anonymous types come from System.Object, so they enable us to call ToString, GetHashCode, GetType, and Equals on the "myBird" object. Let's start by assuming that the application class has defined a static helper function:

```
static void ReflectAnonymousType (object obj)
{
Console.WriteLine("obj is an instance of: {0}", obj.GetType().Name);
```

```
Console.WriteLine ("Base class of {0} is {1}",
obj.GetType().Name, obj.GetType().BaseType);
Console.WriteLine("obj.ToString() == {0}", obj.ToString());
Console.WriteLine("obj.GetHashCode() == {0}", obj.GetHashCode());
Console.WriteLine();
}
```

Now we call on this method from Main by using the "myBird" object as a parameter:

```
static void Main(string[] args)
{
Console.WriteLine("++++ Anonymous Types Meeting++++\n");
// Create the anonymous type that will represent a bird.
var myBird = new {Color = "Black", Species = "Raven", FlightSpeed = 50};
// Reflect over the compiler-generated result.
ReflectAnonymousType (myBird); ...
Console.ReadLine(); }
```

The output should look something like this:

```
++++ Anonymous Types Meeting++++
obj is an instance of: <>f__AnonymousType0`3
Base class of <>f__AnonymousType0`3 is System.Object
obj.ToString() = { Color = Black, Species = Raven, FlightSpeed = 50 }
obj.GetHashCode() = -528093386
```

Notice how our object is listed as type "<>f AnonymousType0`3". The compiler creates the type name, so it cannot be accessed from the C# codebase. But see how there are name/value pairs defined through object initialization that are mapped to a property with an identical name. This is a read-only property that matches the backing field, which is also read-only. Let's analyze the next code block to see how it determines the generated class, representing our "myBird" item.

```
internal sealed class <>f__AnonymousType0<<Color>j__TPar,
<Make>j__TPar, <FlightSpeed>j__TPar>
{
// Here are the read only fields.
private readonly <Color>j__TPar <Color>i__Field;
private readonly <FlightSpeed>j__TPar <FlightSpeed>i__Field;
private readonly <Make>j__TPar <Species>i__Field;
// Constructor.
public <>f__AnonymousType0(<Color>j__TPar Color,
<Make>j__TPar Make, <FlightSpeed>j__TPar FlightSpeed);
// Methods that are overridden.
public override bool Equals (object value);
public override int GetHashCode();
public override string ToString();
// Properties that are read only.
public <Color>j__TPar Color { get; }
public <FlightSpeed>j__TPar FlightSpeed { get; }
public <Species>j__TPar Species { get; }
```

```
}
```

Anonymous comes equipped with overrides for ToString, GetHashCode, and Equals because they come from the System.Object. ToString creates a string from every name/value pair, as shown below:

```
public override string ToString()
{
StringBuilder builder = new StringBuilder();
builder.Append("{ Color = ");
builder.Append(this.<Color>i__Field);
builder.Append(", Species = ");
builder.Append(this.<Species>i__Field);
builder.Append(", FlightSpeed = ");
builder.Append(this.<FlightSpeed>i__Field);
builder.Append(" }");  return builder.ToString();
}
```

Implementation of "GetHashCode" determines a hash value that uses all anonymous types' member variables as the input to the "System.Collections.Generic.EqualityComparer". So, two anonymous types result in the same hash value when defined by the same properties with identical values. Because of this, using a Hashtable container for anonymous types is considered superior.

Pointer Types

We are going to talk about an advanced feature that I rarely used in .NET projects: pointer types. You should know that pointer types require some knowledge of C++. If you don't know any C++, you should take a glance so you have a general idea of what these are. You are also free to skip this section. It should not worry you much because you will rarely encounter cases where pointer manipulation is required, but it's a feature you might want to know about.

In C#, you deal with two types of data: reference types and value types. The third is pointer types. To work with pointer types, you need operators that allow you to avoid memory management of the CLR.

A pointer is a variable that represents a specific location in memory. The following operators are used to create and handle pointer variables:

1. The "*" operator, also referred to as a keyword, in this case, is required to build a pointer variable. It works just like in C++ for pointer indirection.
2. The "&" operator is required to retrieve the address of the variable.
3. The "->" operator is required to gain access to fields of a certain type, which the pointer variable represents.

4. The "[]" operator is needed to index the slot to which the pointer variable points to. If you know C++, you will notice a similarity between this and the interplay between the operator and the variable.
5. The "++" and "--"operators are applied to pointer types to increment or decrement.
6. The "+" and "-" operators work as regular adding and subtracting operators that can be used with pointer types.
7. All comparison and equality operators can also be used with pointer types.
8. The "Stackalloc" keyword is needed to allocate arrays straight to the stack.
9. The "Fixed" keyword is used to fix a variable in order to discover its address.

A quick warning, you are free to explore pointer manipulation, but the .NET runtime will not know what you are doing. So if you are not certain of what you are doing, you are better off not doing it – you might not want those types of consequences.

With that out of the way, let's begin. You might need pointer types when you want to optimize sections of your programs by having direct access to memory outside of CLR. The other scenario is when you want to call a C-focused dll file or a COM service because they require pointers. In this case, you have the option of bypassing pointers and using System.IntPtr.

If you decide to use pointer types, you need to tell the compiler (csc.exe) that you want to use "unsafe code." Here's how you do that:

csc /unsafe *.cs

In Visual Studio, navigate to the build tab inside properties and select "allow unsafe code." Then create a new console app with the setting enabled.]

First, you need to declare your code as unsafe using the "unsafe" keyword. If you don't, it will be considered safe. Here's how:

```
class myApp {
static void Main(string[] args)
{
unsafe
{
// You can play with pointer types inside this block only!
}
        // Pointers have no power in this section!
}
}
```

Inside the method, we can create anything – classes, structures, and parameters, etc. – as long as we make our "unsafe" declaration. Here are some examples below:

```
// Here, we will have an unsafe structure that
// will only work inside an unsafe environment
unsafe struct Node
{  public int Value;  public Node* Left;  public Node* Right; }
// Here we have a safe structure, but the members of Node2 are unsafe.
// However, you can have access to the value from outside of the unsafe
environment,
// except "Left" and "Right".
public struct Node2
{
public int Value;
// You can access these only in an unsafe environment!
public unsafe Node2* Left;
public unsafe Node2* Right;
}
```

Now you can mark the method as "unsafe." Say you have a static method that can benefit from manipulating the pointer. To ensure we can call the method in an unsafe context, we do this:

```
static unsafe void SquareIntPointer (int* myIntPointer)
{
// Perform a test by squaring the value.
*myIntPointer *= *myIntPointer;
}
// This kind of setup requires the caller to call for the
SquareIntPointer.
static void Main(string[] args)
{
unsafe
{
int myInt = 10;
// We are in the unsafe environment.
SquareIntPointer(&myInt);
Console.WriteLine ("myInt: {0}", myInt);
}
int myInt2 = 5;
// Now, you will see a compiler error because we are outside of the
unsafe environment.
SquareIntPointer(&myInt2);
Console.WriteLine ("myInt: {0}", myInt2);
}
```

In cases like these, you don't want the invocation inside an unsafe environment. You have Main updated as unsafe and compile the code.

```
static unsafe void Main (string[] args)
{
int myInt2 = 5;
SquareIntPointer(&myInt2);
Console.WriteLine("myInt: {0}", myInt2);
}
```

```
This is the resulting output:
myInt: 25
```

Summary

In this chapter, we learned the advanced type building methods like indexers and overloaded operators. Then we turned our attention to extension methods and anonymous types. We talked about how they are useful in many situations, but especially when dealing with LINQ-focused API. Anonymous methods are useful for creating shape types at a fast pace, and extension methods add functionality to types without the need for subclasses. In the end, we briefly explored pointer types, although they are rarely used in C#.

CHAPTER 2:

Building Class Libraries

We have mainly built executable applications that contain all their programming logic in a single executable file. We were mostly relying on the base .NET "mscorlib" class library, and nothing else. You can make a wide array of programs with only foundation libraries, but you can begin packaging code in custom libraries so you can reuse it for other applications.

In this chapter, we will look at how to wrap types into a custom library. We will learn how to partition types into namespaces and explore the difference between private and shared assembly. We will also explore the method used by the .NET runtime to determine an assembly's location and learn more about the global assembly cache and several configuration files. Let's start our discussion with custom namespaces.

Defining Custom Namespaces

Before looking at configuration methods of a library, we first need to look at how we package a custom type inside a .NET namespace. So far, you have only worked with small applications that depended on basic namespaces, namely System. When you start building more complex programs, the importance of custom namespaces for your types will become apparent. You should also know that defining a custom namespace is more beneficial than having a ton of dll assemblies because your partners will eventually need a method of referencing the library to use the types you created. It involves importing custom namespaces.

To illustrate the importance of custom namespaces, we will create a new project called "MyCustomNamespaces." Let's pretend we are building a group of animal classes that include

Cat, Dog, and Ferret. Because they have some similarities, we should group them under a single namespace called MyAnimals. The namespace will be of MyCustomNamespaces assembly. We now have two options. Either we have our classes defined in a single file called AnimalsLib.cs, like below:

```
// AnimalsLib.cs using System;
namespace MyAnimals
{
// Cat class public class Cat
{ /* A collection of members... */ }
// Dog class public class Dog
{ /* Another collection of members... */ }
// Ferret class public class Square
{ /* Another collection of members... */ } }
```

Remember that the compiler won't have any issues handling a single code file with all our types, but you will encounter some problems when you try to reuse a class definition to use it in another project. For example, you might need the functionality of the Cat class in a new project. When every single type is defined in one file, you have to work with the whole set. This is the reason to opt for an alternative: dividing the namespaces across code files. All you need to do is ensure that all types are packaged inside the proper logical collection by wrapping them in the same namespace definition. Let's illustrate:

```
// Cat.cs using System;
namespace MyAnimals
{ // Cat class  public class Cat
{ /* A collection of methods... */ }
}
// Dog.cs using System;
namespace MyAnimals
{  // Dog class  public class Dog { /* Another collection of methods...
*/ } }
// Ferret.cs using System;
namespace MyAnimals
{  // Ferret class  public class Ferret
{ /* Another collection of methods... */ }
}
```

With both options, you see the MyAnimals namespace acts as an abstract package containing classes. When we are dealing with a different namespace that needs to access types in a different namespace, we have to apply the "using" keyword.

```
// Example of importing a namespace from the common class libraries.
using System;
// Using the types that are defined inside the MyAnimals namespace.
using MyAnimals;
```

```
namespace MyCustomNamespaces
{
public class Program
{
static void Main (string[] args)
{
Dog d = new Dog();
Cat c = new Cat();
Ferret f = new Ferret();
}
}
}
```

In the example above, we assume the code file defining My Animals namespace is a component of the program holding the file that defines MyCustomNamespaces. What we are really talking about are all the files required for compiling an executable assembly. Just remember that when you define the MyAnimals namespace in an external assembly, you will have to provide the library with a reference before the compilation process takes place. We'll further discuss this topic in sections of this chapter.

Fixing Name Clashes Using Fully Qualified Names

Know that you don't have to always apply the "using" keyword when you refer to a type defined inside an external namespace. You can use the type's entire name, like below:

```
// Keep in mind that we don't have to import the MyAnimals namespace
this time.
using System;
namespace MyCustomNamespaces
{
public class Program
{
static void Main(string[] args)
{
MyShapes.Dog d = new MyAnimals.Dog();
MyShapes.Cat c = new MyAnimals.Cat();
MyShapes.Ferret f = new MyAnimals.Ferret();
}
}
}
```

Usually, you needn't use the entire name because it doesn't improve the code or execution speed. CIL code defines types with the entire qualified name, but C#'s "using" keyword helps you avoid typing it repeatedly. Using a full name has its advantages; it can help you avoid conflicts that arise from multiple namespaces sharing the same names. For instance, if you have another namespace called MyMammals and defines three classes:

```
using System;
namespace MyMammals
{
// Cat class.
public class Cat { }
// Dog class.
public class Dog { }
// Ferret class.
public class Ferret { }
}
```

We are going to update the Program class with the next lines. Notice the compile-time errors that appear because of the two namespaces sharing classes with the same name.

```
using System;
using MyAnimals;
using MyMammals;
namespace MyCustomNamespaces
{
public class Program
{
static void Main(string[] args)
{
// Confusion regarding the namespace we are referencing
Dog d = new Dog();
// We receive a compiler error!
Cat c = new Cat();
// We receive a compiler error!
Ferret f = new Ferret();
// We receive a compiler error!
}
}
}
```

To fix this, we will need to use the full name of the type, like below:

```
// Confusion problem solved.
static void Main(string[] args)
{
MyMammals.Dog
d = new MyMammals.Dog();
MyMammals.Cat
c = new MyMammals.Cat();
MyMammals.Ferret
f = new MyMammals.Ferret();
}
```

Fixing Name Clashes Using Aliases

The “using” keyword can also set up an alias for the type’s full name. Aliases are tokens that stand for the name during compiling time, so it is a valid way of solving name conflicts. Here's an example:

```
using System;
using MyAnimals;
using MyMammals;
// We solve any confusion by creating an alias.
using Dog = MyMammals.Dog;
namespace MyCustomNamespaces
{
class Program
{
static void Main (string[] args)
{
// We are creating a MyMammals.Dog class.
Dog d2 = new Dog(); ...
}
}
}
```

This method allows you to set up aliases for namespaces, too. It is useful when dealing with long namespaces. One example of this is in the base library: the System.Runtime.Serialization. Formatters.Binary, containing the Binary Formatter. Here's how we would set an alias for one:

```
using bfHome = System.Runtime.Serialization.Formatters.Binary;
namespace MyApp
{
class ShapeTester
{
static void Main(string[] args)
{
bfHome.BinaryFormatter b = new bfHome.BinaryFormatter();      ...
}
}
}
```

If you don't know the function of the BinaryFormatter class, it's fine. We were just demonstrating the aliases. Remember that you can utilize the "using" keyword to create aliases for long, difficult to remember type names, and resolve name conflicts. Don't overuse this method, because having too many aliases can confuse you and your colleagues. Colleagues might struggle to figure out what many of those tokens refer to because the field is crowded.

Nested Namespaces

It's possible to set up namespaces inside other namespaces. Interestingly, many base libraries are already doing that, allowing them to provide a well-organized distribution pattern. For example, the IO namespace is defined inside the System. That's why we have System.IO. Now, let's set up a root namespace that will hold "MyMammals" namespace:

```
// How to Nest a namespace.
namespace Tutorial
{
namespace MyMammals
{
public class Cat{ }
         public class Dog{ }
         public class Ferret{ }  } }
```

Root namespaces also offer us the option of having another scope level. So, it doesn't have to define the number of types directly inside its scope. Alternatively, we can define a nested namespace this way:

```
// Namespace nesting 2.0.
namespace Tutorial.MyMammals
{
public class Cat{ }
public class Dog{ }
public class Ferret{ } }
```

The MyMammals namespace is now nested within the Tutorial namespace. Now we need to update our code with the current aliases and directives:

```
using Tutorial.MyMammals;
using Dog = Tutorial.MyMammals.Dog;
```

Notice that when working in Visual Studio, the name of the program's namespace is by default the name of the project. It means you must add future code from the Project > Add New Item menu to automatically insert new types in the default namespace. To rename the namespace, you should click on the Default Namespace option in the Application panel accessible from the Properties tab. Going forward, everything added to your project will be part of the Tutorial root namespace and other namespaces that will use them.

Now, let's discuss the .NET assembly and its benefits.

The Purpose of .NET Assemblies

.NET programs are created by linking several assemblies together. An assembly can be conceived as a binary file hosted within the CLR. Regular binary files like .exe and .dll don't have much in common with older binaries that used the same extensions. So, to understand how it works, we must discuss the benefits of an assembly structure:

1. Code Reusability: While programming in C#, you might have thought your programs are part of the executable assembly, but this isn't so. The programs you have built rely on multiple types found inside the .NET library, or mscorlib.dll and System.Core.dll. The calls library comes as a .dll file containing all the types required for various types of external programs. So whenever we develop an executable assembly, we depend on system libraries and custom libraries to build the application. Note that the class library doesn't have to contain the .dll extension. Assemblies can also use various types from an executable file instead. The .NET framework allows us to reuse any of the types, independent from languages, regardless of how we wrapped a library. For instance, it's possible to build a new library with C# and use it inside another .NET language. We also derive types from those languages. For instance, a base class defined in C# can be extended by a class created with Basic. Interfaces defined in F# can be integrated into any C# structure. When disassembling an executable into a collection of assemblies, we end with code that doesn't depend on a specific language and can be reused in multiple ways.
2. Versionable Units: Assemblies are considered versionable units, meaning they are assigned version numbers that consist of four sections: <major>.<minor>.<build>.<revision>.
   Your assembly will be set to version 1.0.0.0.0 if you don't specify a version. Why does this matter? It means we can use a version number with a public key value to allow different versions of the same assembly to work together on the machine.
3. Type Boundary: The full name of a type is constructed from the prefix of the namespaces added to its own name. The assembly also provides information on the identity type. Imagine we have two assemblies, MyBirds, and YourBirds, both defined in the same namespace: BirdLibrary, which contain the Raven class. In .NET, these are unique types.
4. Self-Describing: Assemblies are considered self-describing because they record all external assemblies they require access to to fulfill their purpose. It means if an assembly needs access to the System.Windows.Forms and System.Core libraries, the dependency will be listed in the assembly's manifest. The manifest is what is called a collection of metadata containing descriptive information like name, version, etc. Also, we have metadata that contains information on the contents of the assembly, like interfaces, classes, constructors, and members of every single type. Assembles are so well-documented that CLR doesn't need to check in the system registry to find the location of external libraries.
5. Assemblies can be configured: Assemblies can be set to private and shared. Private assemblies are found within the same directory as the application that relies on them. On the other hand, shared assemblies are used by multiple programs residing on the same in the same system. They need to be part of the global assembly cache directory. As always,

you can edit and write configuration files; it does not matter how they were deployed. This way, you can tell the CLR to search specific locations for assemblies or load a specific version.

Summary

In this chapter, we learned about .NET class libraries, defining custom namespaces, and nesting namespaces. We talked about how to resolve conflicts that arise from working with multiple namespaces. The more you learn, the more you will be able to configure every detail of your application to maintain it as easily as possible. In the next chapter, we discuss reflection and late binding.

CHAPTER 3:

Type Reflection and Late Binding

Think of assemblies as a basic component for deployment regarding anything .NET. We can explore types inside an application assembly reference using Visual Studio's object browser and similar tools. There are external programs like "ildasm.exe," which allow us to examine metadata, CIL code, and assembly manifest. The alternative is the extraction of the data through the System.Reflection namespace.

This chapter will explore the concept of reflection and the significance of metadata. We will also look at some topics related to reflection. For example, we'll see how the .NET client uses late binding to activate types unknown to it from the compile-time perspective.

Type Metadata

Metadata is important because it describes our types by giving us information about all classes, structures, enumerations, interfaces, and delegates. Many tools that belong to .NET can take advantage of that information. An example is the Windows Communication Foundation, which needs to know the type format at runtime. There are also several compiler tools and IntelliSense. All of them need to know type descriptions.

We examine a type's metadata date with ildasm.exe by using the keyboard shortcut Ctrl + M and opening one of the assemblies you have built. See what happens.

Notice how much information, or content, is in the metadata. It is not something you put in a book. It is a lot. The information about a simple assembly we made can contain multiple pages.

All defined types are described in the document using the "TypeDef #n" token. If a type is defined in another assembly, it is documented as a referenced type with the "TypeRef #n" token. The second example involves a kind of pointer aiming towards the type's whole metadata description inside the external assembly. This means we can summarize metadata as a tabular collection of information describing all type definitions and reference types.

Let's take a look at some of the metadata if you didn't try ildasm.exe yourself:

```
TypeDef #2 (02000003)
TypDefName: CarLibrary.EngineState (02000003)
Flags: [Public] [AutoLayout] [Class] [Sealed] [AnsiClass] (00000101)
Extends: 01000001 [TypeRef] System.Enum
Field #1 (04000006)
Field Name: value__ (04000006)
Flags: [Public] [SpecialName] [RTSpecialName] (00000606)
CallCnvntn: [FIELD]
Field type: I4
Field #2 (04000007)
Field Name: engineAlive (04000007)
Flags: [Public] [Static] [Literal] [HasDefault] (00008056)
DefltValue: (I4) 0
CallCnvntn: [FIELD]
Field type: ValueClass CarLibrary.EngineState
...
```

In the example above, the TypDefName expression determines the name of the type, which is CarLIbrary.EngineState. The "Extends" line describes the base type of all .NET types. It also documents a referenced type called System.Enum. What we did here was display CarLibrary.EngineState.engineAlive's metadata.

Reflection

Reflection involves a runtime type discovery; we can use it to get information obtained in the earlier section using the ildasm.exe tool. For example, we can retrieve the list of all types in an assembly. The list would include everything that is defined by the type, like methods, properties, and fields. We can also gain information about interfaces with specific kinds of supports and the details related to their methods, such as namespaces and classes. Let's use System.Reflection as an example. Below are the items you need to know about:

1. Assembly: It's an abstraction class that contains a collection of members that allow us to load, observe, and manipulate the assembly.
2. AssemblyName: It's the class that lets us learn information pertaining to the assembly's identity, as the version of the assembly.
3. EventInfo: Contains details about specific events.

4. FieldInfo: Contains information about specific fields.
5. MethodInfo: Contains details about specific methods.
6. ParameterInfo: Contains details about certain parameters.
7. PropertyInfo: Provides information about properties.
8. MemberInfo: It determines the behavior of the EventInfo, FieldInfo, MemberInfo, and PropertyInfo classes.
9. Module: This allows us access to a specific module in an assembly made out of many files.

To learn how the namespace is used to read Metadata, we will explore the System.Type class.

The System.Type is used to find the number of members we have access to so we can explore the metadata. The majority of members return types from the reflection namespace. An example of this is Type.GetMethods, which returns an array of MethodInfo items. The list of members like this is very long. You can read the .NET SDK documentation to learn about them.

Getting an instance of type class can be achieved in multiple ways. Remember that you can't build a type object using the "new" keyword because this is an abstract class. Our first option is the System.Object, which defines the GetType method. The method will return an instance of the class with metadata.

```
// We will use a WildBird instance to access the type information.
WildBird wb = new WildBird();
Type t = sc.GetType();
```

Know that this method will only work when you have information about the compile time of the type you are to reflect over. In this case, that type is WildBird. You must also have an instance of it in memory.

This is restrictive. You can now appreciate why a utility like ildasm.exe doesn't retrieve data through a direct call to GetType. By default, these tools aren't compiled in custom created assemblies.

Another option we can use to get this data is the "typeof" operator, as shown below:

```
// Using typeof.
Type t = typeof (WildBird);
```

The operator doesn't need you to build an instance of the object you are trying to get information about. Your codebase need only have compiler time information. Typeof requires a strongly typed name, so remember that.

The more flexible way of getting information is making a call for GetType, a part of System.Type. In this case, the full name of the type you want to access is required. Unlike with the other two options, we won't need compile-time knowledge because Type.GetType gets an instance of System.String. The method will be overloaded so we can set Booleans. One of the parameters will manipulate how the exception is thrown when the type is not found. The second ensures we set the case sensitivity of the string. Let's look at an example:

```
// Acquiring the type info with the static Type.GetType() method.
// Make sure not to throw an exception when WildBird is not found,
ignore case.
Type t = Type.GetType ("AnimalLibrary.WildBird", false, true);
```

In the earlier example, the string passed through GetType doesn't acknowledge the assembly containing the types. In this example, we assume the type set inside the assembly that is being performed on. This means it is easy to access metadata from the external private assembly when we need it.

Fortunately, we can get it by formatting the string parameter with the type's full name, followed by the name of the host assembly. Here's how it looks:

```
// Acquiring type information for a type found inside an external
assembly.
Type t = Type.GetType ("AnimalLibrary.WildBird, AnimalLibrary");
```

We can also add the plus symbol to indicate a nested type. For example, imagine we want to get type information from an enumeration nested inside any class. Here's how you'd do that:

```
Type t = Type.GetType ("AnimalLibrary.WildBirds+Species");
```

You should now have enough knowledge about retrieving metadata during runtime by using core members from the System.Reflection namespace. Reflection services form the basis of some programming concepts like late binding.

Late Binding

Late binding allows us to set up an instance of a specific type and call any of its members during runtime. You don't need to have compile-time knowledge of the existence of the instance. It means a program that binds late to any type belonging to an external assembly doesn't need to reference that assembly.

Programmers often ignore late binding because it takes some effort to uncover the advantage of applying to an object. Binding early to an object is recommended. For example, it is preferable to add a reference to the assembly and designate the type with the "new" keyword. Early binding allows you to discover errors during compile time instead of runtime. But, later binding still has an important role to play if you are creating a program you plan to extend. Before we go any further, let's discuss the activator class.

The Activator Class

Late binding relies on the System.Activator class, which is part of the base library. For now, we are only interested in the CreateInstance method because it enables us to set an instance of a type in a way that allows late binding. Know that the method allows for great flexibility because it's been overloaded several times. In principle, the simplest form of a CreateInstance member accepts a type object containing information of the item you want to assign to memory.

To illustrate, we will create a LateBindApp and import two namespaces: System.IO and System.Reflection. Here's the program class below:

// We are going to set up an object with late binding and load an external library.

```
public class Program
{
static void Main (string[] args)
{
Console.WriteLine ("++++ Late Binding is Soul Binding ++++");
// Try to load a local copy of AnimalLibrary.
Assembly a = null;
try
{
a = Assembly.Load ("AnimalLibrary");
}
Catch (FileNotFoundException ex)
{
Console.WriteLine (ex.Message);
return;
}
if(a != null)
CreateUsingLateBinding(a);
        Console.ReadLine();
}
static void CreateUsingLateBinding (Assembly asm)
{
try
{
// Acquire the metadata for the Raven type.
Type raven = asm.GetType("AnimalLibrary.Raven");
        // Setup a quick Raven instance.
object obj = Activator.CreateInstance(raven);
Console.WriteLine("Created a {0} using late binding!", obj);
}
catch(Exception ex)
{
```

```
Console.WriteLine(ex.Message);
}
}
}
```

We can't execute the program now. First, we need to copy AnimalLivrary.dll – or whichever you created – and put it inside the application's bin\debug folder. We do this because we are calling the Assembly.Load method, which means CLR will perform a sweep inside the folder. Alternatively, we could use the LoadFrom instead of Load to set a path.

Note how the CreateInstance method returns an object instead of a strongly typed Raven, meaning when the dot operator is applied on an obj variable, you won't see the members belonging to the Raven class. How do you fix this? Did you consider an explicit cast? Let's see:

```
// Gaining access to Raven's members with a cast
object obj = (Raven)Activator.CreateInstance(raven);
// Did it work? No. We now have a compile error.
```

Notice how the application does not have a reference to the AnimalLibrary.dll. This means the "using" keyword can't be used to import the AnimalLibrary namespace, which means we can't use explicit casts. We can conclude that the purpose of late binding is to set an instance of an object without compile-time knowledge. You are asking yourself how to call methods of the Raven object inside the System.Object reference. The answer is reflection.

Invoking Methods

Imagine our Raven has a "Flight" method and that sets the state of wings to "immobile" while displaying a message. To extract the MethodInfo of the method, we have to use type method "GetMethod." Once we have the info item, we can call the flight method with "Invoke." The requirement of MethodInfo.Invoke is to transmit parameters needed to the method characterized by MethodInfo. Remember that parameters are described by an array of types from System.Object. The Flight method doesn't require any parameters, so we only need to pass a null value. Now, let's take a look below:

```
static void BuildWithLateBinding(Assembly asm)
{
try
{
// Obtain the metadata for our Raven type.
Type raven = asm.GetType("AnimalLibrary.Raven");
         // Set up the Raven.
object obj = Activator.CreateInstance (raven);
Console.WriteLine("Created a {0} with late binding!", obj);
// Acquire information for Flight.
```

```
MethodInfo mi = raven.GetMethod("Flight");
         // Call method without any parameters.
mi.Invoke(obj, null);
}
catch(Exception ex)
{
Console.WriteLine(ex.Message);
}
}
```

You'll see how the message appears after the Flight method is called. Whenever you are working with late binding to invoke a method that doesn't require parameters, you need to group arguments in an array of items. With that said, here's the AnimalLibrary method defined within the Animal class:

```
public void EnableFlight (bool flightOn, WingsFlapping wf)
{
public void EnableFlight (bool flightOn, WingsFlapping wf)
=> MessageBox.Show (flightOn ? $"Flapping hard{wf}" : "Calmly..."); }
```

Here we have a method with two parameters, a Boolean, which decides whether the bird flies or not, and an enum, which decides the type of flying.

Let's see another method belonging to the Program class that calls EnableFlight. See how we are using values from the enumeration to mention the flight type "fast."

```
static void InvokeMethodWithArgsWithLateBinding (Assembly asm)
{  try
{
// The first step is to acquire the description of the crow's metadata.
Type corvid = asm.GetType("AnimalLibrary.Crow");
         // Next, we need to setup the crow.
object obj = Activator.CreateInstance(corvid);
// Invoke EnableFlight() with arguments.
MethodInfo mi = corvid.GetMethod("EnableFlight");
mi.Invoke(obj, new object[] { true, 2 });
}
catch (Exception ex)
{
 Console.WriteLine(ex.Message);
}
}
```

You should now be able to see the connection between reflection, late binding, and dynamic loading. There is also the reflection API, which we didn't discuss. You will be able to look at it on your own now.

Summary

Reflection is an interesting feature, especially in a solid object-orientated build. In this chapter, we saw how the concept revolves around Type class and the reflection namespace. It involves researching and probing during runtime to answer questions like who, what, where, and why about an object. Late binding involves setting up a variation of a certain type and calling members without knowledge of their names. The concept is related to dynamic loading, which enables you to load an assembly to memory.

Let's move on to concepts that revolve around attributes.

CHAPTER 4:

Attribute-Based Programming

One of the purposes of the .NET compiler is creating metadata for every type, defined or referenced. Moreover, .NET gives programmers a method of embedding custom metadata in the assembly. This is done with attributes. Attributes are a series of annotations used on a specific type – a class, interface, member, method, property, or an assembly.

Attributes are class types that broaden the System.Attribute class. Once you are comfortable with more namespaces, you'll see a large number of attributes you can implement in your projects. You can also develop custom attributes if you want. These will enable you to have full control over your types. You will also be able to build new types from attributes. Let's look at the attributes found in the base class library. Keep in mind we will not list all of them. We will focus on the most popular.

1. CLSCompliant: This attribute forces the annotated object to follow the rules of the common language specification. Note that CLS-abiding type can be used with any .NET programming language.
2. DllImport: This attribute allows your code to call on libraries based on C and C++. This includes the operating system API. However, this attribute is avoided when dealing with COM-related applications.
3. Obsolete: This attribute identifies no longer used elements. Trying to use one of the objects will give you a compiler warning.
4. Serializable: This attribute marks a class with a serializable tag, meaning it will be converted into a stream of bytes to be transmitted to a file or memory.

Know that when an attribute is used inside code, any enclosed metadata will become worthless until another component reflects over the data. Otherwise, embedded metadata is ignored and does not affect anything in the assembly

Attribute Consumers

The .NET framework comes with tools and utilities that heed attributes. For example, one of the many things the compiler does is to look for attributes. This occurs during the compilation process. Let's say the compiler comes across the CLSCompliant attribute. It will verify whether the attributed item displays constructs that are CLS compliant. If we have an object with the Obsolete attribute, the compiler displays the warning. But not all development utilities have the feature preprogrammed.

Methods belonging to the base class libraries are prepared to reflect the number of attributes. For example, when you want the state of an object to carry on to the file, you annotate the class as with the Serializable attribute. The file persists to the file in binary format when the Serialize method detects the attribute. Know that when you develop a program, you can give it the ability to reflect over custom attributes defined by you and those already available. You are able to build a collection of custom keywords that can be read by assemblies.

Attributes in Action

To visualize how attributes are implemented, we are going to develop a small application. We will call it AttributesInAction. We will work on a class called Warrior, which can endure in a binary format. We have to use the Serializable attribute. Know that we can also use the NonSerialized attribute to avoid having a persist field. Here's the code:

```
// We can save the class we are creating to a file.
[Serializable] public class Warrior
{
// The next field will not be serialized.
[NonSerialized]  float strengthOfWarrior;
// The next fields will remain serializable.
bool hasSword;
bool hasDagger;
bool hasArmor;
}
```

For now, we don't have to know how object serialization works. What we are interested in is showing how and when an attribute is used. Look at how attributes have to be declared inside brackets. If you are using the ildas.exe, you will be able to read additional metadata during the compilation process. See how the attributes are registered with the serializable symbol (a red triangle) and the nonserialized symbol attached to the strenghtofWarrior field.

One object can have multiple attributes. Imagine we have a legacy class called HorseCarriage labeled serializable, but it is also an obsolete item. There'd be no need to remove the definition of this class. When you delete things from the codebase, you run the risk of damaging your projects. The wiser thing would be to mark it as with the Obsolete attribute instead. Here's how we would do that:

```
[Serializable, Obsolete ("Upgrade your method of transportation!")]
public class HorseCarriage {  // ... }
You can do the same thing by placing attributes separately in their own
brackets:
 [Serializable]
[Obsolete ("Upgrade your method of transportation!")]
public class HorseCarriage {  // ... }
```

The class name of this attribute is ObsoleteAttribute, not Obsolete. In .NET naming conventions, all attributes are by default attached to the Attribute keyword. Because of this, you don't have to type it every time you use it – C# can tell what you are doing. If you think it would make your code more readable, you can use this naming system. Here's how that would look:

```
[SerializableAttribute]
[ObsoleteAttribute ("Upgrade your method of transportation!")]
public class HorseCarriage {  // ... }
```

If you are going to work with other .NET languages, consider sticking to the naming conventions with the Attribute suffix. Not all languages are as observant as C#.

Constructor Parameters

Obsolete attributes can accept constructor parameters. Right-click on the object in your code editor and look at the definition of the attribute. Select "Go to definition." You will find the attribute will take System.String.

```
public sealed class ObsoleteAttribute : Attribute
{
public ObsoleteAttribute (string message, bool error);
public ObsoleteAttribute(string message);
public ObsoleteAttribute();
public bool IsError { get; }
public string Message { get; }
}
```

Remember that when you use constructor parameters on an attribute, they should first be reflected on by an external utility so the attribute can be allocated memory. The string information will be stored as metadata in the assembly. Now we have our obsolete class, and we can allocate a variation like this:

```
static void Main(string[] args)
{
HorseCarriage horse = new HorseCarriage();
}
```

You can see how the string data is retrieved and displayed in the error list panel and on the problematic code line when you hover your cursor over the obsolete type.

We can conclude a few things:

1. Attributes are classes that are part of System.Attribute.
2. They can't do anything until an object or tool reflects on them.
3. They create embedded metadata.
4. They are applied using square brackets.

We have looked at predefined attributes. Let's see how we can customize attributes and apply them.

Creating and Applying Custom Attributes

To create an attribute, we must first define a class that derives from System.Attribute. We will illustrate the points of this section by sticking to our animal themes examples and building a new library project called AttributedAnimalLibrary. We are going to have a new assembly whose purpose is defining the number of animals. Each one will be described with a custom attribute:

```
public sealed class AnimalDescriptionAttribute : System.Attribute
{
public string Description { get; set; }
public AnimalDescriptionAttribute (string animalDescription) =>
Description = animalDescription;
public AnimalDescriptionAttribute(){ }
}
```

In the example, the AnimalDescriptionAttribute holds on to a section of string data handled through Description, an automatic property. This class derives from the System.Attribute; there's nothing special about the definition. But because of potential security risks, it is advised to create all custom attributes as sealed.

Now we annotate our types how we want. Let's add a number of class definitions to the library we just made:

```
// We need to use a named property in order to assign the description.
[Serializable] [AnimalDescription(Description = "My tired old horse")]
public class Horse { }
[Serializable] [Obsolete ("Get a car!")]
[VehicleDescription("My stallion is too old for this… ")]
public class Volvo { }
[VehicleDescription("A brand new car packed with new features")]
public class Dodge { }
```

The description of the horse has an attribute-based element added, which is named property.

The Description property is used as the constructor of the Vehicle Description attribute, where the string data is prepared. The values are communicated to the Description property when external aspects reflect on the attribute. Then again, we have two types that don't use the property, namely Volvo and Dodge. They are passing string data through the constructor alone. Regardless, when we compile AttibutedAnimalLibrary, we can access the metadata of any types using the ildasm.exe tool. This will show the embedded description of all classes.

Attributes at the Assembly Level

Attributes can be applied to any type belonging to the assembly with the "[assembly:] tag. Say we need to guarantee all members belonging to a public type are defined in the assembly and CLS compliant. Remember, assemblies that are CLS compliant will work on every .NET programming language. It means if you have a few public members that aren't CLS compliant, other .NET-related languages will not be able to rely on them. An example of these are pointer parameters and unsigned data. In a situation like this, you need to ensure that the libraries you create are usable by other languages by verifying their CLS compliance.

To check for compliance, you need a specific assembly-level attribute at the start of your code. Assembly level attributes need to be filed outside the range of the namespace. Below is the pattern you need to follow:

```
// First we need to create our small list of "using" List "using"
declarations.
using System;
using System.Collections.Generic;
using System.Linq;
using System.Text;
// The next step is to declare the assembly level attributes.
// Take note that CLS compliance has to be imposed
// for every single public type that is found in this assembly.
[assembly: CLSCompliant(true)]
// Next, we need the types and namespace.
namespace AttributedAnimalLibrary {  // Types... }
```

Keep in mind that if you start writing some code that is not CLS compliant, you will see a compiler warning.

```
// CLS isn't happy with Ulong types.
public class Volvo {  public ulong notCompliant; }
// Compiler warning.
```

When you navigate to Visual Studio's Solution Explorer and expand the properties tab, you'll see all projects contain a file named AssemblyInfo.cs. You can use it to put all attributes you want at an assembly level in it. Note that the manifest holds the metadata which comes from the following attributes:

1. AssemblyCompany: This attribute contains all information about the company.
2. AssemblyCopyright: This attribute provides copyright info for a specific project.
3. AssemblyCulture: This attribute holds information about languages that are supported by the assembly.
4. AssemblyDescription: This attribute describes the product.
5. AssemblyVersion: This attribute gives you the version of the assembly. The versioning format is as follows: <major.minor.build.revision>.

There are many more attributes out there. To find out more about them, read the documentation.

Reflecting on Attributes with Early Binding

There isn't much use for an attribute if no other component is reflecting its values. Only when an attribute is known can the software component exploit it or manipulate it. Nevertheless, the software element can usually find the attribute through techniques discussed earlier: late binding and early binding. It means you can use early binding, as long as the application has access to the attribute's compile-time definition. The AttributedAnimalLibrary assembly contains a definition of a custom attribute. This is because the attribute is defined similarly to a public class. The best way is to use early binding.

With that said, let's set up a new protect called AnimalDescriptionAttributeReader and refer to the AttributedAnimalLibrary. We will begin by adding the following code to the original .cs file:

```
// Early binding is used to reflect over the attributes.
using System;
using System.Collections.Generic;
using System.Linq;
using System.Text;
using AttributedAnimalLibrary;
namespace AnimalDescriptionAttributeReader
{
class Program
```

```
{
static void Main(string[] args)
{
Console.WriteLine ("*****AnimalDescriptionAttribute Value*****\n");
ReflectOnAttributesUsingEarlyBinding();
Console.ReadLine();
}
private static void ReflectOnAttributesUsingEarlyBinding()
{
// We need to obtain a type which represents the horse.
Type t = typeof(Horse);
        // Fetch all horse attributes.
object[] customAtts = t.GetCustomAttributes(false);
        // Print the description.
foreach (AnimalDescriptionAttribute v in customAtts)
Console.WriteLine("-> {0}\n", v.Description);
}
}
}
```

What's notable is the Type.GetCustomAttributes method, which retrieves an item array that will contain every attribute applied to a member. The member is represented by a type. In this case, it is a Boolean parameter that determines the extension of the search. When the attribute list is retrieved, we iterate over the class and print the value from the description property.

Reflecting on Attributes with Late Binding

In earlier sections, we talked about using early binding to print the Horse's description data. We were able to do this because the AnimalDescriptionAttribute class is defined as a public member in the Attribute Animal Library. But, we can achieve more by introducing late binding and dynamic loading to reflect on attributes. To illustrate this, we will create a project called AnimalDescriptionAttributeExploreLB. For this project, we need to copy the AttributedAnimalLibrary file and paste it into the \bin\debug folder. Let's turn our attention to the code:

```
using System;
using System.Collections.Generic;
using System.Linq;
using System.Text;
using System.Reflection;
namespace AnimalDescriptionAttributeExplorerLB
{
class Program
{
static void Main(string[] args)
{
Console.WriteLine("*****AnimalDescriptionAttribute Value*****\n");
```

```
ReflectAttributesUsingLateBinding();
Console.ReadLine();
}
        private static void ReflectAttributesUsingLateBinding()
{
try
{
// We need to load a copy of AttributedAnimalLibrary.
Assembly asm = Assembly.Load("AttributedAnimalLibrary");
                                        // Retrieve the type info from
AnimalDescriptionAttribute.
Type animalDesc =
asm.GetType("AttributedAnimalLibrary.AnimalDescriptionAttribute");
// Retrieve the type info from the Description property.
PropertyInfo propDesc = animalDesc.GetProperty("Description");
                                        // Retrieve the types from the
assembly.
Type[] types = asm.GetTypes();
// In order to extract the AnimalDescriptionAttributes
// we need to iterate over every single type.
foreach (Type t in types)
{
object[] objs = t.GetCustomAttributes(animalDesc, false);
// Iterate all AnimalDescriptionAttribute and
// print the description with late binding.
 foreach (object o in objs)
{
Console.WriteLine("-> {0}: {1}\n",
t.Name, propDesc.GetValue(o, null));
}
}
}
catch (Exception ex)
{ Console.WriteLine(ex.Message); }}}}
```

Everything in this code is easy to understand if you have been following along. The code is self-explanatory, so go over it a couple of times if you are a bit confused. The only thing different is the GetValue method used to activate a property's accessor.

Reflection, Late Binding and Custom Attributes

Thus far, we have explored these concepts and techniques over numerous examples, but you might be wondering about scenarios they should be implemented in. It's perfectly normal to wonder because we have been exploring aspects of programming that are quite academic. To better understand how these can help in real-world projects, you need to go over the theory. Let's say you are a programmer who is part of a big team, and you are making a new program that needs to satisfy the following conditions.

The program has to be extendable with other external tools. Think about what that means. Think about the IDE we are using: Visual Studio. When it was first created, “doors” were left open in the code to allow third-party software developers to add modules of their own. In this case, developers of this IDE couldn’t define a reference to the external assembly that was not created yet. How did they solve these issues? Let’s see:

1. The first thing to remember is that any extendable program has to offer an input system that enables the user to indicate which modules need to be attached. This part demands dynamic loading.
2. All extendable programs have to establish the module’s ability to support the functionality we need. For example, when we have interfaces that need to be connected to the environment. This step needs reflection.
3. The last thing we need is late binding. An extendable program has to extract the references to a specified infrastructure, like a collection of interface types, and call the members to set off their fundamental functionality.

We can say that an extendable program prepared to query for certain interfaces can tell if the type can be activated during runtime. At its core, it’s a check. Once the verification is passed, the particular type will support extra interfaces that add to its basic functionality.

Summary

In this chapter, we mainly looked at attributes and the purpose of attribute-based programming. We looked at predefined attributes and how to create and apply custom attributes. We looked at ways that early and late binding applies in this context. Just remember that when you use attributes, you improve the fundamental functionality and assembly metadata.

CHAPTER 5:

CIL and Dynamic Assemblies

When developing a .NET program, you will most likely use C# for most programming. After all, it's the reason you're reading this, and working with C# is easy and efficient. If you remember your early lessons, you'll know that the compiler's role is to convert .cs files containing code to a collection of CIL code, metadata, and assembly manifests. Interestingly, CIL is a full-fledged functional programming language that has its own syntax and compiler.

In this chapter, we will learn about CIL, which can be considered .NET's native language. We'll learn the difference between a CIL directive, attribute, or opcode. We'll also explore round trip engineering of an assembly and other CIL-focused utilities. You'll gain the fundamentals of declaring and defining types, namespaces, and members in CIL.

Few programmers learn CIL because it's not used often, so let's explore why we should.

Why Bother with CIL?

As mentioned, CIL is .NET's native language. Whenever you create an assembly using visual basic, F# or C#, the compiler translates it to CIL. Like any language, CIL has its own syntax and tokens because it is a complete programming language. So, you can create an assembly with CIL and compile it with ilasm.exe, CIL's compiler.

Despite its unpopularity, CIL has a great deal to offer. The more knowledge you learn about CIL, the easier you'll progress in advanced programming. Here's a few examples of what you will gain from learning CIL:

1. You will be able to deconstruct a fully-featured assembly, edit its code, and recompile the new version into a custom .NET binary. This is useful when you need to change CIL, so it interoperates with various COM functionalities.
2. Knowledge of CIL will help you create dynamic assemblies through the System.Reflection.Emit namespace. This namespace is an API that allows you to create an in-memory assembly, which can be persisted to disk. If you plan to use your C# skills to developing tools, this will be useful because you'll be able to generate assemblies quickly.
3. You will gain a proper understanding of CTS, especially various functions that can only be found at CIL's level. Note that CIL is the only .NET-related programming language that enables you to control every feature and functionality of CTS. For example, you can define global members and fields through CIL. Remember that this isn't allowed in C#.

If you're still unsure about learning CIL, that's fine. You don't have to learn if all you want is to master C# and .NET base libraries. However, CIL does offer a deeper understanding of programming, and you may find that interesting. You can compare CIL to a C programmer's knowledge of assembly language. The advantage is that programmers with a deeper understanding can come up with advanced, original solutions they wouldn't otherwise come up with. For a chance at becoming a programming guru, you should give CIL a go.

The purpose of this chapter is to teach you the more advanced principles of CIL. We will not explore the syntax from scratch. If this chapter sparks your interest in the language, check out this link and download the official documentation: https://www.ecma-international.org/publications/standards/Ecma-335.htm

CIL Directives, Attributes and Opcodes

When exploring low-level languages like CIL, you'll find strange terms and concepts that seem extremely complicated, even when they are familiar ideas. To illustrate, look at this collection:

{ new, private, public, get, enum, operator, this, unsafe}

As soon as you see them, you know they are C# keywords. But, if you dig a little deeper, you'll notice they have different meanings. For example, enum defines a System.Enum derived type. The "this" keyword references the current object. Unsafe determines whether the CLR can directly observe a code block. The operator enables you to create a hidden method that is only called when you use a specific operator, like the minus symbol. CIL doesn't just define the keywords. The symbols the compiler understands are split into categories, which are in turn categorized based on their meaning. These categories are CIL directives, attributes, and opcodes

– also known as operation codes. All of these categories are depicted through syntax and tokens. Now, let's see the roles each category plays:

1. CIL Directives: CIL tokens that describe an assembly architecture are called directives. Their purpose is to notify the compiler how types, members, and namespaces should be defined in an assembly. Directives are identifiable by how they are separated with a dot prefix, like this: .namespace, .method, and so on. When the compiler is faced with a CIL file with a single namespace directive and two class directives, it will create an assembly that defines one namespace holding two class types.
2. CIL Attributes: Often, CIL directives don't provide sufficient descriptive data to explain a type or member's definitions. Because of this, we can specify many directives using CIL attributes to determine how they should all be processed. For instance, we can add a public attribute to the class directive, together with the extends attribute and implements attribute. The public attribute will determine the visibility type, while the extends attribute describes the base class, and the implements attribute lists interfaces that the type supports. CIL attributes should not be confused with .NET attributes because they are not the same, even conceptually.
3. CIL Opcodes: After defining the namespace and types with CIL directives and attributes, we must add the final piece of the puzzle: logic of the implementation. This is why we have operation codes. Similar to other low-level programming languages, opcodes are difficult to understand linguistically. It means when you are loading a string variable, you will use an operation code called LoadString, but in CIL, it would be ldstr instead. While readability and pronunciation can be a problem, operation codes are only used within the implementation scope.

As mentioned, operation codes like ldstr are necessary for implementing members of a certain type. But, these tokens are essentially CIL mnemonics that stand for binary operation codes. So, let's say we have a C# method written line this:

```
static int Add (int x, int y)
{
return x + y;
}
```

The operation code for the sum of two numbers is oX58. Subtract the two values with the 0X59 opcode. The compiler processes the CIL code in blocks of binary information. It might sound complicated, but all binary operation codes can be written with a mnemonic instead. For instance, in the case of a sum operation, we can use the "add" mnemonic instead of 0X58 to add numbers. Now that you see the difference between binary and mnemonic, you should know that a CIL decompiler automatically converts the binary codes into corresponding mnemonics. The following example is the CIL representation of our Add method:

```
.method private hidebysig static int32 Add(int32 x,  int32 y) cil
managed
{
.maxstack 2
.locals init ([0] int32 CS$1$0000)
IL_0000: nop
IL_0001: ldarg.0
IL_0002: ldarg.1
IL_0003: add
IL_0004: stloc.0
IL_0005: br.s
IL_0007
IL_0007: ldloc.0
IL_0008: ret
}
```

As you can see, it's hard to understand. When creating a program with CIL, you won't have to work with binary operation codes. When CIL programmers talk about using CIL codes, they are referring to mnemonics.

Languages like C# hide all of this low-level nonsense. What's interesting about .NET development is that CIL is a stack-based language. This is hidden, and many people don't realize it. For instance, say we have a Stack <T> class, which forces a value on a stack and takes the top value from the stack to use it. CIL users don't use this type of object to load or unload values. However, the concept itself remains.

There's a component maintaining the values we want to examine. It's called a virtual execution stack. CIL offers several operation codes with the ability to force a value to the top of the stack; this is what is referred to as loading. There are also operation codes that transfer the top stack value to the memory with an action called storing. CIL makes gaining direct access to any points of data possible. This includes type data, method arguments, local variables, and more. But you'll need to load the item to the stack and snatch it for use. Remember, it cannot be executed directly because CIL is a low-level language. Rather it is compiled, and during the process, redundancies are removed. There's an option to enable optimization for your CIL project. Just navigate to the build window in the properties tab. Once the code is optimized, the compiler will remove redundancies.

To better understand how CIL deals with the stack processing mode, imagine a simple C# method that doesn't require any arguments and returns void, like the PrintMessage method. To implement the method, all you need to do is print the value of a string variable to the output stream. Here's how this looks:

```
public void PrintMessage()
{  string myMessage = "Hello World.";  Console.WriteLine (myMessage); }
```

When you see how this method is translated from the C# compiler to CIL, you'll see that the method will define a storage compartment for a variable that relies on the .locals directive. By having the ldstr and stloc.o CIL operation codes, the string is loaded and stored inside the variable. As you know, the first one stands for load string. The second one translates to loading the local argument at index zero. The value from this index is loaded to memory with the ldloc.o operation code, and then the function is returned through the "ret" operation code.

Now that you understand CIL directives, operation codes, and attributes, let's explore CIL programming with real-world applications.

Round Trip Engineering

We already know that "ildasm.exe" utility is used to check the generated CIL code, but you should know it also dumps the loaded CIL from the loaded assembly to an external file. When you have the CIL code, you can edit it and recompile – this is an extremely useful thing. It is called round trip engineering, and it is useful in the following situations:

1. You lost the source code of an assembly, yet you still need to modify it.
2. You are faced with a bad compile that has translated faulty CIL, but you need to edit the codebase.
3. You are building a library for COM interoperability, and you need to take various COM IDL attributes into account, but they vanished during translation.

To illustrate, we will create a new file called HelloApp.cs with any text editor (Notepad is fine) and then declare a class type. If you prefer, set up a console application in Visual Studio. If you do, you must remove the AssemblyInfo file because it will generate CIL code we don't need. Let's have a look at the program:

```
// A basic C# console app.
using System;
// The class will not be wrapped inside a namespace.
// This will lead to a simpler block of CIL code.
class Program {  static void Main(string[] args)
{
Console.WriteLine ("Hello CILly!");
Console.ReadLine();
}
}
```

Save the file in a preferred directory. Then compile the application with the following line:

```
csc HelloApp.cs
```

Using ildasm utility, run the file. Navigate to File and then Dump menu to save the CIL code to a separate file that'll have the .il extension. Save the file in the place where you compiled it. Leave all settings at default values. Furthermore, the ildasm utility will create a .res file when the assembly data is dumped. It is a resource file that you can either delete or ignore – we have no use for it. It contains CLR security data and is irrelevant for our purposes.

Now, we can observe the CIL file with any text editor. Here's how it should look

```
// Here we have the referenced assemblies.
.assembly extern mscorlib
{
.publickeytoken = (B7 7A 5C 56 19 34 E0 89 )
.ver 4:0:0:0
}
// Here we have our own assembly.
.assembly HelloApp
{
/**** TargetFrameworkAttribute data removed for clarity! ****/
.hash algorithm 0x00008004
.ver 0:0:0:0
}
.module HelloApp.exe
.imagebase 0x00400000
.file alignment 0x00000200
.stackreserve 0x00100000
.subsystem 0x0003
.corflags 0x00000003
// Program class is defined.
.class private auto ansi beforefieldinit Program
extends [mscorlib]System.Object
{
.method private hidebysig static void Main(string[] args) cil managed
{
// The method becomes the entry point for the executable.
.entrypoint
.maxstack 8
IL_0000: nop
IL_0001: ldstr "Hello CILly!"
IL_0006: call void [mscorlib]System.Console::WriteLine(string)
IL_000b: nop
IL_000c: call string [mscorlib]System.Console::ReadLine()
IL_0011: pop
IL_0012: ret
}
        // Here we have the constructor.
.method public hidebysig specialname rtspecialname
instance void .ctor() cil managed
{
```

```
.maxstack 8
IL_0000: ldarg.0
IL_0001: call instance void [mscorlib]System.Object::.ctor()
IL_0006: ret
}
}
```

When all externally referenced assemblies are declared, the CIL code file is opened. In the example above, we have a single .assembly token declared for the mscorlib. Remember, if class libraries rely on types that are part of other assemblies, you must add an extra assembly directive. The next step is finding the definition of the assembly with the default version setup because we never mentioned the value. In this case, the version is 0.0.0.0. You can use the AssemblyVersion attribute to create a different version. Furthermore, the assembly is described by several directives like the .module.

The definition becomes that of a Program type once the assemblies are documented and defined. Notice how the class direction holds a number of attributes, which are optional. The majority of the CIL code is a representation of the Main method and constructor's implementation. Both of these are defined with the directed method. Note that when the members are defined through various attributes and directives, they are implemented through a number of operation codes. You need to ensure you understand that. When you work with .NET types within CIL, you must know the type's fully qualified name. Furthermore, the name must be prefixed with an assembly name. In the example below, we implement the Main method in CIL:

```
.method private hidebysig static void Main(string[] args) cil managed
{
.entrypoint
.maxstack 8
IL_0000: nop
IL_0001: ldstr "Hello CILly!"
IL_0006: call void [mscorlib]System.Console::WriteLine(string)
IL_000b: nop  IL_000c: call string [mscorlib]System.Console::ReadLine()
IL_0011: pop  IL_0012: ret }
```

Notice how the CIL code relies on a ldarg.0 instruction, which is also load-focused where the constructor's implementation is concerned. The value must be loaded on the stack. But, it is not a custom value; it is a reference to the current object. Moreover, look at the constructor and observe how it calls the base class constructor.

Labels

In the previous examples, all the lines of code are prefixed with something like IL_xxxx. These are code labels. They can have any name as long as it is not taken. When an assembly is dumped with the ildasm tool, code labels are created automatically, and they follow a particular naming convention. It might be inconvenient; that is why we can customize them. Having more descriptive labels will make our job easier. Let's have a look at an example:

```
.method private hidebysig
static void Main(string[] args) cil managed
{
.entrypoint
.maxstack 8
Nothing_1: nop
Load_String: ldstr "Hello CILly!"
PrintToConsole: call void [mscorlib]System.Console::WriteLine(string)
Nothing_2: nop
WaitFor_KeyPress: call string [mscorlib]System.Console::ReadLine()
RemoveValueFromStack: pop
Leave_Function: ret
}
```

Labels are not mandatory. The only time they are is when we are writing CIL code that relies on certain looping constructs, and you have to use them to distribute logic flow. In our example, however, we can entirely remove labels, and nothing will occur.

Now you understand the structure and composition of a CIL file, so let's do a round trip engineering exercise. The aim is to update code from the .il file, following the process below:

1. Create a reference for the System.Window.Forms assembly.
2. Next, we need to load a local string inside Main.
3. Call for the MessageBox.Show method with the local string as an argument.

First, we add an assembly directive with an "extern" attribute attached to it. It will allow us to mention that it needs the System.Window.Forms assembly. To accomplish this, we must update the code with the following logic:

```
.assembly extern System.Windows.Forms
{
.publickeytoken = (B7 7A 5C 56 19 34 E0 89)
.ver 4:0:0:0
}
```

Note that the value you assign to the ver directive is dependent on the .NET version you're using. To use the right version, navigate to your GAC, and copy the correct values. Next, we must modify the application of Main(). This method is found in our .il file. We should remove the present implementation with the following code:

```
.method private hidebysig static void Main(string[] args) cil managed
{
.entrypoint
.maxstack 8
```

```
// To do list: Type some new CIL code!
}
```

The goal is to force a new string to the stack and then call it with the MessageBox.Show. We use this method instead of Console.WriteLine. Remember, when typing an external type's name, you must use the fully qualified name together with the assembly's name. Remember, in CIL, all methods refer to documents with the fully qualified return type. Now, let's turn our attention back to our Main method and update it with the following code:

```
.method private hidebysig static void Main(string[] args) cil managed
{
.entrypoint
.maxstack 8
        ldstr "I love CIL"
call valuetype [System.Windows.Forms]
System.Windows.Forms.DialogResult
[System.Windows.Forms]
System.Windows.Forms.MessageBox::Show(string)  pop  ret
}
```

Our CIL code now matches perfectly with this C# definition:

```
class Program
{
static void Main(string[] args)
{
System.Windows.Forms.MessageBox.Show("I love CIL");
}
}
```

Compiling the Code

Once you've saved your updated .il file, you can start the compilation process with the CIL's compiler, ilasm.exe. This compiler has a few commands. We'll focus on the most important ones. If you're interested in learning more, use the -? token to see them. With that said, here are the basic options:

1. /debug: this command line flag will add debug information. This includes variable, argument names, and line numbers.
2. /dll: This creates a .dll file for the output.
3. /exe: Similar to /dll, but has a default setting unless stated otherwise.
4. /output: Sets the output name and extension are set. If you don't use this option, the file name will be identical to the name of your source code file.
5. /key: Allow the assembly to be compiled with a strong name.

Now that we have the updated .il file, we can compile it with the following command:

ilasm /exe HelloApp.il /output=NewAssembly.exe

Now you can start the new program, which will show a message box that holds the message instead of the console. This is a basic program, but it demonstrates the concept of round trip engineering with CIL. Just remember that when you create or edit an assembly with CIL as opposed to C#, you should always check whether binary image compilation turned into the correct .NET image. This can be done with the peverify.exe utility by typing the following command:

```
peverify NewAssembly.exe
```

This utility checks every single operation code in your assembly and looks for valid CIL. The tool focuses on semantics, so if you don't clear the stack before you exit function, it will warn you when you try to run the code.

Dynamic Assemblies

When you set out to create a complicated application in CIL, you need to be emotionally prepared. On one side, CIL is highly expressive, allowing you full access and control over any programming construct allowed by CTS. On the other side, writing CIL is time-consuming and tedious, not to mention the high chance of errors. At this point, you are probably wondering how much of the syntax you should memorize. There's no right answer, but most of your programming sessions will not involve any CIL. Understanding CIL concepts will enable you to explore an entirely new concept, namely that of dynamic assemblies.

So far, we've focused on static assemblies, so you're probably wondering what the difference is. Remember, static assemblies are just .NET binaries inhabiting a file on your hard drive. They are requested by the CLR and loaded from the disk. Whenever you compile your code written in C#, the result is a static assembly. On the other hand, a dynamic assembly lives in your memory, with the help of types coming from the System.Reflection.Emit namespace. This namespace allows you to build an assembly with its definitions, modules, and runtime logic. This in-memory binary can be saved to disk, resulting in another static assembly. To create a dynamic assembly, you need a deeper understanding of operation codes.

Dynamic assemblies require advanced programming. They are rarely part of regular programming ambitions, but they can be very useful. For instance, they are important when developing a programming tool that needs to generate many assemblies at a user's command. They are also useful when you want to load a static assembly and add new types dynamically to the binary. With that said, let's look closely at System.Reflection.Emit namespace.

Although developing dynamic assemblies requires a deeper understanding of operation codes, the types belonging to the System.Reflection.Emit namespace hides the intricacies of CIL. For example, you can try out a TypeBuilder class instead of declaring all the required directives and attributes to define the type. Also, you don't need to use a Constructor Builder to define the constructor. You can also emit a special name or ctor token instead. There are multiple members belonging to this namespace, so check the documentation if you want to learn more.

Usually, types belonging to this namespace allow you to represent CIL code programmatically while constructing the dynamic assembly. There are many members like this, but we are mostly interested in the ILGenerator. This member's role is to introduce CIL operational codes to another member. Note that you can't create this type of object immediately because it doesn't contain a public constructor. To obtain an ILGenerator member, you have to call specific methods belonging to various builder-focused types. These types are the MethodBuilder and ConstructorBuilder. Let's look at the code below:

```
// Extract an ILGenerator from the Constructor Builder.
// The object will be called myConstructorBuilder.
ConstructorBuilder myConstructorBuilder =
new ConstructorBuilder(/* ...insert arguments... */);
ILGenerator myGen = myConstructorBuilder.GetILGenerator();
```

When the ILGenerator is ready, you can begin to emit operation codes regardless of the number of methods you have. To learn more about the methods belonging to ILGenerator, go to the documentation. We'll only focus on the Emit method, which operates with Reflection.

Emitting a Dynamic Assembly

To illustrate how an assembly is defined during runtime we'll set up a one file dynamic assembly. We'll name it MyAssembly.dll. Inside the module is a class called HelloWorld, which accepts a basic constructor and a custom constructor we'll use to declare the value of a string type private variable. The class supports a public instance method called SayHi. The method will print a message to the I/O stream and return a private string through the ReceiveMsg method. Here's the example:

```
// The class is built during runtime with the System.Reflection.Emit
namespace.
public class HelloWorld
{
private string myMessage;
HelloWorld() {}
HelloWorld(string s) {myMessage = s;
}
public string ReceiveMsg()
{return myMessage;}
```

```
public void SayHi()
{
System.Console.WriteLine ("The HelloWorld class says Hi!");
}
```

Now, let's look at a scenario involving a console application we'll call DynAsmBuilder. We'll import three namespaces: the System.Reflection, System.Threading and System.Reflection.Emit. We'll then declare a new static method called CreateAsm, which will belong to the Program class. The method is used to determine the assembly's features, implement a new type, and save the assembly to disk. Also, the CreateAsm method will require one parameter: the System.AppDomain type. The parameter is needed to access the assembly builder. With that said, let's work through the code and analyze each step:

```
public static void CreateAsm(AppDomain curAppDomain)
{
// Here, we declare the assembly features.
AssemblyName assemblyName = new AssemblyName();
assemblyName.Name = "MyAssembly";
assemblyName.Version = new Version("1.0.0.0");
// Build a new assembly inside the active App domain.
AssemblyBuilder
assembly =    curAppDomain.DefineDynamicAssembly(assemblyName,
AssemblyBuilderAccess.Save);
        // Remember that we are creating a one file assembly.
// The name of the module will be identical to that of the assembly.
ModuleBuilder module =     assembly.DefineDynamicModule("MyAssembly",
"MyAssembly.dll");
        // Public class named "HelloWorld".
TypeBuilder helloWorldClass = module.DefineType("MyAssembly.HelloWorld",
TypeAttributes. Public);
        // Declare the private String member variable and name it
"theMessage".
FieldBuilder msgField =    helloWorldClass.DefineField("theMessage",
Type.GetType("System.String"), FieldAttributes.Private);
// Setup the custom ctor.
Type[] constructorArgs = new Type[1];
constructorArgs[0] = typeof(string);
ConstructorBuilder
constructor =
   helloWorldClass.DefineConstructor(MethodAttributes.Public,
CallingConventions.Standard,     constructorArgs);
ILGenerator constructorIL = constructor.GetILGenerator();
constructorIL.Emit(OpCodes.Ldarg_0);  Type objectClass = typeof(object);
ConstructorInfo superConstructor = objectClass.GetConstructor(new
Type[0]);
constructorIL.Emit(OpCodes.Call, superConstructor);
constructorIL.Emit(OpCodes.Ldarg_0);
constructorIL.Emit(OpCodes.Ldarg_1);
constructorIL.Emit(OpCodes.Stfld, msgField);
```

```
constructorIL.Emit(OpCodes.Ret);
        // Build the default ctor.
helloWorldClass.DefineDefaultConstructor(MethodAttributes.Public);
// Setup the ReceiveMsg() method.
MethodBuilder receiveMsgMethod =
helloWorldClass.DefineMethod("ReceiveMsg",
MethodAttributes.Public,    typeof(string), null);
ILGenerator methodIL = receiveMsgMethod.GetILGenerator();
methodIL.Emit(OpCodes.Ldarg_0);  methodIL.Emit(OpCodes.Ldfld, msgField);
methodIL.Emit(OpCodes.Ret);
        // Build the SayHi method.
MethodBuilder sayHiMethod = helloWorldClass.DefineMethod("SayHi",
MethodAttributes.Public, null, null);
methodIL = sayHiMethod.GetILGenerator();
methodIL.EmitWriteLine("HelloWorld class says hi!");
methodIL.Emit(OpCodes.Ret);
        // Emitting the type, also referred to as "baking".
helloWorldClass.CreateType();
        // Saving the assembly to disk is optional.
assembly.Save("MyAssembly.dll");
}
```

(Source: Dynamic Assemblies using Reflection.Emit,

https://www.codeproject.com/Articles/18677/Dynamic-Assemblies-using-Reflection-Emit-Part-II-o retrieved in November 2019).

Summary

In this chapter, we learned about the syntax and concepts behind CIL. CIL differs from C# because it doesn't define a keyword collection; it provides directives, attributes, and operation codes. You also learned about several CIL utilities and explored modifying an assembly through round trip engineering. In addition, you learned about working with referenced assemblies, namespaces, members, and types, and developed a new code library that can be executed through the command line. Lastly, we introduced you to dynamic assemblies and the Reflection.Emit namespace. You now have a general idea of how an assembly can be defined in memory during runtime. Working with dynamic assemblies is not something you will often do, but this knowledge expands your thinking in indispensable ways.

CHAPTER 6:

Windows Presentation Foundation

History time! When the first version of the .NET platform was released, programmers who wanted to develop graphical applications had two APIs at their disposal: Windows Forms and GDI+. They are still used today to create old-school graphical interfaces, but Microsoft has released a new GUI system: the Windows Presentation Foundation. This new alternative came out with .NET 3.0.

This chapter will explore this graphical framework to understand core differences between it and the older APIs. You'll also learn the purpose of the Application and Window main classes. Briefly, we'll explore WPF's graphics rendering services. This is a general, introductory chapter about these graphical systems. This section aims to introduce you to other options besides pure C# programming, so you'll be able to make better decisions when deciding on a project's development workflow.

Purpose

Microsoft has developed plenty of graphical user interface systems for a desktop executable. All these APIs come with a codebase representing the core functionality and features of any GUI-focused program. They include elements like windows, controls, menus, dialog boxes, and many others. When .NET was first released, Windows Forms became the industry standard for user interfaces because of its intuitive nature. This API is still in use even today, but in a much more restricted manner because it isn't as visually pleasing or useful as modern ones. Also, Windows Forms didn't have support for various plugins and external modules to extend the functionality.

Windows Forms programmers had to rely on many APIs and object models that weren't connected. Creating these APIs was cumbersome because each had to have a different thought process, although it was all written in C#. For example, attaching data to a grid required different skills from building a 3D rendered animation. It meant Windows Forms developers had to have an extremely diverse toolkit as opposed to specializing. This is where the Windows Presentation Foundation came in.

WPF aimed to combine these different tasks and functionalities into a general mode. It means that if you want to create an animation, you don't have to do any manual programming related to the DirectX API because the functionality is covered in WPF. The most important thing is that all .NET programmers have a single API to meet all their needs. All that is required is learning WPF assemblies and studying XAML to create complex, modern-looking user interfaces. Basics will suffice. XAML is used to develop application UIs through XML markup. The markup can be generated using Visual Studio or Expression Blend (also Microsoft). Then connect it to a C# file.

The more you work with WPF, the easier XAML will become to understand. It offers a great deal of versatility. It allows you to create UI components like buttons and checkboxes, but you can also use it for various animations and videos. With the markup, you'll be able to customize all visuals. For instance, you can make a circular button control element, bringing a logo to life with animation. All that is required is a couple of markup lines. You can customize all controls, and even templates.

Older GUI tools like Windows Forms and MFC handled graphical rendering with a low-level API based on C. It has been a part of Windows for many years, and today it provides enough performance for average business-focused applications. If you want fancy graphics, DirectX is what you'll need. WPF differs from the older model because everything is graphically rendered, whether it's 2D, 3D, or animated. It all relies on the DirectX API. The biggest advantage is that your applications will benefit from various system optimizations and hardware. All WPF programs have access to various services or effects, like blur, transparency, and anti-aliasing – you don't have to program them yourself.

To summarize, the Windows Presentation Foundation is an API designed for applications that integrate several APIs into one model. Moreover, these programs integrate several services. It's a major improvement to the development pipeline because before its introduction, integration was too difficult and complicated to implement. Let's look at the foundational WPF characteristics:

1. WPF contains many layout managers that are highly customizable.
2. Access to a powerful data binding engine that connects content to interface elements.

3. Provides a style engine that enables various themes.
4. Use vector graphics, thus enabling the developers to resize the resolution and size of graphical elements, or screen, so everything fits with the system hosting the application.
5. Both 2D and 3D graphics and animations are fully supported.
6. WPF has a typography API and full support for integrating old GUI systems like Windows Forms and ActiveX.

Now that you see the benefits of working with WPF, let's explore program types that are developed with the API.

WPF Assemblies

WPF can be described as a body of types collected in several .NET assemblies. Check the documentation to explore the many assemblies that must be referenced during the development stage; these are often used to create applications. Visual Studio does the referencing automatically. Let's look at a couple of key assemblies:

1. PresentationCore: This assembly defines a collection of namespaces forming the base of the graphical user interface layer. For example, PresentationCore supports Ink API, some animation primitive types, and a group of rendering types.
2. PresentationFramework: Holds most of the WPF controls, including Application and Window classes. Contains support for interactive 2D graphics and a plethora of data binding types.
3. SystemXaml: This assembly offers namespaces required to program on top of a XAML file. This library allows you to develop various support utilities or provides full control of XAML during runtime.
4. WindowsBase: This assembly is used to define the types forming the entire architecture of the WPF API. It includes multiple threading types, security types, and type converters.

These base assemblies form the group of namespaces, hundreds of classes, structures, delegates, and enumerations that make up WPF. Let's explore the purpose of the most widely used namespaces:

1. System.Windows: Considered the base WPF namespace. It contains all main classes, Application and Window included. These classes are required on every single project.
2. System.Windows.Controls: This namespace holds most of the widgets, and the types used to create menus and tooltips.
3. System.Windows.Data: This namespace holds a collection of types that work with the data binding engine alone.
4. System.Windows.Documents: This namespace contains types that work with documents

API. You need this namespace to add PDF features to your application. Its implementation is done through the XML Paper Specification protocol.

5. System.Windows.Ink: This namespace offers support for the Ink API. This API allows you to record all inputs from a controller, like a mouse, and respond to them accordingly. It's best used for tabled-focused programming.
6. System.Windows.Markup: This namespace defines the types needed for the processing of XAML markup.
7. System.Windows.Media: A core namespace offering root functionality to many namespaces focusing on media features. Inside of these namespaces are types that work with 3D rendering, animations, and more.
8. System.Windows.Shapes: This namespace defines classes that enable the rendering of 2D graphics that respond to the mouse input.

We are going to stop here as these are the most used namespaces. Let's start to explore the Application and Window classes.

The Application Class

The Application class is the global instance of a functioning WPF program. The class has a Run method to run the application and a collection of events like Startup and Exit, including various other events dealing with browser applications. Check the WPF documentation for a better understanding of the many properties. In the meantime, we'll explore the essential ones:

1. Current: This is a static property that gives access to a functioning Application object. It is useful when a window requires access to the object which created it.
2. MainWindow: This property helps us get or set the main window of a program.
3. Properties: This property allows us to find data that can be accessed through a method in the application. It includes windows, dialog boxes, and so on.
4. StartupUri: A URI is set to specify which window will open when the program runs.

All WPF-based programs require a definition of a class extending the Application class. In it, you will declare the Main method (startup point). It will build an instance of its subclass and manage Startup and Exit events. Let's look at an example below:

```
// First, we need to define the application object for the WPF app.
class MyApp : Application
{
[STAThread]  static void Main(string[] args)
{
// Setup the application object.
MyApp app = new MyApp();
                    //  Startup and Exit events.
app.Startup += (s, e) => { /* Launch the app */ };
```

```
app.Exit += (s, e) => { /* Exit the app */ };
}
}
```

In the Startup declaration, all incoming arguments will be processed, and the application will be launched. The Exit, on the other hand, exits the application.

The Window Class

The Windows class stands for a window that is possessed by any class belonging to the application. It is part of the PresentationFramework assembly. It includes all dialog boxes of the program's main window. Note that the Window class holds a collection of classes that add functionality. Check the documentation to learn more about them. We'll discuss those that are important to gaining a rudimentary understanding of WPF.

Content Control class is the parent of the Window class. It is one of the core classes providing derived types that hold a segment of visual data deposited inside the control's surface area through the Content property. The content model allows us to customize the visuals of content control. For example, when you think of the content of button control, you think of a string literal like "Cancel" or "Accept." The value of the content property can be registered as a basic string if you use XAML to make the WPF control. You can declare the property inside the component's definition like this:

```
<!-- Declaring the Content value within the opening element --> <Button
Height="70" Width="90" Content="OK"/>
```

You can set the content to anything you desire. For example, you can have a button containing a text blurb. In the older UI structures, like Windows Forms, you had to create the control yourself. Doing so would've involved a lot of code and a new class that would require your stewardship. With WPF, that is not necessary. In WPF, you don't use an attribute inside the starting definition to assign a content property to a value; instead, you define the data inside the component's scope.

Although WPF controls and ContentControl share the same parent class, they are not the same. The root class provides several base members that provide core user interface functionality. For instance, Control defines properties that control size, opacity, cursor, background color, and more. The root class also offers templating support. WPF is very useful as it offers styles and templates you can modify as you see fit.

WPF for Graphics Rendering

In this section, we will discuss WPF's graphical capabilities: rendering services. WPF offers three methods for rendering graphical information: shapes, drawings, and visuals. Once you understand the advantages and disadvantages of them, your understanding of WPF will increase. You'll appreciate how drawings and geometries are used to render 2D information more flexibly. Also, multiple visual layers optimize the performance of your project.

You might not be interested in creating complicated and graphics-intensive programs right now. Still, the concepts behind these processes apply to various services. WPF depends on a kind of graphical rendering known as retained-mode graphics. It means procedural code generates the graphical rendering. WPF's role is to maintain graphical objects and ensure they are duly redrawn and updated. So when graphical information is rendered, it always exists even when the image is hidden when you place another window above it or minimize it. To make a comparison, when Microsoft's rendering APIs were restricted to Windows Forms, we had immediate mode graphical systems. The programmer had to prepare a model to ensure rendered graphics were managed properly and regularly updated while the application ran. Today WPF takes care of all of that. A Windows Forms program rendering basic geometrical shapes, like rectangles, needed a Paint event to create an object that would draw the shape. Architecture had to be included to ensure the image remained intact when it is minimized. The switch from immediate mode graphics to retained-mode graphics was freeing. Programmers had less graphics code to write and update.

With that said, the graphics API of WPF is not different from older rendering utilities. They all support certain types of brush and pen objects, hit testing techniques, graphical changes, and more. If you are familiar with Windows Forms rendering, you won't have trouble learning WPF rendering.

Rendering Options

As mentioned earlier, WPF is adaptable, offering a plethora of graphical rendering choices. Your options extent beyond XAML or procedural C# code. Here are the three methods offered by WPF:

1. Shapes: The System.Windows.Shapes namespace offered by WPF defines classes for rendering 2D geometric objects, like rectangles, polygons, and more. These are basic types, but they utilize a lot of memory when overused.
2. Drawings: Involves children of System.Windows.Media.Drawing namespace. You'll find classes like ImageDrawing and Geometry Drawing used to render visual data taxing system resources, but it also means fewer features.
3. Visuals: The fastest image rendering method. Visuals allow the use of a visual layer that can only be accessed by C# code, meaning you'll be able to interact directly with WPF's graphical system.

All these methods do the same thing. Differences lie in the details. The main distinguishing factor is performance and memory use. WPF is an intensive system that demands a lot from your system. Still, it is reasonable to expect a program to render thousands of images in one window. That's why choosing to go with shapes, drawings, or visuals will have an impact on your application's performance. Note that in most circumstances, you won't work with one method alone. Developers combine all three, choosing what is most appropriate for each method. It is normal for developers to combine all three.

The accepted standard is using the Shapes namespace when dealing with simple graphical data, like tooltips and mouse inputs. Drawings are mainly used when dealing with vector-based data put together with C# or XAML. Drawings can also be responsive to mouse events and other operations, but you'll have to program that functionality.

Visuals are often used, rendering enormous quantities of visual data because the visual layer offers the fastest, most efficient rendering methods. For instance, let's say you are making an application that is supposed to display a data plot. The visual layer will optimally generate plot points that won't hog your system's memory.

No matter which technique you use, you'll always need various graphical primitives, like brushes and pens, and transformation objects.

Summary

In this chapter, we introduced you to the Windows Presentation Foundation. While we did not dive into too much detail, you should have enough knowledge to get started independently. You explored the basic concepts, like what makes a WPF application come to life, and the options available when formulating your project's design. Now you can use C# and WPF to work with more than console applications.

CHAPTER 7:

ASP .NET

In this chapter, we will learn about ASP.MVC, a web applications framework. The framework appeared out of necessity because the online community demanded a new framework that would follow HTTP and be easier to test than previous frameworks.

In the first section, you will learn about the MVC pattern.

The MVC Pattern

MVC stands for Model View Controller. The pattern originally appeared in the 70s. It was developed for SmallTalk, an object-oriented programming language launched in 1980. The pattern appeared again because it could now be implemented in other languages, like Java, Ruby, and various frameworks like Angular. Around 2007, the pattern was implemented for .NET developers in the form of ASP.NET MVC.

First, we have the model. This represents the application's data, represented by a collection of basic CLR objects, which are the same as the ones in data access libraries. The view models are composed of one or several models designed for the view that will utilize them. To understand them better, imagine these models as database tables. From an academic perspective, models are clean because they don't hold validation logic or similar rules. From a practical point of view, whether a model contains this logic depends on the framework and programming language being used and project requirements. For example, the EF Core holds several data annotations that function as a method for modeling the database tables, containing the validation method inside Core MVC. Normally, data validations and annotations are placed where they make the most sense to reduce potential duplicate code.

Next is the view, which represents the application's user interface. A view will accept instructions and display the results of those instructions to the user. Note that the view must be as light as possible for the commands to be smoothly executed. The controller must address all demanding work. The controller is the intelligence behind the operation. It has two main purposes. The first is to accept user commands, known as actions, and push them to a repository, for example. The second is to transmit any changes to the view. Remember, just like models and views, controllers need to be as light as possible.

It doesn't sound too complicated. But why use MVC instead of any other framework?

ASP.NET MVC was released in 2007, but ASP.NET Web Forms had been growing for six years up until then. Many websites were created using Web Forms. There were no signs of this slowing down. The question is: why did Microsoft develop a new web framework? Before we answer, consider the following.

When Web Forms was released, web development wasn't as complex as it is today. The stateless paradigm we are familiar with wasn't well understood back then, especially by those working on computer applications using Visual Basic. There was a gap between these two types of developers, so it had to be filled. Building websites needed to become easier, and Web Forms accommodated concepts and techniques that only existed for desktop development. Programmers and developers celebrated this, and many switched straight into web development. So a new ecosystem formed around Web Forms and other .NET controls. Everyone is experimenting with stateless web programming, HTTP protocol, and JavaScript.

These developers had a new requirement. They no longer needed a plethora of tools and utilities to fill the gap previously experienced. But they needed more control over rendered views. With each Web Forms update, new features were added. Each one significantly improved applications and led to more complex websites. But, problems surfaced. For instance, the placement of the viewstate inside the rendered page negatively affected performance. Eventually, this led to more problems in .NET, Ruby, and Ruby on Rails. At the time, Microsoft couldn't simply remove the tech because a lot relied on it. A new solution had to be found, and constantly updating Web Forms to fix these issues was not enough. Microsoft had to figure out how to keep current web developers happy while offering a new platform for those who wanted to explore the web further.

That is how ASP.NET MVC came to be. The two models have plenty of differences between them. For instance, the code-behind files, viewstate, and control support were removed. On top of that, testing, dependency injection, control separation, and clean code techniques were better supported. Furthermore, the Razor view engine was developed. Almost everything was improved, but the main drawback is that ASP.NET MVC has some familiarity with HTML, JavaScript, and HTTP functions.

The MVC framework configuration is superseded by convention. In other words, conventions like naming conventions and general architecture have to be followed so that MVC projects reduce the configuration needed.

The MVC Application Template

Now that we have looked at some history and theory, let's look at some code. Visual Studio comes with a full project template designed to assist you when building MVC applications. Navigate to the File tab, select New, and click on the project. In the left sidebar, under Visual C#, is the Web option. Select the ASP.NET Web Application and name it. When the next window pops up, follow the MVC template. There'll be a pre-selected checkbox; it is to "add folders and core references for." In this window, if you would like to create a hybrid program that works with MVC and Web Forms, you can check the box for Web Forms. For the purpose of this section, only choose MVC. There's another option called "add unit tests." A new project will be created with a core framework designed for unit testing if you check it. We will not explore unit testing because it is too big for this book. With that said, before finishing with setup, check out the authentication mechanisms.

Select the "change authentication" option, and a dialogue box will appear. Leave it to default ("authentication set to no authentication") and click "ok" when prompted. When this is done, a set of files and folders will be created.

Be aware that modifying the Project_ Readme.html file from any version of the MVC templates is a project overview feature. It means that when the project is initially loaded, the collection of links to the documentation will be provided, establishing connections between several services. Many of the MVC files have specific locations where they belong. Still, there are some files capable of living outside the root folder. Let's check out some of them:

1. Global.asax.cs: This file enables us to connect to the workflow of the framework. The default template depends on an event handler called the application start. However, there are many others you can connect.
2. Models: This is a folder that is the home to all model classes. A data access library should contain all of your models when you are working on a complex application. This folder is usually used to hold view models like classes created by Visual Studio for the framework's identity.

3. Controller: Contains all of your applications' controller files.
4. Views: All of your MVC views will be put here. There's a specific convention for the architecture of the folder. All controllers need to have their own folder inside the Views folder. They search for their views within the folder that has the same label as the controller. For instance, the Views/Home folder will contain views for the HomeController controller. You will also find a configuration file called _ViewStart.cshtml, inside the root of the main folder. The file belongs to the views inside of its folder structure, and it determines page type. Also, the config file will be executed before views are rendered.
5. Shared: This folder falls under the views folder. Any view can access it. It holds only two files: Layout.cshtml file, and the Error.cshtml file. The first represents the layout determined by the view start configuration file. The second contains the error template for the project.
6. ASP.NET: There are many folders like these, like the App Data folder (a part of the MVC template). The folder contains all file-based information needed by a site. There are others generated to store the code and other resources. You can add a new folder by right-clicking on your project and selecting the Add menu's ASP.NET Web Folder option. These folders will not be seen on the website.
7. App_Start: Older versions of the MVC framework held the configuration code inside a global class. Patch after patch caused the configuration to become too complicated to be handled in one class. So, development is divided into multiple classes. The App Start folder contains all of those classes. The code in there is compiled automatically.

Let's now turn our attention to the BundleConfig class. This class houses bundles and minification settings for the CSS and JavaScript files. Usually, these files are bundled and minified for production purposes. These processes are invisible in debug mode. You can control all of them by tinkering with the class or the web.config files. Suppose you want to shut off bundling and minification. In that case, you must type the following lines in the web section inside the configuration file:

```
<system.web>
<compilation debug="true" targetFramework="4.7" /> </system.web>
```

If you aren't familiar, bundling is the combining of several files into a single one. Bundling boosts a website's speed because web browsers have a limited number of files they can download from the server at a time. Having many small files on your website can decrease performance. The solution is bundling files together to reduce their numbers. Another solution is spreading them across multiple content delivery networks. Regardless of the method you choose, you need to decide on something that is best for you. The building method has the downside of producing a massive file that can slow down the user experience. So, one needs to be cognizant.

On the other side is the minification process. This process speeds up a webpage's loading time. JavaScript and CSS files contain only variables and functions to improve readability. However, size matters, especially when websites are often accessed through mobile devices. Minification solves this problem. It exchanges long names with short ones, removes additional spaces, and more. Changing the format and making everything shorter means fewer bits are transmitted, which translates to shorter loading times. Because of this, all worthwhile frameworks come with two versions of these files: one for production and the other for development.

Summary

In this chapter, we introduced ASP.NET MVC framework, which has become the mainstay of most web application development workflows in C#. It included a set of libraries that add another layer of abstraction from C#. The MVC pattern divides projects into three sections, making them more efficient. Furthermore, we looked at the pattern itself and why it's useful for user interfaces where the separation is between logic application and graphical components. Having internal data representation allows the information to be presented to and accepted by a user more efficiently, making the development of complex programs possible.

CHAPTER 8:

NET Core

In 2016 Microsoft released a new .NET platform called .NET Core. This platform is cross-platform, operating on the three biggest operating systems: Windows, Linux, and macOS. It is based on .NET and C#, which you are much acquainted with now. The platform contains the .NET Core runtime, ASP.NET Core, and the Entity Framework Core. At the time of writing (Jan 2020), the fifth version of .NET core is released, expanding on cross-platform deployment functionalities and many other changes worth exploring.

Unlike other technologies, .NET Core is entirely open source. You can check the code and modify it here and there to see what happens. You can also contribute to the community and development team by helping with your own knowledge of C# and .NET. This is advantageous to regular users because the large community of contributors leads to faster improvement. Furthermore, the documentation is detailed. You can learn a lot from it. You can check it out here: https://docs.microsoft.com/en-us/.

The idea for .NET Core was born when developers requested the ASP.NET platform to function on other platforms, not just other Windows. This led to a project called Project K, with the purpose of dispensing .NET functionality to other platforms. Most of the effort was focused on ASP.NET in order to extend it to other systems, so any dependency on System.Web had to be removed. As you can imagine, removing a component like this doesn't come without consequences. It means they had to write the framework almost from scratch and return to deciding whether they were adding much-needed components. So it was decided that there needs to be a framework that can be used by all web-based applications. This led to the MVC platform and the Web API merging.

The Entity Framework was introduced because the platform needed a new data access layer. The new platform was named .NET Core.

It makes one wonder what will happen with the other .NET frameworks. Will support for them end? Will you have to rewrite your applications to be supported by Core? The answer is no. C# and the .NET platform are continuously being developed, even though there hasn't been very exciting development recently. But all of these technologies are well developed, and it doesn't look like they'll be replaced anytime soon. Look at WinForms and Web Forms; they are still used by many products even if there isn't much chat about them.

The Purpose of NET Core

.NET Core wasn't just about extending .NET functionality. Remember that .NET has existed since 2002. Technology has changed a lot since then. Developers have become more experienced, computers are more powerful, and the number of users has increased. These are the obvious things that have changed since 2002. With that said, here's a list of .NET Core goals and functions:

1. Cross-platform support: Core functions on all three major operating systems and their versions. Now, support for Android, iOS, and Xamarin has been added.
2. Performance: Performance remains one of the .NET Core's most important goals. Frequent releases ensure that the framework keeps improving.
3. Portable class libraries: Core now includes .NET Standard. This is a specification that implements some uniform behavior in the .NET runtime.
4. Deployment: Core applications are portable. They can also be deployed as a standalone product. In other words, they can come with the framework, or Core system installation.
5. Command-line support: The platform supports a full command line.

A .NET Core application can be developed anywhere because Visual Studio is now available on Mac. There is no need for virtualization. You can also use cross-platform utilities from Core development to work on any system. What's also attractive is the wide range of deployment choices, with no reliance on Windows. For instance, Linux servers are the standard choice because they are cheaper to run and maintain, especially today in a cloud-based environment. So, an option to deploy an application straight to the cloud cuts costs. This might explain the proliferation of new startups, since it has become cost effective. Now, small teams of developers can build their own products.

Core also offers Containerization, which is one of the impressive things about Core. Core applications receive containerization support. It means containers like Docker can simplify how applications are released from one environment to another. For instance, Core makes it easy to move an application from a development environment to a testing environment. Project files are bundled together into a single container, hence the term Containerization. The container can just be duplicated, with no need for installations. Things are much easier now as Windows supports Docker. This means you will be able to develop an app in a container and move the container when you deploy, meaning you don't have to do installs – no more deployments and no more installs.

Most applications developed with ASP.NET Core produce high benchmark test scores. As you know, performance is one of the most important things to a developer. The original .NET framework is old, and developers have gotten out of it what they can. It's one of the reasons they wrote Core. Starting over allowed them to optimize it from the start. In other words, performance became the central driving force.

Components

Here's the basic structure of .NET Core:

1. The Core runtime.
2. Framework libraries.
3. SDK tools and a dotnet application host.
4. Language compiling.

The Runtime (aka CoreCLR) is the root library of .NET Core. It contains a garbage collector, base .NET types, the JIT compiler, and many libraries. It is what connects all these libraries with different operating systems. The only things dependent on operating systems are classes. The class libraries themselves come in independent NuGet packs. Runtime tries to reduce the amount of code to leave some implementation of the class to itself. All of these contribute to a flexible codebase that can change and be deployed quickly. However, CoreCLR doesn't do a lot on its own. Defined library code is compiled to the CoreLib assembly, which isn't used outside Runtime. CoreCLR also provides tools like ILDASM and ILASM.

The Framework libraries, also known as CoreFX, are a collection of base libraries containing classes for file systems, collections, console, XML, and more. These libraries construct CoreCLR and provide us with materials for other frameworks. However, other than the many CoreCLR elements contained in the libraries, these libraries are runtime-focused. You can conclude that the CoreCLR and CoreFX build .NET Core.

We also have SDK tools and the dotnet App Host (part of SDK). The command-line interface is integrated into the toolkit because it is required to create Core libraries and applications. The dotnet host is the engine of operating CLI commands. The host's role is launching commands and Core applications. You can check yours by typing the following in any command line:

```
dotnet --version
```

The command initiates the dotnet host and will display the installed version of the Core SDK. The CLI has many useful commands. Make sure to check them out at Microsoft's documentation.

Next to the CLI commands are frameworks that offer many other command-line options. For instance, the Entity framework adds instructions that can be used to update or migrate the databases.

The language compiler, called Roslyn, offers us several compilers for C# and Visual Basic. Remember that these compilers are open source and come with APIs for code analysis. Also, Visual Basic was added fairly recently, but C# remains the dominant force in the .NET Core ecosystem.

Remember, don't confuse .NET Core with the full .NET framework, because there are several distinguishing features between them, even though they have many identical APIs and rely on C#. Here are some of those factors:

1. Core offers additional platform support for every system.
2. Although Core is supported and maintained by Microsoft, it is open source.
3. Fewer application models are being introduced.
4. Core has fewer APIs.

We've already discussed the first two differences. It's worth noting that Core doesn't support every single app model that is part of the full framework. This statement is even truer for models created over Windows technologies. Also, Core applications can be described as either console applications or class libraries.

Core would have fewer APIs because the full Framework is gigantic. So, trying to change all of the APIs is impractical. Core developers follow agile design principles, so their goal was to offer stripped-down products as version one, fulfilling minimum requirements. While it sounds bad, it doesn't mean developers were lazy. With each new iteration, the number of supported APIs increases. For example, version 2.0 introduced another 32,000 APIs.

With that said, the .NET Core is a brand new technology that is under heavy development. Still, it is quickly proving itself to be indispensable.

Summary

In this chapter, we explored the structure and goals of the .NET Core. We learned about important distinguishing features between Core and the full .NET framework. As you practice, you will find that creating Core applications isn't very different from creating general .NET Framework applications. You simply have a smaller number of frameworks and APIs. Everything is still C# programming. Core's advantage is its open-source nature, meaning it gains from thousands of developers worldwide. This means bugs are fixed, and tools and new features are implemented at increasing speeds. This may seem like a downside because developers might struggle to keep up, but this is positive because it makes your job easier.

CONCLUSION

What a journey! You have started from the very beginning the C# programming guide for beginners, and now you have finally completed the advanced course. Congratulations to you. You have come a long way. A lot of people don't go this far in their education. We admit that the framework is intimidating. That is why these guides were made in a way that assists you in your learning.

Our purpose was to give you the fundamental tools you need to start your journey of being an advanced C# programmer, working with tools like ASP .NET MVC, .NET Core, and more. You have reached a stage where books aren't enough; you have to jump into the documentations and learn. This is not a journey you will take alone. There are plenty of communities online that share a common goal. Learn with them. So get out there, contribute to projects, and never stop learning.

REFERENCES

Burns, S. (2019). Hands-on network programming with C# and .Net Core: build robust network applications with C# and .Net Core. Birmingham: Packt Publishing.

Miles, R. (2018). The C# Programming Yellow Book: Learn to Program in C# from First Principles, independently published.

Sharp, J. (2018). Microsoft Visual C# Step By Step. Place of publication not identified: MICROSOFT.

Stellman, A., & Greene, J. (2013). Head first C♯. Beijing: OReilly.

Strauss, D. (2019). Exploring advanced features in C#: enhance your code and productivity. New York, NY: Apress.

Made in United States
Troutdale, OR
11/18/2024

25020530R00343